ISRAEL'S COUNTERTERRORISM STRATEGY

COLUMBIA STUDIES IN TERRORISM AND IRREGULAR WARFARE

COLUMBIA STUDIES IN TERRORISM AND IRREGULAR WARFARE

Bruce Hoffman, Series Editor

This series seeks to fill a conspicuous gap in the burgeoning literature on terrorism, guerrilla warfare, and insurgency. The series adheres to the highest standards of scholarship and discourse and publishes books that elucidate the strategy, operations, means, motivations, and effects posed by terrorist, guerrilla, and insurgent organizations and movements. It thereby provides a solid and increasingly expanding foundation of knowledge on these subjects for students, established scholars, and informed reading audiences alike.

For a complete list of titles, see pages 407–8.

Israel's Counterterrorism Strategy

ORIGINS TO THE PRESENT

Boaz Ganor

Columbia University Press
New York

Columbia University Press
Publishers Since 1893
New York   Chichester, West Sussex
cup.columbia.edu

Library of Congress Cataloging-in-Publication Data
Names: Ganor, Boaz, author.
Title: Israel's counterterrorism strategy : origins to the present / Boaz Ganor.
Other titles: Columbia studies in terrorism and irregular warfare.
Description: New York : Columbia University Press, 2021. | Series: Columbia studies in terrorism
and irregular warfare | Includes bibliographical references and index.
Identifiers: LCCN 2020053410 (print) | LCCN 2020053411 (ebook) | ISBN 9780231199223
(hardback) | ISBN 9780231199230 (trade paperback) | ISBN 9780231553001 (ebook)
Subjects: LCSH: Terrorism—Israel—Prevention. | Terrorism—Israel. | National security—Israel. |
Arab-Israeli conflict. | Palestinian Arabs—Politics and government. | Israel—Politics and
government.
Classification: LCC HV6433.I75 G357 2021 (print) | LCC HV6433.I75 (ebook) |
DDC 363.1/6095694—dc23
LC record available at https://lccn.loc.gov/2020053410
LC ebook record available at https://lccn.loc.gov/2020053411

Cover design: Noah Arlow

CONTENTS

ACKNOWLEDGMENTS

Israel's Counterterrorism Strategy: Origins to Present summarizes a research project spanning many years that has examined Israel's counterterrorism strategy since its inception in 1948 through the end of the second decade of the twenty-first century. It is based on an analysis of literature and publications that saw light in either Hebrew or English on Israel's policy within the examined time frame. The book also relies on a large number of interviews conducted over the years with the most senior Israeli decision makers: prime ministers, defense ministers, chiefs of staff, directors of the Israeli Security Agency (ISA, or Shin Bet) and Mossad heads, counterterrorism advisors to the prime minister, and others.

Rarely does a researcher get the opportunity to review his research topics or a part thereof by observing the decision-making process in real time. I have been fortunate to have been exposed to some of the topics dealt with in this book not only through secondary material (documents, articles, and books) or even primary material (personal interviews I conducted with the decision makers themselves); at certain periods examined in this book, I found myself observing, closely and in real time, terror attacks and their harsh outcomes in Israel as well the affect they had on the Israeli counterterrorism decision-making process and the decision makers themselves. That exposure occurred during my military service or in my various roles as an advisor in the Office of the Prime Minister, the Bureau of the Advisor to the Prime Minister on Counter-Terrorism, the Ministry of Defense, the Ministry of Transportation, and the National Security Council, as well as my meetings with prime ministers and other decision makers who are the subjects of this research.

The book therefore gives the reader a peek into Israel's counterterrorism activities over a period of seventy years and the decision-making processes, challenges, dilemmas, and considerations at the core of these activities.'

Note that I have translated Hebrew literature cited in the notes into English.

I would like to thank everyone who has assisted me with my research, translation, and publication of this book, especially my translator, Ariel Rodal-Spieler; my research assistants, Dafne Beri and Arielle Goldfarb; and, above all, my deputy at the International Institute for Counter-Terrorism (ICT) and my right-hand man, Stevie Weinberg, who orchestrated this effort.

Special thanks to ICT's Board of Directors, led by its chairman, Shabtai Shavit. Together we have established and led the ICT since its creation in 1996. I am also thankful to the partners who have supported us over the years, in particular the Jusidman Foundation and Ambassador Ronald Lauder, president of the World Jewish Congress, who established the Ronald Lauder Chair for Counter-Terrorism, which I have the honor of holding at IDC Herzliya.

And above all, a big "thank you" to Professor Uriel Reichman, who, from the beginning of my professional career, believed in and supported me and has since served as a mentor and role model.

I want to thank my family, who have been with me throughout my professional career and shared my many experiences connected to the events described herein: my parents, Shulamit and David Ganor (RIP); my children, Lee, Tom, and Dan; my grandson, Omer; and first and foremost, my beloved wife, Amit.

Special thanks are due to Caelyn Cobb and Bruce Hoffman at Columbia University Press, and to the reviewers who have had a major contribution in building the structure of this book.

CHRONOLOGY

Prime Ministers of Israel and Timeline of Major Events (1948-2018)

1948: Declaration of the State of Israel

1948: Outbreak of the War of Independence.

1948–54: First David Ben-Gurion Administration

1953: Qibya raid (Operation Shoshana)

1954–55: Moshe Sharett Administration

1956: Suez Campaign

1955–63: Second David Ben-Gurion Administration

1963–69: Levi Eshkol Administration

1967: Six-Day War

1969–74: Golda Meir Administration

1972: Munich Olympics Massacre

1973: Yom Kippur War

1974–77: First Yitzhak Rabin Administration

1976: Entebbe Operation

1977–83: Menachem Begin Administration

1978: Operation Litani

1979: Camp David Accords and Signing of the Israel-Egypt Peace Treaty

1982: First Lebanon War (Operation Peace for Galilee)

1983–84: First Yitzhak Shamir Administration

1984–86: First Shimon Peres Administration

1986–92: Second Yitzhak Shamir Administration

1987: Start of the First Intifada

1991: Madrid Conference

1992–95: Second Yitzhak Rabin Administration

1993: Signing of the Oslo Accords

1994: Israel-Jordan Peace Treaty

1995: Oslo II Accords

1995: Assassination of Yitzhak Rabin

1995–96: Second Shimon Peres Administration

1996–99: First Benjamin Netanyahu Administration

1998: Wye River Agreement

1999–2001: Ehud Barak Administration

2000: Start of the Second Intifada

2000: Camp David Summit

2001–2006: Ariel Sharon Administration

2002: Operation Defensive Shield

2005: Israeli withdrawal from Gaza

2006–2009: Ehud Olmert Administration

2006: Kidnapping of IDF Corporal Gilad Shalit by Hamas

2006: Second Lebanon War

2008: Operation Cast Lead

2009–18: Second Benjamin Netanyahu Administration

2010: Mavi Marmara Flotilla

2012: Operation Pillar of Defense

2014: Operation Protective Edge

ISRAEL'S COUNTERTERRORISM STRATEGY

INTRODUCTION

The Israeli-Palestinian conflict can best be understood as the result of con-flicted national aspirations on the part of Jews and Arabs in the land of Israel. In addition, some believe it stems from the resistance of the Muslim world to the existence of a Jewish entity in the heart of the Middle East. The origins of the conflict are rooted in the late nineteenth century, with the beginning of Zionist immigration. The first Zionist immigration to Israel was spurred by a strong connection to the country and a desire to establish a Jewish homeland. These Zionists joined the existing Jewish community, who lived among locals. Nevertheless, the political and military confronta-tion between the two sides began only after World War I and the end of the reign of the Ottoman Empire in the region.

The Balfour Declaration, with which the British recognized the Jewish right to a national home in Israel, created a sense of deprivation among the Arabs living there, which was expressed in widespread outbreaks of anti-Jewish violence in April 1920 and May 1921. Tension persisted in the years that followed and reached a new peak in August 1929, when Arab con-ducted riots against the Jews of Hebron and Safed. During this period, the Palestinian national movement began to organize itself, and armed gangs, choosing the path of military actions against the Jews and the British, began to operate. The leader of these gangs, Sheikh Izz al-Din al-Qassam, has since been considered a hero in the eyes of Palestinian organizations. (The military wing of Hamas, the Izz al-Din al-Qassam Brigades, is named after him.) Waves of violence between the Jewish and Arab populations continued to erupt, reaching new heights in the late 1930s, until they were suppressed by the British government. A period of calm lasted approximately a decade.

The Arabs in Israel opposed the November 29, 1947, United Nations (UN) resolution to partition the territory between the Jordan river and the Mediterranean Sea into two nation-states—one Arab and one Jewish. Hostilities against Jewish targets began the next day, signaling the start of the War of Independence and the entry of Arab states into a cycle of conflict with Israel in an attempt to prevent the establishment of the Jewish state. The cease-fire agreements signed at the war's end set the de facto borders of the state of Israel, leaving the Palestinians without an independent country, as refugees (in Jordan, Lebanon, and Syria) or as residents of Israel.

After 1949, the "Palestinian agenda" became one of the key issues in the Arab world, with Arab heads of state declaring their commitment to the Palestinians at every opportunity. In reality, in many instances the Arab states exploited the plight of the Palestinians to promote their own domestic and regional interests. For Israel, this exploitative activity quickly became a major security threat and the cause of several wars between Israel and its Arab neighbors. It also served as the backdrop for the various waves of terrorism perpetrated by Palestinian terrorist organizations, which have resulted in numerous casualties since the establishment of the state.

This book examines the development of terrorism threats faced by Israel throughout the years, the evolving challenges faced by its decision makers in light of this threat, and the doctrines and strategies developed by Israel to cope with them.

Over the years, the challenge of Palestinian terrorism faced by Israel has taken different forms, and it has been necessary to adapt Israeli policy to the changing characteristics of the terrorist attacks and to their various perpetrators. Since the establishment of the state of Israel, the following eight periods can be distinguished. Each period displays a unique dimension of Palestinian terrorism, and each has posed a different challenge to Israeli decision makers and security forces. The eight periods have been divided as follows:

- 1948–67: Confrontation of the Fedayeen
- 1967–74: The challenge of Palestinian national terrorism—dealing with terrorist attacks abroad (contending with hijackings)
- 1974–77: The challenge of cross-border terrorism (contending with hostage barricade situations)
- 1978–86: Confrontation of the military forces of Palestinian terrorist organizations (contending with artillery attacks)
- 1987–91: The challenge of the first intifada and the activities of Islamist organizations (contending with popular violent activities)
- 1992–99: The need to deal with terrorism during the peace process (contending with suicide attacks)
- 2000–2004: The challenge of the second intifada following the breakdown of the peace process (contending with mass casualty attacks)
- 2005–18: The challenge of Hamas in Gaza (contending with rockets and "lone wolf" attacks).

In light of these different types of challenges involving terrorism, each prime minister and government adopted particular responses, policies, and strategies and employed different operative counterterrorism measures. These strategies reflect the Israeli governments' and prime ministers' ideological outlooks and value systems. Their actions also reflected their perceptions of the nature and level of the terrorism threat that Israel was facing and the legal, operational, and political challenges—including domestic pressures and international constraints—that they faced in countering terrorism during their terms.

Israeli's Counterterrorism Strategy: Origins to the Present is divided into ten chronological chapters covering the years 1948 to 2019 and explores the dynamic interactions between the evolution of terrorism and Israel's responses. Each chapter examines the particular threats and responses pursued in each period by the respective government. Chapter 1 sets out the research questions and hypotheses of the book, as well as conceptual models that will help in examining the Israeli counterterrorism decision-making process in each of the chapters that follow. The models will also help in comparing the counterterrorism policies of each era's government and will be used in the closing chapters to draw the lessons learned from the Israeli counterterrorism experience that are relevant for other democratic countries that are contending with terrorism.

In order to elucidate the way in which the challenge of Palestinian terrorism was seen by Israeli decision makers, each chapter includes interviews that were conducted with prime ministers, defense ministers, IDF chiefs of staff, Mossad, ISA, and ilitary intelligence directors, advisors to the prime ministers for counterterrorism, directors of the Counter-Terrorism Bureau, and others.

Chapter One

THE ISRAELI COUNTERTERRORISM STRATEGY AND DECISION-MAKING PROCESS

Conceptual Models

The terrorist threat to Israel has taken on different forms over the years and has manifested in various waves of terror, including abductions and hostage-taking, airplane hijackings, suicide attacks, lone-wolf attacks using cold weapons, and attacks against Israeli targets abroad. The identity of the perpetrators of terrorist attacks has also changed over the years, beginning with Palestinian terror attacks carried out on behalf of the Arab states during Israel's early days, to nationalistic and Islamist terror by Palestinian terrorist organizations. Each group had a slightly different motive and ideology; some were influenced by global extremist ideologies, and others followed Islamist-jihadist terrorism practices spurred by a combination of extreme national, religious, and political motivations. Some of the attacks were carried out by operatives of terrorist organizations, some by local independent networks, and others by individuals who underwent a process of radicalization and acted under the inspiration of one terrorist organization or another, or as a result of deliberate incitement.

Israel used of a variety of tools and methods that have taken the form of intelligence, offensive, defensive, deterrent, legislative, and punitive measures, as well as educational and information campaigns aimed at fostering resilience among the Israeli public. In all of these activities, Israel has been required to strike a balance between its desire to achieve maximum effectiveness in its counterterrorism measures and the need to preserve the state's liberal-democratic values. The Israeli "democratic dilemma" in counterterrorism today characterizes the struggle that all liberal-democratic countries face in dealing with the threat of terrorism.[1]

This book presents four postulates that are examined throughout the following chapters, which review different periods during which Israel was forced to deal with various forms and magnitudes of terrorism.

1. Israel has never had a written policy to address counterterrorism. Israeli policy in this area is dynamic and has changed over the course of time, to a large extent in accordance with changes in the challenges, scope, and characteristics of terrorism faced by each Israeli government and its leaders.

2. Israel's counterterrorism strategy evolved through a combination of cumulative experience, different policies, and operative steps that have been taken by various Israeli governments over the years.

3. The methods employed by Israeli governments to counter terrorism to a large degree reflect the worldview and objectives set by their leaders (the prime minister [PM], ministers of defense, and heads of the defense and security establishment). The counterterrorism response also reflect the influences and pressures stemming from the internal Israeli system and the external, international system vis-à-vis Israeli counterterrorism activities.

4. Israel has never exhausted its capabilities in its actions against Palestinian terrorism. In many cases, Israeli governments have chosen to limit their counterterrorism activities due, among other factors, to ethical, moral, and legal considerations as well as external international pressure.

THE SEVERITY OF THE TERRORIST THREAT TO ISRAEL

Any state's counterterrorism doctrine, and the means and methods derived from it, results from the scope and characteristics of the terrorist threat. When dealing with the tactical threat of sporadic terrorist attacks with limited damage and casualties, the state will have a certain kind of reaction. When dealing with a large number of frequent, multi-casualty attacks, and when terrorism is causing significant harm to the country's economic stability, morale, and security, it is reasonable to assume that the state's policy in response to terrorism will be different.

As noted, Israel has contended with varying levels and types of terrorism for more than seven decades. However, it can be stated generally that since its establishment, Israel has had to contend with a very large—and possibly unprecedented—magnitude of terrorist attacks relative to its size and population and compared with terrorist activities in other countries. It is no wonder that the need to take counterterrorism action quickly became a crucial issue, significantly impacting the public and political discourse in Israeli society.

Israeli security policy in general, and counterterrorism policy in particular, has largely been the result of Israeli decision makers' assessment of the scope and characteristics of the terrorist threat during their respective terms in office. As one would expect, their answers to the question of whether terrorism poses an existential, strategic, or tactical threat to Israel, or whether it is at most a nuisance, affected Israel's handling of this phenomenon and its defensive, intelligence, and offensive measures in relation to the Palestinian terrorist organizations.

Israeli decision makers' assessments of the danger posed by terrorism can be learned from their answers to this question during my interviews with them. These interviews indicate that most of the decision makers, who were forced to deal with terrorist threats of varying degrees of intensity depending on the period, believe that terrorism often caused many casualties, affected the public's daily conduct and sense of security, and had an impact on the economy. In some cases, they noted, the threats dragged Israel into extensive military operations and even wars. However, terrorism has never succeeded in reaching a level at which it threatened the existence and survival of the state of Israel. For example, former counterterrorism adviser to the prime minister Rafi Eitan argued, "Terrorism against Israel has never constituted an existential danger. Never. On the contrary, it led to internal cohesion and unity and never achieved its goals. However, it did strike a serious blow to morale."[2]

Former Israel Defense Forces (IDF) chief of staff Gabi Ashkenazi agrees with Eitan and explains what constitutes an existential threat to Israel:

> An existential threat to the State of Israel would be an army that could occupy territory and conquer the state. If the Syrians had succeeded in crossing Jordan in 1973, that would have been an existential threat. . . . [Terrorism is] a nuisance—yes, a major disruption to normal life—yes, a blow to one's sense of personal security and to societal resilience—yes, but I do not think it is an existential threat.[3]

Former prime minister Yitzhak Shamir recommended reserving the definition of an existential threat for situations that require the full concentration of
all of the state's resources in order to deal with such a threat. Therefore, "one
should not vulgarize the subject by defining terrorism as an existential war."[4]

Another PM, Shimon Peres, clarified that he sees "terrorism more as
a threat to Israel than as a war."[5] However, terrorism might lead to wars.
Actually, terrorist and guerilla attacks have led Israel to launch large-scale
military operations several times throughout its history (for example,
Operation Protective Edge in Gaza in 2014) and even full-scale wars (such
as the First Lebanon War in 1982 and the Second Lebanon War in 2006).[6]
This is the reason that, according to former prime minister Ariel Sharon,
terrorism poses a strategic problem for Israel: "Unlike in other places where
terrorism is a tactical problem, in our region it is a strategic problem.
Because . . . all of the wars actually began with terrorist acts. . . . I think
that the era of great wars is over. We are facing limited wars. This will also
be the case in the world."[7] Former Mossad chief Meir Dagan explained the
strategic nature of the terrorist threat to Israel:

> Terrorism is not a direct strategic threat, but its ramifications certainly have
> strategic implications. I will give a few examples. Terrorism has its finger on
> the trigger, ready to cause harm to the diplomatic [peace] process. This has
> a strategic impact. From an economic perspective, terrorist attacks harm, for
> example, the willingness of foreign companies to invest in Israel, to tourism,
> and something much deeper that cannot be measured at a given moment—
> terrorism erodes the resilience of people over time. . . . The strategic ramifi-
> cations of terrorism can therefore be seen in almost every area of life.

At the same time, Dagan argues that although terrorism is only a strategic
threat to Israel, at a cumulative level, it might pose an existential threat to
the state. "If you want to smash a stone, then a blow of a hammer is war,
[and terrorist attacks are] drops of water that ostensibly do not appear to
be an existential threat, but if they continue for many years, in the end the
stone will cease to exist."[8]

In reference to the accumulated impact of terrorism, another Mossad
chief, Shabtai Shavit, argues that the level of such cumulative threats posed
to Israel should be regarded differently from the perspective of time, as
they occurred in different eras:

On the axis of time, at first, in the 1970s and until the mid-1980s, terrorism was only a tactical problem, like a stinging wasp. It wasn't pleasant, but it wasn't fatal. From the mid-1980s and during the 1990s, I think that terrorism took on a strategic aspect, and this is based on the test of whether the resilience and national strength of the people of Israel have been harmed—and I think the answer is yes. They have been harmed not because of terrorism alone but as a result of a combination of historical, social, economic, and political circumstances that terrorism was able to exploit.[9]

Many Israeli decision makers emphasize that terrorism has had a strategic impact on Israeli: Palestinian relations, the prospects for peace, and the possibility of the creation of a Palestinian state. (Some refer to this impact as positive and others as negative.)[10] Former IDF chief of staff Amnon Lipkin-Shahak argued, "Had it not been for Palestinian terrorism . . . today we would not find ourselves in the real dilemma of partitioning the land between us and the Palestinian Authority. . . . I can say that, to a large extent, if it were not for terrorism, the Palestinians would not have achieved their goals."[11] Yigal Pressler, former adviser to the PM on counterterrorism, continued this line of thinking: "If there had been no attacks in Jerusalem or in the West Bank, there would have been no Oslo Agreement."[12] Another former adviser to the PM on counterterrorism, Rehavam Ze'evi, sums up: "The Intifada [the Palestinian popular uprising in 1987] gave us the Palestinian state."[13]

Other Israeli decision makers stress that although the physical damage caused by terrorism is usually marginal, the anxiety and panic that accompanies this phenomenon might turn what is a negligible threat into a strategic danger.[14] Thus, for example, Meir Amit, who served as head of both the Military Intelligence Directorate and the Mossad, argued, "Terrorism can be described as a nuisance that has a cumulative psychological effect and an effect on morale that somewhere reaches the point at which quantity becomes quality."[15] Or as another former head of military intelligence, Shlomo Gazit, put it,

In objective terms, terrorism is of marginal significance . . . but public hysteria, which is to a large extent fueled by a leadership that does not know how to deal with this issue properly, turns it into a monster [which causes] the diversion of resources and the unjustified changing of priorities.[16]

Thus, most of the Israeli decision makers who dealt with terror in the 1980s, 1990s, and 2000s agree that terrorism has never reached the point at which it became an existential threat to Israel. However, for various reasons and in various aspects, this phenomenon poses a strategic threat to the state. The assessment of the extent of the danger posed by terrorism in each of the periods examined in this book is a precondition for understanding the methods, strategies, and measures that Israel has taken in dealing with terrorism.

ISRAEL'S COUNTERTERRORISM STRATEGY

Whether or not terrorism constitutes a strategic threat to Israel, the scope and characteristics of terrorist attacks against Israel over many years have forced it to employ a wide variety of counterterrorism measures in the areas of intelligence, offensive, and defensive activity. But has Israel's vast accumulation of experience in dealing with terrorism since its establishment led to the formulation of a clear and structured doctrine or a written counterterrorism strategy? According to Israeli decision makers, Israel's knowledge and experience in the field of counterterrorism has never been consolidated into a coherent strategy—neither a written nor a spoken one.

When asked whether Israel had a counterterrorism strategy, Ariel Sharon replied, "I do not know of a strategy. . . . I have not seen a consistent line."[17]

Shabtai Shavit also stressed that Israel did not develop a coherent counterterrorism strategy, attributing this to the need to bring many immediate operational solutions to rising terrorist threats:

> Israel has never had a counterterrorism strategy, nothing set out in an orderly fashion. I do not know of any system or entity whose job was, or who was given a mandate to deal with, the issue on a strategic level. But in the absence of a strategy I would not jump straight into tactics. In my opinion, in the normative world, there is a third level between these two levels—an operational one. Our policy against terrorism throughout the years has been operational—there was thinking all the time, but the thinking was operational—how to provide a solution for the near future.[18]

Meir Dagan agreed with this argument and added,

The state of Israel, as in many other things, never had a written doctrine on the matter. . . . The reason that the doctrine was not written is not a technical one. People are not stupid. They did not want to tie themselves down to limitations that would not stand the test of reality. Politicians are more aware than others [of the fact] that principles are born to live with and not to die for, so you do not want to make a policy that you then become captive to. You set a policy that is a guideline, and then when you reach a tight spot, there is no point in pouring out the baby with the bathwater.[19]

Prime Minister Benjamin Netanyahu also questioned the need for a written strategy for fighting terrorism. "A written policy is ineffective because people enslave its principles to a political agenda," he said.[20]

On the face of it, the absence of a defined and written counterterrorism strategy serves the political echelon and gives them room for maneuvering and contradiction. Reserve Brigadier General Nitzan Nuriel, who served as head of the counterterrorism bureau at the National Security Council under Netanyahu, added,

There is no strategy, because I think there is a great fear of commitment. The leadership prefers to respond to events or to act while the events are taking place rather than to create a clear directive that it must stand behind and that all the organizations should focus on. This way, the prime minister can say that we don't negotiate with terrorists but still conduct negotiations with terrorists.[21]

Nevertheless, there are those who find operational advantages, not just political ones, in the absence of a written strategy. Former IDF chief of staff Ashkenazi addressed the question of strategy, saying,

I do not think that there are only disadvantages to this. It requires us to rethink these things all the time. Necessity is the mother of all invention, and necessity has taught Israel to think all the time. I also think that there are differences between the various forms of terrorism. I think it would be a mistake to formulate something that applies to all kinds of terrorism all the time. I think things and circumstances change all the time.[22]

The absence of a written counterterrorism strategy therefore contributes to the Israeli out-of-the-box thinking and innovative approach to counterterrorism that has developed over the years.

Another argument against the need for a written counterterrorism policy was raised by Lipkin-Shahak:

> Written policy has limitations because it often finds its way to the media, and then public debates arise, which can reduce the effectiveness of the operational fight against terrorism. But it is necessary that the policy be clear and not left up to [the interpretation of] those carrying it out. In other words, the responsible political leaders must set out a clear policy, which, as far as I'm concerned, can also be written. It does not need to involve too many procedures. It should certainly have its own logic and comply with the laws and rules of the state. One cannot place the entire responsibility of policy making at the level of those carrying it out.[23]

Dagan agrees. Although he explains (as mentioned previously) the logic behind the absence of a written Israeli counterterrorism strategy, he argues that there is still a need to develop a clear guideline that will direct all operational agencies engaged in countering terrorism in a simultaneous and synergetic counterterrorism effort.

> There need to be guidelines that work in everyday life, in routine, because not everything rises to the decision-making level of the political echelon. 99 percent of daily decisions go through many other layers before they reach the decision maker, and because of this you have to determine very clear guidelines. . . . You can't call the head of the Shin Bet every morning and tell him that today you want him to do this and tomorrow you want him to do something else. The only way to solve this is by defining a policy.[24]

It would seem, in fact, that those who perform the duty of carrying out a counterterrorism policy in Israel—the heads of the security agencies—yearn for a kind of counterterrorism Magna Carta to explicitly define the objectives of counterterrorism, the guidelines for achieving these objectives, and the boundaries for action and maneuvering. In the absence of such a clear doctrine, the responsibility placed on the shoulders of these agencies is immeasurably greater. As such, it appears that at times the heads of the security forces have tried to take the initiative to formulate a written doctrine themselves, as noted by Yaakov Perry:

> I remember that several times over the past few years in the Shin Bet we composed documents that we submitted to the Israeli government, the Knesset Foreign Affairs and Defense Committee, the minister of defense, and the prime minister, in which we expressed how we see the [counterterrorism] objectives, the goals, and the paths to achieve them. It is true that in Israel there was never a discussion held in the cabinet under the title "the State of Israel's counterterrorism policy," but I think that in practice things are done very regularly.[25]

Dagan notes that at least once in the history of Israeli counterterrorism, there was an attempt to set out a written policy, but that policy was limited to counter only one type of terrorism—suicide terrorism—and has become anachronistic, as it has not been updated since.

> A policy is something that needs to be updated and every once in a while revised, as a policy always relates to the current reality. You could say there was once an attempt to do this. In 1996, after the major terrorist attacks, when the counterterrorism bureau was founded, headed by Ami Ayalon, I was his deputy. We wrote down the state of Israel's policy at the time, and the government ostensibly accepted it. In theory, it still applies to this day. You could say that since 1996, Israel has had a policy, but that policy, when you examine its essence, was directed at dealing with suicide bombings.[26]

Former prime minister Shamir, on the other hand, did not agree with the assumption that the counterterrorism strategy should be determined at the level of those executing it. According to Shamir,

> not everyone who knows how to fight this phenomenon in practice knows how to turn it into a doctrine. These are two different things. I would perhaps even say something more drastic—that someone who knows how to write a doctrine does not know how to carry it out, and vice versa. He who carries it out wants to turn everything he comes up with into a doctrine, so he also makes mistakes. One must be wary of doctrines. Not everything has to be turned into a doctrine.[27]

Ze'evi summed up by saying that Israel's counterterrorism policy was strongly influenced by the identity of the Israeli PM and their worldview at any given time:

> There is no such concept of a coherent, written policy that is passed on from one leader to another. The policy is a function, first of all, of the personality of the prime minister. Of all the prime ministers, the one who dealt most seriously with this was Rabin. . . . The others [prime ministers] dealt with it only to the extent that it was brought before them. When they came to Golda and told her that the murderer of the athletes was roaming around Europe, she dealt with it. . . . Not even Shamir, who arose from terrorism, and not Peres, who was deputy defense minister and defense minister.[28]

ISRAELI DECISION-MAKING PROCESSES REGARDING COUNTERTERRORISM

Given the absence of an official Israeli counterterrorism strategy, it is even more important to understand how decisions on counterterrorism were made in Israel. What was the decision-making process? Did this process differ from other such processes with regard to other subjects? Who are the relevant actors in this process? And what are their considerations?

Perry assessed the uniqueness of the Israeli counterterrorism decision-making process, arguing that internal (emotional) and external (international) considerations are taken into account. Perry pointed out three main typical characteristics of this unique process:

> Most important is secrecy, with the least amount of people in on the secret. This ultimately reduces the variety of opinions. The less opposition there is, the fewer dissenters exist. The second thing is emotion. On the issue of terrorism, the state is very emotional, and justifiably so . . . and when emotion gets involved in considerations that need to be very cold and very rigid, it tips the scale. The third thing is "what will the world say about us?" Other countries are less sensitive about this issue. . . . This effect greatly impacts the intensity of the fight, the resoluteness of the fight, and the staunchness of the decision. The United States, Britain, or France are much less sensitive to what the "gentiles" will say about them. Not because they are "gentiles" but because they are stable enough and strong enough.[29]

Shamir, on the other hand, highlighted the element of time in the counterterrorism decision-making process. According to him, the decision-making process on this issue is not very different from the process in relation to other issues, but "it has to be faster. You have no time to lose. In other matters, it may be possible to devote time to a period of reflection and deliberation, but here you need to decide quickly. But the decisions must be the correct ones."[30]

This sense of urgency can be explained by the fact that many of these decisions and initiatives in counterterrorism were taken over the years as an immediate response to severe terrorist attacks in Israel, or in light of a concrete intelligence warning of an expected attack. The PM's adviser on counterterrorism during the Rabin administration, Yigal Pressler, who was tasked with helping to deal with the new phenomenon of suicide bombings in the mid-1990s, argues that "most of the proposals in counterterrorism always came after attacks, never before them. . . . Once terrorist attacks are taking place, almost every counterterrorism proposal will be approved. After attacks, there are no financial restrictions. There are no interest groups."[31]

Who, then, initiates Israeli counterterrorism activity? Is it a bottom-up or a top-down process? It seems that the former head of intelligence and the military establishment of the time had a different view on this than Israel's political leaders.

According to Lipkin-Shahak, the initiation of counterterrorism activity usually takes place at the field level and is then brought before the decision makers for approval. "I assume that in the best-case scenario, the PM understands the ultimate intention, the main idea. But the activity, the goals, the path, and the timing come from the bottom up in the vast majority of cases." This process does not change even after the occurrence of major attacks, according to Lipkin-Shahak, who maintained that after such attacks, the government asks, "what do we do?" And the security services come up with recommendations.[32] Shavit refers to this as a two-way process:

On the one hand, the initiatives came from below. On the other hand, there was a demand from above. But there was quite a large gap between these two poles so I, as head of the Mossad, or the heads of other agencies, interpreted the decision maker's [wishes] even if he did not explicitly say that he expected and wanted to see initiatives from below.[33]

Benjamin Netanyahu presented the process differently: "In the policy arena, the initiative is top-down, totally."[34] Netanyahu was referring to steps aimed at applying pressure on Arafat to take action against terrorism during his first term as PM in the late 1990s. "When it came to initiating action [against terrorism], the general directive came from me and sporadic initiatives came from the field."[35] Peres stated, "It comes from above when it has a political slant; for example, reaching an agreement with the Palestinians. That is a political initiative. But whether to target the 'engineer' (Yahya Ayyash) or not? That comes from below."[36]

Carmi Gillon, former head of the Israel Securities Authority (ISA), took an intermediate position on the question of who takes initiative for counterterrorism activities:

> It works both ways in that the prime minister gives direction . . . and then in the end you go to the office and think about things and synthesize what you can bring to the table and what you can't. There are many bottom-up initiatives. In the end, the head of the organization filters ninety-five percent. And there is a meeting of minds here. . . . You know in advance that if you have the operational feasibility, then you are expected to do something.
>
> You need to remember one thing about the political echelon. However professional, however good, they are political people. This is something people often forget. Yitzhak Shamir was a political man even though he ran the system under him in a very rigid and institutionalized manner. The same definitely goes for Begin, and Rabin too. It all comes down to the ballot box at the end of the day. Now there is a lot of populism in this matter . . . because when the political leader looks at the big picture, he takes into consideration whether an operation is right or not, what the price of a mishap may be, what the price of success may be, and so on, he is very influenced by the environment in which he lives.[37]

Shamir, on the other hand, said,

> There should be a degree of freedom of action that would prevent unnecessary restrictions or loss of time or such things. We must avoid any bureaucracy. But there must be a report, and it is important that the people who are politically responsible for these matters be one hundred percent involved in everything that has been done or not done. This is very important because

the political echelon always knows things that those who are carrying it out do not know.[38]

Shamir claimed that dealing with terrorism did not take a lot of time from his daily agenda. "I do not think it distracted me or prevented me from dealing with other things," he said. "But I tried to make sure I knew a great deal about this matter, and one of the ways to learn is to read raw material, not just general summaries. And personal meetings are also very important. You learn a lot from them."[39] Pressler, Rabin's adviser, said that the subject of terrorism took a considerable part of the PM's time: "It depends who the prime minister is and whether he has a defense minister," he said. Rabin was both prime minister and defense minister, and Shamir had a defense minister. "About 80 percent of Prime Minister Rabin's security dealings had to do with terrorism. Most of the military activities were only to do with terrorism."[40]

The difference in the amount of time each PM devoted to dealing with counterterrorism stemmed, of course, from the scope of the terrorist threat during their term of office. But their decisions in the field of counterterrorism were also a result of their degree of determination and their ideological worldview. On this point, Shavit said,

> Each prime minister has his own personality and is exposed to different people and advisers with different approaches. Shamir was more determined in his worldview than Rabin was on the issue of targeted killings. In most cases, the Mossad was more active, pushing more for an active war against terror and its leaders. Military Intelligence often presented the potential prices we may pay as a reaction to [counterterrorism activities], which sometimes led doubt to be cast regarding how worthwhile these actions were. The Shin Bet had an operational perspective. The Shin Bet's answer was to try and see whether a particular action would have an immediate, operative effect on areas that were within its responsibility.[41]

THE COUNTERTERRORISM DECISION-MAKING PROCESS
CONCEPTUAL MODELS

So what can be learned from the interviews with decision makers regarding the challenge that terrorism poses to Israel, decision-making processes in counterterrorism, and the Israeli strategy in countering terrorism in general?

Israeli decision makers and heads of the security establishment believe that terrorism poses a unique and critical challenge compared with other security threats and challenges facing Israel. These decision makers also argue that despite the severity of the strategic threat that terrorism poses, the state never constructed a comprehensive, systematic written counterterrorism strategy. Instead, the growing Israeli experience in its never-ending efforts to counter terrorism has accumulated over the years to become a kind of oral guideline to lead the counterterrorism establishment. These guidelines were changed and interpreted by different Israeli governments and decision makers according to the level and characteristics of the terrorism that the state was facing during their terms while taking into consideration both internal and external influences, pressures, and constraints.

All of the respondents emphasized the importance of Israel's key decision maker, the prime minister, in the counterterrorism decision-making processes. The following conceptual model examines the factors—the formal and informal actors—that play a role in or influence the decision-making processes in this area. It alsolooks at the main considerations—both internal and external—that each decision maker takes into account when examining the methods of action or tools needed to combat terrorism in the given period (such as targeted killings, the deportation of terrorists, or the demolition of houses).

As we have seen, many factors influence the decision-making processes in counterterrorism. Ultimately, however, most of the strategic decisions on this issue are made by the Israeli cabinet and by the person in charge of it—the PM. These players will be the ones to decide on, among other things, major counterterrorism operations, targeted killings, negotiations with terrorist organizations over the release of hostages, humanitarian activities, diplomatic processes with regard to terrorist organizations and the populations they purport to represent, concrete reactions in the wake of major terrorist attacks, and the degree of intensity of the use of various counterterrorism methods. Although formally the decisions on these issues are made by either the entire Israeli government or the smaller security cabinet, in many cases the ministers accept (following a discussion and perhaps even a debate) the PM's preferred course of action.

The prime minister, for his or her part, brings personal, ideological, and emotional baggage, as well as personal experience, to the discussion table. Most of the PMs came from within the Israeli security establishment, in which they served before and after the founding of the state. Some even held the highest offices within the defense establishment, such as Ben-Gurion, Begin, Shamir, Rabin, Sharon, and Barak. Others were elected to the post of prime minister following many years of political experience within their party and in the political and diplomatic spheres (for example, Golda Meir and Ehud Olmert). Others represent a mix of the two backgrounds. (Netanyahu, for example, has an esteemed military record, though he never held a senior commanding post, along with extensive political and diplomatic experience.)

The PM makes decisions in light of his or her cumulative professional experience and value system. Naturally, he or she is influenced by the educational system in which he or she was raised (which is sometimes affiliated with a particular ideological doctrine) and the education received at the parents' home. All of these factors shape the PM's worldview, which is usually presented to constituents before he or she is elected. This worldview becomes the leader's moral North Star that guides his or her decisions, but in certain cases the PM's declared ideology can act as a millstone around his or her neck that prevents the making of necessary decisions.

In addition to the foundation of the ideological and moral core that shapes the Israeli PM's worldview, there are many additional (and sometimes even contradictory) concrete influences, in the form of formal and informal players who have the leader's ear. These voices, too, affect his or her stances and decisions in dealing with terrorism. Included in the informal influences are family members, friends, and other close associates whose opinions the PM values. Alongside them are various advisers who, in most cases, accompanied the him or her along the bumpy political path to the lofty position and who won trust and respect along the way. Some of these advisers are political consultants whose job it is to liaise between the PM and other bodies in the political system, such as parliament, the government coalition, or the PM's own party. Beyond the political advisers who mediate between the party and the PM, the party and its members also have direct channels of influence on his or her decisions on various issues, including counterterrorism, through various party institutions. (The influence of these institutions on government decisions was greater during the state's early years than it has been in recent decades.)

Along with the informal and semiformal actors that influence the government and its leader, there are formal and sometimes even statutory channels of influence. For example, for many years (until 1996), prime ministers used to appoint a special adviser on terrorism, whose task was to coordinate the counterterrorism activities of the various security agencies and ministries and to provide advice on the issues. The adviser on counterterrorism had more influence on the PM's decisions in dealing with terror than did other advisers. However, the adviser often found himself competing for the leader's ear with the heads of the security agencies, who expressed different and even contradictory positions on the issues on the agenda. Traditionally, the adviser was appointed by the prime minister himself. His background was in security, and he had extensive experience in dealing with terrorism. Above all, however, the counterterrorism adviser was in many cases a personal friend and confidante of the PM, and as such, he gained the respect of the Israeli security community, which gave him more influence among that community.

The decisions of the Israeli government as a whole and of the prime minister in particular on how to deal with the phenomenon of terrorism are influenced primarily by the positions adopted by the official bodies responsible for thwarting terrorism—the Israeli security forces and their heads: ISA, Mossad, IDF, Military Intelligence, and, to a certain extent, the police. These bodies, as we have seen, not only convey to the PM their recommendations about what to do when a decision on counterterrorism must be made but also, in many cases, initiate action and bring it to the government for approval. Other formal players influencing decision-making processes and the PM's decisions on counterterrorism are the National Security Council and the relevant ministers: of defense, foreign affairs, internal security, and sometimes the minister of intelligence, as well as other cabinet ministers who have extensive experience in security or who are the heads of the political parties that make up the coalition.

As noted, the phenomenon of terrorism takes center stage when it comes to public interest and media attention in Israel and therefore constitutes a difficult and constant test for the Israeli leadership, especially the prime minister. The PM is a political figure who holds office by the will of the voters in the democracy of Israel, and therefore he or she must reflect and, to

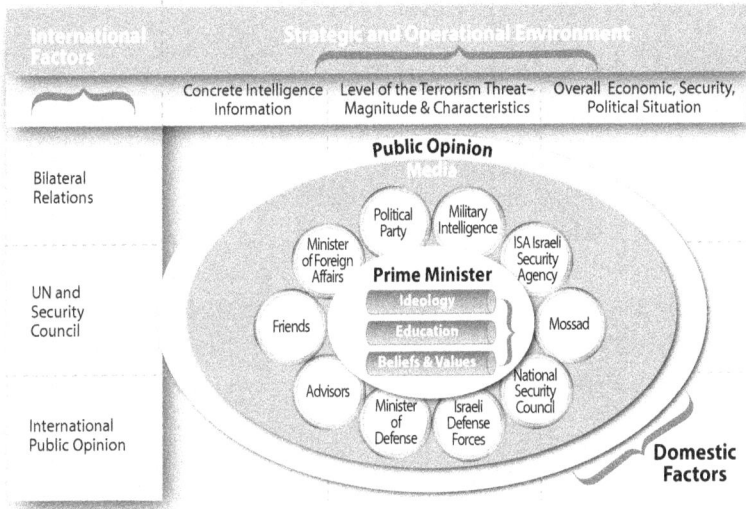

FIGURE 1.1. Factors influencing the Israeli counterterrorism decision-making process

a large extent, satisfy the wishes of the voters and fulfill their expectations (or what the PM perceives as being the public's expectations. The people, public opinion, and the Israeli media therefore play an important role in and have a significant influence on the decision-making processes of the leadership in dealing with terrorism (figure 1.1).

All of these factors are the domestic influences that shape the policies adopted by the PM and the government's actions in the field of counterterrorism. However, Israel's decision-making processes are also subject to external and international influences and constraints. Israel, to its chagrin, is constantly under international scrutiny when it comes to its attempts to deal with Palestinian terrorism. The bloc of states composed of the Arab, Muslim, and nonaligned countries—most of which do not recognize Israel's right to exist and do not maintain diplomatic relations with it—has always had an almost automatic majority in international institutions, first and foremost in the various UN bodies. This reality has led to unprecedented and relentless criticism by these institutions of Israeli counterterrorism measures. Furthermore, Israel's friends among the Western nations are often critical of the actions Israel takes to combat terror (whether to appease and maintain good relations with the Arab and Muslim states, or because of their genuine expectation that their friend, Israel, one of the only democracies in the Middle East, meet the highest standards of liberal-democratic values). This criticism by Western countries has often reflected the negative sentiment and condemnatory attitude of the public and the media in these countries vis-à-vis Israel. All of these elements make up the system of international influences and constraints on Israeli governments and their leaders that had to be taken into account when deciding on whether or not to carry out counterterrorism activity.

The considerations, influences, and constraints described in this chapter do not exist in a vacuum. The decisions that Israeli decision makers have been required to make in the field of counterterrorism have generally been made in light of certain circumstances and very specific and concrete needs, including those stemming from the security situation at the time. (An example is the degree of stability of Israel's relations with its neighbors and the risk of descending into all-out war as a result of a decision to carry out a military operation against terrorist targets in the territory of a neighboring state.) Other considerations that have had to be taken into account are those related to the economic, political, and diplomatic situation in the country at the time of the decision, as well as analysis and assessment of the level of terrorism. For example, have there been a large and ongoing number of terrorist attacks? Is it a rising wave or one that is at its peak or on its way down? Does it represent a new type of attack that is posing a challenge to Israel? How many casualties? And finally, of course, there is the consideration of whether or not a concrete intelligence alert exists that requires immediate action.

These are the actors and the systems of constraints that influence the Israeli prime minister when he or she makes decisions on how to confront terrorism. These considerations and constrictions can be illustrated using the Counterterrorism Dilemmas Conceptual Model, which presents two axes that reflect the central, permanent tensions faced by the various Israeli governments and that shaped their decisions on how to deal with terrorism.[42]

A. The "democratic dilemma" axis. At one end of this axis is action that is very effective in combating terrorism, and at the other end are the liberal-democratic values of the state. The tension between the two extremes of the democratic dilemma axis is expressed in the fact that an increase in the level of effectiveness is, most likely, liable to threaten the state's liberal-democratic values. An effective fight against terrorism might cause damage to citizens' rights to privacy, freedom of expression, freedom of assembly, protest, a fair trial, and more.

On the other hand, stricter adherence to these democratic and liberal rights might reduce the effectiveness of the fight against terrorism. Thus, on issues of counterterrorism the decision maker finds himself or herself in constant tension between the desire to maximize the effectiveness of the fight against terrorism and the desire to preserve the liberal and democratic character and values of the state. This tension, known as "democratic dilemma in counterterrorism,"[43] essentially dictates the decision-making process in dealing with terrorism, especially with regard to the means and methods of action used in counterterrorism activity.

In reference to the aforementioned model of influencing factors on Israeli counterterrorism decision-making, it is only natural that Israeli security agencies (Mossad, ISA, Military Intelligence Directorate, police, etc.) strive to maximize the efficiency of counterterrorism activities. On the other hand, legal counsels, human rights organizations, and sometimes close friends and associates often present a position that assigns paramount importance to the preservation of liberal-democratic values even if such preservation curbs counterterrorism activity. It should be noted that the democratic dilemma axis is a zero-sum game continuum according to which one can review various counterterrorism activities, as well as overall counterterrorism policy executed over a certain period, through their positioning on the axis at a point that is closer to the end, reflecting maximal efficiency, or closer to the other end, which reflects maximal preservation of the liberal-democratic values of the state.

B. *The "dilemma of restraint in counterterrorism" axis.* This axis reflects the influence of domestic factors versus external factors on the decision-making processes in counterterrorism and the constant tension between them with regard to the degree of restraint required in Israeli counterterrorism activities. In Israel, as a country that suffers from terrorist attacks, internal public pressure exerted on decision makers (particularly after the occurrence of severe terrorist attacks) naturally reflects a demand for more effective and determined action and less restraint when it comes to offensive, punitive, retaliatory, and deterrent measures against the terrorist organizations, the perpetrators, and their dispatchers. At the same time, the pressure exerted on Israeli decision makers by external and international actors—UN institutions, international organizations and tribunals, friendly countries, international media and public opinion, and the like (as reflected by the International Factors in the aforementioned model of influencing factors on the Israeli Counterterrorism Decision-Making)—is designed to achieve as much restraint as possible with regard to the state's counterterrorism activity, to minimize the use of coercive measures, and especially to reduce the expected collateral damage. In other words, compliance with domestic pressure stands largely in contradiction to the pressure applied on Israel by international players.

Here, too, one must address the restraint axis as a continuum, according to which one can review various counterterrorism activities as overall counterterrorism policy executed over a certain period through their positioning on the axis at a point that is closer to the end, reflecting maximal restraint, or closer to the other end, which reflects no restraint at all. These two dilemmas can be illustrated by using the conceptual model in figure 1.2.

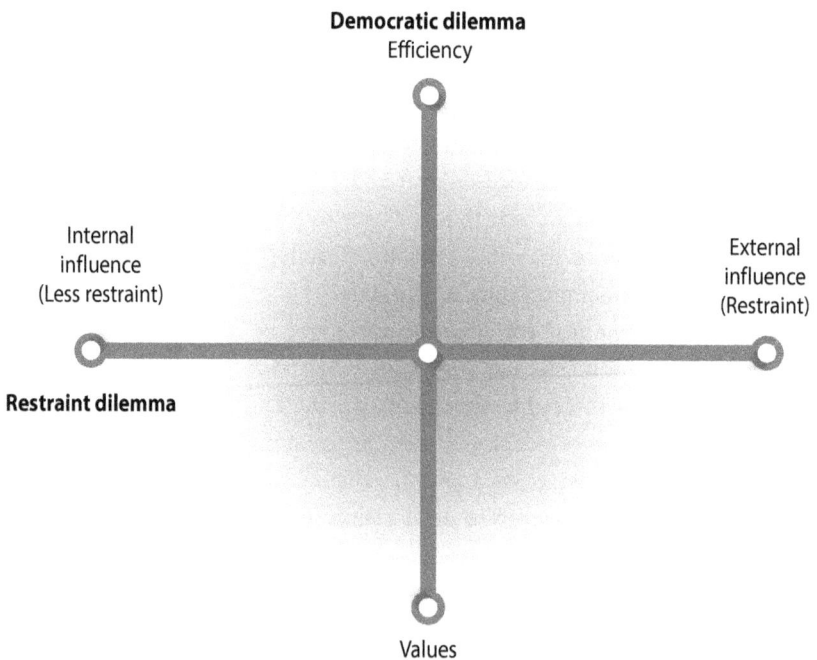

FIGURE. 1.2. Counterterrorism Dilemmas Conceptual Model

We can therefore position the various Israeli governments' counterterrorism activities on these axes in the conceptual model and see how far they are from the point that reflects the delicate balance between the various tensions stemming from the democratic dilemma and the dilemma of restraint. We can also see whether they are closer to the extremes of each continuum.

This Counterterrorism Dilemmas Conceptual Model will be utilized at the end of each of the following chapters as a basis for analyzing the features of the Israeli government's counter-terrorism activities in the period discussed in the chapter. At the end of the book, the model will help us compare the counterterrorism policies of the various governments. The proposed model will thus serve as a tool for analyzing Israel's "art of counterterrorism" throughout the years—the art of finding the required balance between different and sometimes contradictory methods and strategies for dealing with terrorism. In addition, this conceptual model will enable us to draw conclusions from the Israeli experience in confronting terrorism, which will also be relevant for other democratic countries dealing with this phenomenon.

Chapter Two

THE "FEDAYEEN PHENOMENON"

The David Ben-Gurion and Moshe Sharett Administrations (1948-63)

THE FEDAYEEN

In 1948, the newly minted Israel faced the first of many wars against its Arab neighbors. The state was forced to confront a coalition of Arab states that were disgruntled by the 1947 United Nations Partition Plan for Palestine in what became known as the War of Independence. In 1949, Israel signed a set of armistice agreements with its Arab neighbors, Egypt, Lebanon, Jordan, and Syria. The Armistice Lines have since become known as the "Green Line" and allowed Israel to maintain control over 78 percent of the territory formerly known as Mandatory Palestine.[1] After the signing of the armistice deal, the Palestinians who evacuated their homes ended up as refugees in Egypt, Syria, Lebanon, and especially Jordan.

In the years following establishment of the state of Israel, many refugees tried to infiltrate into Israeli territory, sometimes in an attempt to return to their abandoned homes and sometimes to carry out property crimes or terrorist attacks. These intrusion attempts were referred to as *histaninuyot*, or infiltrations. Common among all of these infiltrations were that the perpetrators were residents of the neighboring Arab countries and that their actions involved penetrating into Israel through the armistice demarcation lines.[2] The individuals who infiltrated Israel became known as Fedayeen.

Over the years, changes occurred in the type and volume of infiltration. Between 1952 and 1956, intrusions into Israel decreased from 16,000 in 1952 to 7,018 in 1953,[3] 4,638 in 1954, and 4,351 in 1955.[4] However, at the same time, it appears that there was an increase in the number of personal injuries as a result of infiltrations. In 1951, 137 Israeli civilians and soldiers were injured by infiltration units (mainly from Jordanian territory). In 1952, the number of wounded rose to 147; in 1953, 162 people were injured; in 1954, there were 180 injuries; and in 1955, 258 Israelis were wounded by the actions of the Fedayeen.[5] Benny Morris estimates that between 1949 and 1956, infiltrators killed between 200 and 300 Israelis (not including soldiers who were killed or injured in border clashes with Arab armies), and wounded between 500 and 1,000.[6]

Beyond the physical harm that the infiltrators caused, to both property and human lives, the primary damage was psychological—to morale. The repeated attacks on Israeli soil caused much anxiety among the public, and the state was forced to allocate considerable resources to protecting the border communities. Indeed, the psychological damage from the infiltrations into Israel and particularly on the border settlements had serious direct and tangible consequences in the form of an exodus of residents of the border communities to central Israel. These settlements were mainly populated by immigrants, who bore the physical and emotional burden of repeated assaults. Their abandonment of the border communities severely damaged Israel's strategy following the War of Independence, which was intended to assert and protect Israel's borders and prevent infiltration through the establishment of approximately 350 new settlements along the borders between 1948 and 1953.[7]

Israeli leaders attributed the blow to the morale of the residents of these communities to the fact that they lacked the resilience that characterized those who had lived in Israel longer, as these new immigrants had fled primarily from Arab countries on the eve of Israel's independence.[8] Some of the new settlements were abandoned altogether, and many others were left only partially populated.[9]

Morris categorizes the phenomenon of infiltrations in the years between 1949 and 1956 as "innocent infiltration," driven by economic motives, and "violent infiltration," which was politically motivated. Most of the infiltrations in the state's early years fell in the first category, reflecting Palestinian attempts to return to their homes, cultivate their land, and regain property they had left behind. However, the second group comprised intrusions by Palestinian refugees and soldiers and citizens of Egypt, Jordan, and Lebanon, who infiltrated Israel for the purpose of killing, inflicting damage, and gathering intelligence. It should be noted that in some cases, infiltration originally intended for economic purposes actually ended in the death and injury of civilians.[10]

One of the recurring questions that has arisen in studies of the phenomenon of these infiltrations has been the degree to which they were organized by the Arab states. The extent of Arab countries' direct and indirect involvement varied over the years and with the different borders. However, Israel adopted an official position to deal with infiltrations across the board. From the state's point of view, the fact that the infiltrators crossed the cease-fire lines from the territory of a neighboring Arab country was enough to impose full responsibility for the infiltration and its consequences on that country.[11]

This was not the only difficulty faced by Israeli governments in assessing the situation. Another question that had to be addressed was the gap between the policies of government officials and decision makers in neighboring countries toward infiltrations into Israel and the position of officials on the ground. There were sometimes significant differences between the positions of these actors, which made it difficult to carry out the decisions and policies laid down by central Arab governments. This reality threw into question the degree to which Arab states had the power to cease infiltrations into Israel.[12]

In any case, it seems that after the War of Independence and in the early 1950s, the Fedayeen's activities were spontaneous for the most part and typically criminal in nature, though sometimes their actions were executed for political reasons and directed by the Grand Mufti of Jerusalem and his flock in the West Bank and Gaza Strip.[13] The phenomenon of infiltration quickly took shape and adopted characteristics of a war of attrition through which Arab countries were able to remain involved in the conflict without risking deterioration into all-out war with Israel, which they might have found themselves losing. Using the bands of Fedayeen as a strategy of guerilla warfare against Israel was particularly suited to the conditions on the ground and Israel's long and winding borders, which, as they were formulated in the postwar armistice agreements, lacked any landforms or natural barriers.

Of the Arab states bordering Israel, it was Egypt that led the way in organizing, initiating, and directing the cells of Fedayeen, particularly between 1954 to 1956.[14] During these years, Egypt began to organize squads of Fedayeen to carry out infiltrations into Israel not only from the Gaza Strip and the Israeli-Egyptian border but also from Israel's borders with Jordan and Lebanon.[15] According to Israel's prime minister at the time, David Ben-Gurion,

> Our neighbors were not satisfied with violating the principles of the UN Charter and infringing on our rights as they were secured in the ceasefire agreements, but rather organized guerrilla attacks against Israeli civilians. . . . Cases of this began in the early years following the signing of the armistice agreements, but continued to escalate, especially from 1951 onwards. . . . Egyptian groups called Fedayeen were specially organized by the dictator of Egypt. . . . According to the confession of the Egyptian dictator himself, as well as reliable information that was received by ambassadors of countries friendly to Israel, groups of Fedayeen were sent by the military junta in Egypt to Jordan and Lebanon, although the authorities in these two countries did not approve of these actions.[16]

HANDLING THE FEDAYEEN PHENOMENON

Shortly after the War of Independence, Israel began to take extensive steps toward fortification and self-defense. Fences were erected along the borders and around the border settlements, and mines and explosives were buried along the fences. Israel also used booby-traps, including tripwire mines and "jumping" fragmentation mines. Devices such as irrigation pipes and water pumps were booby-trapped. To reduce the ability of the Fedayeen squads to penetrate into Israeli territory, Israel also bolstered its troops stationed along the border and at potential points of intrusion. This task was assigned to a new unit that was established in the early 1950s, *Mishmar Hagvul*, or border police, whose troops carried out patrols and ambushes along the border.[17] Between 1949 and 1956, the state spent $1 million annually to protect the border settlements, which did not include expenses for the IDF, police, and physical protection of the settlements.[18]

Israel's efforts to effectively seal its land borders failed, as the task was beyond its capacities and limited resources. Attempts to reach an understanding and operational agreement with its neighbors to prevent the infiltration of the Fedayeen into Israeli territory were also unsuccessful.[19] The failures of both the Israeli defense system and attempts to reach an understanding with the neighboring Arab states led the young state's decision makers, particularly its military leaders, to adopt an active approach of reprisals in an attempt to stop Fedayeen infiltration. This retaliatory action was aimed mainly at Palestinian and Arab communities along the borders in neighboring Arab states, which served as bases for the Fedayeen's actions.

In general, the Israeli reaction at this point (the early 1950s) was not based on any political or military doctrine but, rather, on the unsystematic organization of individuals or military forces, as opposed to a military force that was trained to carry out this particular task. The motives behind the Israeli response included a combination of a desire for revenge and the achievement of deterrence, rather than a methodical military doctrine. According to the Jerusalem district commander at the time, Colonel Michel Shaham,

> 1952 was full of failures. IDF soldiers demonstrated a lack of persistence and professionalism. There were places where reprisals took place, or where they were meant to have taken place; and these are all unpleasant to remember. Beit Jalla, Beit Sira, Idhna, Wadi Fukin, Furik, Deir Ballut, and more. It is fortunate that these reprisals were not published in the Israeli press. It was better that way. It was better for the people of Israel to think that the IDF, for political and other reasons, was employing a policy of restraint, rather than to be aware of the army's military failures.[20]

Ian Lustick noted that at the time, the attacking units "displayed both cowardice and ineptitude."[21] Ariel Sharon (later prime minister), who was summoned by Colonel Shaham to assist in stabilizing the area, described the situation at the time as follows:

> It was a total state of failure in terms of the security situation. The War of Independence ended. . . . After the war there was already a decline. The army took on a different character. It was organizing itself. A very large percentage of officers had been released and had gone home. Especially commanders of field units. Then a wave of terror began . . . the situation deteriorated, and the IDF, then at its lowest point in terms of its capability, tried to carry out a

series of actions that usually ended in failure. Each time, I had a feeling that it could have been done differently, but I was a student in Jerusalem, a battalion commander in the reserves in the Jerusalem brigade. I assume that I said as much to the brigade commander, Michel Shaham, of blessed memory. He was very close to Ben-Gurion and spoke with him about the matter.[22]

Indeed, Colonel Shaham understood the need for a trained military unit suited for special missions of this kind. Shaham received the approval of his superiors and initiated the establishment of what was to be called "Unit 101," commanded by Major Ariel Sharon. This decision was contrary to the position of Head of Operations Moshe Dayan, who believed that every military unit needed to be capable of such actions, not just special units.[23]

The unit's test mission was to blast the home of one of the Fedayeen leaders, Mustafa Samueli, from the village of Nabi Samuel.[24] The mission was deemed a success, despite the fact that Samueli had not been sleeping in his home that night and was therefore unharmed.[25] Unit 101 soon made a name for itself as an elite IDF unit charged with carrying out actions on Jordanian and Egyptian territory against the Fedayeen and their dispatchers. Due to the sensitivity of these operations, the unit's activities were kept secret, and Israel generally did not accept public responsibility for its actions. Moreover, members of the unit did not wear IDF uniforms and were armed with weapons captured from Arab armies and the Fedayeen themselves, to conceal any Israeli involvement. In several cases, when asked, Israeli officials claimed that by their assessment, these activities were carried out spontaneously by Israeli citizens.[26]

The establishment of Unit 101 was not followed by a substantial change in the goals and targets of Israeli retaliation. Rather, the change was reflected in the skills of the combat forces and the success of their missions. The unit and its members, who carried out the majority of their operations across the border, set new standards of combat and served as role models to the entire military, bolstering the IDF spirit for years to come.[27] In describing the principles that guided the activities of Unit 101 at that time, its commander, Ariel Sharon, quoted then-IDF Chief of Staff Moshe Dayan as saying, "you cannot guard every tree in the orchard and every water pipeline in the field, and it is impossible to secure the lives of all Jews everywhere, but we need to set a high price for attacks against Jews that will make them think twice before attacking."[28]

As a direct continuation of the sporadic retribution attacks that characterized Israel's policy until the establishment of Unit 101, many reprisals in the years 1952 to 1955 (after the unit's establishment) were directed against civilian targets such as settlements, facilities, and homes. The primary course of action was penetrating a civilian settlement in the West Bank (which was then under Jordanian control) and bombing a building or several buildings, sometimes along with their inhabitants. The decision to carry out an operation on one target or another was generally based on prior intelligence indicating that Fedayeen cells operating in Israel were using it as a base for its mission, or that the villagers were collaborating with the Fedayeen. Unsurprisingly, Israel's retaliatory actions sparked harsh international criticism, expressed by repeated condemnations from the United Nations and criticism from various countries.[29]

Another guiding principle of the unit's activities was "an eye for an eye and a tooth for a tooth." When a member of the unit, Yitzhak Jibli, was captured by Jordan during an Israeli retaliatory raid in June 1954, in the months that followed, a number of actions were carried out to take members of the Jordanian Legion hostage and bring them to Israel in order to obtain Jibli's release. Four months later, a prisoner exchange did take place, and Jibli was returned in exchange for four members of the Jordanian Legion.[30] According to Dayan, the reprisals were designed to create explicit, defined rules specifically aimed at the Arab states and "to establish rules regarding what was permitted and was forbidden in [Israel's] relations with the Arab states and their inhabitants, and be careful not to surrender."[31]

According to Morris, at the same time, Israel launched a strategy of "indirect deterrence." Because it was impossible to target those anonymous infiltrators who carried out attacks in Israel, it was only natural that the deterrence be directed toward Arab states in order to make it clear that it was their responsibility to prevent this type of activity.[32] In fact, the retaliations were not only intended to deter Arab states and prevent the infiltrators from continuing their activities against Israel but also to make it clear to the Arabs that they would not succeed in destroying the state.

Aharonson and Horowitz define additional goals of Israeli reprisals as "latent functions," which include creating an atmosphere in which the superpowers would choose to abandon policy initiatives that might threaten the status quo.[33] They argue that some Israeli policy makers believed that a military confrontation with the Arabs was inevitable and that time was on their side, and therefore the reprisals could be used as a means of controlled escalation. The retaliatory attacks were used to improve the standard of combat and raise morale among IDF soldiers. The Israeli retaliations also affected the morale of the public. According to Aharonson and Horowitz, the recent historical emotional experiences of the Holocaust and the rebirth of the Jewish people in Israel created public pressure for a response to any provocation.[34]

Morris notes that the raid on the village of Sharafat in February 1951 was in retaliation for an attack by infiltrators in West Jerusalem earlier that month. The reprisal was in accordance with the "eye for an eye" principle defined by Dayan, and it resulted in nine Palestinians deaths, including women and children. One of the most lethal reprisals carried out at the time by the IDF against Fedayeen bases took place on October 14, 1953, in the village of Qibya. This operation, which was triggered by the murder of a mother and her two children in the Jewish town of Yehud by a group of infiltrators from Jordan, led to the death of sixty-nine residents of the village. Israeli officials denied involvement in the Qibya raid. Five days after the operation, prime minister and defense minister David Ben-Gurion made the following declaration in an address to the nation:

> We carried out a thorough investigation and it is clear beyond a doubt that not a single Army unit, even the smallest one, was absent from its base on the night of the Qibya attack. The border settlers in Israel, mostly refugees from Arab countries and survivors of the Nazi concentration camps, have for years been the target of murderous attacks. The Israeli government gave them weapons and trained them to protect themselves, until some people in these border settlements lost their patience and after the murder of a mother and her two children in Yehud, they attacked, last week, the village of Qibya across the border, one of the main centers of the gangs of murderers. Every one of us regrets and suffers when blood is shed anywhere and nobody regrets more than the Israeli government the fact that innocent people were killed in the retaliation act in Qibya. All of the responsibility rests with the government of Jordan.[35]

However, in a later account given by IDF commander Major General Rehavam Ze'evi, he relayed that the Qibya raid was dubbed "Operation Shoshana" after the Jewish girl who was murdered, along with her mother and brother, Reuven. Ze'evi also said that Ben-Gurion had given an order to collect and burn all written material relating to the raid—operational commands, maps, and reports. It would seem that Israel's policy of taking no responsibility for retaliatory attacks was not unique to the Qibya operation. Morris claims that over the course of the years 1949 to 1953, Israel almost always denied involvement in reprisals, with government spokespersons repeatedly maintaining that they did not have any information about what happened, or that it was the independent initiative of "vigilantes."[36]

Sixteen years after the incident, in a lecture to a group of teenagers in Tel Aviv in January 1969, Defense Minister Moshe Dayan acknowledged Israel's responsibility for the Qibya operation:

> During the Qibya operation, I was not Chief of Staff, but I was Chief of Operations, and I know that it was not the intention of the government of Israel or the IDF to kill residents of Qibya. The intention was to destroy houses. A special unit went into the village and the Arabs locked themselves up inside their homes and shuttered the windows. The unit thought that the village was empty and that everyone had fled because there had first been an exchange of gunfire. Several houses were blown up and it later transpired that they had been blown up along with their inhabitants. It turned out that the men had fled, leaving their wives and children at home. The stain of the Qibya operation has still not been erased.[37]

The trauma of the Qibya raid had an impact on the Israeli government and led to a change in its policy. Moshe Sharett, who at the time was serving as foreign minister and was among the chief opponents of Israel's reprisals policy, used the harsh impact made by the actions in Qibya to pressure Ben-Gurion to change the government's decision-making processes concerning retaliations. Up to that point, Ben-Gurion was the only person who approved these operations. But as a result of Sharett's pressure, it was agreed that from that point on, the defense minister would be consulted before a decision was made, and a dispute occurred, the decision would be passed on to the Cabinet.[38]

At the same time, the guidelines regarding retaliatory operations were changed. At the end of 1953, new IDF operational orders were drafted, detailing that IDF activity would be carried out in a transparent manner;

there would be no deliberate targeting of civilians, women, or children; the choice of target would not necessarily be linked to the attack for which the reprisal was carried out; the retaliatory response would be as swift as possible and as near as possible to the original attack; and the chosen targets would be essential military and police installations.[39] However, the Israeli government continued to lay most of the blame for the Fedayeen's actions on the neighboring Arab countries. In light of this, the Israeli government announced in November 1955 that it was

> as ready as ever to honor the ceasefire agreements in all their detail, to the last letter. But the other side must also follow through on its commitment. An agreement that is violated by the other side will not apply to us as well. If the ceasefire lines across the border are opened to terrorists and murderers, they will not be closed to those defending themselves. If our rights are violated by violence via land or sea, we maintain the freedom to protect ourselves in the most active way.[40]

And, indeed, in 1955–56, the majority of Israeli retaliations focused on Jordanian and Egyptian military and police targets. The objective underlying these actions was to cause significant damage to Arab armies and governments in order to pressure them to stop their support for the Fedayeen and to act to prevent Fedayeen forces' infiltration into Israel from their territory. Meir Amit dubbed Israel's policy at the time the "billiard ball method"—"You're hitting a ball there in order for it to come back here."[41]

The transition of retaliatory actions from a focus on civilian to military targets was intended to improve Israel's image in the world. However, this new policy effectively served Palestinian interests insofar as it escalated tensions in the region and was liable to lead to an outbreak of fighting between Israel and its neighbors, and perhaps even to an all-out war.[42]

Opinions vary with regard to the effectiveness of the Israeli retaliatory actions against Arab states. Morris, for example, highlights the negative consequences of the reprisal in Gaza in 1955. According to Egyptian media and some Egyptian officials in Gaza, the reprisal led some to sympathize with the Fedayeen.[43] However, he admits that after the raid, Egyptian authorities embarked on a large-scale operation to limit infiltration out of fear of an uncontrolled deterioration of the situation.[44] He says,

throughout most of the period in question (1949–1956), the Arab governments and their armies denounced infiltration attacks, mainly due to fear of
IDF retaliation. . . . The retaliatory raids were, above all, acts of punishment
and deterrence. But they lifted Israelis' spirits, helped forge a unified nation
from a multifaceted immigrant society, certainly helped Mapai (the ruling
party) retain power and relegate the more vocal and militant right, and without a doubt, prepared the IDF for a second round.[45]

In contrast, Aharonson and Horowitz stress that despite the fact that the
reprisals were a means to preserve and enhance Israel's deterrence, created
a "safety valve" that prevented the need for all-out war and, in the main,
strengthened the public status of the Israeli political elite, it is difficult to
establish ironclad rules with respect to the effectiveness of retaliations,
because it is impossible to assess what the situation would have been had
these activities not been carried out.[46]

Zaki Shalom argues that in order to examine the effectiveness of the reprisals, one must look at two main criteria: the objectives that this policy was
supposed to achieve, and the alternative situation that would have occurred
in its absence. He believes that originally, policy makers were not inclined to
attribute far-reaching goals to the reprisals policy but, rather, thought that it
was intended primarily to prove that the government was undertaking security measures against infiltration, and this goal seems to have been achieved.
Shalom concludes, however, that "the debate over the effectiveness of the
reprisals policy as a means of deterring Arab nations is the kind of debate
that has never been resolved and probably never will be."[47]

Even the opposition in the Knesset at the time criticized the government's policy from two opposing poles. The left questioned the usefulness
of the reprisals, which it claimed served only to inflame tensions and hatred
in the region and did not actually prevent terrorist attacks. The right argued
that the retaliatory attacks had no point on their own and that the government should instruct IDF soldiers to remain in the territories they took
control of during the reprisals rather than withdraw immediately after the
operation.[48] Ben-Gurion curbed the criticism from both sides of the political spectrum by making the following statement:

I know the details of every operation, I know the topographical and other
conditions in which they took place, and I declare that we will do everything

that is humanly possible to reduce the number of casualties to a mini-
mum. . . . Even in a defensive operation, offensive actions must be taken.
For the most part, the most effective way to protect oneself is via offensive
actions. And if we must defend ourselves, we will not sit in our homes and
defend ourselves. We are going to move the war to the other side and defend
ourselves with full-fledged aggressive acts, because some defense requires
offensive measures.[49]

In his speech, Ben-Gurion also hinted that he believed there was room
to reconsider certain aspects of Israel's retaliatory actions, but he strongly
opposed the opposition's proposal of "liberating land" as a response to
Fedayeen actions. In any case, the debate between the various approaches
ended shortly after the operation in Qalqilya in late October 1956 with the
outbreak of the Sinai Campaign, in which Israel aimed to put an end the
Fedayeen's actions in the south.[50] Indeed, at the end of the war, calm befell
the southern front with the end of infiltrations and Israeli retaliations.

The 1950s and early 1960s marked the start of the shaping of Israel's
counterterrorism policy. Israeli security officials and decision makers
treated terrorism and sabotage as a military problem requiring consideration separate from other security challenges. Consequently, special operations units were established, and special methods of warfare and measures
were developed that were also incorporated into other combat units, and
above all, experience in offensive counterterrorism was amassed. An integral part of this activity was the domestic and international criticism it
garnered, which led to both the shift from civilian targets to Arab military
targets and a change in goals—from deterring the Fedayeen and lowering
their morale to putting pressure on the Arab countries. This forced them
to stop infiltration from their territories into Israel while simultaneously
strengthening the morale of the Israeli public.

THE BEN-GURION AND SHARETT ADMINISTRATION'S COUNTERTERRORISM POLICIES IN LIGHT OF THE COUNTERTERRORISM DILEMMAS MODEL

In conclusion, this period, which encompassed the first decade of the
establishment of the state, was a challenging time in terms of security.
The many terrorist attacks, both organized and unorganized, on Israeli

territory constituted a strategic threat to the nascent state. The mechanisms of transparency, regulations, and checks and balances that characterize a liberal democratic state did not exist at the time. Much of the state's counterterrorism activity was carried out secretly, with no one taking responsibility, and led to many casualties among Palestinian civilians suspected of being supporters or accomplices of the Fedayeen and, subsequently, of the terrorists.

During the period under discussion, many governments rose and fell. The first government, headed by Ben-Gurion, was established in 1949 and replaced the provisional government that was established with the founding of the state. Ben-Gurion also headed the next three governments (until January 1954), with Moshe Sharett replacing him to head the following two governments—the fifth and sixth (until November 1955). Ben-Gurion then returned to head the next four governments until the tenth Israeli government ended its term in June 1963.

An examination of the positions of the Israeli governments in dealing with terrorism in the period under discussion using the Counterterrorism Dilemmas Conceptual Model (figure 2.1) proposed in the previous chapter shows that the first Israeli government headed by Ben-Gurion, as well as the subsequent governments that he headed, tended toward the end of the scale of the democratic dilemma axis, indicating a preference for effectiveness in counterterrorism at the expense of liberal democratic values. In the state's early years, these Ben-Gurion governments also preferred to respond to domestic considerations and pressures that required less restraint in Israeli counterterrorism activity with very few ethical-moral considerations than to the external pressures calling for restraint and international criticism voiced against Israel in the wake of its actions to combat the Fedayeen. This policy was based on reprisals that, as noted, did not take into account the collateral damage caused to Palestinian civilians in the attempt to create a balance of deterrence and put pressure on the Palestinian public and on the governments of the Arab states bordering Israel to prevent the Fedayeen from embarking on attacks from their territory.

This tendency of Ben-Gurion's governments can be understood when considering the fact that the Israeli public, and especially the residents of the border communities—Holocaust survivors and refugees who had fled Arab countries—were in a constant state of anxiety from the relentless attacks on their communities and were applying pressure on the government to

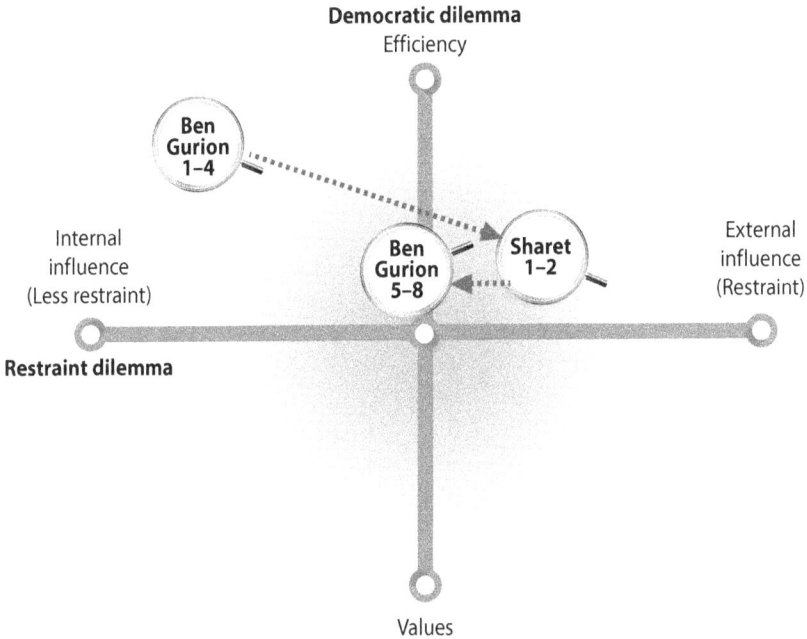

FIGURE 2.1. Counterterrorism Dilemmas Conceptual Model—Ben Gurion and Sharett administrations

remove this threat. The Ben-Gurion government was not, however, indifferent to international pressure and criticism. It resolved the dilemma and tension created between the conflicting domestic and external pressures by avoiding responsibility for the retaliatory actions that caused civilian casualties in Arab countries, even claiming that these activities were carried out by vigilante groups from the border communities who were seeking revenge for the attacks carried out on their homes. The turning point was the Qibya operation in October 1953, which caused many civilian casualties, and the subsequent Moshe Sharett governments, which were established beginning in January 1954. Sharett, who opposed Ben-Gurion's policy of reprisals, altered Israeli policy; the targeting of Arab civilians in retaliatory attacks was prohibited, and only military, police, and government targets were selected. The rules of engagement regarding when to open fire were changed, and the objectives of military operations were carefully chosen. This change in Israeli policy reflected a transition from considerations solely of effectiveness to a combination of practical considerations and ethical and moral considerations while taking into account international pressure and criticism. The institutionalization of Israeli counterterrorism policy during the Sharett governments, the establishment of internal regulatory mechanisms, and the professionalization of the security forces and government bodies had a strong influence on the Ben-Gurion governments that came afterward.

Chapter Three

PALESTINIAN NATIONAL TERRORISM AFTER THE SIX-DAY WAR

The Levi Eshkol and Golda Meir Administrations (1963–73)

RENEWAL OF TERRORISM POST-FEDAYEEN

Terrorism against Israel was not renewed until in the mid-1960s. In 1959, a number of Palestinian students led by Yasser Arafat established Fatah (Palestinian National Liberation Movement) in Egypt. Fatah followed two basic principles: the independence of the Palestinian national movement from any Arab rule, and the primacy of armed struggle as the sole means of liberating Palestine. On January 1, 1965, after a long period of organization, a Fatah cell operating from its base on Jordanian territory carried out the organization's first terrorist attack, on Israel's National Water Carrier. The organization still marks its founding on this day.

Over the months that followed, Fatah continued to carry out attacks against Israel from Jordanian territory and the Gaza Strip. Israel responded by renewing retaliatory actions on Arab territory. On July 14, 1966, the air force was activated for the first time in a retaliatory attack on heavy engineering equipment operated by the Jordanians in their water project in the Jordan Valley. One of the most striking reprisals of this period was the assault on the Jordanian village of Samu, near Hebron, on November 13, 1966. The operation was carried out after three soldiers were killed and six others injured when their vehicle hit a mine. In response, an Israeli infantry force raided the village, for the first time in broad daylight, blowing up thirteen houses and the local police station. To Israel's surprise, the Jordanian Legion intervened during the operation, which ended with ten Israeli soldiers injured and one dead. Speaking about the Samu operation, Prime Minister Levi Eshkol said that it reflected a policy of "defensive deterrence."[1] Yitzhak Rabin, then IDF chief of staff, described the Israeli policy during this period as follows:

> We tried to improve the means of detection and advance warning of terrorist infiltration. But preventative measures alone were never enough. The actions against Syria had to be aimed at official government targets, military or civilian. The situation was different in Jordan and Lebanon, whose leaders did not want to take action against Israel, but whose citizens in the border areas assisted terrorists and provided them refuge, against the wishes of the authorities. There we targeted mainly civilian, not government, targets, to deter them from collaborating with terrorists and assisting those that attacked Israel. . . . In a long series of reprisals in Jordan and Lebanon, culminating in the operation in Samu on November 13, 1966, which was carried out during daylight hours and resulted in the Jordanian army rushing to the aid of the village and dozens of casualties, there was only one fallen Israeli soldier. . . . I cannot say that the retaliations prevented terrorist activities, but I am certain that they prompted the Jordanian and Lebanese authorities to take action against the terrorists, thereby undermining them.[2]

Despite Israeli decision makers' assessment that the reprisals accomplished the goal of achieving deterrence, this was not reflected by a decrease in acts of terrorism and sabotage against Israel in the 1950s and mid-1960s. From January 1965 until the outbreak of the Six-Day War, Palestinian groups carried out over 100 terrorist attacks, in which several dozen Israelis were killed or wounded.[3] Seven terrorists were killed (three from Arab fire), and two were captured.[4] These attacks continued, much to the chagrin of the Arab states, until the Six-Day War broke out in June 1967.

ISRAEL AFTER THE SIX-DAY WAR

The Six-Day War had considerable influence on how Palestinian nationalism materialized, as well as on the scope and characterization of Palestinian terrorism. The defeat of the Arab states shattered the illusion of a possibility of freeing Palestine in a coordinated Arab attack against Israel, at least for a short while. However, the Palestinian organizations' assessment, led by Fatah, was that the "1967 disaster" only intensified the "1948 disaster" (the establishment of the state of Israel). And the fact that most of the Palestinian nation was now under Israeli occupation allowed, in their eyes, for the broadening of Palestinian grassroots campaigns against Israel. Fatah announced the relocation of its headquarters and the diversion of the main terrorist effort to the West Bank and Gaza Strip. The organization's leadership, headed by Arafat, who himself had infiltrated the West Bank, attempted to focus the resistance to the occupation on two simultaneous efforts: acts of terror against Israel and an attempt to organize a civil rebellion along with popular protest.

ISRAEL'S STRATEGY AFTER THE SIX-DAY WAR

The new situation created a substantial challenge for Israel. After the Six-Day War, Israel found itself ruling approximately one million Palestinian Arabs, who did not accept its authority. At the time, Israel's borders were prone to repeated infiltrations by terror cells, and the War of Attrition with the Arab armies continued. Israel was therefore required to establish military and civil rule in the West Bank while allowing residents to conduct their lives in a reasonable manner. These two goals did not always coincide, and the tension created between Palestinian civil life and the Israeli military activity that accompanied Israeli rule in the West Bank went on for many years.

According to the minister of defense at the time, Moshe Dayan, Israel's policy in the West Bank included two opposing elements: one hand wrapped in a silk glove, the other an iron fist.[5] The imposition of martial law made it clear to West Bank residents that they were entitled to have normal lives and to enjoy a number of privileges, such as free passage to Jordan for trade and familial visits, permission to work in Israel, and more, only if there was no terrorism or civil disobedience in their areas. Using this bipolar approach, Israel attempted to counteract the considerable efforts that Fatah had made to agitate the Palestinian population in the West Bank.

As part of the "iron fist" strategy, Israel used military decrees to conduct administrative punishments. This system included administrative regulations that bypassed the long and cumbersome legal procedures and allowed for punishment of Palestinians who had carried out terror attacks or assisted in them immediately after their capture and without trial. Included among the administrative punishments that Israel implemented was the demolition of the houses of convicted terrorists, deportation of agitators and terrorists, limitation on freedom of mobility for the residents of the West Bank, curfews, closures, and more.[6] At the same time, Israel allowed the Palestinians to turn to the Israeli High Court of Justice when they felt they had been subjected to arbitrary actions.

The policy dictated by Dayan in the West Bank was often subject to resistance and criticism from various sources, both military and political. Major-General Rehavam Ze'evi emphasized, for example, that "in a regular forum held by Moshe Dayan, which dealt with the topic of West Bank and Gaza," for over six years Dayan argued "for the closure of the Jordanian bridges and for them to serve only as exit points."[7] In contrast, Abraham Ahituv, head of the Israeli Security Agency (ISA) at the time, supported the open-bridge policy and claimed that the organization always

> attempted to defuse the situation as much as possible, and to dull the motivations for organization. . . . We attempted to eradicate the motivations. It reminds me of the argument I had with Ghandi [Rehavam Ze'evi] when he was assistant head of the IDF Operations Directorate, regarding opening the bridges. At a meeting with Moshe Dayan, I personally supported opening the bridges, and Ghandi was against it; I also had opponents in the agency. It was obvious to me: dull the stingers, constantly work on defusing the situation. Indeed, I supported these goals and I consider them no less important than the war on terror.[8]

That being the case, it would be incorrect to detach Israel's direct operative activity in preparation for the war on terror in the West Bank from its policies regarding all other aspects of life, such as employment, welfare, the economy, society, freedom of religion, and freedom of mobility. Israel's policies in those respects determined Palestinian society's attitude toward the Palestinian terror organizations and their willingness or unwillingness to support, cooperate with, and join them. Thus, immediately after the Six-Day War, this policy brought about the failure of Fatah's attempts to organize a civil rebellion in the West Bank and to recruit the residents to carry out terror attacks against Israel.

However, the notorious carrot and stick policy in and of itself was not enough to meet the challenge of terrorism and civil rebellion in the West Bank. This was mainly attributed to the fact that Fatah members did not hesitate to use violent means and methods against their own people in order to tip the scales in their favor, even going so far to as carry out terror attacks against Palestinians from the West Bank and Gaza Strip who worked in Israel. Therefore, the Israeli security forces needed to locate the terror cells and neutralize them. Such actions required reliable, precise, and up-to-date intelligence, which did not exist.

It quickly became clear to policy makers in Israel that in order to prevent terror attacks and to ensure calm, they must establish a new intelligence apparatus that would be reliable and effective. Most of the intelligence burden fell on the Israeli Security Agency (ISA, or Shin Bet), which, after the war, was tasked with thwarting hostile terror activities. (Prior to the war, gathering intelligence about the Fedayeen was the military intelligence units' responsibility.) The ISA was required to create something from nothing and quickly set up an intelligence network in the West Bank. This was not an easy task, especially considering the collective memory of residents of the Gaza Strip, who knew what had become of individuals suspected of having cooperated with Israel during its brief control of the strip after the Sinai War.[9] The professionalism of those in the ISA, along with the cross-agency cooperation among the ISA, the Military Intelligence Directorate of the IDF, martial law, and the various IDF special units brought about desired success in a relatively short time. The ISA's ability to grant or deny various benefits to the residents of the West Bank, such as employment opportunities in Israel and passage by bridges, provided them with effective measures to obtain cooperation from residents of the West Bank.

This policy, which proved itself in the early years of Israeli rule in the West Bank and managed to bring about calm and normalcy in the months after the Six-Day War, did not fit the conditions in the Gaza Strip at the time. The Gaza Strip, with a different topological structure than the West Bank and highly influenced by densely populated refugee camps and poor living conditions, presented a serious challenge to Israeli security forces. The terror organizations, which had the population's support—whether out of coercion or genuine desire—took advantage of the meager IDF presence in the strip in general and in the refugee camps in particular, and essentially controlled the camps during the night and throughout most of the day. Indeed, terrorists' control of the populated centers in the Gaza Strip was quickly translated into terror attacks against IDF forces, Israelis, and Palestinians who worked in Israel or were suspected of cooperating with the Israelis. The number of attacks was immense. Barely a day went by without a terror attack against Israel. In two years (1969–70), 931 attacks were carried out in the Gaza Strip, killing 11 IDF soldiers and 15 Israeli citizens and wounding 161 soldiers and 68 civilians.[10]

The Israeli policy in the Gaza Strip had a number of goals. The first was to demonstrate to residents, in hopes of neutralizing the population's support for terrorists, that the IDF controlled the territory. The second was to deepen the IDF's knowledge of the terrain in refugee camps and Palestinian towns in order to locate terrorists' hiding places and weapons caches. The third goal was to minimize terrorists' ability to carry out attacks on the main roadways. The fourth was to maximize encounters with terror cells in order to harm and arrest them. Finally, the policy aimed to provide safety and security to the Palestinian civilians who were interested in returning to a daily routine and working in Israel.

Along with the overt and illustrative operations in the strip, the IDF began working covertly with undercover forces, who disguised themselves as Palestinians and moved freely inside the refugee camps. Ariel Sharon described such activity as follows:

> The undercover personnel which I operated was made up of joint Jewish and Arab units . . . usually I had mixed units of three Jews and two Arabs or two and two. The Arabs were usually terrorists which we took to work for us. The Jews would be silent and the Arabs would talk. Through a long line of operations in the camps, we managed to bring the terrorists out.[11]

One of the methods employed by the IDF in the Palestinian refugee camps during this time involved widening roads and building new ones in order to allow rapid and safe passage for military forces and access to any area in which military presence was required. Shlomo Gazit stated that the decision to build these roads was made by Defense Minister Dayan:

> His plan was to divide the camps into small sectors, where the passage from one sector to the other requires exposure. This was to be done by tearing

down a row of houses along the existing alleyways so that each alley becomes a wide road that allows patrols and inspection.[12]

These actions, as well as others, achieved their goal, and the number of terror attacks in the Gaza Strip declined from 473 in 1969 to 64 in 1972.[13]

INFILTRATION OF TERROR CELLS INTO ISRAEL

In addition to its actions in the West Bank in the late 1960s and early 1970s, the IDF was required to deal with the grave phenomenon of infiltration by terror cells into the West Bank and Israel via the country's borders (mainly from Jordan). The purpose of these infiltrations was, for the most part, to transfer weapons, instructions, and money to the West Bank; broaden the terror organizations' combat forces; and carry out terror attacks. The situation required Israel to return to the traditional policy, which included strengthening security measures along the border in order to prevent the infiltrations as well as retaliations in Arab territory.

The new long border with Jordan became a penetrable barrier immediately after the Six-Day War. Although this border was more convenient to protect compared with the previous one, given that it was straight and extended along the natural boundary of the Jordan river, its length proved to be a challenge because it was difficult to provide a constant and efficient defensive response.

After the Six-Day War, Israel decided to invest considerable resources on establishing a physical defense system along its borders. The system included parallel fences with land mines planted between them, as well as an electronic alert system. Adjacent to the fence was a dirt road with guard and observation towers established along its entire length. The IDF patrolled the border by foot and mounted patrols, and pursuits were initiated when an infiltration was detected. The system was put into effect along the borders with Jordan and Syria in 1968 and along the border with Lebanon in 1970. By 1972, a border fence had been erected along all of Israel's land borders.[14]

As part of their attempt to overcome the physical obstacles and prevent pursuits, the terror organizations endeavored to find new and original methods that would enable them to cross the border. They began to blur their tracks with branches and walked backwards in order to lead the IDF's trackers to conclude that the terrorists were exiting the country rather than entering it. Some terrorists carried others on their backs to give the impression that the cell had fewer members than it actually did. In some cases, the infiltrating terrorists wore sheepskin on their shoes, and in other cases, they sprinkled pepper to confuse the tracker dogs.[15] However, none of these methods proved to be useful for the infiltrating cells. By the end of 1968, the IDF had eliminated or arrested about two-thirds of the Palestinians who had infiltrated through the Jordanian border.[16]

Ze'evi, who was head of central command at the time, explained the principles of the policy he established during that era:

> I blocked the Jordan Valley for three months since I received the Command . . . I closed it with soldiers. I built a fence. . . . When we blocked the Jordan Valley the terrorists looked for new channels, so they went to the Dead Sea. So we blocked it with the means we had at the time: dovish—lookouts. But we were raised on an offensive approach, so we began to conduct raids on the eastern side of the Dead Sea.[17]

And, indeed, as mentioned, in addition to defensive actions, Israel renewed offensive retaliatory actions. However, unlike in the past, this time Israel did not settle for responses to multicasualty terror attacks but, rather, carried out what it defined as "active defense." This strategy of offensive preemptive actions included bombings from the air or sea, artillery fire, and especially ground operations and patrols in the neighboring Arab countries in order to attack the terrorists in their bases and during their preparations.[18] At first, the offensive actions focused on Jordan; only later (from the early 1970s onward) did they shift to Syria and Lebanon. The notable retaliatory action in this period took place in March 1968.

THE BATTLE OF KARAMEH

The Battle of Karameh became a milestone in the development of the Palestinian national movement and a magnet for Fatah's new recruits. On March 18, 1968, a bus carrying Israeli students hit a land mine that had been placed by a Fatah cell that had infiltrated Israel from Jordan. In the attack, a teacher and a doctor who had traveled with them were killed, and twenty-eight students were injured.[19] It was the height of a sequence of terror attacks carried out by infiltrating cells that had occurred since the beginning of that year. On the day of the attack, Israel delivered a complaint to the UN Security Council and announced that it would take any measures it considered necessary for self-defense. The meaning of this was clear. Israel prepared for widespread retaliatory action against Palestinian bases in Jordan, and its preparations were not hidden from the Palestinian organizations.[20]

Arafat decided not to evacuate Fatah's stronghold in Karameh and to combat the Israeli forces when they attacked. And indeed, three days after the terror attack, numerous Israeli forces infiltrated Jordanian territory, surrounded the Palestinians in Karameh, and attacked their strongholds. The Palestinians received significant support from the Jordanian army, expressed mostly as artillery fire toward IDF troops, which caused many casualties among the attacking Israeli force: —28 killed and 90 wounded.[21] According to Fatah's statistics, 93 Fatah members were killed and many were wounded, and 128 Jordanians were killed or wounded.[22] Although Israel severely damaged the organizations' infrastructure in Karameh and achieved its tactical goals, the Israeli combat forces suffered a large number of casualties. The weapons that remained in the area enabled the Palestinians to turn the tables on Israel, and it seemed that the Palestinian organizations, led by Fatah, were the ones to win the battle.

Fatah gained control almost overnight. Its position at the top of the hierarchy of Palestinian organizations was now indisputable, and Arab states showered the group with praise. Egyptian president Gamal Abdel Nasser, who was impressed with Fatah's determined struggle, strengthened his ties to the organization and sent weapons to compensate for those lost in the battle.[23] Many volunteers joined Fatah's ranks in Jordan and the entire Arab world. On May 20, 1968, thousands of Egyptian students and former soldiers reached out to the organization. Arafat's position within Fatah was strengthened infinitely.

Following the actions in Karameh, Arafat abandoned his anonymity and became Fatah's official spokesperson[24]. The Palestinians' position in general, and that of the terror organizations in Jordan in particular, strengthened. The organizations' activists did not hesitate to travel with their weapons along the roads and in major Jordanian cities. The establishment of Palestinian organizations in Jordan, and the formation of ex-territorial areas that were controlled exclusively by the terror organizations, soon created tension with the Hashemite government and King Hussein. This tension grew, given the sensitive geopolitical situation in Jordan, in which the Hashemite minority essentially ruled over a Palestinian majority. Another reason for concern for the Jordanian government was the knowledge that the Palestine Liberation Organization (PLO) was widely supported at all levels of the government and had deeply infiltrated the Jordanian military and security forces. The real concern was not of the possibility of a coup against the government but, rather, that Fatah would attempt to establish a national Palestinian identity and use it for its own purposes at the expense of the legitimacy of the Hashemite rulers.[25]

The strengthening of the terror organizations in Jordan and their activities against Israeli targets from within Jordanian territory was abhorrent in the eyes of the decision makers in Israel as well. Israel's proactive policy in Jordan was meant to harm the terrorists' infrastructure, especially in the areas of the Jordan Valley near the border, while simultaneously motivating the Jordanian government to act forcefully against the terror organizations in their own territory.

CONFRONTING ATTACKS AGAINST ISRAELI AND JEWISH TARGETS ABROAD

After the Six-Day War, Palestinian terrorist organizations, led by the Popular Front for the Liberation of Palestine, headed by George Habash, opened another front in the campaign of terrorism against Israel—airline terrorism. This campaign saw Palestinian terror cells, sometimes aided by affiliated international terrorist organizations from Europe, Japan, and other countries, carrying out hijackings on El Al planes and on foreign airlines that flew to Israel, as well as attacks at airports and elsewhere. As a country surrounded by hostile states, without the option of crossing to the rest of the world via land, Israel had to ensure a safe and regular air and sea connection with the world. Among other things, the vital air channel served economic purposes (export and import) and an important source of income in Israel: tourism.

The first hijacking was carried out in July 1968. El Al flight 426 took off from Rome and made its way to Lod airport in Israel. A terrorist cell belonging to the Popular Front for the Liberation of Palestine (PFLP) took control of the plane and diverted its course to Algeria. The terrorists held the plane and its thirty-eight passengers and ten crew members hostage in

Algeria, demanding the release of Palestinian terrorists from Israeli prisons in exchange for the hostages' freedom. Following thirty-nine days of negotiations, Israel released twenty-four terrorists, and the hostages were released. The attack marked the beginning of a wave of hijackings that soon spread to a number of other airlines. This tactic was also adopted by other terrorist organizations.[26]

In another attack in August 1969, members of the PFLP hijacked TWA flight 840, which was flying from Los Angeles to Tel Aviv via Rome. The plane, which was carrying seven crewmembers and 120 passengers who were citizens of a number of countries, was made to land in Damascus. Two days later, all passengers were released except for six Israelis. Four of them were women and were released after a short time, while the two Israeli men remained in captivity in Syria for three months before being released in a prisoner swap with Israel in exchange for 71 Egyptian and Syrian soldiers. On February 18, 1969, an El Al plane was shot at during its ride on the tarmac at the airport in Zurich. A number of passengers and crewmembers were injured, and the terrorists, members of the PFLP, were arrested after the head of the cell was killed by a security guard on the plane. The guard, Mordechai Rahamim, was arrested by authorities in Switzerland and put on trial, though he was ultimately acquitted and released.[27] During the guard's trial, it was revealed that Israel had begun to secure El Al flights with professional air marshals. Seven months later, on September 8, 1969, as part of a multipronged attack on Israeli targets and embassies across Europe, an El Al office in Brussels was attacked with hand grenades. Two months later, El Al's Athens office was also attacked.

In February 1970, three members of a PFLP cell fired guns and grenades at El Al passengers at Munich airport as they made their way by bus from the terminal to the plane. One Israeli passenger was killed and eleven were wounded. The terrorists were caught, arrested, and deported. In the same month, Swissair flight 330 was blown up immediately after taking off from Zurich airport on its way to Tel Aviv. The plane was carrying thirty-eight passengers (including fifteen Israelis) and nine crew members. During the attack, which was most likely carried out by the PFLP-General Command (the so-called Jibril Front), a bomb triggered by barometric pressure was planted in the plane's cargo compartment.[28]

September 1970 witnessed one of the worst terrorist attacks in the history of civil aviation. On September 6, members of the PFLP hijacked three

planes on their way to New York and landed two of them at Dawson Airport in the Jordanian city of Zarqa. One was TWA flight 741 from Tel Aviv
via Frankfurt (with fifty-five Israelis on board), and the other was Swissair
flight 100 from Zurich (which included twenty Israelis). On the same day,
there was also a foiled attempt to hijack El Al flight 219 from Amsterdam;
one of the hijackers was killed and another, Leila Khaled, was arrested.
The other members of the cell hijacked Pan Am flight 93 en route to New
York from Amsterdam via London. The plane was forced to land at Beirut
airport and was then flown to Cairo. Three days later, BOAC Flight 775 was
hijacked in Bahrain and forced to land at the airport in Zarqa. The hostages
were released in Amman after a few days, on September 11, with fifty-three
Israeli and Jewish passengers remaining in captivity. The terrorists blew up
the three empty planes at the Zarqa airport and two weeks later freed all of
the hostages in return for the release of PFLP terrorists.[29]

On May 30, 1972, a terrorist attack was carried out at the Lod airport in
Israel. Three Japanese terrorists, members of the Japanese Red Army terrorist organization, acting on behalf of the PFLP, entered Israel on an Air
France flight from Paris. After receiving their bags, the terrorists opened
fire using weapons stashed in their suitcases and hurled grenades at the
passengers in the arrivals hall. The attack killed twenty-four people and
wounded seventy-one. Two members of the cell, who had been trained at
PFLP bases in Lebanon, were killed, and the third, Kozo Okamoto, was
captured and sentenced to life imprisonment.

On August 16, 1972, a bomb exploded on an El Al flight making its way
from Rome to Lod Airport. The bomb was planted in a booby-trapped
record player that terrorists had given to two female British tourists. The
detonation caused limited damage, most likely due to special reinforcement in the plane's cargo compartment that was designed to absorb a
blast. The pilots succeeded in landing safely at the airport in Rome.[30] This
attack marked one of a series that were thwarted over the years involving
terrorists who were trying to smuggle explosives onto aircraft via innocent travelers who were unaware that that they were being utilized for this
purpose. On May 8, 1972, Sabena flight 571 was hijacked on its way from
Brussels to Lod Airport. Black September terrorists equipped with forged
Israeli passports landed the plane at the airport in Israel and demanded
the release of 317 terrorists imprisoned there. The following day, a team
from the elite IDF unit Sayeret Matkal led by Ehud Barak and including

Benjamin Netanyahu, who posed as technicians to fix the aircraft, took control of the plane and neutralized the explosives that had been placed in it. The terrorist cell's commander and his deputy were killed, and two female terrorists were caught and sentenced to life imprisonment. About 100 of the hostages were freed without injury, two passengers were injured, and one passenger was killed during the takeover.[31] On September 5, 1973, five Black September terrorists tried to fire shoulder-launched SA-7 missiles at an El Al plane on the runway at the airport in Rome. The terrorists were apprehended, and the attack was thwarted.[32] This was one of many foiled attacks on El Al planes and those of other airlines flying to Israel during this period. PFLP-General Command announced in February 1970 that these attacks exemplified the transition from aircraft hijackings to indiscriminate attacks on planes with the aim of killing as many passengers as possible.[33]

Merari and Elad offer six reasons that the PFLP diverted its efforts to actions outside Israel during this period:[34]

1. *Criticism of Fatah*: The PFLP criticized Fatah's strategy of armed struggle, one of direct confrontation with Israel, because of the restrictions imposed on Palestinians by their host countries, the pointlessness in confronting Israel's military superiority, and the fear of the erosion of Palestinian military forces in these confrontations.

2. *The military argument*: The PFLP claimed that attacks abroad avoided a direct confrontation with Israel and allowed for the exploitation of its power in the most effective manner.

3. *International propaganda*: This was a key motive that stemmed from the assessment that these actions would attract a great deal of media attention.

4. *Internal moral-psychological motives*: There was a goal to rouse the Palestinian people and convince them that there was no political solution to the conflict with Israel.

5. *Defining the enemies*: The attacks signaled that the PFLP defined the enemy not only as Israel but as a much wider group of "imperialist and reactionary forces" that required carrying out attacks abroad.

6. *The organizational motive*: After the Six-Day War, an increasing number of voices within the PFLP called for intensifying the struggle against Israel. The launch of its campaign abroad was thus a direct response by the PFLP to internal pressures.

The activities of the PFLP under Habash against Israeli targets abroad garnered harsh international, Palestinian, and Arab reactions. The Democratic Front for the Liberation of Palestine (DFLP), led by Nayef Hawatmeh, argued that because these actionswere carried out by individuals, they turned the Palestinian masses into nothing but a passive audience and further distanced them from the goal of a popular war. In contrast, Fatah claimed that international attacks harmed the Palestinians' political status in the world and undermined the PLO's international achievements.[35] Even the PFLP's patron—the Soviet Union—protested its terrorist activities abroad. As a result of criticism and pressure applied to the PFLP, in October 1971, the organization decided to stop the hijackings but not to refrain from attacks on "imperialist interests around the world." This decision caused dissent within the PFLP, which led to the departure of some of those responsible for terrorist activities overseas that were headed by Wadie Haddad.

Israel also took the airline attacks very seriously. In response to the hijacking of an El Al flight to Algeria, in December 1968, the IDF attacked the Beirut airport and destroyed thirteen airliners on the ground. IDF Chief of Staff Bar-Lev said regarding the Beirut operation, "Our security is more important than our desire to be popular." In a meeting with military reporters, he added, "I hope and believe that the IDF raids on the Beirut airport will make Arab airlines and Arab governments do everything possible to stop terrorist groups from targeting our aircraft, and not just our aircraft, but any target abroad. It was a deliberate action, and I hope it achieves its goal."[36]

Merari and Elad note that the Beirut raid had two goals: to deter further terrorist attacks against flights to and from Israel and to pressure Lebanon to suppress terrorism from its territory. Israeli foreign minister Abba Eban presented the raid as part of Israel's war for survival; in response to a question about whether or not the international reaction to the raid in Beirut would affect Israel's retaliation policy, he said, "We have no policy of retaliation. We have a policy of survival. If retaliation helps survival, we are for it."[37]

The second wave of attacks carried out under the leadership of the Black September organization[38] focused on Israeli interests and symbolic targets abroad, such as Israeli embassies and officials, Jewish targets, and the like. Black September was not averse to attacks against Israeli, Jordanian, and

Arab civilian targets, and it drew the wrath of many countries, including Arab states. The first terrorist attack for which Black September took responsibility was the assassination of the Jordanian prime minister, Wasfi al-Tal, on November 28, 1971, when he was in Cairo attending an Arab summit.[39] But the most infamous attack by this terrorist faction took place on September 5, 1972, against the delegation of Israeli athletes at the Munich Olympics. Salah Khalaf, also known as Abu Iyad (Yasser Arafat's deputy, who, according to Israeli intelligence, was among the leaders of the faction), said that Black September's leadership decided to carry out the attack after the Olympic Committee denied the PLO's official request to send a delegation of Palestinian athletes to the games. He said that the attack was designed to achieve three main goals: "To confirm the existence of the Palestinian people in defiance of the world, to take advantage of the extraordinary concentration of mass media in Munich to draw international attention to the Palestinian cause, and to secure the release of over 200 Palestinians jailed in Israel."[40]

THE ISRAELI RESPONSE TO ATTACKS AGAINST ISRAELI TARGETS ABROAD

The prevailing view is that the Israeli decision to carry out targeted killings was made only after the attack on the Israeli athletes at the Munich Olympics. However, Merari and Elad stress that such actions were carried out prior to Munich and that, in fact, calls to target the heads of Palestinian terrorist organizations were voiced in Israel beginning in mid-1972, following the heinous attack on Lod Airport. Indeed, three weeks after that attack, a spokesman for the PFLP, Ghassan Kanafani, was killed in a Beirut car bombing. His replacement, Bassam Abu Sharif, was seriously wounded in the explosion of a booby-trapped book, and other Palestinian leaders were also injured when letter bombs that were sent to them exploded.[41]

Although the Israeli policy of targeted killings preceded Munich, the brutal attack at the Olympic games, which shook the Israeli public, required decision makers to show resolve and adopt tough new responses. Against this background, the government, headed by Golda Meir, implemented an operational policy of targeted killings around the world focusing on all those involved in the initiation, planning, preparation, management, and execution of the Munich attack. In this regard,

Prime Minister Meir announced after the attack that the war against Arab terrorists could not be limited to defensive measures but must also be active, saying, "We have no other option but to strike terrorist organizations wherever they are."[42]

Salah Khalaf attributed to Israel a long list of assassination attempts on Fatah activists and PLO representatives throughout Europe. He claimed that Israeli intelligence sent parcel and letter bombs to a large number of Palestinian activists, including attacks in Beirut, Algiers (where PLO representative Abu Khalil was mortally wounded), Tripoli (where PLO representative Mustafa Awad Zaid was blinded and paralyzed), Cairo (where Fatah leaders Farouk Qadummi and Hayal Abdel Hammid escaped unharmed), Stockholm (where Omar Sufan, director of the Red Crescent, lost the fingers on both of his hands), Bonn (where Adnan Hamad of the Palestinian student organization was seriously wounded), and Copenhagen (where Ahmed Awadallah had to have his arm amputated). Following the killing of PLO representatives in Paris and Rome—Zuwaiter and Hamshari—the PLO's representative in Nicosia, Hussein Abu Al Khair, was killed on January 25, 1973, and the list goes on.[43] According to Salah Khalaf, a "war of shadows" soon developed between Israeli intelligence and Palestinian terrorist organizations led by Fatah. Three days after the killing of Abu Al Khair, in Madrid, Black September killed a member of Israeli intelligence who went by the name Baruch Cohen but whose real name, according to Abu Iyad, was Moshe Hanan Yishai. And on March 12, 1973, Black September murdered an Israeli citizen named Simcha Giltzer in Nicosia, claiming he was an Israeli intelligence officer. About a month later, on April 9, two attacks were carried out in Cyprus, one on the residence of the Israeli ambassador and the second on an El Al plane parked at the airport. The following day, an Israeli commando unit landed in Beirut and killed three Palestinian officials: Yousef Al Najjar (Abu Yousef), Kamal Adwan, and Kamal Nasser.[44]

Not all of the Israeli retaliation operations ended successfully. In August 1973, Israel intercepted a Lebanese civilian aircraft and forced it to land at an airport in the north of the country. Based on intelligence, Israel was led to believe that the plane was carrying the head of the PFLP, Habash. Immediately after landing, it became apparent that Habash was not on the plane, leading to international condemnation of Israel for its action.

In light of international criticism, in the years that followed, Israel preferred to focus on retaliations targeting the infrastructure of the terrorist organizations in neighboring countries. Four days after the Munich massacre, the Israeli Air Force attacked eight terrorist bases in Syria and three in Lebanon. In a television interview, IDF Chief of Staff David Elazar said that the strikes against the terrorist bases in Syria and Lebanon were not only a reaction to the murder in Munich but part of the war Israel has to wage against terrorists as long as they continued to attack it.[45] The IDF's retaliation did not end with the aerial attacks; a number of days later, an infantry force blew up about 150 homes belonging to terrorists and collaborators in the central area of south Lebanon.

Following 1972's multi-victim attacks in Munich and Lod, the opposition party Herut repeated its previous arguments that Israel should not settle for retributions against terrorist organizations but should initiate large-scale operations in order to force Arab countries to expel terrorist groups from their territory. Ezer Weizmann, former commander of the air force and one of the architects of Herut's security doctrine, recommended that the IDF occupy southern Lebanon and oust the PLO from the area. He did not rule out the possibility of the initiation of a war for the purpose of eliminating terrorism, saying, "A country does not only go to war when faced with the immediate danger of annihilation."[46]

Attacks against Israeli targets abroad in the late 1960s and early '70s constituted a serious escalation in terrorism and required the appropriate organizational and operational preparedness. Against this background, a number of proposals regarding the reorganization and redeployment of security forces were presented to the Israeli political leadership, aiming to provide a suitable response to the situation. After the hijacking of the flight to Algeria, Isser Harel (former head of the ISA and Mossad) suggested that Defense Minister Moshe Dayan establish a special body to direct and operate all entities involved in the war on terror in order to perform special missions. Following the attack in Munich, Ariel Sharon proposed the establishment of a special command to combat terrorism comprising all of the parties involved—the ISA, Mossad, and the IDF—and the launch of an extended offensive against the terrorist organizations. However, the political leadership rejected all of these proposals. The only organizational change following the attack in Munich was the appointment of Aharon

Yariv as Prime Minister Golda Meir's advisor on counterterrorism,[47] a position that involved consultation and the coordination of activities in the field for combating terrorism, but which lacked the authority to make decisions and direct the various bodies.

THE ESHKOL AND MEIR ADMINISTRATIONS' COUNTERTERRORISM POLICIES IN LIGHT OF THE COUNTERTERRORISM DILEMMAS MODEL

In summary, after the Six-Day War, there were many changes in the nature of the terrorism perpetrated against Israel. Palestinian terrorism was institutionalized and carried out primarily by seven Palestinian organizations. Chief among them was Fatah, the largest of the Palestinian terrorist organizations, as well as the "Communist fronts": the PFLP and DFLP. Also involved were the organizations supported by Arab states, such as PFLP-General Command (backed by Syria and Libya), the Palestinian Liberation Front (supported by Syria and Libya), and As-Sa'iqa (an organization founded by Syria). The seventh organization was the Arab Liberation Front (established by Iraq).

Moreover, Israel's control of the territories in Judea, Samaria, and the Gaza Strip, which it occupied during the war, gave Palestinian terrorists direct access to Israeli population centers; and the wave of terror against Israeli targets abroad and on the airlines posed new challenges that necessitated a change in Israel's counterterrorism policy. During the Eshkol and Meir administrations, a policy that aimed for a balance between rewards and punishments using the carrot and stick method was formulated under the leadership of Defense Minister Moshe Dayan. This approach was directed at the Palestinian population in the West Bank in an attempt to prevent its involvement in terrorist attacks and its assistance to the Palestinian terrorist organizations.

Thus, in reference to the Counterterrorism Dilemmas Model (figure 3.1), it seems that, all things considered, the governments of both Levi Eshkol and Golda Meir managed to strike a balance between domestic and international pressures in deciding on counterterrorism operations during this period, which was reflected in the carrot and stick policy employed in the territories.

These Israeli governments also invested considerable effort in defensive measures deployed along the borders and at crossings into Israel from the

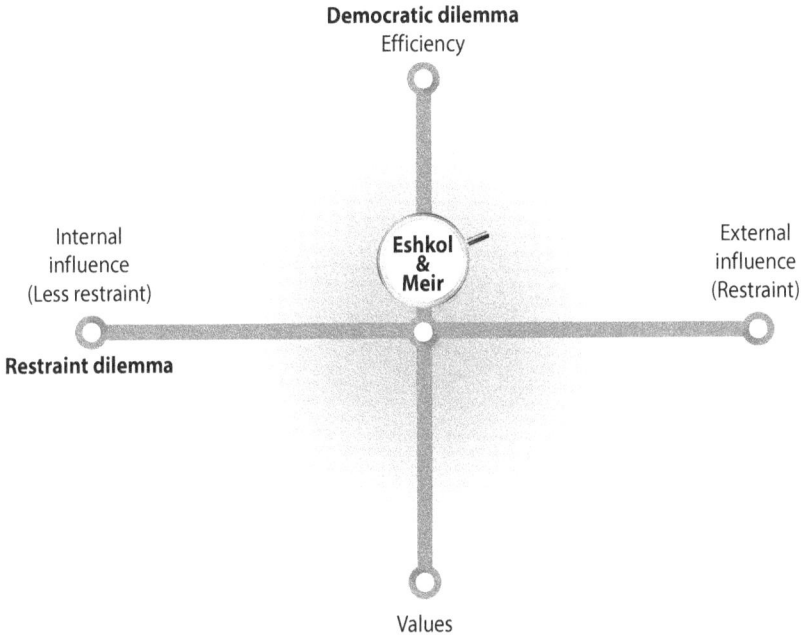

FIGURE 3.1. Counterterrorism Dilemmas Conceptual Model—Eshkol and Meir administrations

territories. This was in addition to the renewal of offensive action against terrorist bases in neighboring countries—especially in Jordan, Lebanon, and Syria—and the carrying out of reprisals in these countries as a reaction to the wave of attacks against Israel. In the wake of the attacks abroad, which reached their peak with the murder of the Israeli athletes in Munich, Israel renewed and intensified its policy of targeted killings, pursuing terrorist operatives in various countries around the world. These actions generated much international criticism (though Israel generally did not take responsibility for these actions in foreign countries). Israel, however, chose to ignore this criticism and declared that its counterterrorism activities were necessary in order to ensure its survival in the face of repeated terrorist attacks.

Along with condemnation by the international community, the Israeli government also was forced to contend with harsh criticism at home from the main opposition party, Herut. Herut blasted the government's policy of retaliation, maintaining that the Israeli counterterrorism policy needed to be more powerful and proactive. In light of the overall counterterrorism policy of Eshkol and Meir governments, it would seem that the policy of carrying out targeted killings in foreign countries following attacks on Israeli targets abroad constituted a departure from their balanced approach and reflected an attempt to achieve more effective deterrence against terrorism, even at the expense of violating international values and principles.

Chapter Four

CROSS-BORDER TERRORISM AFTER THE YOM KIPPUR WAR

The Yitzhak Rabin Administration (1974-76)

THE RABIN DOCTRINE

In the 1970s, Palestinian terrorism intensified on all fronts—within the "Green Line" in Israel, across borders in attacks involving the infiltration of terrorist cells from neighboring Arab states and especially Lebanon, and abroad. The number of attacks on Israeli and Jewish targets abroad actually decreased significantly in the late 1970s due to the Palestinians' political achievements in the international arena and their decision to avoid these types of attacks, which tarnished their image in the eyes of the world.

One of the most notorious terrorist attacks carried out abroad during this period was the hijacking of Air France flight 139 from Tel Aviv to Paris on June 28, 1976. The aircraft was carrying 246 passengers and 13 crew members.[1] Two of the hijackers belonged to the armed wing of the PFLP, at the time under the leadership of Wadie Haddad, also known as Abu Hani, and Wilfried Böse and Brigitte Kuhlmann were from the German terrorist organization the German Revolutionary Cells (RZ). The plane was forced to land in Libya, where three other Palestinian terrorists joined the hijackers before the plane continued to Entebbe, Uganda. The terrorists, who were granted protection by Ugandan leader Idi Amin, separated the Jewish passengers from the others, who were released after two days. The terrorists demanded the release of 53 Palestinian terrorists (40 of them were imprisoned in Israel and thirteen in other countries). They also demanded a total of $5 million from the French government.[2]

According to Prime Minister Yitzhak Rabin, on the eve of the hijacking, Israeli security forces warned that the Palestinians were liable to carry out an attack, even specifying the "soft underbelly" of "foreign airlines and airports who have not adopted the strict security arrangements practiced on El Al and at Ben Gurion Airport in Lod."[3]

On learning of the hijacking, the Israeli government assessed the situation and determined that responsibility for the hostages' safety rested on the shoulders of the French government because they were taken captive on a plane belonging to France's national airline. However, due to the aircraft's location, a military takeover was not possible, and the government decided to begin negotiations with the hijackers for the release of prisoners in exchange for freeing the hostages. Rabin writes, "at the beginning of the meeting I turned to the IDF Chief of Staff and asked, 'Is it possible for the IDF to extract the hostages in a military operation? If the answer is yes, then that option is our preference. If the answer is no, we will consider negotiating with the hijackers."[4] This fundamental decision reflected the policy of the Rabin government at the time, known as the "Rabin Doctrine," and it was also adopted by future governments in cases involving negotiations with terrorists. This policy dictated that if a military rescue option is available, it is always preferred, and if it is not, then negotiations can be held in order to release the hostages. Thus, when Rabin was told that Israel had no military rescue option, he recommended to the government that negotiations be conducted.

> We have no right to abandon the hostages. If we cannot rescue them by force, even when there is a risk involved, we need to exchange them for the terrorists that we are holding. And I do not mean deception or a tactical ruse, designed to buy time, but serious negotiations that Israel will follow through on.[5]

Rabin stressed that a decision of this magnitude, with the associated risks, should be taken by the entire government.

> This time, because of the sensitivity of the matter, a murmur of agreement from the ministers was not sufficient. I demanded a vote. The government

unanimously approved the proposal to conduct negotiations for the release of hostages, even in exchange for those detained in Israel.[6]

In order to achieve broad support from the government for this move, the prime minister turned to the opposition, saying, "the decision to surrender to the terrorists if there was no other way of saving the lives of the hostages weighed on [him] heavily. The support of the opposition relieved that weight to a certain extent."[7] Rehavam Ze'evi, who served as the prime minister's advisor on counterterrorism, explains the logic of consulting with the opposition in such cases:

> When the Air France flight was hijacked and brought to Entebbe, Yitzhak Rabin consulted with the Cabinet to get a consensus regarding negotiations with the Front for the Liberation of Palestine and the willingness to return their prisoners in exchange for our hostages. It was a very difficult decision. Yitzhak was under very strong pressure from the families of the hostages, who had been demonstrating in front of IDF headquarters, among them people from the defense community. And as someone who is attentive and doesn't shut out voices, he took the decision. I didn't entirely agree with it, but I also couldn't identify an alternative at that point. Still, I suggested that he let Menachem Begin, the head of the opposition, in on the secret.[8]

Indeed, the Entebbe affair reflected another feature of the decision-making processes in such cases, one that is perhaps unique to Israel: the pressure on decision makers by the families of the hostages. In this context, Rabin said that "relatives of the hostages broke into the Kirya (the IDF headquarters in Tel Aviv) through the guarded gate. I could understand them. I received a delegation of emotional relatives. I informed them of the government's decision."[9]

Rabin goes on to describe a meeting he had with the father of one of the hostages, who held a senior position in the defense establishment, in which he was asked, "how long will [Rabin] play roulette with the lives of [their] children?" This was a difficult sentiment for Rabin, who said,

> The words pounded my heart like heavy stones. "Roulette with the lives of our children." I could not help but remember that the hijackers of the Air France flight to Entebbe had previously hijacked a plane carrying oil

ministers from OPEC countries . . . and to demonstrate the seriousness of their intentions, they did not hesitate in killing two of the hostages.[10]

The moment the prime minister was told that the defense establishment believed there was a military option to release the hostages, he took it to the government to pass a motion that would change its previous decision and support military action. He was aware of how risky and ambitious the decision was to carry out a military operation approximately 3,800 kilometers from home, in the territory of a country hostile to Israel, with several terrorists who were receiving assistance from Ugandan soldiers holding civilian hostages surrounded by explosives. Such a complex operation had never before taken place. Rabin made this clear to the government on the eve of the vote to approve the operation. His opinion was that "there will be victims in this rescue operation, both the hostages and their liberators."[11] Rabin stated that "even if 15 or 20 people are killed," he supported the action. "Even if the price is high," he believed that it was mandatory to use a military option given that it was available, and thus he refused to give in to the terrorists.[12]

The operation was carried out on July 3, 1976, a short time before the ultimatum posed by the terrorists expired. It was dubbed "Operation Yonatan" after Yonatan Netanyahu (brother of future prime minister Benjamin Netanyahu), commander of the elite unit Sayeret Matkal, who led and was killed in the operation. The action was highly complex militarily and required precise intelligence, as well as a plan for the Israeli forces to land in the airport in Uganda. The operation also involved an unprecedented exercise in deception during which the Israeli commandos posed as members of the convoy for Ugandan president Idi Amin. In a vehicle assumed to be Amin's, they arrived at the terminal building where the hostages were being held. The Ugandan army and terrorists were caught completely by surprise, and the operation led to the release of about one hundred hostages. Three hostages as well as Yoni Netanyahu were killed, and one IDF fighter was seriously injured. One hostage, Dora Bloch, was murdered after the operation while she was in a hospital seeking medical treatment during the rescue operation).

The Entebbe operation has become a symbol of Israel's operational counterterrorism policy and has served as proof of Israel's long arm in confronting terrorism, notably through its determination to persevere in this mission, ability to obtain accurate and up-to-date intelligence, integrated actions between intelligence agencies and operational units, and outside-the-box thinking reflected in complex undercover operations. The conduct of the Israeli government throughout the entire hostage affair encapsulates Israel's policy in dealing with hostage situations. This includes assigning responsibility for the safety of the hostages to the governments on whose sovereign territory the attack was carried out, a willingness to negotiate with terrorists in the absence of a military rescue option, and even the significant price of releasing imprisoned terrorists in order to ensure the safety and release of hostages. However, if a rescue option is possible, even if it is very complex with a low chance of success, it is preferred by the Israeli government.

TERRORISM AGAINST ISRAEL ON THE DOMESTIC FRONT AND CROSS-BORDER ATTACKS

The PLO leadership and heads of Fatah, who, in the early 1970s, sought international recognition, quickly realized that Palestinian terrorist activity abroad, led by communist terrorist organizations and the Habash Front, was threatening the Palestinians' achievements in the diplomatic sphere. Thus, in July 1974, the PLO leadership made an unprecedented decision to cease terrorist attacks against Israeli and Jewish targets abroad. In order to make clear the seriousness of their intentions to all of the organizations, PLO leaders declared that if the hijackings continued and led to the killing of hostages, severe penalties would be imposed on the perpetrators, including execution. According to Merari and Elad, the PLO is an exceptional example of an organization making a calculated decision to avoid a particular kind of terrorism, not as part of a formal or secret agreement but as the result of a cost-benefit analysis. Merari and Elad call it a timely decision that led to political gains and boosted the PLO's international status.[13]

In parallel with these diplomatic efforts and the PLO's decision to stop attacks overseas, in the mid-1970s, PLO member organizations and Palestinian rejectionist organizations increased their efforts to carry out terrorist attacks inside Israel and in the West Bank and Gaza Strip, referred to as internal attacks. Palestinian organizations also increased attacks from neighboring countries into Israel, or cross-border attacks. This activity was reflected in the decision of the Palestinian National Council in March 1977 that "emphasize[d] that the struggle in the occupied territory in all its forms—military, diplomatic and popular, is the central component of its battle plan."[14]

At this stage, the armed struggle was intended to create a campaign of attrition that would lead to Israel's withdrawal from the territories occupied in 1967. And as part of a multiphased strategy, it was intended to bring about the first phase of the establishment of a Palestinian state in the area, which would eventually serve as a platform for Israel's destruction. An immediate reflection of this goal was the large number, relative to previous years, of mass-casualty attacks in 1974.(That year saw seven such attacks, whereas in the years prior, there had never been more than two mass-casualty attacks per year.)[15] The cross-border attacks for the most part resulted in multiple casualties and were intended to indicate strength. They were planned either as hostage-taking attacks or as indiscriminate killings, directed mainly at Israeli civilian targets.

Most of the cross-border attacks during this period were carried out from Lebanese territory against Israel's northern villages through either land or sea borders. This activity reflected a change in the Palestinian terrorist organizations' pattern, which, until the early 1970s, used Jordanian territory as its main base for terrorist attacks, crossing Israel's eastern border. This change resulted from the expulsion of the Palestinian terrorist organizations' military forces and headquarters from Jordan and their relocation to Lebanon at the end of 1970.

BLACK SEPTEMBER AND CROSS-BORDER ATTACKS

The PFLP hijacking of three planes to Jordan's Dawson's airport near Zarka in September 1970 embarrassed Jordan's King Hussein and challenged his leadership and sovereignty over Jordanian territory. This was the straw that broke the camel's back and a continuation of the arrogant and provocative behavior exhibited by the Palestinian organizations operating in Jordan. The Jordanian government was not able to sustain the state-within-a-state that had been created; areas de facto were out of its control, in which Palestinian organizations set up road-blocks, carried out carjackings, extorted businessmen, raped women, and generally created anarchy.[16] The words of Abu Daoud, who served as commander of the Fatah forces in Jordan, testify to the atmosphere at the time:

> [Fatah] had the feeling that not only could we eliminate Hussein, but that we had to. Secondly, I must tell you in all honesty that this was not only the feeling of the so-called leftists and radicals of the guerrilla organizations; it was also the feeling and the desire of most of us in Fatah—the fighters and the young officers. Amongst ourselves, we talked about the possibility of removing Hussein very seriously and very sincerely. We even talked about our views with Arafat and I told him more than once that I thought we were making a grave mistake by not taking action against Hussein.[17]

The bombing of the planes in Jordan took place only a few days after the failed assassination attempt on King Hussein as he made his way to the airport in Amman. In addition, during that time, members of the Palestinian organizations declared the city of Irbid in northern Jordan a liberated area. The culmination of these events was that on September 16, 1970, Hussein ordered his army to destroy the terrorist groups' military forces in Jordan. The fighting, which began in the capital city of Amman, quickly spread to northern Jordan and from there to other areas. The Palestinian forces, which received extensive aid from the Syrian army, were eventually defeated. This episode became known as Black September.

The costs of the war were heavy on both sides, with some 600 Jordanian soldiers killed and 1,500 wounded, and between 5,000 and 7,000 people defected from the legion.[18] Between 910 and 960 Palestinians were killed, of whom some 400 were Fatah members and 200 were members of the PLA. About 1,500 to 3,500 Jordanian citizens died, most of them Palestinian residents of Amman.[19] The Black September campaign against the Palestinian organizations in Jordan led to the virtual elimination of their strongholds in that country. Many members were killed in battle, others were jailed, and the rest were expelled from or fled Jordan. Rehavam Ze'evi, at the time head of Central Command, said, "I absorbed one hundred ten to one hundred fifteen terrorists. We explained to them how to and where to cross [the Jordan River]. Some of them became agents."[20]

With the loss of their Jordanian base and the defeat of the PLO's military forces by the Jordanian Legion, the Palestinian organizations invested their resources and efforts in reestablishing themselves in Lebanon. Lebanon quickly became the main base for launching terrorist attacks against Israel and strikes on Israeli communities near the border. And, indeed, between 1974 and 1977, many cross-border attacks occurred in which Palestinian terrorists infiltrated Israel to conduct hostage barricade situations. Here are some examples:

- On April 11, 1974, the Jibril Front (PFLP-GC) committed a mass-casualty attack in Kiryat Shmona, causing the deaths of 18 civilians and wounding of 15.
- A Democratic Front for the Liberation of Palestine (DFLP) cell took over a school in the community of Maalot and held some 100 children hostage. In the IDF operation to take control of the school and neutralize the terrorists, 23 teenagers were killed and 64 were injured.
- On November 19, 1974, a DFLP cell entered a residential building in Beit She'an and took some of the residents hostage. During the attack, one of the hostages was killed and some 20 were injured, including children, after they jumped from the upper floors of the building.
- On March 6, 1975, a Fatah terrorist cell landed on the beach in Tel Aviv after shooting at passers-by on the boardwalk, and proceeded to take over the Savoy Hotel. Eight hostages and three soldiers were killed during the rescue attempt, and 12 were wounded.
- On June 15, 1975, a terrorist cell belonging to the Arab Liberation Front, a pro-Iraqi Palestinian terrorist group, seized a building on Moshav Kfar Yuval. During the attack, three hostages were killed and four were wounded.

The waves of attacks from Lebanese territory and the many casualties they caused led to retaliatory actions by the IDF, thus turning Lebanon into a central arena for Israeli military operations by air, land, and sea. IDF operations in Lebanon, which increased in the late 1970s, included both reprisals for major attacks in Israel as well as preventive offensive measures designed to thwart attacks and disrupt those in the planning stage, cause damage to the terrorist organizations and deter them, as well as demoralize the terrorists and their supporters. According to Sayigh, the intense Israeli operations in Lebanon are what pushed Lebanon toward civil war in 1976. He says that in th same year, Israel launched 1,437 shelling attacks and 44 air raids, which killed 67 civilians and injured 142. This number does not include casualties among the Lebanese security forces and the military forces of the Palestinian terrorist organizations.[21]

ISRAEL'S HANDLING OF CROSS-BORDER ATTACKS

Israel's actions to prevent cross-border attacks were not limited to offensive means. Hanan Alon lists several defensive actions in the 1970s that were intended to help in this endeavor. This included a large-scale project to cover dirt roads with asphalt to prevent the laying of mines along the northern border. This move was effective in reducing the number of mines. Israel also built shelters in the northern towns to protect civilians from artillery fire from the organizations across the border. By 1975, Israel had completed the sheltering of all the communities located up to fifteen kilometers from the border. Perimeter fences and guard towers were built around all border communities and crucial facilities such as power plants, water pumps, fuel facilities, and factories, and reserve troops were stationed to defend them.

Beginning in 1970, members of civil defense groups were stationed as guards to check people entering crowded places such as playgrounds, beaches, and sports stadiums. Parents were tasked with guarding school gates, and after the Yom Kippur War, the Civil Guard was established, a voluntary body under the auspices of the Israeli police. At its peak, the Civil Guard included tens of thousands of volunteers who patrolled their neighborhoods at night in order to help ensure residents' safety and security. The Israeli police established a special unit for detecting and neutralizing explosive devices, and the public was called on to be alert and call the police in case of suspicious activity.[22]

The effectiveness of these measures appeared to be limited. Terrorist cells continued to infiltrate and attack from Lebanese territory, and waves of internal terror attacks inside Israel continued. Many bombings, shootings, and grenade attacks occurred, mainly in Jerusalem and Tel Aviv but also in Be'er Sheva, Ashdod, Petah Tikva, Netanya, and Afula These attacks targeted crowded areas such as markets, shopping centers, buses, bus stops, and cinemas.[23]

During these years, the challenge of dealing with terrorism was placed on the doorstep of the first Yitzhak Rabin administration, which was sworn in in June 1974 and remained in power until June 1977. Rabin explains the steps his government took in dealing with terrorism as follows:

> Soon after I became Prime Minister, I appointed Major General Res. Reha-
> vam Ze'evi [Gandhi, as everyone called him] as an advisor on the war on
> terror. . . . I tasked Gandhi with determining the exact regulations that would
> define the areas of responsibility of the army and the police. . . . We fortified
> the Lebanese border and built an effective system there to prevent infiltra-
> tion into Israel. The Civil Guard was established, [with] its practical role in
> securing [Israeli] communities and neighborhoods.[24]

However, the growing number of cross-border attacks and the large number of casualties led to a sense of insecurity and demoralization among
Israelis. It also led to public criticism of Israel's policies against the terrorist organizations, with many voices calling for more offensive action and
even revenge attacks. The main opposition party, the Likud, maintained
its critical line, claiming that the IDF's retaliatory actions were ineffective
and that Israel should not shy away from extensive military operations to
seize areas near the border if necessary, in order to drive terrorist groups
out of the northern communities. According to the leader of the opposition, Menachem Begin, there was a need for "constant and relentless
attack to defeat these murderers anywhere, anytime. They are within . . .
reach."[25]

In the West Bank and Gaza Strip as well, the terrorist organizations did
not remain dormant in the 1970s. Following a lull in the West Bank in
the late 1960s and in the Gaza Strip in the early 1970s, these organizations
continued to organize cells to carry out sporadic attacks in the West Bank
and Gaza Strip and within Israel proper. From time to time, in response to
various events in the local or international arenas, mass demonstrations
and protests also broke out among Palestinians in the territories.

In general, however, the Israeli government was satisfied with the state
of affairs in the West Bank and Gaza Strip, and proposals for change or

a reexamination of policy were rejected. The main criticism against Israel's policies in the territories was that Israel refrained from restricting the growing influence of the PLO on Palestinian streets and from taking steps to fight it. The entrenchment of the PLO in the West Bank was reflected in its transferring of money there, as well as its control over local government institutions, unions, student organizations, and the like. This criticism was expressed in an October 1974 document prepared by the commander of the West Bank, Brigadier General Aryeh Shalev, after the Arab League's summit in Rabat. Shalev stated, "so far we have done nothing to stop or interfere with that process, and it is very possible that the local residents mistakenly interpret our behavior as a sign of weakness."[26] He therefore recommended deterring and punishing any expression of support for the PLO in order to encourage the moderate elements and pro-Hashemites among the Palestinians. Additionally, he suggested supporting the establishment of a local Palestinian government, strengthening Israel's position on the ground by reinforcing its military presence, establishing new Jewish settlements, and supporting civilian projects that demonstrated Israel's intentions to remain in the area, all the while improving the local population's standard of living.[27]

Two years later, in March 1976, head of Central Command Yona Efrat recommended adopting a "hard-handed," zero-tolerance policy in the West Bank and Gaza Strip regarding expressions of opposition to Israeli rule, fearing that they would intensify.[28] However, despite criticisms of Israel's policy that began in the early 1970s, Ben-Rafael notes that Israel was not above employing severe coercive and punitive actions in the territories, including the expulsion of terrorists and the demolition of their houses. These steps, he claims, were intended to minimize the PLO's involvement and presence in the territories as much as possible, and to limit the Palestinians' involvement in terrorist activity.[29]

In the second half of the 1970s, the strengthening of the PLO in the West Bank and Gaza Strip was clearly reflected in local elections held in 1976, in which PLO supporters won the majority in many towns and municipalities in the West Bank. Immediately after the elections, the Israeli military began efforts to neutralize the PLO's political significance as much as possible.[30]

The short tenure of the Rabin government was characterized by tremendous tensions and crises that reflected the personal rivalry between

Prime Minister Rabin and his defense minister, Shimon Peres, and the conflicts among the various parties that formed the coalition. In the end, the prime minister decided to resign and dissolve the government in late 1976, in the wake of a crisis that developed between the secular and religious factions. In the elections that took place in the mid-1977, a revolution took place for the first time in the history of the state of Israel; the right-wing Likud party took power and formed the new government.

THE RABIN ADMINISTRATION'S COUNTERTERRORISM POLICY IN LIGHT OF THE COUNTERTERRORISM DILEMMAS MODEL

In conclusion, tension in Israel grew during the time of the Rabin government due to the deployment of the terrorist organizations in Lebanon and the infiltration of terrorist cells into Israel from Lebanese territory. On the other hand, Israel's dazzling success in releasing the hostages from Entebbe raised the Israeli public's morale, strengthened its confidence in the government, and even brought about enthusiastic support for Israeli counterterrorism efforts in the international arena. This enabled the Rabin government to find the necessary balance between meeting Israelis' expectations with regard to combating terrorism and avoiding harsh international criticism. Israel's preventive defensive measures, including bolstering the ground barrier along the Israeli-Lebanese border and increased security measures, did not provoke international reproach, and the military operations and aerial and artillery attacks that Israel carried out from time to time against terrorist bases in Lebanon were usually met with understanding by the international community in light of the many Israeli casualties of terrorist attacks by cells infiltrating from Lebanon. Most of the domestic criticism directed at the Israeli government revolved around the accusation that it had refrained from taking steps that would deter the PLO from its ongoing efforts to increase its influence over Palestinians in the territories. However, in practice, the government did not refrain from punitive measures in the West Bank, including the expulsion of terrorist operatives and the demolition of their homes.

In light of the Counterterrorism Dilemmas Conceptual Model (figure 4.1), it would seem that the Rabin government generally succeeded

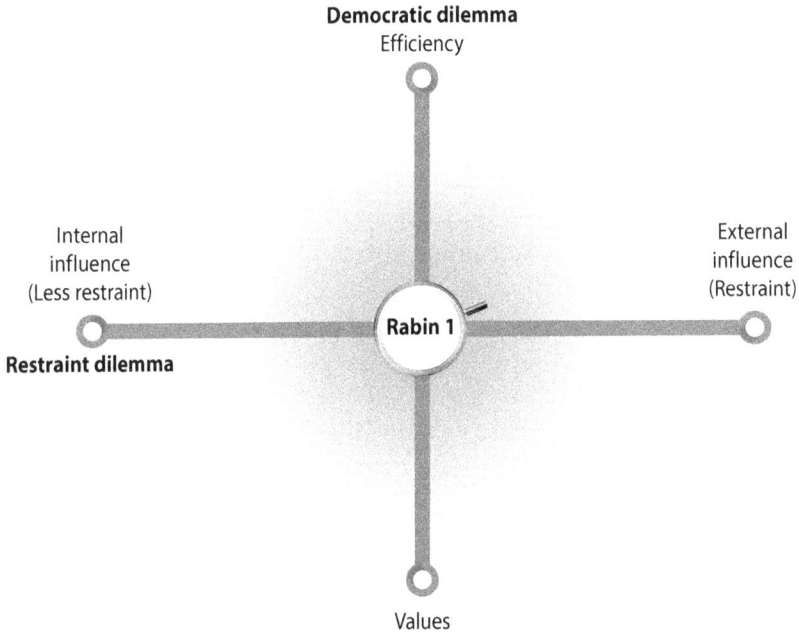

FIGURE 4.1. Counterterrorism Dilemmas Conceptual Model—Rabin administration (1974-76)

in finding a delicate balance between effective counterterrorism and the preservation of liberal democratic values, as well as between the pressure exerted by those in the Israeli opposition to escalate counter-terrorism activities and the persistent international demand to exercise restraint.

Chapter Five

TERRORISM AGAINST THE BACKDROP OF THE LEBANON WAR

The Menachem Begin, Yitzhak Shamir, and Shimon Peres Administrations (1977–86)

On June 20, 1977, following the Likud's victory in the elections, the first Begin government was established. The government's crowning accomplishment was achieved at the beginning of its term when the Egyptian president, the sworn enemy of Israel, embarked on a creating peace initiative and visited Israel in November 1977. This was the first visit of an Arab leader. Following negotiations that lasted over a year, Israel and Egypt signed a peace agreement in March 1979.

The Egyptian peace initiative had a direct impact on the Palestinian arena. President Sadat's moves toward peace with Israel and the Egyptian leader's visit to Jerusalem only strengthened the nationalistic trend among Palestinians in the West Bank and Gaza. In October 1978, a number of activists in the West Bank established the National Guidance Committee, stating that

> peace is not possible without a complete Israeli withdrawal from the occupied Arab territories and as long as the Palestinian people are not allowed to return to their homeland, determine their future, and establish an independent state in their country and homeland, with Jerusalem as its capital.[1]

On November 28, 1978, several days after the establishment of the committee and Sadat's visit to Israel, Avraham Orly, coordinator of government activities in the West Bank and Gaza Strip, presented to the minister of defense a list of recommendations that was meant to change Israeli policy toward the Palestinians in those areas. Among the recommendations was encouragement of those Palestinians who supported Sadat's initiative, organization of groups of Palestinians who wanted to be involved in the Cairo talks between Israel and Egypt, and suppression of those who support the PLO. But these steps did not succeed in neutralizing the opposition of the PLO and its supporters to the Israeli-Egyptian peace process.[2]

In an attempt to limit the strengthening of the PLO in the territories, Israel tried, in addition to its punitive actions, to make its mark in the Palestinian political arena by establishing and empowering elements that would act as a counterweight to the PLO.[3] For example, beginning in 1978, Israel supported a newly established organization in the West Bank called the Village Leagues. Mustafa Dodin, a former Jordanian minister, and a group of Palestinian activists created the Village Leagues as a social-administrative body.[4] Dodin's goal was an organization that would work to promote a settlement with Israel. However, due to its ties with Israel and lack of a real political support base in the territories, the Village Leagues was short lived.

As part of its efforts to neutralize the power of the PLO, Israel also refrained from interfering with the Muslim Brotherhood's efforts to expand its influence in the West Bank and Gaza Strip (which included heightened religious activity as well as social welfare initiatives among the Palestinian population).[5] At the time, this seemed to be the right policy to defuse the PLO's power in the territories, as the Muslim Brotherhood was not engaged in terrorist activity. But in retrospect, this policy backfired when, in 1987, the Brotherhood established its military wing, Hamas, which began to carry out brutal terrorist attacks against Israel.

The rise of the right-wing Likud party in the late 1970s enabled party leaders to change Israel's counterterrorism policy in all arenas. Directed by the political leadership, the IDF and the Civil Administration (the governing body in charge of the West Bank and Gaza Strip) adopted a strong-arm policy in the territories in order to undermine the PLO and prevent Palestinian cooperation with terrorist organizations. This policy did not achieve its goals; in fact, following the signing of the Israeli-Egyptian peace treaty in 1979, unrest in the territories increased. After the murder of six yeshiva students in Hebron in May 1980, the Israeli government deported

Hebron mayor Fahad Kawasma, Halhoul mayor Mohammed Milhem, and Sheikh Rajab Al-Tamimi, the chief *Qadi* (magistrate of an Islamic court) of Hebron.[6] As a result, a wave of violence broke out in the territories, which did not cease despite the IDF's strong-arm policy.

In the early 1980s, the Likud government decided to toughen Israeli actions in the West Bank and Gaza Strip, in total contrast to the policy that was employed in the early 1970s. According to Gazit, due to the worsening of security problems in the territories, while Menachem Begin was acting defense minister, the military intensified its involvement in decision-making, and civil and administrative considerations became of secondary importance.[7] Among the guidelines included in the new Israeli policy was to prohibit mayors and dignitaries from engaging in political activities, ban mayors and dignitaries from traveling freely outside Israel, and punish anyone who violated the guidelines by conducting meetings with members of the PLO. The free transfer of funds to the territories was also prohibited, and the National Guidance Committee was outlawed, with special supervision imposed on its members.[8] The culmination of all of these steps came in March 1982, when Israel fired mayors Bassam Shaka, Kareem Khalaf, and others. These dismissals led to the outbreak of an unprecedented wave of protests, riots, and attacks on military outposts throughout the territories.[9]

OPERATION LITANI

On the Lebanese front, at this stage, Likud leaders were able to implement the policies they had been advocating for since the 1950s throughout the rule of the Labor government, such as the use of military force to eliminate terrorism, or at least to drive the Palestinian organizations' outposts farther from Israel's borders. Prime Minister Begin and his defense minister, Ezer Weizmann, disagreed about the timing of offensive operations in Lebanon. According to then IDF chief of staff Lieutenant General Rafael Eitan, Begin adopted the notion that counterterrorism operations in Lebanon should not come as retaliation against attacks by terrorist organizations. In contrast, Weizmann preferred that operations be in reaction to terrorist provocations. Eitan claimed that he supported Menachem Begin's position:

> If Israel wants to punish those responsible for an attack after the attack has taken place, its hands are tied: First, it has to pay the price of the attack (and

this is often a very high price), and then it needs to identify the culprits, find them and punish them. When Israel decides to take the initiative and prevent attacks or the ability to carry them out, it has a much wider range of options.[10]

The first expression of a significant change in Israel's policy came on March 18, 1978, with the beginning of Operation Litani. Seven days earlier, Israel had suffered one of the worst terrorist attacks in its history, the Coastal Road Massacre. The attack was carried out by Fatah terrorists, who hijacked a public bus on the coastal road, shooting at and throwing grenades at passing vehicles. After stopping a second bus and forcing its passengers to join the passengers on the first hijacked bus, the terrorists drove it along the road, and the attack ended in a firefight with Israeli forces. The result was the death of thirty-seven Israelis and one American, and seventy-one others were wounded.[11]

The Israeli public's shock and anger forced the government to take unprecedented action against the terrorist organizations in Lebanon. According to the cabinet secretary at the time, Arye Naor, after this brutal attack, no one in the government had any doubt that there must be a large-scale response. The chief of staff presented a plan of action, while Begin and his ministers dealt with questions on the diplomatic side. What would be the ramifications of action within Lebanese territory on the political process and on relations with Egypt the United States? After deliberation, the IDF's plan was approved unanimously. Its goal was the destruction of the terrorists' bases, infrastructure, and weapons along the entire Lebanese-Israeli border at a depth of six miles, from the Mediterranean Sea in the west to Mount Hermon in the east. A political goal was not set explicitly, but it was clear that following such an extensive operation, a new situation would be created in southern Lebanon that might open the door to a fundamental change, creating a buffer zone and unification of the Christian enclaves under an Israel-friendly leadership.[12]

Operation Litani appeared to have an additional goal: revenge. Shortly after the government meeting, Prime Minister Begin made the following announcement in the Knesset:

We shall not tolerate, under any circumstances, a situation in which murderers, more vile than at any time since the Nazis, operate. . . . And in Beirut they will continue to glorify these murders and promise to continue and to intensify them. . . . We shall hit these murderers at any given time, in all places, with all our might, by sea, by air, by land, until they are no longer able to carry out their murderous schemes against Israelis only because they were born Israelis, against Jews because they were born Jewish.[13]

After the IDF's plans were approved, Israel launched a campaign to conquer the southern part of Lebanon from the Israeli border to the Litani River, an area that served as a base for Palestinian terrorist organizations. Israel swiftly defeated the organizations' military forces and, on its withdrawal from these territories, left control in the hands of their allies among the Lebanese Christian community, who would decide whether or not to prevent the return of the PLO to these areas. The name that Israel gave this area—the "security zone"—indicated its strategic significance. This strip of territory quickly proved itself to be an effective deterrent and prevented many attempts to enter and attack Israel.

In a speech on the eve of the tenth Knesset elections, Prime Minister Begin summarized his government's policy with respect to the war on terror and compared it with that of the previous Labor governments:

We have fundamentally changed the way we protect our people against terrorist murderers. In the days of the Labor governments there was the retaliation policy. We do not disparage this. The terrorist murderers would come, take hostages, kill a man, a woman, a child, and then our army would find the terrorists and make them pay. We have changed that system radically. No more retaliation. We are now acting preventatively. We are going to them, infiltrating their bases and making them pay there. We do not wait until they come to us and shed our blood. This is effective, real defense of our nation, our children, our wives, and this is the type of defense that will continue in the future.[14]

Nevertheless, attacks on the northern border continued. The terrorist organizations tried every possible method to infiltrate Israel: by land (attempting to cross the border fence using various means, including tunnels and springboards), by air (using aircraft, including hang gliders and hot air balloons), and by sea.

OPERATION PEACE FOR GALILEE

The move of the Palestinian terrorist organizations' military forces from Jordan to Lebanon after the events of Black September in Jordan in the early 1970s, as well as the need to deal with IDF operations in Lebanon and its allies in the South Lebanon Army in the late 1970s, led those organizations to formally establish their military forces in Lebanon. Similar to the process that began in Jordan and led to their expulsion from that country, the organizations began to take over areas from southern Lebanon to the city of Beirut, as well as the region of the Bekaa Valley in the east of the country. They spread their military forces throughout these areas, established bases, and set up checkpoints on major traffic arteries. These activities challenged Lebanese sovereignty, and for the second time in a decade, the Palestinian organizations sought to establish a state within a state—exclusively Palestinian-controlled territory within Lebanon.

The process of institutionalizing terrorist military forces manifested in the massive procurement of various weapons (mostly self-propelled heavy weapons), establishment of military units in the organization's quasi-regular structure and hierarchy, and participation in military training and exercises through friendly armies. Apparently, the accelerated build-up of military forces and the Palestinian organizations' successful control of a large area of Lebanese territory distorted reality in the eyes of some of the leaders of the organizations. Sa'd Sayel, for example, commander of Fatah's military forces in Lebanon, believed that Fatah might reach the level of a regular army and that there could even be a direct confrontation between the Palestinian and Israeli armies. "Regular war is actually the best kind of war to resolve situations quickly and decisively," he claimed.[15]

Repeated efforts by terrorists to infiltrate Israel by land, air, and sea failed. The arming of military units in Lebanon with artillery weapons led to increased use of this type of attack. The new method was encouraged by Syria, whose leaders saw the artillery amassed by the Palestinians as an effective means of serving its own interests in Lebanon as well as a way to weaken Israel.

In many cases, terrorists responded to IDF attacks on targets in Lebanon by firing artillery and Katyusha rockets at northern communities. These actions created a chain reaction, with a terror attack leading to Israeli reprisal on Lebanese targets, which in turn would lead to artillery fire on northern Israel. To the Palestinians, such action seemed to reveal Israel's soft underbelly. They quickly discovered that they could severely disrupt life in northern Israel using artillery weapons against civilian communities without entering Israeli territory and without risking the elimination of the terrorist cell before the attack. Sa'd Sayel concluded that in order to carry out meaningful action against Israel, the Palestinians needed "to focus firepower against a defined target."[16] The heavy weapons available to the organizations gave them deterrent capabilities against Israeli offensive operations on PLO positions in Lebanon. This recognition led to the accelerated armament of mobile artillery weapons and the preparation of ammunition depots and supplies that would enable a prolonged conflict with Israel.

Following an Israeli attack on PLO strongholds in Lebanon shortly after the Likud victory in the 1981 elections, the terrorists responded with artillery fire aimed at the northern communities. The next few days saw an escalation in the exchange of fire between Israel and the terrorists, with the Israeli air force attacking deep inside Lebanon and in the city of Beirut, and the terrorists bombing all of the northern communities with artillery and Katyusha rockets. The terrorists concealed their artillery and rocket launchers as well as their weapons stores within the hearts of densely populated towns and villages, forcing Israel to be highly selective in its ground and air raids against them. But even so, Israeli offensive operations resulted in casualties among Lebanese and Palestinian civilians. Naor notes that Begin's instruction was to do everything possible to minimize casualties among the civilian population. Marks were carefully selected, and pilots targeted them with a great degree of precision. Still, when the air force attacked a crowded urban area, the media reported more than 100 dead and 600 wounded.[17]

The United States' reaction was severe. The Reagan administration imposed sanctions on Israel, and Israel was criticized in the court of public opinion. The PLO responded to the air attack by bombarding Israel's northern communities. For twelve days, more than 1,200 shells and Katyusha rockets were fired from Lebanese territory, which paralyzed life in northern Israel.[18] These artillery battles were given the operational name *Avir Psagot* ("mountain air"). A document seized at the PLO headquarters in Sidon addressed to Hajj Ismail (commander of Fatah's Castel Brigade, which controlled southern Lebanon) outlined how to use artillery fire. Dated July 8, 1981, and signed by the PLO's Supreme Military Council, the document reads: "The Supreme Military Council has decided to concentrate on destroying the settlements of Kiryat Shmona, Metula, Dan, She'ar Yashuv, Nahariya and the immediate environs."[19]

The Palestinians' control in southern Lebanon, held by Fatah, allowed them to divide areas and tasks among the various organizations in order to streamline their operations and achieve maximum efficiency. Their military bodies operated under a unified command in the framework of the joint forces. This was expressed in an operational directive to fire artillery from Yasser Arafat to one of his soldiers on July 18, 1981.

> Greetings to the revolution! I am strengthening you! You will prove your importance as a glorious son of your nation and your revolution! We are expecting the heavy shelling of Safed and Rosh Pina with heavy Katyusha rockets tonight because of its great importance. You must also shell the villages near the border using 120 and 160 mm mortars. Act immediately. You should also put combat patrols in place, either of your own soldiers or those of the "joint forces", to position ambushes along the border and deep into the occupied territories.[20]

Israel escalated its attacks and hit the organizations' targets in Beirut and remote areas deep inside Lebanon. It struck Lebanese infrastructure as well; for example, bridges connecting southern Lebanon to the rest of the country. None of these actions resulted in the cessation of Palestinian artillery fire. After two weeks of artillery battles, with the help of the air force and in light of U.S. and international pressure on Israel, a ceasefire was reached in Lebanon on July 24, 1981. The ceasefire was welcomed by the Palestinians as an unprecedented achievement and as a de facto recognition of the PLO.[21]

According to Schueftan, three elements turned the new threat of the PLO into a political success. The first was Israel's vulnerability, the second was the immunity of the Palestinian artillery arsenal from complete annihilation, and the third was American fear of escalation.[22] PLO leaders understood that any provocation of Israel in the future, and certainly a flagrant violation of the ceasefire, would lead to a harsh Israeli response that could include ground incursions against PLO forces in Lebanon. Therefore, the Palestinian organizations maintained the ceasefire on the Lebanese border but continued with their attempts to attack Israel from Jordanian territory. Israel did not accept the Palestinian interpretation of the agreement, announced that it would view any action against it in any arena as a breach of the ceasefire, and began preparing for a large-scale ground operation in Lebanon.

After the attempted assassination of the Israeli ambassador in London, Shlomo Argov, Israel decided to carry out air strikes deep inside Lebanon and in Beirut. The Israeli government was looking for an appropriate trigger to initiate the campaign in Lebanon and to eliminate the strategic threat established by the Palestinian forces, especially their artillery forces aimed at Israel's northern settlements. Former IDF military intelligence chief Shlomo Gazit said,

> they made up poor Shlomo Argov in London, in order to actualize Ariel Sharon's strategic plan. I was in London before the break of war, I was friendly with Argov; he invited me for lunch and we analyzed the situation. To the two of us, it was clear that the war in Lebanon was about to happen. We pondered what would be the excuse. Whether it would be in a week or a month, we didn't know.[23]

The Israeli attack was countered with massive artillery fire from the Palestinian organizations toward the north of Israel, and from there the path to all-out conflict was short. Israel decided to implement its military plans of action for the occupation of southern Lebanon and the destruction of the Palestinian military forces, plans that it had prepared long before. In his remarks at a cabinet meeting on the eve of the operation in Lebanon, Prime Minister Menachem Begin described the considerations that motivated him to approve it:

> I do not want anyone to think that it is with a light heart that I offer this option . . . it will cost us casualties. . . . We know there is no war without casualties. But we cannot accept for there to be two types of citizens in the country: citizens in Tel Aviv, living quietly and peacefully, and citizens in Nahariya and Kiryat Shmona, living in shelters. . . . There will be no end to this, and if we don't act now we'll have to act later, to once and for all remove the threat from the Galilee! . . . The intention is to push back the terrorists and destroy their weapons in a 40 mile range, so that no heavy artillery of theirs can harm our communities.[24]

To demonstrate the goals of the large-scale operation in Lebanon, the Israeli government decided to dub it "Operation Peace for Galilee." At first, when the IDF entered Lebanon, only a few voices among members of the opposition criticized the decision to launch the operation in Lebanon as well as its scope and timing; the majority of the public supported the operation.

Milstein notes that Operation Peace for Galilee signaled a strategic change in Israel's counterterrorism policy. Prior to the action, Israel had fought terrorism through reprisals, intelligence warfare, and preventive measures and obstacles. This type of warfare left the initiative in the hands of the enemy, who possessed advantages that Israel found difficult to counteract. In contrast, Operation Peace for Galilee allowed Israel to apply all the methods of regular warfare against the terrorist organizations and bring them into its field, in which Israel held all of the advantages.[25]

It soon became clear that this was not just another campaign to strike terrorist bases, and the operation progressed beyond the forty kilometers that were necessary to distance the terrorists' artillery from Israel's border. As the operation went on, the IDF suffered significant casualties, and the opposition began to criticize the government, claiming it was using the operation in Lebanon to change the political map in the region and impose peace on Lebanon. In the words of Yitzhak Rabin, who was a member of the opposition at the time,

> until the war in Lebanon, the security and defense agencies agreed . . . that the IDF was never intended to play a political role or to replace the negotiating table. . . . The war in Lebanon is characterized by the premise that permanent diplomatic solutions can be reached through military action. . . . The Lebanon War had three immediate objectives and a fourth long-term goal: the first was based on the assumption that it was possible to eliminate the PLO as a military player, "that no terrorist would remain in Lebanon", in the words of the Prime Minister. The second objective was the removal of Syrian forces from Lebanese territory, and the third, which was dependent on the success of the first two goals, was that the Israeli military presence in the Lebanese capital would allow for the establishment of a Lebanese government favorable to Israel that would "sign a peace treaty with it." . . . Early on in the war in Lebanon it was clear that the first three goals were not achieved.[26]

THE END OF THE LEBANON WAR AND ISRAEL'S
UNITY GOVERNMENT

Approximately one year after the outbreak of the war in Lebanon, and
after Prime Minister Begin resigned in September 1983, Yitzhak Shamir
was appointed prime minister of Israel. At the time, IDF forces were heavily deployed in Lebanon, preparing to retreat from the Shouf Mountains,
and moving to redeploy along the new line at the Awali river.[27] The Lebanon War left its mark on the PLO and the Palestinian terror organizations,
whose main strongholds were in Lebanon. Their military infrastructure was
destroyed. The organizations split into various factions, and their members
were driven into Beirut and north Lebanon. Eventually, the terrorists who
were loyal to Arafat were forced to leave Lebanon for eight faraway Arab
countries.

On October 10, 1983, Prime Minister Shamir presented his government
to the Knesset, and some two weeks later, car bombs exploded in Beirut
at compounds of both the U.S. Marines and the French forces. The attacks
were carried out by Shiite suicide bombers who belonged to the new Lebanese Shiite terrorist organization established by Iran, Hezbollah. Hundreds
of French and American soldiers were killed and injured in the attack due
to the collapse of their barracks. Shortly thereafter, on November 4, a suicide bomber drove a car packed with explosives into the headquarters of
the Israeli military governor of Tyre. The explosion caused the building
to collapse, killing sixty people (including twenty-nine Israeli soldiers and
security personnel) and injuring forty-three (of whom thirty-one were
Israeli security forces).[28] The Shiite organizations' pressure worked, and
American, British, and Italian forces began to evacuate Lebanon at the end
of February 1984.

About a year later, on January 14, 1985, the Israeli government decided on
a phased withdrawal from Lebanon. That day, two roadside bombs exploded
in the western region of Lebanon, killing two IDF soldiers and injuring
seven. Six days later, Israel began to withdraw its forces from the Awali river
line. The terrorist organizations tried to attack the IDF forces as they altered
their deployment in Lebanon, and the growing number of IDF casualties
resulting from Lebanese guerrilla attacks continued to make headlines.

In light of these attacks on its forces, Israel continued to carry out its
policy of phased withdrawal. On April 13, 1985, the IDF completed its

evacuation of the Nabataea Triangle in the center of Lebanon's southern district. In May 1985, the next phase of the IDF's withdrawal from Lebanon was completed, with its return to the lines of the security zone,[29] and on June 10, the withdrawal was finally complete. From the beginning of the war in Lebanon until that date, 1,216 IDF soldiers had been killed in Lebanon.[30] After the withdrawal from Lebanon, Defense Minister Yitzhak Rabin, who was the architect of the withdrawal plan, said,

> We found a different security policy for the problem of terrorism from the Lebanese border. I would like to mention that in the last six months, two Israelis were killed. Every casualty is a loss. But, in six months no citizen was killed. In Lebanon, the situation is less stable than in any of the other three fronts.[31]

Rafael Eitan, IDF chief of staff during the war in Lebanon, strongly criticized the government's policy and the decision to withdraw in stages. He claimed that the Lebanon War accomplished all of the goals that were set for it to achieve. The terrorists had been annihilated, their bases had been destroyed, the Syrian influence in Lebanon had declined significantly, and Syria's involvement in Lebanese affairs had been blocked. Eitan points out that an agreement was signed with the Lebanese government and that multinational forces were stationed in Lebanon in order to ensure stability for Amine Gemayel's government. Because Israel was behind these achievements, he claims that it allowed for the tables to turn by withdrawing its forces from the Shouf Mountains and evacuating the Beirut-Damascus road. Eitan maintains that Israel's withdrawal was a result of impatience, short-sightedness, and submission to domestic pressures. Israel enabled Syrian forces to return to Lebanon, the agreement with Lebanon was canceled, the multinational forces were expelled from Lebanon by terrorist attacks, and the IDF was forced into the security zone. Eitan believes that this was a serious mistake and led the IDF to total failure in its war against terrorism in Lebanon.[32]

The head of military intelligence at the time, Ehud Barak, also opposed the redeployment of the IDF in Lebanon, but for entirely different reasons. According to Barak, the characteristics of the new deployment in Lebanon created a line of outposts along major axes similar to the Israeli line of strongholds along the Suez Canal on the eve of the Yom Kippur War.

From now on, he claimed, Israel would be forced to protect those posts and essentially wage a defensive war. In order to maintain the posts, Israel would have to send supply convoys and would find itself with large forces in Lebanon just in order to protect itself.[33] Ehud Barak's assessment did in fact materialize in the late 1980s and throughout the 1990s.

THE BEGIN, SHAMIR, AND PERES ADMINISTRATIONS' COUNTERTERRORISM POLICIES IN LIGHT OF THE COUNTERTERRORISM DILEMMAS MODEL

This chapter examined the period encompassing 1977 to 1986, during which four administrations governed: two headed by Menachem Begin, one headed by Yitzhak Shamir, who replaced Begin after his resignation, and a unity government with Shimon Peres as prime minister and Shamir as foreign minister. This period began with political upheaval that, for the first time in the history of the state of Israel, saw the rise of the center-right Likud party headed by Begin.

When it was in the opposition, the Likud party urged the Israeli government to adopt a tougher policy toward the terrorist organizations operating from Arab countries, while calling for the occupation of territories and creation of a demilitarized zone along the Israeli border in order to remove the Palestinian terror threat from the borders. And indeed, the Begin governments launched two large-scale military campaigns against the Palestinian terrorist organizations in Lebanon to achieve these goals, following significant terrorist attacks and massive artillery fire into Israeli territory. The first military operation (Operation Litani) was carried out in 1978 and the second (the Lebanon War) in 1982.

The Likud party had also argued that Israel should have done more to counter the PLO's attempt to increase its influence over the Palestinians in the West Bank and Gaza Strip. The party, with its rise to power under Begin's leadership, took steps to strengthen Israel's hold on the West Bank (contrary to the policies adopted by previous governments). The government took firm measures against the Palestinian municipal leadership that affiliated itself with the PLO and accepted the authority of the Fatah movement. These measures included the dismissal of the heads of local authorities, expulsion of pro-PLO leaders, prevention of the transfer of funds to the territories, and more.

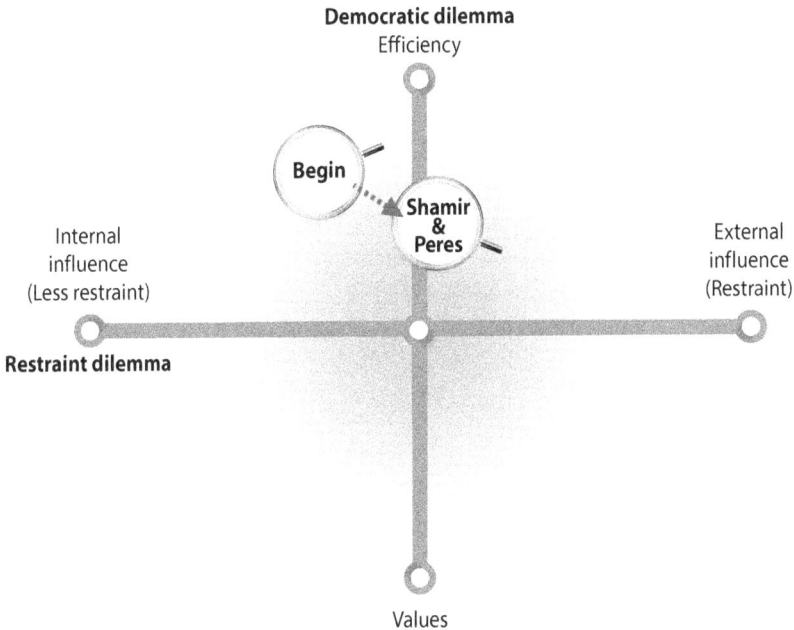

FIGURE 5.1. Counterterrorism Dilemmas Conceptual Model—Begin, Shamir, and Peres administrations

In reference to the Counterterrorism Dilemmas Conceptual Model (figure 5.1), all of these actions indicate a clear tendency on the part of these Israeli governments (especially the Begin governments) to seek greater effectiveness in the fight against terrorism by deterring the terrorist organizations and their supporters in the territories as well as the states offering them protection and territory. First and foremost among these areas was Lebanon, and by causing serious damage to their operational infrastructures, Israel severely impaired the organizations' ability to continue carrying out attacks from Lebanese territory. These steps were taken sometimes even with the risk of infringing liberal democratic values, with little consideration for external international pressure (from the Reagan administration as well as other sources). The Israeli governments sometimes employed measures that previously had been reserved to fight terrorism in order to battle against Arafat's political influence in the territories. And in the Lebanese arena, military means were used not only to cause significant harm to the terrorist organizations but also to exploit the momentum of military success to achieve political gains in Israeli-Lebanese bilateral relations.

The Shamir and Peres governments, on the other hand, toned down the Israeli position on both of these fronts. They began a phased withdrawal of the IDF from most of the territories occupied in Lebanon during the war, sought to restore diplomatic relations with the countries that had severed ties with Israel due to the war, and worked to strengthen the relationships between Israel and its friends around the world. In the Palestinian arena, these governments agreed to renew the diplomatic process to achieve autonomy for Palestinians based on the parameters of the Israeli-Egyptian peace agreement.

Chapter Six

THE FIRST INTIFADA AND ACTIVITIES OF THE PALESTINIAN ISLAMIST ORGANIZATIONS

The Yitzhak Shamir Administration (1987–91)

THE RISE OF PALESTINIAN ISLAMIC JIHAD

The mid-1980s brought a new trend in terrorist activity in Israel and the territories. In addition to the established terrorist organizations, "lone wolves" and local independent networks began to organize to carry out terrorist attacks. These groups consisted of a few individual Palestinians and residents of the territories who, on their own initiative and without any assistance, involvement, or orders from the various terrorist organizations, initiated attacks in the territories and Israel proper. These attacks usually involved the use of cold weapons and improvised devices that could be prepared independently, such as knives, Molotov cocktails, and pipe bombs made of makeshift explosive material. It is likely that this increase in terrorist attacks by the local independent networks in the territories stemmed from the intensification of Palestinian nationalist sentiments. Perhaps another cause was effort by Abu Jihad and Fatah to establish a sociopolitical infrastructure for youth movements in the territories (*Shabiba*), whose members saw themselves as committed to the armed struggle and made do with improvised weaponry.[1]

During these years, the religious-educational activities (*Dawah*) of the Islamic organizations in the territories, headed by the Muslim Brotherhood in the Gaza Strip under the leadership of Hamas founder Sheikh Ahmed

Yassin (who was released from prison as part of the Jibril Agreement in 1985), continued to expand. These activities were viewed as an educational indoctrination phase preceding the establishment of an Islamic state in Palestine. The nonviolent approach taken by the Muslim Brotherhood was perceived by some of the organization's members as insufficient and passive. These activists withdrew from the organization and established a number of factions, Islamic Jihad, in the Gaza Strip and West Bank. The goal of these factions was to put into practice the principle of violent jihad and focus on perpetrating attacks on Israel. Beginning in the mid-1980s, Islamic Jihad, aided by the infrastructure of the Palestinian terrorist organizations in the territories, began to carry out attacks against Israeli targets in the territories and Jerusalem.

The first action leading to the establishment of Islamic Jihad in the West Bank took place in 1985. In May that year, the unity government freed 1,150 Palestinian prisoners in exchange for three Israeli soldiers who had been abducted by the Popular Front for the Liberation of Palestine (PFLP). At the time, the organization was headed by Ahmed Jibril, and the deal became known as the Jibril Agreement.[2] Following this prisoner exchange, hundreds of Palestinian terrorists, most of whom were convicted of murder and terrorist attacks, returned to live in the West Bank and Gaza Strip. This mass release of terrorists led to the establishment of the Palestinian Islamic Jihad (PIJ) movement, headed by Sheikh Assad Bayud Al-Tamimi (a former preacher from Jerusalem who had lived in Jordan since 1970).[3] The founders of the Jihad factions were deeply influenced by the Islamic Revolution in Iran several years earlier and encouraged by what they saw as the success of jihad in Lebanon: the activities of the Islamic organizations that forced the Israeli army to withdraw from Lebanon.[4]

Arafat, who, even before the intifada, had identified the dangerous trend of the return to Islam, worked to establish contact with the Islamic Jihad factions in the territories. The task of uniting the Palestinian factions was assigned to Abu Jihad, who was helped by those of his aides who had Islamic leanings, particularly Bassem Sultan, known as Hamdi. The tenuous link that developed between Fatah and Islamic Jihad was maintained by the Organization 77 Committee, part of Fatah's strike forces (the Western Sector).[5] Among the most heinous attacks by Islamic Jihad in cooperation with the 77 Committee was on IDF Givati Brigade recruits and their families at the Western Wall in Jerusalem in October 1986.

It soon became clear that the most prominent of the PIJ factions was that led by Fathi Shaqaqi. A June 1994 interview with Hani al-Abed, one of the organization's senior military operatives, sheds light on PIJ's ideological principles:

Q: Do you believe that terrorist attacks can advance you further towards your goal?
A: Not too much.
Q: How would you define Islamic Jihad's goal?
A: A state in all of Palestine. We do not believe in the theory of stages. The role of the Islamic organizations inside Palestine is not the liberation of Palestine, but the spreading of the spirit of jihad within the population. The liberation will come from outside, through the military. Secular nationalist movements are disappearing in Arab countries. The Islamic regimes that will be established in Arab countries will topple Israel.[6]

Indeed, as noted by Byman, PIJ "was an Islamist group that believed that violence was a necessary step towards defeating Israel and creating an Islamic Palestinian state."[7]

PIJ operatives organized into small cells of five to seven members and began to carry out harsh attacks in Israel and the territories. The cell members were ordered to maintain secrecy and not to reveal their affiliations and views. As a result, many also refrained from exhibiting signs of religious piety, such as growing beards or wearing *jalabiyas*.[8] PIJ viewed itself as loyal to the armed struggle against Israel, though its leaders understood the limitations of the armed struggle and therefore reiterated the basic assumption that the task of liberating Palestine was the responsibility of the Arab armies. However, unlike Fatah in the past, PIJ saw its role not as a catalyst for an Arab war against Israel but, rather, as a key to the weakening of Israeli society by fostering anxiety, anarchy, and damage to morale. According to Islamic Jihad leader Fathi Shaqaqi, the armed struggle (terrorist activity) undermined Israel's staying power and at the same time strengthened Palestinian society. Despite its might, Israel could not stand the death of "one hundred of its sons in a car explosion. Such an event is considered a national disaster."[9] Sheikh al-Tamimi called on his supporters in the territories to draw encouragement from what he called "the political, economic, and spiritual erosion of the Jews" due to the blows they were receiving from the Palestinians, and to be strong, because time was on their side, and the longer they fought against Israel, the more Israel would lose its confidence.[10]

HAMAS IS BORN

The rise of Islamic Jihad forced the Muslim Brotherhood to become directly involved in the uprising in the territories. To his dismay, the movement's leader, Sheikh Yassin, conclued that in order to maintain the movement's relevance and prevent its members from joining the ranks of the PIJ (after years of propaganda, religious education, and welfare activity), the movement must take an active part in events in the West Bank and Gaza Strip. For this purpose, the Muslim Brotherhood established a military wing, Hamas, and exploited the violence in order to harm groups and individuals who they said were "corrupting Palestinian society" (such as drug dealers and homosexuals). As explained by Byman, "Much of Hamas's agenda involves social behavior; its members oppose moral permissiveness, favor Islamic law over secular law, and are dedicated to eradicating corruption."[11] Hamas began publishing leaflets calling for strikes, demonstrations, and large-scale disturbances, different from those of the Unified National Leadership (Fatah-PLO leadership). Despite the clear divisions between the PLO and Hamas, the two succeeded in avoiding a direct confrontation in order to prevent a civil war and not play into Israel's hands.

Hamas's ideology was based on a combination of Palestinian nationalism and the aspiration to establish an independent state under Islamic sharia law in all areas of Palestine. In contrast to PIJ, Hamas was careful to retain its independent status and not become the satellite of any Arab or Muslim state (including Iran), even though it was prepared to accept any assistance it could from these countries. Like PIJ, Hamas set its own psychological goals for its terrorist activity during the intifada, including fracturing and undermining Israeli society from within, leading to a change in Israel's political positions and withdrawal from the Gaza Strip and West Bank.[12]

During this time, Hamas refrained from initiating terrorist attacks inside Israel within the Green Line border. Shabi and Shaked point out that in addition to the concept of jihad, Hamas added another important element from the Muslim Brotherhood's doctrine, *Sabr* (patience or perseverance). In a 1993 interview with the Saudi newspaper *Al-Hayat*, Hamas spokesperson Ibrahim Ghousha said, "Hamas alone will not be able to liberate Palestine, but it is the spearhead in a war of attrition that could last for thirty, forty years, until the Zionist enemy understands that the land does not belong to them."[13]

The return to Islam, expressed in the establishment of Hamas and PIJ and the joining of many activists to their ranks, was also reflected in the secular Palestinian organizations, which began to make use of religious concepts in their statements and propaganda. On March 21, 1988, for example, for the first time, Fatah's Executive Committee added to an official announcement the opening statement, "In the name of the merciful God," and quoted a number of *Surahs* (chapters) from the Koran.[14]

On the eve of the intifada (the popular uprising in the territories) at the beginning of 1987, a change had already begun in Israel's policy toward the Islamic organizations in the territories. In the late 1970s and early 1980s, the Israeli Civil Administration saw the fundamentalist Islamic elements as a rising power, balancing or limiting the PLO's influence in the territories. However, from the mid-1980s onward, this administration became more and more convinced that the inherent danger in the rise of fundamentalist Islam in the territories surpassed any possible benefit it represented in relation to the PLO. This change in view was reflected in the Civil Administration review distributed in January 1987, which described the risks posed by radical Islam as follows.

In principle, the fundamentalist Islamic groups in the Gaza Strip are the most dangerous to Israel in the long term, due to their fanatic and uncompromising religious and political views, according to which Israel is perceived as a heretical act that contradicts Islam, with redemption reliant on its destruction in a holy war. In this outlook, there is no room for any compromise with Israel. . . . The starting point in the treatment of the issue is that the eradication of [the Islamic element] in one fell swoop is not possible. However, its further spread can be curbed by controlling measures and appropriate action in the field.[15]

The outbreak of the intifada and Hamas's terrorist attacks only confirmed the Civil Administration's assessments, and in September 1989, the Hamas movement was outlawed, which facilitated the prosecution of its members.

OUTBREAK OF THE INTIFADA

On May 18, 1987, six PIJ activists escaped from the central prison in Gaza, including Imad Saftawi, who had been tried for murdering six Israeli civilians. The news of the daring escape spread like wildfire in the territories. The escapees were showered with praise as it became clear that despite being wanted by Israel, they were not hiding but continuing to carry out terrorist attacks. The PIJ escapees' boldness and defiance of the Israeli security forces, combined with Hezbollah's achievements in Lebanon, damaged the IDF's deterrent capability, symbolized the success of the Islamic groups in the eyes of Palestinian youths in the West Bank and Gaza, and inspired them to rise up in resistance of Israel.[16]

The activities of the independent local networks and the strengthening of Islamic Jihad were only a prelude to the events of the intifada. One can point to a variety of nationalist, religious, and social factors that led to the outbreak of mass demonstrations and riots in the Gaza Strip in December 1987 and, later, in the West Bank. These factors can be classified as processes that had a prolonged and cumulative effect. Each factor can be understood as a catalyst having an immediate effect. Among the long-term processes were the following.

1. *Disappointment with the secular Palestinian terrorist organizations.* Palestinian organizations suffered a severe blow in the Lebanon War. This included the destruction of their military infrastructure, exile to other countries, and the feeling that inhabitants in the territories were not being adequately represented in the PLO institutions. This severely limited their influence on the Palestinian decision-making process and strengthened the conviction of the youth in the territories to take their fate into their own hands, dictating moves that would affect Israel, the PLO, and the entire arena.

2. *The Islamic awakening.* The rise of fundamentalist Islam among movements and organizations in Arab countries, inspired by the Khomeinist revolution in Iran, also influenced the youth in the Palestinian territories. The economic situation there, the daily experience of life under occupation, disappointment in the secular organizations in contrast to Hezbollah's achievements in Lebanon, and the Islamic movements' welfare activities in the territories all led to a growing trend of a return to Islam among the younger generation. In this context, the conclusion drawn by PLO/Fatah leaders, expressed in Hani al-Hassan's remarks, is especially interesting:

"We reached a very dramatic conclusion: we found that the silent majority of our people in the occupied territories supported radical Islam with their hearts, if not with their actions."[17]

3. *Economic problems.* Gad Gilber emphasizes the social and economic processes that underlay the intifada. Among them, he discusses the drastic annual population growth in the six years preceding the intifada, which resulted from a natural increase and a decline in emigration. The early 1980s also marked a turnaround in economic development in the West Bank and Gaza. In the 1970s, these areas enjoyed the most significant real growth, but from 1981 to 1982, there was a sharp downturn in their gross national product, which was accompanied by an increase in unemployment in the territories.[18]

4. *Frustration stemming from a rise in education.* In the fifteen years preceding the intifada, there was a steady increase in the attainment of both secondary and higher education among residents of the territories. Universities were opened to meet the growing demand, and many young people left to study abroad. After graduating, they found themselves unemployed or employed in Israel doing manual labor, which did not require professional skills and was neither socially respected nor financially rewarding. All of this created frustration and bitterness among young educated people.[19] Hillel Frisch notes that, paradoxically, the prosperity of blue-collar workers in the 1970s enabled them to afford to give their children a high school and postsecondary education. However, no changes were made in the labor market that would enable the absorption of the new educated workers.[20]

5. *Humiliation resulting from direct contact with Israeli society and the Israeli occupation.* The many young Palestinians who set out to find a livelihood in Israel were quickly exposed to the profound gaps between the quality of life in Israel and that in the territories. The frustration and anger generated by these disparities were further fueled by the disdainful and hostile attitude of segments of Israeli society. For example, Shiff and Yaari state that most of the detainees in the early days of the riots were young people who worked in Israel and had experienced humiliation by Israelis.[21]

6. *The generation gap in Palestinian society in the territories.* The fact that the younger generation, aged fifteen to twenty-five, took responsibility for the uprising in the territories reflected a process of generational change in Palestinian society, which involved transferring the burden of the struggle from the parents' generation to the younger generation. This process undermined the authority of the father figure in the Palestinian family due to his difficulty in earning a living, as well as criticism of the passivity of the generation who first experienced the occupation.

In addition to the ongoing processes that prepared the ground for the outbreak of the intifada, a number of specific events can be identified that also influenced the popular uprising in December 1987.

1. *A car accident in Gaza*. On December 8, 1987, a serious road accident in the Gaza Strip occurred in which an Israeli truck hit a Palestinian car. Four of the passengers, Palestinian workers, died at the scene and others were seriously injured. Because of the accident, rumors spread in the territories that this had been a deliberate action by Israeli extremists and not an accident. The rumors were reinforced by a leaflet, likely printed by students of the Islamic College in Gaza, as well as by a headline in the *Al Fajr* newspaper the day after the accident, claiming that there was malicious intent behind the accident. Following the funeral of those who were killed, thousands of mourners attacked an IDF outpost, and the riots continued well into the night. The following day, the intifada began.[22]

2. *The escape of PIJ activists from the Gaza prison in May 1987*. As mentioned, the success of the escape and the terrorist attacks carried out by the escapees damaged the IDF's deterrent capability in the territories. PIJ's contribution to the outbreak of the uprising (at least in their eyes) can be observed in the first leaflet distributed by PIJ at the beginning of the intifada:

> O Muslims, oh Mujahideen! Islamic Jihad was the first to ignite the fire of the uprising and called for demonstrations in the mosques, which was the dawn of the popular Islamic revolution for the liberation of the Holy Land and the prophets from the Zionist impurity. The Mujahideen sacrificed and are sacrificing more and more casualties.[23] In this context, it should be noted that the deaths of the escapees in an encounter with IDF forces in the Gaza Strip on October 6, 1987, also had an impact on the outbreak of the uprising. PIJ actually sees that date as the day the intifada began.[24]

3. *The glider attack*. About a month before the outbreak of the intifada, a terrorist from the PFLP/GC-"Jibril Front" infiltrated Israel from Lebanon using a hang glider. He landed near a Nachal Brigade army encampment in Kiryat Shmonah and killed seven soldiers. The fact that a single terrorist had succeeded in killing so many soldiers initiated a public debate in Israel following the incident, focusing on the issue of the sentry having fled his position as the terrorist entered the base, also contributed to weakening the IDF's deterrent capability in the territories and strengthening the ethos of Palestinian daringness. A pamphlet distributed in Jabalya Camp on the fourth day of the uprising read, "Today they (the Jews) are

repeating the words of the sentry's father: We want to live as we are, instead of dying as heroes. Today they understand that the future belongs to us and that they have reached the end of the escapade of the Zionist dream."[25]

4. *The IDF's response to the riots in the Balata refugee camp*. Shiff and Ya'ari claim that the IDF had long been hesitant to act in response to the rise of the *Shabiba* Movement in the Balata refugee camp and the numerous instances of disturbances, riots, and throwing of stones and Molotov cocktails in the camp. This hesitation influenced Palestinian activists in other areas of the territories as well.[26]

From Israel's perspective, the intifada in the territories constituted a major crisis that required the active involvement of decision makers, the formation of policy and of responsive and punitive measures, military and diplomatic deployment, and the channeling of resources and laborers to deal with the problem. The riots began on December 9, when Palestinians took to the streets in protest following the crash in which the Palestinian workers were killed. On that day, the IDF killed a seventeen-year-old Palestinian and wounded sixteen others.[27] In the early stages of the intifada, Israeli decision makers underestimated the gravity of the problem and thought that the main damage would be media related. Ariel Sharon said in this context that he

> remember[ed] what Rabin, of blessed memory, said, as well as Shamir: "It's a wave, a ripple, it will all pass," and so on. They did not read the situation correctly. By the way, the Shin Bet did warn us. They said that we are conducting an all-out war. But nothing, they didn't take it seriously.[28]

Prime Minister Yitzhak Shamir's mood at the time can be gauged from his statements shortly after the outbreak of the intifada, when international media were extensively covering the beating of Palestinians by Israeli soldiers:

> We are not allowed to kill; we are not allowed to expel; we are not allowed to beat. You ask yourself, what are we allowed to do? Only to be killed, only to be wounded, only to be defeated? . . . We have plenty of "friends" in the world who would like to see us dead, wounded, trampled, and suppressed— and then it is possible to pity the wretched Jew. When Jews are killed in this country, does the United Nations discuss it? It has never yet happened. But we do not want to be deserving of pity, we want to fight for our lives.[29]

The violent incidents quickly spread throughout the territories, threatening to spill over into Israel, and involved thousands of the territories' residents. The demonstrations became more and more frequent, included more and more participants, and were accompanied by the throwing of stones and Molotov cocktails. In addition to protests and violence, there were also acts of civil disobedience, which included days of general and trade strikes, the cessation of tax payments, the resignation of local police officers and transportation workers, and pressure for local councils and municipalities to quit and establish an alternative system of self-rule free from Israeli control. At this point, Israeli decision makers still believed that the intifada could be stopped by military means. Defense Minister Yitzhak Rabin hoped to erase the violent demonstrations from the agenda. In January 1988, IDF chief of staff Dan Shomron estimated that the IDF's punitive measures would lead to calm within two to three weeks. The goal, for the chief of staff, was not only to quash the uprising but also "to create a reservoir of deterrent memories that would have an effect in the future"[30]—in other words, to deal with the uprising in a way that would ensure that the population would be prevented from repeating it.

At the same time, a debate developed in Palestinian society over the question of how nationalist goals should be realized, whether through "popular struggle" (intifada) or "military struggle." PIJ secretary-general Shaqaqi tried to resolve the dispute by stating that there was no contradiction between the two types of struggle. He proposed separating the grassroots activity that formed the basis of the intifada from the equally vital armed struggle, saying that this would deprive Israel of the possibility of excessive aggression in suppressing demonstrations.[31] Accordingly, some of the Palestinian organizations tried to express their support for the intifada and take an active part in the uprising by engaging in terrorist activity in Israel and infiltrating its borders, as well as by shooting artillery from Lebanon into northern Israel. However, this activity was only a secondary effort alongside the uprising.

There is a debate regarding the role of the PLO in initiating and directing the popular uprising in the West Bank and Gaza Strip. Many scholars believe that the PLO was surprised by the outbreak of the intifada.[32] In any event, the PLO leadership tried, through Abu Jihad, to do all it could to control events in the West Bank and Gaza Strip, and for this purpose, the Unified National Leadership of the Uprising (UNLU) was established, headed by Fatah activists. The UNLU issued leaflets with instructions for carrying out demonstrations and strikes, throwing stone, and more. Fatah organized its young activists into action committees in the territories, which, like their counterparts in the Islamic organizations, planned popular activities and took action against suspected collaborators with Israel.

ISRAELI RESPONSE TO THE INTIFADA

Israel, for its part, was also surprised by the intifada. The IDF's initial response was to use firearms in an attempt to restore order and prevent violent demonstrations. This resulted in a large number of Palestinian casualties, which led IDF to attempt to reduce the flames by means of punitive measures and deterrents such as curfews in riot areas and administrative detentions. The Israeli forces also began to operate undercover military units, members of which disguised themselves as Palestinians and planted themselves inside the violent demonstrations, helping to locate and arrest the inciters. The close and direct contact between IDF forces and rioters in the territories led to cases of severe violence against Palestinians. These incidents, dubbed "the policy of beating," were filmed by Israeli and foreign media outlets and broadcast around the world, drawing harsh criticism of Israel. Defense Minister Rabin described the background of the formulation of the beating policy as follows.

> I decided to deal with the problem just as the enlightened and democratic police of London, Paris, New York, Seoul, and Brussels do, assaults with clubs and beatings of the rioters. . . . There is nothing wrong with this. The decision to use force, including beatings, instead of live ammunition to take control of violent riots was made after hearing from soldiers and commanders in the field and from senior security officials. . . . I did not consider renouncing it for a moment nor will I do so in the future. . . . It turns out that close-ups of beatings with clubs and blood are more harmful to Israel's image than shooting live ammunition and killing. Despite the harsh criticism, I decided to give the command to continue to operate as much as possible using clubs rather than bullets, blows rather than shots. It was important to me and to everyone that there be fewer casualties both among IDF soldiers and among the Palestinians.[33]

Despite the defense minister's ostensibly well-thought-out policy, things began to spin out of control. The use of force was intended not only to carry out arrests and take control of disturbances but also to punish rioters and deter others from engaging in similar acts. Examples of severe actions taken in the territories were revealed in a trial held in the Southern Command's military court in May 1989, in the case of the death of Hani al-Shami Ben Dib from the Jabalya refugee camp. Known as the Givati Trial, the case dealt with the IDF's policy of beating. After hearing testimonies, including from some of the IDF's most senior officers, the judges harshly criticized the military's policy.[34]

Due to condemnation of the beating policy around the world and from various circles in Israel, and in light of the verdict of the Givati Trial, it was decided that Israel's policy in the West Bank and Gaza needed to be reevaluated. In March 1988, a new line was adopted based on a combination of military and diplomatic measures. This policy included activities aimed at exhausting the Palestinian population through military and administrative punitive actions for disturbances in their areas. At the same time, Rabin sought a diplomatic solution to the problem.[35] The challenge of the intifada at this stage, and the policy that guided Israel's actions at the time, can be understood from Rabin's words:

> The goal assigned to the IDF and other security forces by the political echelon—the government, through the defense minister—is to bring about maximum calm and maintain a system of municipal government and civil administration which will function for the benefit of the civilian population. . . . There is no one single system or means that can bring about calm. Therefore, we are operating on the basis of three systems: The military presence must deal with the suppression of violence and not allow it to develop further. . . . The second area of action is the punishing of the organizers and instigators who are carrying out violent activities . . . with the goal being broad arrests, first and foremost of the inciters, the organizers, and the perpetrators of these actions. . . . The third area is the operation of a system of administrative and economic measures. We try to be more selective in the economic sphere, although we cannot always stay that way. The purpose of all three of these systems is not only to suppress the violence, but also to sow motivation to change the atmosphere, so that it will lead to a longer calm.[36]

At this stage, the directive was to reduce the extensive use of clubs and to avoid, as much as possible, direct physical confrontation with rioters;

rather, the aim was to take control of the violence from a certain distance.[37] It was clear to policy makers that the challenge of the intifada necessitated a search for new methods and measures that had not been used to deal with terrorism in the past. For this purpose, special teams were established to develop nonlethal methods and means to take control of rioters and prevent disturbances. Among the new developments were plastic, rubber, and paint bullets, the use of which was designed to deter and hinder the main inciters, as well as *hatsatsit* (half-tracks with mechanisms mounted on them that scattered gravel at demonstrators), armored vehicles, and special sheets for extinguishing burning tires.[38]

The plastic bullet, 5.56 mm in length, was supposed to be nonlethal when fired within certain ranges. In an affidavit of response given in a petition filed against the minister of defense regarding the use of plastic bullets, deputy chief of staff Major General Ehud Barak explained the need to switch to the use of this type of weapon:

> The use of plastic bullets led to a turning point in the IDF's struggle against the violent disturbances in Judea and Samaria and the Gaza Strip, as they were an effective means of preventing disturbances, dispersing them, and apprehending the rioters. If the plastic bullet had not been put into use, the number of violent disturbances and their scope and severity would have increased significantly, as would the number of casualties. . . . This weapon also contributed significantly to the restoration of the IDF's deterrent capability in its ceaseless efforts to reestablish order in these areas and ensure the safety of both soldiers and residents.[39]

During the intifada, the regulations determining when IDF soldiers should open fire were also changed. The procedure dictated a warning call, warning shots fired in the air at an upward angle of at least 60 degrees, and then, if the suspect continued to flee, shooting aimed at injuring the legs. According to these regulations, as they were formulated in August 1986, live ammunition could be fired in only two cases: if a soldier was in mortal danger, and as part of an arrest procedure if the suspect was suspected of committing a serious crime.[40] In January 1989, it was determined that a soldier may open fire "at whoever poses a concrete danger, and one such danger, for example, is the erection of barriers".[41] On July 6, 1989, the "Apprehension of Suspects Procedure for Individuals Wearing Costumes or Masks Under Suspicious

Circumstances" was published. In essence, it permitted the apprehension or arrest of an armed masked individual using live ammunition, and under suspicious circumstances, it permitted the arrest of an unarmed masked individual using plastic bullets, not live ammunition.[42]

In light of Israel's inability to halt the intifada, one of the questions that arose was how Israeli citizens living in the West Bank would respond to the daily hardships and harm it caused. However, despite intensification of the intifada and violent incidents against Israelis, Jewish settlers in the territories refrained from taking the law into their own hands and initiating "counter acts" of terrorism.[43]

Overall, the years of the intifada, 1988–90, marked a significant change in Israel's punitive policy toward the terrorist organizations and their collaborators in particular, and toward Palestinian residents of the territories in general. The administrative punitive methods and measures that were in place prior to the intifada—such as detentions, the demolition and sealing of houses, deportation, closures, curfews, and the like—which Israel used in a specific and selective manner during the 1980s, 1970s, and even earlier, became routine during the intifada against large groups of instigators and participants in disturbances. Although these steps were unsuccessful in ending the intifada, according to Shalev, this does not mean that they had no influence on the level of violence on the ground. It is possible that had such methods not been employed, the scale of violence would have been much greater.[44]

Demolition and Sealing of Houses

During the intifada, the number of cases in which the houses of those convicted (and sometimes only suspected) of engaging in terrorist activity against Israel, collaborating with terrorist organizations, inciting violence, and organizing riots increased significantly. Prior to that time, the punishment of demolishing or sealing a house was considered severe and employed only in the most extreme cases, such as murder, attempted murder, and the throwing of grenades or explosive devices. However, during the uprising, the security forces used this punishment much more frequently, as it was no longer limited as a response to serious terrorist attacks. It was used to punish Palestinians who threw Molotov cocktails (even if no damage was caused), who acted against other Palestinians suspected of collaborating with Israel, and even those who threw stones. The punishment of demolishing and sealing houses was sanctioned by the court even before the intifada. The High Court of Justice (HCJ 698/85) ruled that

> there is no basis to the petitioner's complaint that house demolition is a form of collective punishment. In their opinion, only the terrorists and criminals themselves should be punished, and house demolition punishes additional family members who will be left without shelter. Such an interpretation, if accepted by us, would leave the above Regulation and its orders void of content, leaving only the possibility of punishing a terrorist who lives alone.[45]

The court emphasized the deterrent purpose of this punishment:

> [The deterring effect] should apply not only to the terrorist himself but also to those around him. . . . He should know that his criminal acts will not only hurt him, but are apt to cause great suffering to his family. From this point of view, the sanction of house demolition is no different than the punishment of imprisonment imposed on the head of a family, a father whose small children will be without a supporter and a bread winner.[46]

The large number of punitive house demolitions and sealings led the defense establishment to adapt its punitive procedures for the needs on the ground. It was permitted, in urgent and exceptional cases of serious attacks and rapid apprehension of the criminal, and in a short and reasonable time following the attack, to immediately apply the sanction in accordance with Regulation 119 without having to grant the right to plead one's case.

The state attorney's office believed that "a short and reasonable time" was forty-five days from the date of the offense until the day of demolition, during which, in urgent and unusual cases, security forces would be allowed to demolish the house without giving the victim the right to be heard. The Military Advocate General's office believed that this period could be extended to ninety days. Defense Minister Rabin and the Israeli Security Agency (ISA, or Shin Bet) pressured the Military Advocate General's office to allow demolition in this accelerated manner even after ninety days, as often a long time would pass between the incident and the apprehension of the culprits.[47]

Following the demolition of thirteen houses in the village of Beita in April 1988, whose owners were denied the right to plead their case, the Association for Civil Rights in Israel petitioned the High Court of Justice. Over the course of the hearing, the judges proposed a compromise whereby a two-stage process would take place in extreme and exceptional cases that required the defense establishment to take immediate steps to demolish the house. First, the house would be seized and immediately sealed, and it would be demolished only after the owner had been given the right to plead his case and the plea had been rejected by the military commander or High Court of Justice. To Rabin's dismay, the judges' motion quickly turned into a high court decision. Even after changes in government and the appointment of Moshe Arens to replace Rabin, the defense ministry continued to pressure the Military Advocate General's office to adjust its position and allow administrative punitive measures with shorter proceedings.[48]

The thoughts and feelings of Israeli decision makers regarding this type of punishment can be gleaned from the words of then-prime minister Yitzhak Shamir, who, when asked what he meant when he said they should "get what they deserve," replied,

> To show these bastards who kill us mercilessly that there is someone who knows how to strike back. We have to prove to all these murderers, to all these "martyrs," that before they reach "Muslim Paradise," we will take revenge on them in any way we see fit. . . . We can prove to the terrorist organizations and their leaders, to Arafat's gangs, to Islamic Jihad, and to all those who are involved in Palestinian terrorism, that acts of terrorism will harm them more than they harm us, for example by way of demolitions of the murderers' homes and the expulsion of all those who collaborated with them.[49]

The demolition of a terrorist's home is far from a trivial act; it is a difficult undertaking that involves overcoming emotional difficulties, as testified by then-OC Central Command Major General Amram Mitzna after the detonation of four houses in the Ras al-Ain neighborhood of Nablus in October 1988. These houses belonged to members of a "shock committee" cell suspected of murdering three "collaborators" with Israel. Mitzna said,

> I know that this is a very difficult act. It is very difficult for us as well. It is only with the recognition and deep understanding that we have no choice that we

are able to withstand such difficult things. [The destruction of houses] sends a clear message: we will fight to the end and do everything in our power to capture those who harm local Arab residents.[50]

Military Advocate General Straschnov also expressed his misgivings during the intifada when he was asked to approve the demolition of houses, saying he believed that the punitive measure was even more severe than expulsion. He added that the assumption that demolishing the house of a terrorist was an effective deterrent to terrorist attacks had not been proven with certainty in any empirical study, and that despite the use of this measure, terrorist attacks continued.[51]

The Israeli security community's assessment regarding the effectiveness of demolishing and sealing houses was reflected in then-Central Command chief Amram Mitzna's reply affidavit to the High Court of Justice, in which he presented data proving the policy's success:

According to the data available to us, this policy [i.e., applying the sanction in Regulation 119] has resulted in a significant decrease in the number of Molotov cocktail throwing incidents (since it was introduced). Thus, for instance, during July and the first half of August, "only" 113 incidents of Molotov cocktail throwing were recorded in the Judea and Samaria area. In my estimation, a significant component of this decrease, which we hope will continue in the coming months, can be attributed to the influence of Regulation 119, in its full severity and immediacy, against the houses of those who throw Molotov cocktails.[52]

However, the effectiveness of house demolitions and sealings was never proven—neither the intensive manner in which it was used during the intifada nor the specific and selective manner in which it was employed in the time preceding it. Aryeh Shalev points out two factors that explain, in his opinion, the decrease in this punishment's effectiveness and deterrent capability. One was the PLO's decision to grant financial compensation to the families of the targets, and the second was the boomerang effect; that is, increased hatred and opposition to Israel.[53]

In a round of interviews with people who played central roles in counterterrorism decision-making during the intifada, various—and even contradictory—opinions were presented regarding the effectiveness of this type of punishment. On the one hand, the former counterterrorism advisor to Prime Minister Rafi Eitan maintained that he had "always been against it. It has never been effective."[54] On the other hand, another former advisor to the prime minister on counterterrorism, Yigal Pressler, believes that there is great benefit to this punitive measure, because the terrorist's family, who are usually aware of the intent to commit a terrorist attack, know that they will pay for their family member's actions.[55] In contrast to these two approaches, the majority of respondents supported the demolition and sealing of houses, but in a highly selective and case-by-case manner, and certainly not as it was done during the intifada. Shimon Peres, for example, did not rule out the measure, but he suggested that it be used selectively. "It's like DDT; when you use it too frequently, it loses its effectiveness . . . it is necessary to be very careful not to erode its effect, so you need to be very selective in number and target."[56] Yaakov Perry, former head of the ISA, agreed.

> There have been places where a house was demolished and this had an effect on peace and quiet in the area, and for a relatively long period. There were places where it had the opposite effect . . . the more routine it becomes, the more this tool loses its effectiveness. The more it is used in a focused manner, the better the effect that is obtained.[57]

Administrative Detentions

One of the best-known and most effective measures of administrative punishment during the intifada was detention. Detention was intended to temporarily neutralize the hostile element who was inciting violence or perpetrating attacks without a public trial and without disclosing evidence to the public and the defendant himself. It was meant to make it easier for security officials to deal with cases in which the disclosure of evidence was likely to harm national security due to exposing the identity of the source or intelligence methods through which the information was obtained.

Like the other types of administrative punishment, detention was also based on the Defense (Emergency) Regulations. In the period leading up to the intifada (1983–87), it was used in a limited and on a case-by-case basis against those suspected of perpetrating or aiding terrorist attacks, as well as those suspected of belonging to terrorist organizations. During the intifada, the use of administrative detention also increased. On the eve of the outbreak, only 200 Palestinians were administratively detained in the West Bank and Gaza Strip, but in the three years of the intifada, some 14,000 residents of these areas were detained.[58]

The widespread use of this kind of punishment obliged the legal systems (especially the Military Advocate General's office) to prepare accordingly and to adapt legal procedures to conditions on the ground. One of the main problems encountered by the defense establishment was the issue of "automatic supervision" of administrative detention, according to which the detainee had to be brought before a judge within ninety-six hours of arrest to examine the circumstances of detention. Given the large number of detainees, the inability of the military justice system to meet this requirement led, in certain cases, to the release of detainees who were not brought before a judge in time. In accordance with a proposal made by the military advocate general on March 17, 1988, the "Injunction Regarding Administrative Detainees (Temporary Order) (Judea and Samaria) (No. 1229), 1988" was amended, and afterward the equivalent injunction for the Gaza Strip was also changed. Through these amendments, the requirement of automatic supervision by a military judge within ninety-six hours of arrest was revoked, as was the requirement of a periodic reexamination every three months; however, the detainee was given the option of appealing his detention before an appeals committee.

The authority to issue an administrative detention order was granted to every military commander, not just to the commander of IDF forces in the area. The amendment of the injunction enabled the administrative detention of thousands of Palestinians in the territories in a short time, and for this purpose, a special detention facility in Ktziot was prepared.[59] Straschnov attested to the fact that the prevalence of this punitive measure did not cause any harm to proper legal proceedings (within the framework of administrative detention) and that before the military commander signed the administrative detention order, he was required to obtain the opinion of the regional legal advisor. This advisor had to determine whether there was a sufficient legal basis for the arrest, that the information on the detainee was based on more than one intelligence source, and that the information was crosschecked, reliable, and well founded.[60]

In November 1988, following the urgent need to renew the administrative detention protocol for all detainees of the first wave of the intifada six months after their arrest, security forces requested an extension for the maximum period of detention from six months, as the injunction specified, to one year. This demand was rejected by the Military Advocate General's office, but the request was made again in August 1989, and the order was ultimately amended.[61] In light of the tightening of punitive measures during the intifada, Palestinian lawyers in Gaza began to strike. This continued for more than half a year, during which there were no appeals to the Israeli High Court of Justice and no appeals on administrative detentions. However, when the Palestinians realized that this strike was working against their best interests, they began to use the High Court of Justice appeals process to take a stand against administrative punishment.[62] Of the 14,000 administrative detainees during the intifada, approximately 10,500 filed appeals against their arrest; about 5 percent of the appeals submitted were accepted by the military judges, most of them resulting in the shortening of the detention period, and a few resulting in the immediate release of the detainees.[63]

The military establishment believed administrative detention was one of the most effective tools at its disposal for dealing with the intifada, and its leaders—first and foremost the defense minister—viewed the number of reduced administrative detention sentences as a disgrace.[64] B'Tselem (the Israeli Information Center for Human Rights in the Occupied Territories), on the other hand, vehemently criticized the policy of administrative detentions during the intifada. According to the organization, international law permits the detention of civilians without trial only in exceptional and necessary circumstances, emphasizing that this preventive measure must not be used as a substitute for punishment. Israel, however, according to B'Tselem, made administrative detention a punitive method, changed the detention and appeal procedures illegally, and held the detainees under inhumane conditions.[65]

Some of interviewees in this book, individuals who helped shape Israeli policy during this period, also expressed hesitation about the legitimacy of the extensive use of this method, though others highlighted its great effectiveness. Former defense minister Moshe Arens said he did not approve of the large number of administrative detainees.[66] By contrast, Yaakov Perry, head of the ISA during the intifada, emphasizing its usefulness, maintained that it would have been impossible to deal effectively with the events of the ntifada without administrative detentions, especially when the intelligence organizations could not reveal information or bring evidence to court or when the number of detainees was so large that it was not physically possible to arrest everyone.[67] However, Yigal Pressler, former advisor on counterterrorism to the prime minister, stated unequivocally that he is against administrative detentions and claimed that if the facts that prove the offense cannot be made public, the suspect should not be arrested until the necessary facts are obtained.[68] As was the case regarding his position on house demolitions and closures, former defense minister and prime minister Shimon Peres also recommended a "meticulous number" of administrative detentions, opposing the massive use of this measure. Explaining the dilemma, Peres said,

> When a nation is at war, its instinct toward the law is different. When war is distant, the law takes precedence. In wartime, the army is a deity; everything is forgiven. . . . One must distinguish between the eve of war, a state of war, postwar, and distance from war. The nation's perceptions change in each of these four phases, and things you can do in phase A, you cannot do in phases B and C.[69]

Deportations

Until the intifada and following it, Israel used deportation as a severe administrative punishment against senior members of terrorist organizations and those who incited and instigated violence, and not necessarily against those who were caught perpetrating terrorist attacks (the latter were usually tried and sentenced to prison). Until the intifada, and in its first year, deportation was considered the most severe form of punishment against these offenders and a practical means of distancing an inciter from the area. Although deportation could cause temporary tension and escalation in the area, in the long run, the benefit of deportation exceeded any temporary damage. This was expressed by then-IDF chief of staff Dan Shomron, who said that "deportation from the territories is a deterrent and effective punishment, even though in the short term it can cause agitation. Deportations will continue, but there will be no mass deportations."[70]

As mentioned, with the outbreak of the intifada and escalation of violent incidents in the territories, Israel employed every punishment in its arsenal, but with much greater frequency and scope. The number of deportations also increased in comparison with the years preceding the intifada, but the increase was in percentages of tens, not hundreds, as was the case with other punishments. In other words, despite the large number of deportations, Israel was careful about using this severe measure, employing it specifically and meticulously. During the era of the Shamir and unity governments, between 1983 and 1991, 114 Palestinians were deported from the territories. In 1983, no Palestinian was deported; in 1984, only one was deported; in 1985, the number of deportations was twenty-nine; ten in 1986;eight in 1987[71]; thirty-two in 1988; twenty-six in 1989;none in 1990; and eight in 1991.[72]

In January 1988, as part of the government's attempt to calm the situation in the West Bank and to reduce violence, four principal activists involved in organizing the riots were deported. In response to a question in the Knesset, Defense Minister Rabin responded that deportation was "an effective means for individual cases. This measure was never used against large numbers of people."[73] Rabin maintained that all of the deportees were involved in hostile terrorist activity and were chosen as part of an effort "to remove organizers and instigators and ensure that they would not continue to cause provocations in the area."[74] Following the deportations, the Security Council convened and unanimously issued a statement of condemnation, expressing "grave concern over the situation in the occupied Palestinian territories" and Israel's deportation of the Palestinians, and responded with a number of points. The Security Council took the following actions.

1. Reaffirm[ed] once again that the Geneva Convention relative to the protection of civilian persons in time of war, of 12 August 1949, is applicable to Palestinian and other Arab territories, occupied by Israel since 1967, including Jerusalem,

2. Call[ed] upon Israel to refrain from deporting any Palestinian civilians from the occupied territories;

3. Strongly request[ed] [that] Israel, the occupying Power, abide by its obligation arising from the Convention;

4. Decide[d] to keep the situation in the Palestinian and other Arab territories occupied by Israel since 1967, including Jerusalem, under review.[75]

The deportations affair helped the PLO jump on the bandwagon of the intifada and reap political dividends from the violent incidents in the West Bank and Gaza Strip and the harsh scenes that were broadcast around the world. To this end, the PLO prepared for a wide-ranging propaganda campaign. It leased the ship *Sol Phryne*, changed its name to *The Return*, and prepared it for voyage to Israel with a number of deportees and several journalists on board. On Saturday, February 13, 1988, a car exploded in Limassol containing three senior Fatah commanders who were involved in the ship's preparation as well as in many past acts of terrorism.[76] The next day, a number of devices exploded on *The Return*, and it sank in the port of Limassol. On February 16, a PLO spokesperson accused Israeli intelligence of perpetrating the attack and promised revenge. Prime Minister Yitzhak Shamir, who was visiting Rome at the time, said that he had learned about the event in Limassol only from the media and could not comment.[77] A few days later, a rubber boat sank on the Lebanese coast carrying a terrorist squad on its way to attack Israel. The attack was planned as an act of revenge for the sinking of *The Return* and the killing of the three terrorists in Cyprus. Two of the terrorists on the raft were killed, and three swam ashore.[78]

In early April 1988, while Israeli settler children were hiking near the village of Beita, clashes broke out in which Tirza Porat, a girl from the settlement of Elon Moreh, and an Arab youth were killed. The incident led to violent protests by the settlers against the Arabs of *Shabiba* (Fatah's youth movement in the territories) and to settler criticism of the IDF, including a call to dismiss the chief of staff.[79] A short time later, it was decided to deport eight residents of the territories, and another twelve deportation orders were issued, six of them to residents of Beita. According to Israeli security sources, the deportation was carried out as part of the IDF's deterrent policy.[80] Reserve Brigadier General Aryeh Shalev stressed at the time that decisions on deportations were made at the highest level of government, not by IDF General Staff. Moreover, before such a decision was made, a system of very thorough checks was conducted by all of the security forces and judicial bodies, as such a step had to pass the test of the Israeli High Court of Justice. Shalev also explained that deportations had a dual purpose: to deter others from incitement and to minimize the damage caused by those who were being deported.[81] At the same time, the high court rejected the petitions of three candidates for deportation. Its president noted in the decision that "the [Geneva] Convention does not mention, or even allude to, the expulsion of a terrorist or an enemy agent from the area, but rather the protection of an entire civilian population from deportation."[82]

In April 1988, sixteen Palestinians were deported from the territories. In August 1988, twelve were deported to Lebanon, six from the West Bank and two from the Gaza Strip, who were charged with being senior operatives of terrorist organizations, engaging in incitement, and organizing riots.[83] The deportations continued: in January 1989, thirteen Palestinians were deported from the territories,[84] and on June 29, 1989, eight residents were deported to Lebanon. These eight were key Fatah and DFLP activists who were deported after being detained for about ten months on suspicion of incitement and organizing the uprising in the territories.[85]

Following this series of deportations, the Israeli government abstained from further deportations for a year and a half. This punitive action was renewed only after dissolution of the national unity government and reshuffling of the post of defense minister. In December 1990, during Moshe Arens's tenure as defense minister, and following the stabbing to death of three Jews in Jaffa, deportation orders were issued against four Palestinian residents of Gaza, with the deportation carried out in January 1991. In May 1991, four more Palestinians were deported, and in January 1992, another twelve deportation orders were issued.[86]

As the intifada continued, calm remained elusive, and deportations multiplied, doubts were raised among various parties regarding whether this measure was achieving its objectives. According to security officials' assessment, the effectiveness of this means of punishment was limited mainly by the lengthy legal procedure involved in deportation and the long periods between when the deportation order was issued, the legal proceedings was completed, and the actual expulsion occurred. International criticism and condemnation of Israel as a result of the deportations reinforced doubts regarding the usefulness of the punishment. In February 1989, the minister of defense informed the Knesset Foreign Affairs and Defense Committee of a change in policy, saying that the IDF had decided to reduce the number of deportees because of doubts about the effectiveness of this punitive measure.[87]

In June 1989, the defense minister tried to quiet unrest in the area not through the threat of deportations but, rather, by stating that calm on the ground would enable deportees to return to their homes. After the deportation of June 1989, Rabin announced that if a lull in the territories could be achieved, the possibility of returning these deportees to their homes within three years would be considered, subject to the cessation of all terrorist activity against Israel.[88] This promise did not achieve the desired goal. In the months that followed, Israel refrained, as mentioned, from deporting Palestinians from the West Bank and Gaza Strip. At the same time, in May and June 1989, the defense minister asked the justice minister and attorney general to find a legal solution that would enable the expulsion of inciters and those suspected of violent acts within seventy-two hours to seven days of issuance of the order.[89] Following this request, the ministers of defense and justice established an inter-ministerial team to examine all measures taken against the residents of the territories, including deportation. One of the solutions proposed at the time was to examine the possibility of a process of expedited deportation from the territories, and to convert the right to an early plea to an appeal that could be filed in the deportee's absence through a representative.[90] In July 1990, the military advocate general was instructed to examine the possibility of deporting inciters and riot organizers from their homes, without their families, to other areas in the territories for a limited time.[91]

In the late 1990s, it was decided that deportation orders against Palestinians in the territories would be resumed, despite the fact that the military establishment and the judicial system had failed to find an appropriate way to expedite the deportation proceedings.[92] Even after the resumption of deportations, the military and political echelons tried to find new solutions to the problem. In May 1991, IDF chief of staff Barak presented a proposal to the Knesset Foreign Affairs and Defense Committee to deport Palestinians from the territories for limited periods in order to allow for the more frequent use of deportation. In his opinion, deportation for a fixed period of eighteen months would not lead to harsh international criticism.[93]

Despite the government's dissatisfaction with the deportation process, and questions regarding the effectiveness of this punishment, the Shamir and unity governments maintained a policy of limited individual deportation. The number of deportees each year, including the years of the intifada, was extremely limited, totaling no more than a few dozen cases. Former ISA head Perry sums up the question of the effectiveness of deportation by saying, "All in all, I think that the tool of deportation has proven itself, but not in all cases. It depends why you are deporting, whom you are deporting, and where to you are deporting them. If you have good answers to these three questions, deportation can be effective."[94]

Collective Punishment? Closures and Curfews

Besides personal administrative punishments, Israel employed punitive measures against the populations of certain areas throughout the years of its rule in the West Bank and Gaza, especially during the intifada, in order to bring calm and prevent riots and violent incidents in that area. In this context, Israeli security forces imposed local curfews (preventing residents from being out in the streets in a certain area) and closures (preventing Palestinians from moving from one area to another, and from the territories to Israel). The military also adopted measures intended to make it difficult for Palestinians to support and participate in the intifada, mainly through fines imposed on participants or parents of children who took part in riots and/or stone throwing.

As mentioned, curfews were one of Israel's most-used measures. During curfew, residents of the area were allowed to leave their homes for only a short time each day when the curfew was temporarily lifted in order to allow them to purchase food. Such actions were perceived by the international community as a collective punitive measure in which many were required to pay the price for violations of law and order by only a few. In Israel, these were considered legitimate preventive measures. Few rightwing decision makers criticized the government for not using these and other measures as collective punishment against the Palestinian population. They called for the use of harsher measures in an attempt to convey the unequivocal message that residents should not enlist, participate, and assist in violent activity against Israel in general, and terrorism in particular, and to raise the price the population would be required to pay for the events of the intifada. For example, Ze'evi, the prime minister's counterterrorism advisor in the 1970s and later a minister in the government, claimed the following:

> We have to look for what hurts them and we do not do this. We are scared, for example, of collective punishment, despite the fact that it works exceptionally well. Disturbances in Beit Fajar will lead to a prohibition against exporting stones via the Allenby Bridge. If there are disturbances in Hebron,

the grapes from the Hebron vineyards will not be sent to Jordan! If you say this is immoral, I will reply that it is more than moral, because in this way we cause less blood to be spilled, both Jewish and Arab alike. But people object to taking these steps, because it is collective punishment. The government lives in fear of the media and under the threat of criticism by parliament and by its own members. . . . Shamir is not a coward, but I do not have to explain why the government opposes collective punishment.[95]

In contrast to Ze'evi, Minister Ariel Sharon presented a position whereby he would "reduce and reject collective punishment of Palestinians in the territories."[96] In order to end the intifada, he said, it was not necessary to take more stringent steps but, rather, different steps. "The most important thing is to distinguish between Palestinian Arabs working against us and the non-active part of the population, and then to fight against them."[97]

With the transition from spontaneous demonstrations to organized popular action coordinated by local and regional leadership and action committees, actors in the intifada adopted a number of objectives in the late 1980s. Havakook and Shakib highlight the goals:

- The disruption of Israeli control of the Gaza Strip and the West Bank—causing damage to government institutions, administration, local administrative institutions, and so on;
- the building of alternatives to the Israeli ruling and welfare mechanisms in an attempt to achieve maximum independence;
- boycott of the Civil Administration in the territories and the neutralization of elements within Palestinian society working for it (police, taxation, etc.); and
- mobilization of the masses to engage in unarmed violent conflict with the IDF and settlers in the territories in order to obtain media coverage and to influence public opinion in Israel and around the world.[98]

An examination of the intifada's achievements with these goals in mind shows that in most cases, the objectives were achieved. Following the wide-ranging media exposure and extensive coverage of the events, the intifada rose to the top of the agenda in the Arab world and in international public opinion. Avraham Sela notes that the intifada brought the Palestinians many successes. The Palestinian issue was restored to the center of public interest in Western Europe and the United States. King Hussein, whose political status in the West Bank suffered a mortal blow, severed of the legal and administrative ties between the banks. The PLO quickly succeeded in taking over the intifada and neutralizing the local leadership, making it financially and politically dependent on the PLO. A direct (though low-level) dialogue was opened between the United States and the PLO, which reflected recognition of the organization.

The polarization of Israeli society over the fate of the territories was exacerbated, and the national unity government was forced to embark on a diplomatic initiative that defined Palestinian residents of the territories, for the first time since 1948, as the main partner in negotiations, with an incentive given for the building of a Palestinian state and institutions free from Israeli rule.[99] However, one of the most important achievements of the intifada was solidification of the status of the West Bank and Gaza residents in all of the relevant arenas. Going forward, the PLO leadership could not ignore the needs, aspirations, and leadership of the residents of the territories, and their status within the PLO was significantly strengthened.

Another of the most important achievements of the intifada in the eyes of Palestinians was that Jordan's influence in the territories was downgraded. If, before the intifada, the PLO and Jordan competed for status and support in the West Bank, the intifada brought about a clear PLO victory. Hussein, who was unable to understand why Israel could not suppress the riots in the first months of the intifada, soon became anxious that the uprising in the territories would spill over into his country and draw in the Palestinians living there. The crossing of barricades by the traditional Jordan loyalists in the West Bank and their joining the ranks of the PLO and the Islamic organizations following psychological and physical pressure by intifada activists made it clear to Hussein that Jordan had no choice but to officially disengage from the territories. In late July 1988, the king broadcast that administrative and legal ties between Jordan and the West Bank were severed. Jordan's renunciation of sovereignty in the West Bank was ostensibly intended to clear the way for the PLO, but Hussein likely hoped that the severing of economic ties and cancellation of the Jordanian $1.3 billion five-year plan to develop the territories would prompt the Palestinians to ask him to retract his decision.[100] One of the first practical manifestations of Hussein's step was the Jordanian government's decision of August 4, 1988, to fire all of the 21,000 Palestinians living in the West Bank who received salaries from Jordan and to exchange all Jordanian passports in the territories with travel documents.[101]

From Israel's perspective, the intifada severely damaged its image in the eyes of the international community, undermined its hold on the territories, caused casualties among the security forces and Israeli civilians, completely disrupted the routine activities of the IDF and other security forces (which had to reinforce the territories with many additional forces and cancel training exercises), and harmed the deterrent power of the IDF (which had refrained from using military force against unarmed civilians). At the same time, it also strengthened the PLO and Palestinian terrorist organizations in the territories (especially the Islamic fundamentalist organizations); neutralized Jordan as a key player in the arena; and forced Israel to seek diplomatic moves that would satisfy the Palestinians, restore calm in the area, and meet international demands and pressures. Former Mossad chief Reserve Major General Meir Dagan described the change in the Palestinian challenge to Israel following the intifada as follows.

They became a half-political authority. This trend started at the beginning of the 1980s, but it really reached its peak in the Intifada. As soon as the Intifada broke out and they realized that it could bring them political achievement . . . from that moment, the organization, while not deviating from terrorism, used popular violence as the main tool of the war, with the understanding that this tool had the best chance of succeeding. They did not abandon terrorism. Previously, terrorism took the lead, and in second place were the political institutions that supported terrorism. It was now reversed; the political arm began to lead, and terrorism was designed to serve the political factors. That is the change that occurred within Fatah.[102]

THE YITZHAK SHAMIR ADMINISTRATION'S COUNTERTERRORISM POLICY IN LIGHT OF THE COUNTERTERRORISM DILEMMAS MODEL

This period of 1987 to the end of 1991 saw three governments under the leadership of the Likud party headed by Yitzhak Shamir—two unity governments and a government with a right-wing coalition led by Likud. The most prominent challenge of this period was the outbreak of the Palestinian popular uprising (the intifada). This security challenge took the Israeli security forces and government by surprise and required a reassessment of defense policy in order to contend with the Palestinian violence, in which the component of terrorism, although present, did not play a central role.

At the same time, Israel was faced with a new diplomatic challenge when, in late 1988, PLO chief Yasser Arafat declared the organization's recognition of Israel. This opened the door for negotiations between the United States and the PLO, while Israel continued its refusal to negotiate with Arafat and the PLO. The end of this period was marked by the 1991 Gulf War, during which Israel suffered a few dozen Scud missile attacks from Iraq but refrained from responding militarily at the behest of the United States, in order to prevent the disintegration of the U.S.-led military coalition against the Iraqi army, which included various Arab states.

In light of the new and serious security challenge Israel was facing—the intifada—there was a sharp escalation in the use of Israeli counterterrorism measures during this period, particularly in the punitive and deterrent measures against the Palestinians in an effort to stop the violent events. This escalation is reflected in the Counterterrorism Dilemmas Conceptual Model (figure 6.1) by positioning the Shamir governments in the less restrained and more efficiency-driven part of the model, given the far more frequent and substantial use, relative to the past, of severe punitive measures such as deportations, administrative detentions, curfews, the demolition and sealing of houses, and, in the early days of the intifada, limited violence (beatings) to neutralize violent demonstrators, and an easing of the regulations determining when to open fire.

The major escalation of violence in the territories and its prolonged duration, as well as the massive use of punitive measures—especially the disturbing images transmitted via the global media—led to unprecedented waves of worldwide protest and criticism of Israel and to direct and indirect pressure on the Israeli government to change its policy. Moreover, pressure was applied on the domestic front to take every possible step to end Palestinian violence and the ongoing danger it presented to Israeli citizens. Although the Israeli governments during this period did not have to contend with a right-wing opposition that demanded intensified counterterrorism activity (as in the past), they faced pressure from the public, and especially from settlers in the territories, who suffered more than others from Palestinian violence.

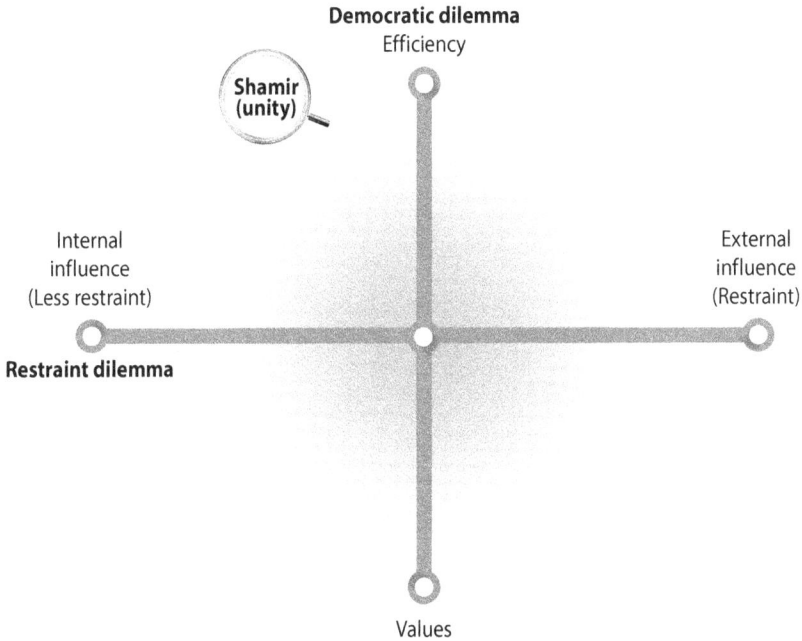

FIGURE 6.1. Counterterrorism Dilemmas Conceptual Model—Shamir administration

Thus, during the period under discussion, there was additional intensification (compared with the previous period) of Israeli policy, with the heavy use of punitive and deterrent measures considered to be effective at the expense of liberal democratic values, and with more priority given to responding to the expectations and demands of the Israeli public than to the pressures exerted on the government in the international arena.

Chapter Seven

COUNTERING TERRORISM DURING THE PEACE PROCESS

The Yitzhak Rabin Administration (1992-96)

PEACE PROCESS AFTER THE INTIFADA

The Israeli government's counterterrorism policy during the period 1992–96 was managed by two governments: that of Yitzhak Rabin, which served from July 13, 1992, until the prime minister's assassination on November 4, 1995, and the Shimon Peres government, which served from November 1995 until June 19, 1996.

With the cessation of the intifada, the PLO quickly realized that its achievements would be measured by the extent to which it succeeded in transmitting to the diplomatic arena international sympathy for the Palestinian problem. The PLO was also clear about what it was required to do in order to move the diplomatic process forward. At the Arab Summit held in Algiers in early June 1988, an unsigned document, which later became known as the "Abu Sharif Document" (named after Arafat's advisor), was distributed only to foreign journalists and denied the Palestinians' intention to destroy Israel. In his opening speech at the nineteenth session of the Palestinian National Council (PNC), held in Algiers in November 1988, Arafat addressed U.S. president-elect George H. W. Bush directly and asked him to adopt a balanced policy.[1]

With a majority of 253 votes in favor, 46 against, 10 abstentions, and 29 absentee delegates, the PNC approved the diplomatic resolution that adopted UN Security Council Resolutions 242 and 338. These resolutions were accompanied by a Palestinians right to self and were a basis for Palestinian participation in an international peace conference in the Middle East. However, all this was not enough to satisfy the United States. U.S. Secretary of state George Schultz even refused to grant Arafat an entry visa, thus preventing him from speaking at the UN General Assembly in New York.

The PLO's next move took place on December 7. While Arafat was meeting with a group of American Jews in Stockholm, a document was circulated, again unsigned, explaining the PNC's decisions and stressing that the council accepted Israel's existence in the region and rejected all forms of terrorism. On December 13, Arafat spoke at a special session of the UN General Assembly in Geneva. Secretary Schultz gave Swedish foreign minister Sten Andersson a letter in which he explicitly stated what Arafat needed to say in order for the Americans to agree to renew its dialogue with the PLO.[2] Despite American attempts to coordinate the wording of the speech with Arafat, Arafat continued to use vague and ambiguous phrasing, though at a subsequent press conference in Geneva, he asserted the declarations demanded by the Americans. These remarks satisfied the U.S. administration, which then announced the opening of a dialogue with the PLO.[3]

On March 6, 1990, U.S. secretary of state James Baker presented a peace plan calling for separate bilateral talks between Israel and Syria, Lebanon, and a Jordanian-Palestinian joint delegation. The PLO opposed the American proposal, and in Israel, the Likud's unwillingness to agree to the government's support for the plan led to a political crisis and the fall of the Israeli government.

On August 2, 1990, under Saddam Hussein, Iraq invaded Kuwait. Hussein ignored the demands of the international community and American ultimatums to withdraw from Kuwait. After the formation of a coalition led by the United States, which included Arab states, a large-scale military operation against Iraq was launched on January 17, 1991, dubbed "Operation Desert Storm." This was the beginning of the Gulf War, which lasted a month and a half and ended with an Iraqi military defeat and the liberation of Kuwait. The Gulf War had an immediate effect on the Israeli-Palestinian conflict. Israel, which was hit by forty Scud missiles fired from Iraq, agreed to the American plea for restraint and refrained from joining the fight for fear of harming the fragile U.S.-Arab military coalition. During the campaign, the United States found itself needing to advance the diplomatic process, and in exchange for participation by the Arab countries in the coalition, it was even willing to force its ally Israel to hold direct talks with Palestinian representatives. The PLO and its leader, Arafat, found themselves on the wrong side of history after publicly supporting Saddam Hussein and Iraq's invasion of Kuwait. Thus, at the end of the Gulf War in February 1991, the PLO was in a difficult position politically and economically.

There was more bad news for Arafat at that time, resulting from a shift in the demographic balance in the area in Israel's favor due to the influx of Russian Jewish immigrants that began after the fall of the Soviet Union. Until then, PLO leaders believed that time was on their side. They were convinced that the high birth rate among the Palestinian people in the territories, in contrast to the growth of the Jewish population in Israel, would ultimately dictate the processes and developments in the region and bring about a Palestinian victory. Arafat himself understood the power of Palestinian growth, stating that "the womb of the Arab woman" is his "greatest strength."[4]

The end of the Cold War and the Soviet Union's decision to allow its Jews to immigrate to Israel greatly troubled the Palestinians and might have been a catalyst for the PLO's decision to focus on the diplomatic track. The waves of immigration from Russia were accompanied by threats by the Palestinian organizations. An Islamic Jihad leaflet distributed in the territories in February 1990 threatened the immigrants, stating that "the area will spit them out, as was done in the past with the Tatars," and that "Islamic Jihad will hit them to prove that this is not a land flowing with milk and honey but a land of death for its invaders."[5]

THE MADRID CONFERENCE

Against this backdrop, the American administration, together with Russia, orchestrated the Madrid Conference in November 1991, with the participation of Israel, Syria, Lebanon, Egypt, and a joint Jordanian-Palestinian delegation. This multilateral track was created to discuss the establishment of Palestinian self-government. The PLO's leadership had no choice but to agree to the participation of a Palestinian delegation within the Jordanian delegation, all of whom would be Palestinians from the West Bank and Gaza Strip (not PLO members or Jerusalem residents).[6]

In a way, the Madrid Conference was imposed on the Shamir government by the United States, and Israel reluctantly participated in the multilateral track in Madrid and the bilateral Israel-Palestinian track that followed in Washington, D.C. With the establishment of the Rabin government in July 1992, the Israeli government changed its policy regarding the process for engaging in dialogue with its Arab neighbors and the Palestinians. Shimon Peres asserted that one of the reasons (if not the central one) for the political stalemate that characterized the process until establishment of the Rabin government was the Shamir government's insistence on neutralizing any sign of direct involvement by the PLO in the negotiations. He claimed that this created a strange situation in which those who made the decisions on the Palestinian side did not participate in the talks and those who participated in the talks did not make the decisions.[7] Peres acted quickly to change this policy, and in a series of decisions and agreements with the Palestinians, the Rabin government, in which Peres served as foreign minister, in effect canceled the restrictions on the negotiation process imposed by the previous government.

Despite the willingness of the new Israeli government to cancel all restrictions imposed by the previous government on the participation of PLO members and residents of East Jerusalem in the Madrid talks, this negotiating channel quickly hit the skids. However, in addition to the official Madrid channel, Arafat maintained direct Israeli channels with members of political parties, academics, and others, the most important of which was the Oslo channel.[8]

THE OSLO TALKS

The Oslo talks, which began as an academic meeting sponsored by the Norwegians, took an important turn to become the main Israeli-Palestinian channel after Rabin approved the participation of official Israeli representatives in the talks. The meetings in Oslo, which began in mid-1992, a week before the Israeli elections, focused on the idea of "Gaza first," according to which the first Israeli step in the agreement to be signed with the PLO would be to withdraw from Gaza. (PLO representatives insisted that, as part of this step, Israel withdraw from Jericho as well, making it "Gaza and Jericho first.")

According to Yossi Beilin, who was serving as deputy foreign minister at the time and who was one of the architects of the Oslo talks, at this early stage, he refrained from informing Israeli decision makers of the existence of the unofficial Oslo channel. The negotiations in Oslo came to the attention of decision makers only in February 1993, after Israeli academics Pundak and Hirschfeld submitted a proposal to the Palestinians in Oslo for an interim agreement and annexes dealing with Israeli-Palestinian cooperation in various areas.[9]

Several months after the Rabin government was established in December 1992, following a number of terrorist attacks, and in the wake of the kidnapping and murder of border police officer Nissim Toledano by Hamas terrorists on December 17, the Israeli government decided to deport the largest number of Palestinians involved in acts of terrorism and incitement: 415 members of Islamic fundamentalist groups were deported to Lebanon.[10] Most of the deportees belonged to Hamas's civilian propaganda and political infrastructure, people responsible for the distribution of donations, spokesmen, and political activists—not necessarily terrorists who were directly involved in carrying out attacks. Rabin described the deportation as an attack on Hamas's "outer shell," not the hard core of terrorist operatives.[11] Their deportation was intended to weaken the supportive environment within which Hamas operated, thereby strengthening the peace process and the PLO, as well as to demonstrate the government's determination to fight terrorism and calm the Israeli public.[12]

On December 18, 1992, the UN Security Council passed Resolution 799 condemning the deportation and calling on Israel to ensure the immediate return of the deportees. Fierce demonstrations broke out in the West Bank and Gaza Strip, in which a number of Palestinians were killed or wounded.[13] The deportees refused to leave the area in Lebanon to which they were expelled and continued to live in tents under harsh conditions, with journalists from all over the world covering their situation on a regular basis. Hezbollah offered to sponsor the deportees and provided them with assistance and operational training that included military exercises, preparation of explosive devices, and new methods of attack.[14] Four days after the deportation, the deportees organized a protest march back into Israeli territory, and they were not stopped until the South Lebanese Army fired shells at them. The Lebanese government refused to allow the transfer of international humanitarian aid to the deportees, and on December 25, the Israeli government made the same decision regarding the area under its control. However, in the following days, Israel announced that a small number of the deportees had been deported by mistake and that they would be allowed to return to Israel.[15]

International pressure on Israel increased as the media continued to cover life in the tent encampment in Lebanon. In addition to international pressure on the Israeli government to rescind its decision and allow the deportees to return to their homes in the territories, Arafat ordered the cessation of direct talks with Israel in Madrid. Rabin, who was intent on progressing with the negotiations with the Palestinians, found himself split between his unwillingness to rescind the deportation and the inability to return to the negotiating table. The Oslo channel, which, unlike Madrid, was conducted directly with the PLO, allowed Rabin to renew talks in Washington after they were stopped by the Palestinians. However, according to Mamdouh Nofal (a former senior DFLP activist who served as an aide to Arafat), the Palestinians understood from Shimon Peres and Abu Alaa that in order to advance the channel of direct negotiations with the PLO in Oslo, any progress on the Washington channel had to be thwarted. According to Nofal (and denied by Peres),

> [Peres] told us that Rabin would agree to bring Faisal Husseini into the talks and that the Americans would offer to publish an official paper [in Madrid] and he said that what was needed was to thwart this round and not give in to the temptations offered by Rabin and the administration. . . . Abu Alaa . . . was convinced that Peres was right and that hampering the Washington talks was the only way that Rabin would be persuaded to officially adopt the alternative Oslo channel. . . . When we heard this, we decided in Tunis to thwart the ninth round of talks in Washington between April 27 and May 13, 1993. Arafat . . . instructed them to take tough positions. . . . He issued a written order to the delegation to oppose a tripartite meeting between the US, Israel and the Palestinians even though in the past the PLO had been very interested in such a meeting.[16]

At the same time, during the sixth meeting in Oslo in May 1993, the level of talks was raised following an agreement between Rabin and Peres, with

Israel represented by Foreign Ministry director-general Uri Savir. According to Beilin, "when Savir and Abu Alaa shook hands, Israel in effect recognized the PLO, and this was a new asset for the PLO that it did not exploit."[17] When the need arose to legally formulate the Oslo Accords, jurist Joel Singer joined the Israeli team. Singer proposed that the principle of mutual recognition between the PLO and Israel be included in the Oslo agreement, but Rabin was not convinced. After receiving a report from Peres and Savir, Rabin sent a letter to Peres stating that the Oslo channel was dangerous because it was being used by the PLO to torpedo the talks in Washington. Rabin objected to the agreements formulated in the Declaration of Principles and claimed that they had been devised without prior coordination with him. He therefore demanded that the Oslo talks be suspended until the resumption of talks in Washington.[18]

In the end, the Declaration of Principles between Israel and the PLO was signed on August 19, 1993, in Oslo by Uri Savir and Abu Alaa, still without mutual recognition, but the path to recognition of the PLO was short. According to Beilin, on August 22, he received a phone call from the prime minister, during which

he asked whether the agreement contained a reference to the cessation of terror. I told him that the preamble to the agreement is a mutual commitment to peace, but the PLO commitment to stop terrorism exists only in the mutual recognition agreement . . . that was not signed. I heard discomfort on the other end of the line. "Yossi, for me the main issue is terrorism. Even the Intifada is less important, because the agreement will end it. But we cannot sign an agreement with the Palestinians without the PLO committing to stop terror. Talk to Holst and see what can be done." I spoke with Holst but it was clear that he, too, was unable to issue a commitment to stop terrorism from an entity we did not recognize. Almost right until the historic signing, Rabin wavered between his reluctance to recognize the PLO and his desire to reach a binding agreement with the Palestinians . . . his desire for a firm commitment to put an end to PLO terrorism, a commitment only the PLO could have given. In the days that followed, the need for a commitment to stop terrorism won over the reluctance to recognize the PLO.[19]

Rabin's expectations of the agreement with the PLO can be gleaned from an interview he gave on the eve of the signing in Washington.

I hope that there will be a partner who will be responsible for internal problems in Gaza . . . who will deal with Gaza without the problems of the High
Court of Justice, without the problems of B'Tselem,[20] without the problems
of all kinds of bleeding hearts, the mothers and fathers. . . . Ask me if the PLO
is a sympathetic client—not at all . . . they are a terrorist organization. . . .
They are murderers. You make peace with your enemies, including despi-
cable enemies. I will not romanticize them.[21]

On September 13, 1993, the Declaration of Principles was signed between
Israel and the PLO on the White House lawn in Washington, with the two
sides recognizing the existence of the other. Carmi Gillon explains that the
Oslo Declaration of Principles constituted a revolutionary change. The PLO
renounced terror, which meant that the largest Palestinian organization,
Fatah, was emerging from the cycle of terror and violence. However, whereas
Fatah was participating in a diplomatic process, other organizations—
chief among them Hamas, Islamic Jihad, and the PFLP—announced that
they would continue and even increase terrorism, with the aim of preventing a peace process.[22]

Following the signing of the agreement, Rabin declared to the Knesset
Foreign Affairs and Defense Committee,

[He] see[s] the PLO as a partner, and the real test . . . is the cessation of terror,
and their willingness to talk and to take risks. [Israel] will continue to wage
war against the Palestinian terrorist organizations. On the other hand, whoever has stopped terrorism becomes a secondary priority in this respect.[23]

In October 1993, talks began on what was called the Gaza-Jericho Agreement, headed by Amnon Lipkin-Shahak and Nabil Sha'ath. That same
month, 750 Palestinian prisoners were released, most of them over the age
of fifty, under the age of eighteen, women, the sick, and those who had
already served most of their sentences—and no terrorists who had been
convicted of murder or injury (those with "blood on their hands").[24] On
November 29, the interim agreement was signed in Cairo. This agreement
stipulated that Israel would be responsible for the security and public order
of Israelis everywhere. It also defined the areas of Gaza and Jericho that
would be transferred to the PLO's autonomous control and the timetable for
the evacuation of these areas. Joint security mechanisms were established;

coastal security measures, maritime space, and air space were decided on; and Israel agreed to the release of some 5,000 Palestinian prisoners who had not harmed Israelis or been arrested for hostile activity after the signing of the Declaration of Principles.[25]

TERRORISM IN THE WAKE OF OSLO

The terrorist attacks that took place after the signing of the agreements did not change Israel's position. Thus, despite two terrorist attacks in the Gaza Strip in November 1994, which cost the lives of ten Israelis, seven of whom were soldiers, talks with the PLO continued on the condition that they step up the fight against terrorism. Terrorism, though not a factor that thwarted or delayed the peace process, perhaps accelerated it. According to Uri Savir, in March 1995, he offered the Palestinians a package deal: if they would apply a comprehensive security policy and show determination in the war against terrorism, Israel would agree to accelerate negotiations on the interim agreement with hopes of completing it by July 1, 1995.[26]

Palestinian autonomy under the control of the PLO-led Palestinian Authority (PA) was established in the territories from which Israel withdrew in the West Bank and Gaza Strip. The extent of the changes that the PLO underwent after establishment of autonomy in the territories was defined by Palestinians as a "transition from revolution to statehood."[27] This transition entailed a complex process that required changes in structure, ideology, goals, ways of thinking, and behavior. According to Barry Rubin, it meant a change from a revolutionary movement to a state that was required to serve the needs of 2.5 million Palestinians. It was a change from a loose coalition of independent groups to a government that would coordinat law enforcement with a monopoly on key services, a change from dependence on violence (which often meant harming Israeli civilians) to a responsibility to halt Palestinian terror against Israel, and a shift from the dream of total victory—the establishment of a Palestinian state from the Jordan River to the Mediterranean Sea—to a new goal—a Palestinian state in the West Bank and Gaza Strip with East Jerusalem as its capital). No longer desperate exiles, Palestinians would experience rehabilitation in the homeland; from being a dispersed few, they would become a nation. Autonomy meant a change from referring to the United States as a central, anti-Palestinian enemy (in cooperation with the Russians to fight Western imperialism) to reliance on the United States; from reliance on the Arab states and a pan-Arabist ideology to Palestinian nationalism; and from the aspiration of building a utopian society that would serve as a model of Islam, socialism, democracy, and rapid development to facing the unpleasant reality of slow development and limited resources.[28]

Arafat's policy in the first years after the establishment of autonomy in the West Bank and Gaza Strip was one ambiguity; he was a "master of double talk."[29] On the one hand, the Palestinian Authority condemned terrorism and, ostensibly at least, acted against the Islamic terrorist organizations Hamas and Islamic Jihad, but on another hand, it viewed the attacks as means of exerting pressure on Israel and promoting Palestinian interests within the framework of the diplomatic process.

The establishment of autonomy in the areas of Gaza and Jericho, and later in additional parts of the territories, effectively gave the Islamic terrorist organizations the independent, secure, and protected territory that the secular Palestinian organizations had sought in the past. This territory was very close to Israeli population centers, had no defined border with Israel, and was not separated from Israeli territory by physical or geographical obstacles. Therefore it allowed for quick and easy travel to the target of an attack and for safe shelter for perpetrators following an attack. The establishment of the Palestinian Authority also signified a fundamental change in the identity of the Palestinian organizations that continued to carry out terrorist attacks against Israel. Fatah, which perpetrated most of the attacks in the territories and in Israel until the establishment of the PA, for the most part ceased its involvement in terrorist attacks. However, the Islamic organizations, led by Hamas, quickly took its place and intensified attacks on Israel. This change in the perpetrators of the attacks was accompanied by an escalation in the type of terrorist attacks employed by the organizations.

Beginning in 1993, Islamic organizations began to use a new type of attack, suicide bombings ("an operational method in which the very act of the attack is dependent upon the death of the perpetrator").[30] This method, known as the "smart bomb," made it possible for perpetrators to be precise in the timing and location of the attack and thus cause maximum damage to life and property. Suicide bombings allowed them to demonstrate their determination and the depth of their religious faith and Palestinian patriotism. It involved material compensation (payment to the family of the suicide bomber and a rise in social status) and the belief in a heavenly reward (eternal life in paradise alongside seventy-two virgins).[31] All of these factors made suicide bombings the preferred method of attack for Islamic Jihad and Hamas operatives.

The transfer of power to Arafat enabled Hamas to further establish itself and prepare to launch attacks from the territories. The fundamental change in Hamas's policy on terrorist attacks after establishment of the Palestinian Authority was in the element that limited the organization's activities. On the eve of the PA's establishment, the IDF controlled the West Bank and Gaza Strip. The presence of the IDF and the ISA on the ground made it difficult for the organization to recruit, train, and arm operatives and send them to instigate terrorist attacks. When the movement had built up the capability to execute the attack, it was carried out. After establishment of the PA, these restrictions were almost completely removed. Hamas had no difficulty locating individuals who were willing to participate in an attack or obtaining or preparing a few kilograms (or even much more) of explosives, making a bomb, and sending off these recruits to complete their mission. The factor that limited the scope and type of attacks carried out by Hamas from this time forward was no longer the movement's operational capability but, rather, its interests and the motivation of its decision makers to initiate attacks at any given time. The manner in which Hamas attacks were carried out starting in the mid-1990s can be understood from the words of then IDF intelligence head Major General Moshe Ya'alon in April 1998:

> When Hamas carries out a suicide attack, it is the result of a decision made by the system, by the leadership that is mainly based abroad, in Jordan, in Damascus in part, and in other countries. These figures formulate a strategy for terrorist attacks that are then passed on to the field. On the ground there is always the potential but it is not executed without a directive from above.[32]

Based on Ya'alon's statement, one can distinguish between two kinds of attacks: self-initiated and organized. Self-initiated attacks are carried out by an individual ("lone wolf") or a few operatives for personal reasons or out of a desire for revenge, without the directive or involvement of a terrorist organization. Sometimes such attacks were carried out as a "tryout" for a terrorist organization or by Palestinians suspected of collaborating with Israel as a step toward purification or a demonstration of patriotism and nationalism. Organized attacks are perpetrated by a terrorist cell belonging to a particular organization. These attacks usually occur in accordance with the ideology and interests of the organization, taking into account timing and location, and in many cases are more complex and result in more casualties than self-initiated attacks.

Some of the factors influencing Hamas's and Islamic Jihad's interests and motivation to launch or refrain from launching institutionalized terrorist attacks in Israel after the establishment of Palestinian autonomy were as follows.

- *The Palestinian Authority*: This involved the PA's (and Yasser Arafat's) policy toward Hamas and Islamic Jihad and its willingness to act against the organizations' infrastructure and activists.
- *Palestinian public opinion*: The fundamentalist Islamic organizations, primarily the Hamas movement, were attentive to the feelings of the Palestinian population. The public's stance played a role in shaping the terrorist organizations' policy on attacks. (It should be noted that the PA had indirect control of terrorist organizations' policy on attacks, due in part to its control over mass media and ability to mold Palestinian public opinion according to its will.)
- *Israeli policy*: This influence entailed Israeli positions in negotiations with the PA; willingness to transfer additional territories to Palestinian control, release prisoners, and more; and Israel's counterterrorism policy vis-à-vis Hamas and Islamic Jihad.

Arafat, who refrained from disarming Hamas and Islamic Jihad and harming their operational capability for engaging in terrorist attacks, chose to "ride the tiger" in order to preserve the organizations' terrorist capabilities in case of need and even to use them as a catalyst for Israeli withdrawal from other areas of the territories. The fundamentalist organizations' terror attacks also helped to build Arafat's image as the only moderate actor in the Palestinian arena to offer a nonviolent alternative and a prospect of peace in the Israeli-Palestinian conflict, thus making him an important force to be supported and strengthened. At times, when Arafat determined that terrorist attacks at a given time might boomerang and lead Israel to refrain from withdrawing from additional parts of territories, signing more agreements with the PA, or fulfilling its obligations under the signed agreement, Arafat demanded that the Palestinian Islamist organizations temporarily desist from carrying out attacks and even reached ad hoc agreements with them.

To this end, Arafat used his powers of persuasion and sometimes even threatened these organizations, claiming that such actions were harming Palestinian national interests. Furthering these interests, Arafat demanded that during certain periods, organizations withhold attacks or a certain type of attack. When it seemed that his efforts of persuasion were not bearing fruit and some organizations were not listening to him, he added a concrete threat, which was expressed in a wave of arrests of Hamas and PIJ activists, again in the name of national interests. However, even at their peak, Arafat's counterterrorism activities focused only on limiting the terrorist organizations' motivation to attack Israel; he did not act to significantly impair the operational capabilities of these organizations. Arafat did not try to change the Palestinian narrative about Israel and continued to incite his people through state media, school textbooks, and other methods. From Israel's perspective, the policy Arafat adopted was like sitting on a barrel of explosives.[33] The establishment of the Palestinian Authority changed the characteristics of terrorism against Israel and posed new challenges to Israeli decision makers in shaping counterterrorism policy.

THE IDENTITY OF THE PERPETRATORS OF TERRORIST ATTACKS

The rise of organizations such as Hamas and Islamic Jihad in the territories and the embedding of Hezbollah in Lebanon in effect represented the passing of the baton for terrorist attacks to these organizations. The signing of the Oslo Accords and Fatah's declared cessation of terrorist attacks against Israel brought this process to its peak. Some secular Palestinian organizations (such as the PFLP, PFLP-GC, and other factions that left Fatah) continued to try to carry out attacks, but their part in the terror campaign was negligible.

The greater the role of the Islamic fundamentalist terrorist organizations in hostile activity against Israel, the more the motives that guided the perpetrators changed. From the establishment of Fatah in the mid-1960s to the end of the 1980s, the main (in fact, the only) driver that united the wide range of Palestinian terrorist organizations was nationalism, the aspiration to establish an independent Palestinian state in all of "Palestine." With the growth and strengthening of the fundamentalist Islamic organizations, the basis of the conflict between Palestinians and Israel transformed from a national struggle for control over parts of Israel/Palestine to a religious conflict between Muslims and Jews. The national motive was swallowed up by a series of religious commandments, laws, and guidelines. (Some of the spokesmen of fundamentalist Islamic organizations even went so far as to state openly that the conflict was no longer about control of the territory but, rather, about the presence of Jews in this part of the world.) This change in the perpetrators' motives regarding the attacks has, on the face of it, far-reaching implications regarding the nature of the conflict and the possibility of agreement on a solution. Whereas a conflict over a particular area of land might be solved by territorial compromise between the parties, a religious dispute over the mere presence of a particular side in the region must lead to all-out war. This was the prevalent view among policy makers during this period.

Israeli decision makers made a practical and ethical distinction between the Islamic fundamentalist organizations and the PLO led by Arafat. This distinction, though not necessarily in line with reality on the ground, made it easier for decision makers to interpret events for both themselves and the Israeli public in a black-and-white manner: the PLO, the supporter of peace, versus the Islamic organizations, the opponents of peace. This view was expressed in, among other things, Israel's long-standing refusal to consider Hamas spokespersons' offers of a cease-fire. Rabin referred to such a Hamas proposal in November 1994 as follows.

> Israel will not negotiate with extremist Islamic organizations as long as they do not change their policy and continue to engage in terrorism against Israelis. Hamas and Islamic Jihad are the enemies of peace and indiscriminately murder innocent civilians in Jerusalem, in the heart of Tel Aviv, and kidnap soldiers to use as bargaining chips. As long as this is their policy, I see no sign of change. . . . The main test is to prevent them from murdering peace, with the thought that we will fight them with all of our capabilities.[34]

Gillon explained the difference in Israel's attitude toward the two Palestinian streams by saying that, unlike the PLO, there was no situation in the present or future in which Hamas would change its ideology, which advocates for the annihilation of Israel, whereas the PLO (at least ostensibly) did indeed make such an ideological change.[35]

CHANGING THE MODUS OPERANDI: SUICIDE BOMBINGS

In the period under review, suicide bombings were the most prominent type of attack in the Palestinian terrorist arsenal. These attacks were executed by suicide bombers who carried explosives on their bodies or in their bags or hid them in vehicles they were driving. A suicide attack is especially difficult to thwart once the terrorist has set out on his mission armed with a bomb. Moreover, the perpetrators can precisely target the site of the attack and the timing of its execution, thereby ensuring harm to many victims. This type of attack also draws media and public attention due to the degree of the terrorist's resolve. The willingness to commit suicide raises a great deal of interest in the perpetrators' motive, thus lending indirect legitimacy to the action. The suicide attack is easy to arrange and carry out and does not require particularly lengthy preparation. Additionally, due to the nature of the attack, in which the attacker dies, the chance that security forces can capture him is small, reducing the possibility that the enemy can obtain intelligence information.[36]

The first suicide bombing of this period was carried out on April 16, 1993, near the Mehola Inn in the Jordan Valley. A bomber from PIJ detonated a car bomb in the inn's parking lot near a group of soldiers, killing one and injuring eight. From then until the year 2000, there were an additional nineteen suicide attacks within the Green Line and in the territories, in which 132 Israelis were killed and 727 wounded.[37] The suicide attack posed a new challenge to Israeli security officials and policy makers. In order to formulate ways of contending with such attacks and learning attackers' motives, a special team was formed in the IDF Intelligence Branch that studied the subject of suicide by radical Muslims in various parts of the world, including Iran and Afghanistan.[38]

Rabin and his cabinet quickly understood the danger inherent in this type of attack, which caused a large number of casualties and exacerbated the public's anxieties about terrorism. In a lecture to ISA agents, the prime minister said, "Since the beginning of suicide bombings on buses and car bombs, which endanger the continuation of the peace process, terrorism has in fact become a strategic threat, and in order to thwart it, most of the ISA's resources must be channeled to this end."[39]

Though Rabin viewed the suicide attacks as a strategic threat to Israel, he denied the claim that this type of attack was the result of the Oslo Accords.

The first suicide bombing was in April 1993 in Mehola, when no one knew or dreamed of the possibility of the Oslo Accords. This was a development that was typical of the same radical Islamic element in Lebanon, Hezbollah. . . . It was not dependent on the Oslo Agreement, it would have developed in any case, and the fact is that this began before any agreement with the Palestinians.[40]

After the suicide attack at the Netzarim Junction in November 1994, during which a terrorist riding a bicycle loaded with explosives detonated them near an IDF outpost, killing three soldiers and injuring eleven, Rabin said that Israel is "facing a phenomenon of a new kind of terrorism, the terrorism of a suicide bomber who knows he has no place to run. Anyone who says that there is a hermetic solution is not to be believed. There is no choice but to deal with this terrorism using our tools."[41]

In a briefing with journalists, Rabin added that Israel must draw lessons from the change in the nature of terrorism, which was now carried out mainly by suicide bombers. As such, "the death penalty is irrelevant."[42] Foreign Minister Shimon Peres explained the complexity of the war on suicide terrorism according to his worldview, saying that in dealing with terrorism, two problems must be overcome:

The first is military-operational—how to fight suicide bombers. The second is broader—how to prevent public support for them. The right way to combat suicide bombers is to find out before they do anything, and that requires intelligence efforts from us and from the Palestinians. But it is impossible to solve the problem with weapons alone. We must create an economic situation that will divert broad support for Hamas to the alternative government.[43]

"WE WILL FIGHT TERRORISM AS IF THERE IS NO PEACE PROCESS AND PURSUE PEACE AS IF THERE IS NO TERRORISM"

The suicide bombings and mass killings that accompanied advancement of the peace process posed a grave challenge to Israeli decision makers.[44] On the one hand, Rabin and his government saw the Oslo Accords and subsequent agreements as a strategic option for Israel. On the other hand, it was clear to decision makers that public support for agreements with the Palestinians depended on the degree of calm and personal security that these agreements would bring. In an effort to reconcile the difficulty of advancing the peace process while mass-casualty attacks were taking place, Rabin coined the saying that Israel will continue to "fight terrorism as if there is no peace process; pursue peace as if there is no terrorism."[45]Indeed, Byman notes that "from the start Rabin tried to insulate the Oslo negotiations from terrorism."[46] In theory, this separation between the peace process and the terrorist attacks enabled the government to sever all ties between the two issues, but in reality, it was an artificial separation and did not fulfill its primary and most important mission.

The Israeli public was not prepared to accept a situation in which the peace process continued amid terrorist attacks, which led to continued erosion of the public's support for the process. However, from the outset, this position could not stand the test of time, because it was inherently contradictory. The interim arrangements between Israel and the Palestinians, by their very nature, dealt a significant blow to Israel's ability to deal with terrorism. The limitations on the war on terror resulting from the peace process can be divided into two categories: first, limitations resulting from the actual signed agreements, and, second, restrictions stemming from the leadership's self-restraint (as a result of resistance to being dragged into an escalation of the situation and endangering the peace process).

LIMITATIONS STEMMING FROM THE PEACE AGREEMENTS

The agreements that the Israeli government signed with the PLO involved considerable risks regarding all aspects of the fight against terrorism, some of which resulted from a lack of attention or the prioritization of the overall goal of achieving peace over minor security details. Most of them, however, were inherent in the agreement itself and constituted a radical departure from Israel's counterterrorism strategy, because, per the agreement, from its signing onward, an important part of Israel's war on terror would rely on the Palestinian Authority's security and intelligence services and the activities of the Palestinian police. Thus, a situation was created in which the prevention of terrorist attacks depended first and foremost on the success or failure of a foreign element. Then-OC Southern Command Major General Shaul Mofaz best articulated this in April 1995:

For the first time in my career, my responsibility to fight terrorism depends on another authority, which is not doing what the job requires, not in accordance with the understandings, and not in accordance with the agreements. . . . When I talk about a total failure, I am also talking about Yasser Arafat. . . . [He] represents the Palestinian Authority and the ability of its security apparatus. And he failed, failed, failed.[47]

Prime Minister Rabin described it in a less blunt manner in August 1995:

The basic understanding between us and the Palestinians is that with the transfer of all authority and the IDF's exit from all Palestinian population centers in the Gaza Strip, the responsibility for maintaining public order and security for those traveling on their roads and ours is also theirs. . . . We do not see the Palestinian Authority making a serious effort to deal with those who oppose the agreement. . . . In this reality, we demand that the Palestinian Authority do its job.[48]

Israeli policy makers' expectations of the PA regarding the fight against terrorism can be understood from the prime minister's remarks in April 1995:

Israel demands that the Palestinians intensify their activity against Hamas and Islamic Jihad. . . . The main responsibility for preventing the organization of suicide bombers and the procurement and preparation of explosives for terrorist attacks is the Palestinian Authority's.[49]

Secure Travel on Palestinian Authority Roads

Israel's reliance on the PA's mechanisms in all aspects of counterterrorism was reflected in a number of areas, including the security of Israeli traffic on routes bordering PA territory. For example, at the beginning of negotiations on the security arrangements under the Gaza-Jericho Agreement, the Israeli negotiators promised the IDF exclusive control over the 300-meter security zones along the routes to the Gush Katif settlements. As the negotiations progressed, the security zones shrank to 100 meters, and in the Cairo agreement, no security zones were mentioned at all; the IDF was given control only of the road itself.[50] Indeed, in April 1995, the prime minister stated that "responsibility for the transportation of Israelis to and from the settlements falls on us."[51] But given the lack of control over security zones along the roads in the Gaza Strip and West Bank, it was almost impossible to thwart attacks against Israeli vehicles on these routes.

The Pursuit of Terrorists Into PA Territory

During negotiations of the Gaza-Jericho Agreement, Israel insisted on the principle of "hot pursuit" of terrorists who had harmed Israelis. In November 1993, Rabin told the Knesset Foreign Affairs and Defense Committee,

> We are insisting on our right to a "hot pursuit" of terrorists. But if there is information about elements in Gaza planning terror attacks, the local police will deal with the matter, and we will focus on protecting the settlements. If this arrangement does not work, it will endanger the entire agreement.[52]

According to this principle, during negotiations, Israeli decision makers promised the military echelons that the IDF would reserve the right to hot pursuit of terrorists even if they fled to PA territories. In practice, the IDF was not allowed to pursue terrorists except in the case of a fatal terrorist attack, and even then, pursuit was virtually impossible. This inability to pursue the perpetrators of attacks seriously damaged the IDF's deterrent capability.[53] The terrorists knew that after an attack, it would be easy for them to flee to safety to an area where the IDF's maneuverability and movement were limited or even nonexistent.

"Cities of Refuge" in the Palestinian Authority

Israeli security officials feared that when the IDF left Arab towns, they would create a security vacuum that would become extraterritorial areas in which the IDF could not set foot and in which terrorist cells could operate unhindered. In other words, the areas to which wanted terrorists and perpetrators of attacks would seek shelter from the long arm of the Israeli security services would become cities of refuge for terrorists. The political echelon in Israel disagreed with the military echelon's assessment of this issue. Decision makers believed that the PA would take steps to prevent from turning into a haven for terrorists. The prime minister said at the time, "with our pulling out of the large Palestinian population centers, we expect that a similar effort will be made to ensure that the vacuum created by our exit is handled in such a way as to prevent the area from becoming a base for attacks against us or against Palestinians."[54]

Shortly after implementation of the Gaza-Jericho Agreement, it became clear to Israeli security forces that they had been right and that their grim predictions had materialized. The PA turned a blind eye to the activities of Hamas, Islamic Jihad, and other organizations in its territory, allowing them to operate freely, prepare for the execution of terrorist attacks, and amass a large and varied supply of arms. At a cabinet meeting convened after the double suicide bombing at Beit Lid Junction in January 1995, IDF chief of staff Amnon Lipkin-Shahak said that the PA was not fulfilling its obligations and that Gaza and Jericho had become cities of refuge. Three months later, Major General Mofaz explained the significance of the chief of staff's remarks in greater detail, saying that there were dozens or perhaps hundreds of wanted terrorists in the PA's territories, and that the Gaza Strip had become a hotbed of terrorist activity. The terrorists there had many weapons and considerable freedom of action. "Hamas and Islamic Jihad have never enjoyed such freedom of action," he said.[55]

Foreign Minister Peres tried to minimize the harm this situation caused to Israel's security, stating that in an age of suicidal terrorism, the existence of cities of refuge had no importance. At a meeting of the Knesset Foreign Affairs and Defense Committee in January 1995, he said, "the phenomenon of terror perpetrated by suicide bombers is extremely difficult. They are not seeking refuge in Gaza or in Jericho, but in hell or in heaven."[56] Peres chose to ignore the location of the leaders of the organizations, the commanders and dispatchers of the suicide bombers, the planners of the attacks, the bomb makers, and all of those who aided the terrorist cells—almost all of them lived and operated in the territory of the Palestinian Authority.

The Relationship Between the IDF and the Palestinian Police

After establishment of the PA's police force, a strange relationship was created between it and the IDF. On the one hand, Palestinian officers were, in theory, the IDF's partners in maintaining security and order in the territories and foiling terrorist attacks. This was expressed in, among other things, joint motorized patrols along traffic arteries and in problematic areas. On the other hand, the Palestinians did not meet the conditions set for the establishment of their police force in terms of the number of police officers, their identity, and their weapons.

In May 1994, 70 operatives of the Fatah Hawks (an organization that had been involved in twenty-two shooting incidents with IDF forces in the Gaza Strip after the Oslo Accords were signed) were serving in the Palestinian police, along with a number of wanted individuals.[57] Furthermore, twenty-four of the sixth graduates of the Palestinian police course that ended in mid-November 1994 were wanted by Israel. The person who was named the course's outstanding trainee was Jamal Shahawan, a wanted terrorist from the Qalqiliya area. During the ceremony, graduates of the course listened to a number of statements, including that the Palestinian struggle "must continue in Haifa, Ashdod, and Beit Shean [Israeli cities within the "green line"])."[58]

Even before formal establishment of the Palestinian police, Arafat decided that the liaison committee between the PLO and IDF would be headed by Rashid Abu Shabak, founder of the Black Panther Movement (Fatah's operational arm in the West Bank and Gaza during the intifada) and a wanted person who had fled from Gaza. Abu Shabak did not change his views on Israel after his appointment, and he even hinted that he did not intend to fight to protect Israel's security interests. In April 1994, he declared, "Shimon Peres's statement that Fatah must not become close to Hamas is out of line. This is a Palestinian issue, and we are not going to let anyone intervene in our internal affairs."[59]

The reality of Israeli-Palestinian security cooperation first hit during the events at Erez checkpoint in July 1994. Palestinian police joined an unruly mob of rioters at the checkpoint and even fired at the IDF soldiers stationed there. The Israeli government objected to the incident, but its spokespeople emphasized that the objection stemmed from the Palestinian police's lack of experience. As then deputy minister Yossi Sarid said, "The Palestinian police should not be thrown out with the events at Erez checkpoint."[60]

In the interim agreement, dubbed "Oslo II" and signed in Washington, D.C., on September 28, 1995, Israel demanded the right to approve the appointments of Palestinian policemen. It also demanded that those already serving immediately cease to employ those convicted of serious crimes, and that anyone proven to have been involved in terrorist activities after their recruitment have their weapons and police documentation confiscated. As can be gleaned from what was *not* said in this agreement, Israel de facto agreed to the inclusion of persons wanted for murder and other terrorist activities in the Palestinian police force provided they had not been convicted of serious crimes and had not committed terrorist acts after their recruitment.

Intelligence Gathering for Defensive and Operational Purposes

Intelligence plays a key role in the ongoing struggle against terrorism. It should provide vital information about terrorist organizations' intentions and make it possible to thwart attacks before they occur. Intelligence should also provide information on the location of the perpetrators, their dispatchers, and their bases so that they can be successfully attacked. With establishment of Palestinian autonomy, the importance of intelligence increased tenfold and was supposed to compensate for the loss of control in the area by providing advance warning of terrorist organizations' intentions. As long as the IDF controlled the areas in which the terrorists prepared for attacks, it was able to disrupt their activities in the initial stages of organization. Even routine security measures (without prior intelligence) were sometimes sufficient for preventing terrorist attacks. But after the IDF evacuated Palestinian areas, enabling the free passage of people and goods between the territories and Israel, security forces were forced to rely almost entirely on intelligence to prevent terrorist attacks.

Moreover, before establishment of the PA, Israel could secure cooperation from the Palestinians by granting benefits, licenses, and jobs or by threatening to revoke various rights. Control over the area gave Israel's intelligence services direct contact with people on Palestinian streets and facilitated the collection of information vital to combating terror and preventing attacks. Israel's withdrawal from Palestinian areas turned the tables. Palestinians' motivation to provide information to Israeli intelligence services disappeared completely. The bitter fate of those suspected of collaborating with Israel during the intifada and the Palestinian security services' focus on tracking down Israeli agents in the territories after establishment of the PA did not help matters.

At the beginning of negotiations with the Palestinians, heads of the Israeli intelligence services presented various explanations in an attempt to reassure the public with regard to the anticipated decrease in the amount and quality of intelligence about terrorist organizations operating in the Palestinian territories. However, as early as January 1995, chief of staff Lipkin-Shahak was prepared to admit that there was "no answer to the suicide bombers. Eight months have passed since [Israel] left Gaza, and [they] have fewer intelligence sources."[61] In September 1995, the head of the Military Intelligence Research Division, Brigadier General Amidror, stated even more categorically, "Israel's intelligence capability in the Gaza Strip has fallen to zero, and a similar situation is likely to be created in the West Bank when we transfer control to the Palestinian Authority."[62]

The severe blow to the Israeli security services' intelligence capabilities in the autonomous Palestinian areas made them dependent to a large extent on the PA's intelligence and security services. Indeed, those Palestinian services acquired excellent intelligence capabilities after the establishment of autonomy. The large number of Palestinian security and intelligence mechanisms, the employment of many intelligence personnel to run them, and the integration of these mechanisms into the fabric of Palestinian society (whose *Hamula* [extended families] structure meant that some members of a family could be active Hamas operatives while others worked in one of the Palestinian intelligence apparatuses), gave the PA a tremendous amount of intelligence in real time. In February 1995, Major General Sagi, head of Israeli military intelligence, appeared before the Knesset Foreign Affairs and Defense Committee and said, "the Palestinian police have the intelligence and military ability to get to every terrorist's headquarters and home, and they do so when they receive the appropriate instructions."[63]

Given the steep decline in Israel's intelligence capabilities in the autonomous Palestinian areas, it was only natural for its intelligence services to gain the assistance of their Palestinian counterparts in obtaining early intelligence about terrorist attacks. But this was not clear-cut. Palestinian intelligence services generally withheld intelligence regarding plans for attacks. If they had such information, in the best-case scenario, they themselves acted to prevent the attack (if it was in the PA's interest at the time to do so). Sometimes the Palestinians did nothing with intelligence information, even after receiving it from Israel. At a Labor faction meeting in September 1994, the prime minister said,

> If they do not take steps against terrorism and do not make a reasonable effort, it will make the process very difficult. We demand that they fulfill

their obligations. The steps they have taken so far have been more warning measures and not actions against terrorism. We demand that Arafat take action against the organizers and perpetrators of terrorist attacks. We cannot tolerate a situation in which even when we pass on information to them, and even when they know, they do not do what they can.[64]

In other cases, Palestinian security services acted to prevent certain terrorist attacks or arrested perpetrators as a result of intelligence information passed on to them from Israel.[65] However, such cooperation involved serious damage to Israeli intelligence sources. Sometimes, when information was received from Israel about plans to carry out an attack, Palestinian security services would warn the attack's planners and perpetrators in advance, and in other cases, they would foil the attack and immediately afterward take steps to locate and neutralize the Israeli intelligence source.

The Palestinian security service's attitude toward suspected collaborators with Israel is evident from the statements by Muhammad Dahlan, head of the Palestinian security service in Gaza: "there are some people who have provided information that led to the elimination of a Palestinian, and some who have themselves killed one of their own people. If we catch them, we will chop off their heads."[66] However, the Palestinian intelligence services were not satisfied with merely locating and eliminating Israeli intelligence agents. In some cases, they turned them into double agents and used them to gather intelligence on the Israeli security services. In April 1995, it was discovered that an Israeli intelligence agent exposed by Jibril Rajoub's intelligence apparatus had been asked to continue to behave as if he was working with Israel and to steal information from the ISA about others who were cooperating with Israel.[67] Those suspected of collaborating with Israel feared Palestinian intelligence officials so much that in order to clear their name and that of their family, they were even willing to volunteer to carry out suicide bombings in Israel.[68]

THE PEACE PROCESS AS A MEANS OF THWARTING TERRORIST ATTACKS

In addition to the restrictions on counterterrorism efforts stemming directly or indirectly from the security and diplomatic agreements between Israel and the PLO, the Israeli government imposed a series of limitations and prohibitions on itself. It wanted to avoid being drawn into a situation in which steps to combat terrorism would endanger the peace process and lead it to be halted or suspended.

Based on assessments by Israeli security officials and policy makers that the main goal of Hamas and other fundamentalist terrorist organizations was to stop the peace process, Rabin dictated a policy according to which the peace process would not be harmed should mass-casualty terrorist attacks occur. Therefore, the government generally refrained from threatening to suspend the process. Rabin had already underlined this position when he appeared before the Knesset Foreign Affairs and Defense Committee in March 1993, announcing that he did not intend to make the continuation of diplomatic talks conditional on a cessation of terror, as such a demand would, in effect, grant Hamas veto power over continuation of the talks, which was exactly what Hamas aspired to do. The government's concern that the process would be halted or slowed because of such a stipulation effectively prevented use of the peace process as a means of thwarting attacks. Government spokespeople responded to every call to threaten the suspension of negotiations with the reiteration that they did not want to play into the hands of the terrorists and enable Hamas to achieve its goal: the halting of the peace process.

Following the attacks in Kfar Darom in April 1995, Rabin said "the goal of the terrorist organizations is to kill Israelis and Palestinians in order to murder peace."[69] The Israeli government's decision to refrain from exploiting the diplomatic process to stop terrorist attacks stemmed from, among other things, the assessment that this was a transition period and that domestic and foreign security would improve after completion of the peace process. According to the assessment of Israeli decision makers, the benefits of peace in the future required acting with restraint during the transitional period, even when it demanded making sacrifices in order to achieve peace.

Ignoring the Palestinian Authority's Failure to Stop Terrorism

The Israeli government's decision not to suspend negotiations due to terrorist attacks led it, consciously or unconsciously, to turn a blind eye to Arafat's unwillingness to act decisively against Hamas and Islamic Jihad and to thwart terrorist attacks in Israel. In an effort to avoid harming the peace process, the government was prepared at first even to ignore acts of terror by Fatah itself,[70] even though the prime minister said at the time that "if there was any suspicion that the PLO-Tunis was involved in terror attacks, it would change the whole picture."[71]

In December 1994, Muhammad Ghneim (Abu Maher), who was responsible for recruitment and organization in the PLO, said in an interview with the Jordanian paper *Al-Aswak* that as long as the demands for withdrawal, dismantling of the settlements, right of return, and establishment of a Palestinian state were not met, the armed struggle would continue. "Therefore, there were many special joint operations of the Fatah fighters with fighters of other factions like Hamas and the Popular Front. These joint activities [would] continue as long as the occupation continues."[72]

At first, Israeli leaders explained the PA's inaction in thwarting terror as birth pangs and the difficulty that Arafat and his people were having in accommodating the possession of control in the territories. In the next stage, members of the government explained Arafat's helplessness against perpetrators of the attacks in Israel by claiming that although he was indeed interested in thwarting such attacks, he was incapable of doing so. For example, the prime minister wondered in September 1993 that if Israel had not succeeded, "shall the Palestinian police succeed?"[73] Such arguments by Israel effectively removed responsibility for terrorist attacks in Israel from the shoulders of the Palestinian Authority. Declarations of this sort by Israeli decision makers, which excused Arafat's failures in thwarting terrorism, eventually came back to haunt them. When Rabin met with Arafat in August 1994 and demanded that he take action against the Hamas movement's terrorist activities, Arafat responded, "You too did not prevent terror in Gaza."[74]

The claim that Arafat was unable to prevent terrorism was repeated by Israeli officials every time there was a mass-casualty attack in Israel. Sometimes the claim was accompanied by a comparison of the forces available to Israel in the West Bank and Gaza with the "meager" forces at Arafat's disposal. This comparison was fundamentally erroneous, given that Arafat had excellent intelligence capabilities with regard to the Palestinian population in the territories, far beyond the capabilities of the Israeli security services even when Israel had controlled those areas. With these capabilities, Arafat could have thwarted almost every attack against Israel.

The claim that Arafat suffered from a lack of capability and not a lack of will in thwarting terrorist attacks during the period under review lacked any basis in reality. In August 1994, then-chief of general staff Ehud Barak said, "I believe that the Palestinians' main problem is will and determination. If they insisted on doing what they took upon themselves, I believe that they would succeed and that there would be security for Jews and Arabs."[75]

Support for this assessment came in August 1994, when news agencies in Gaza reported that Arafat had restrained the commanders of the security forces who wanted to act aggressively against the extremists. The commander of the Palestinian police said in this context that his forces were capable of putting an end to the Hamas attacks, but that it depended on "the decision of the political echelon"—that is, Arafat. Such a decision was never made.[76]

This situation ultimately forced the Israeli government to recognize that Arafat was not doing everything in his power to prevent terrorist attacks in Israel. In August 1995, the prime minister stated in an interview that the Palestinian Authority had not made a serious effort to deal with Hamas and Islamic Jihad and that the PA was capable of doing much more in the fight against terrorism.[77]

However, even though Israeli policy makers understood that Arafat was not acting decisively against terrorism, they preferred to attribute his inaction not to the maliciousness of the Palestinian Authority but, rather, to erroneous judgment on the PA's part.[78] But, in fact, this was not a mistake of judgment. After mass-casualty attacks, Arafat would take empty demonstrative actions, such as ordering senseless arrests of Islamic activists, sending warnings to the leaders of the fundamentalist organizations, and paying lip service through public condemnations. These actions only testified to what Arafat was capable of doing to fight terrorism if he had been interested in doing so. The Palestinian Authority's policy at the time was expressed by Nabil Shaath when he said, immediately after the suicide bombing at Beit Lid Junction (January 22, 1995), that the PA would take more aggressive measures against Hamas and Islamic Jihad: "this time it will not be a performance that lasts two or three days."[79] But even that promise was baseless. According to then-OC Southern Command Shaul Mofaz in April 1995,

The main problem with the implementation of the security agreement is the lack of decisiveness and determination on the part of the Palestinian Author-ity and the Palestinian security forces in their activity against Islamic Jihad and Hamas. . . . In this area, they have been a total failure. . . . These are two things that the PA did not do: Firstly, it did not make a decision to confiscate the weapons of members of the Islamic organizations, and secondly, it does not persecute them. If the Palestinian Authority wants to, its security appa-ratuses know how to reach every Hamas activist's door and every Izz al-Din al-Qassam cell member and catch them.[80]

In August 1994, the prime minister declared that he did not

demand 100 percent security from Arafat, but the exhaustion of all the Pal-estinians' abilities to provide security. If that does not happen, it will place a question mark over the possibility of implementing the transfer of authority to the Palestinians over the course of the negotiations that opened this week.[81]

Other voices from the government also declared that they demanded that Arafat devote 100 percent effort to prevent terrorism, not a 100 percent success rate in thwarting attacks. This declaration effectively enabled the Palestinian Authority to evade its responsibility for preventing attacks, as its activities or omissions were not measured quantitatively on the basis of the number of attacks against Israel but by the abstract measure of effort. Arafat, who immediately understood the advantages inherent in the Israeli demand, announced in his meetings with Rabin, "We cannot prevent 100 percent of the terrorist acts, but we will do our best."[82]

In conclusion, the situation after the signing of the Oslo Accords and the establishment of Palestinian autonomy required the Israeli government to formulate a new framework for counterterrorism. This policy was based on a number of basic assumptions that were laid out for policy makers by the Israeli intelligence agencies:

- Arafat and Fatah made a strategic decision to materialize the peace process with Israel. This included renouncing the use of violence and terrorism against Israel.
- The primary goal of the Palestinian Islamic fundamentalist organizations, most notably Hamas, was to stop the peace process.

- Hamas and Islamic Jihad are irrational organizations. They are not deterred by retaliation against them and will never reach an agreement with Israel.
- Palestinian Authority decision makers understand that terrorism does not serve the Palestinians' national goals, and therefore they do everything in their power to thwart attacks and strike against terrorist organizations.

The conclusion from all of the above was that any harming, cessation, or suspension of the peace process due to terrorist attacks serves the interests of the fundamentalist Islamic organizations.

In reality, however, it turned out that some of the basic assumptions underlying Israeli policy at that time were questionable.

- Hamas, in fact, as a grassroots movement firmly tied to Palestinian public opinion, could not and would not act in a way contrary to its stances and to Palestinian national interests.
- Hamas saw eye to eye with the Palestinian Authority leadership in regard to Palestinian national interests; namely, Israel's withdrawal from the territories and the establishment of a Palestinian state. (The Islamic organizations, however, aspired to establish an Islamic republic in Palestine, whereas the PLO sought a secular democratic state.)
- The struggle against the peace process according to this approach was a central goal of Hamas, but not the only one. Hamas' da'wah (religious-social activity) was more important than the movement's other goals because it was vital for ensuring the existence, growth, and expansion of Hamas among the Palestinian public.
- Both the PA and Hamas feared a civil war in the territories, and therefore they were not interested in a direct confrontation. This fear, and the concern that the PA might interfere with Hamas's da'wah activities, gave the PA significant leverage over Hamas, which could have been used to prevent attacks in Israel.

Thus, during this period, the PA had the ability to influence Hamas's policy of terrorist attacks, both directly, by damaging the organization's military and civilian infrastructure in the territories (thereby undermining its ability to carry out terrorist attacks), and indirectly, by reducing Hamas's motivation to carry out attacks in Israel through persuasion and sometimes even threats. This indirect effect also could have been achieved via Palestinian public opinion and the creation of an atmosphere not conducive to attacks, as the PA controlled all of the media in the territories. However, the PA made a strategic decision to refrain from physically harming Hamas's military and civilian infrastructure, either to prevent escalation to the point of a Palestinian civil war or to maintain the option of violence in the next stages of peace negotiations with Israel through Hamas attacks.

Israel did not realize at the time that in order for the Palestinian Authority to use its leverage over Hamas, the Israeli government had to spur motivation among the PA leadership, which would be achieved only when the PA was forced to understand that terrorist attacks harmed Palestinian national interests. In other words, Israel should have made use of the peace process as a key element of a carrot and stick policy to thwart terror attacks and make it clear to the PA that in the absence of terrorist attacks, when Palestinian violence is not used against Israel, the peace process would continue as usual and Palestinian national interests would be realized. However, if the Palestinians used violence and terror against Israel, the peace process would be delayed and with it the realization of Palestinian national interests.

Offensive and Operative Action: The Boomerang Effect

The establishment of Palestinian autonomy in the territories in effect changed the rules of the game with respect to the operative and offensive counterterrorism activity that was common in previous governments. Chief of staff Ehud Barak spoke about this issue in September 1994: "it was clear from the outset that the IDF would not carry out actions to prevent, thwart, or otherwise deal with terrorism within the autonomous areas. That was handed over to a very clear address, and this address is now being tested in Gaza and Jericho."[83]

The decision to leave the responsibility for counterterrorism activity in the autonomous areas in the hands of the PA stemmed from several considerations. They included the complexity of activity in these areas (within a hostile and armed population), an unwillingness to harm the sovereignty of the PA, which had just taken over responsibility for security in the area, and the lack of desire to damage Arafat's standing and image internally in a way that would endanger the continuation of the peace process. However, this principled policy of the government did not last long. When it became clear to Israeli decisionmakers that the fundamentalist Islamic organizations were continuing to carry out mass attacks in Israel, and that the PA was not doing everything in its power to stop them (or was unable to, as some policy makers believed), the policy changed, and policy makers instructed security forces to operate in the autonomous areas as well, albeit discreetly.

This activity was assigned to undercover units and Special Forces and focused on the elimination of senior operatives of the terrorist organizations who were wanted for the initiating, planning, preparing, and carrying out terrorist attacks in Israel. Following a suicide bombing in the heart of Tel Aviv in October 1994, in which twenty-one people were killed and forty-three were wounded, Rabin announced that he had instructed security forces to take out the terrorist leaders. "We must seek, find and arrest or eliminate those who organize this terrorist activity."[84] According to the British weekly paper *The Observer*, this directive was given at an emergency meeting of the cabinet, which was attended by the heads of Mossad, the ISA, and Military Intelligence. Fifty-one days later, Hani al-Abed, a senior Islamic Jihad figure in the Gaza Strip, was killed. Israel did not take responsibility for the killing, but Islamic Jihad blamed Israeli security forces. In January 1995, Foreign Minister Peres reiterated the government's commitment to act against the terrorist organizations and told the Knesset Foreign Affairs and Defense Committee that Israel must take all necessary measures to locate the terrorists and attack them before they carried out their plans, without limiting how or where they act.

During this period, Israel continued to target killings of senior members of Palestinian terrorist organizations. As mentioned, it adopted this method against terrorists in the territories and autonomous areas. Former ISA head Gillon notes that between March 1995 and February 1996, twenty-three people were removed from the list of wanted persons, ten of whom were killed during their capture and the rest of whom were arrested.[85] Gillon mentions elimination of the so-called Hebron Cell, which was responsible for a series of major attacks against Israel, as being among the interceptions.

In addition to the ISA's ongoing interceptions, during this period, a number of targeted killings were carried out in which several senior operatives were eliminated. (It should be noted that in most cases, Israel did not explicitly take responsibility for these killings.) Among the operatives that were taken out during this period were Hani al-Abed; Kamal Kahil, a key Hamas operative in Gaza; Mahmoud al-Hawajah, a senior member of Palestinian Islamic Jihad's military wing; Fathi Shaqaqi, head of Palestinian Islamic Jihad; and Yihye Ayyash, "the Engineer," a senior Hamas figure who was a main player in initiating and preparing suicide attacks.

Al-Abed was killed in Gaza in an explosion that was set off when he started his car. He had been imprisoned there until his release. The day after the killing, at a ceremony commemorating fallen Nahal Brigade soldiers, Rabin declared, "with one hand we shake hands with the kingdom of Jordan and with the other hand we pull the trigger to hit the murderers of Hezbollah and Islamic Jihad."[86] With this statement, Rabin tried to illustrate his government's policy of supporting continuation of the peace process and the war on terrorism in parallel, two lines operating side by side but not affecting each other. Sheikh Abdullah Shami, one of the leaders of the Islamic Jihad in the territories, accused Israeli intelligence of carrying out al-Abed's killing, saying that "this assassination is part of the plot that Rabin promised when he said that his long arms will hit Muslim extremists wherever they are." Shami vowed that Islamic Jihad would carry out a "revenge attack in Tel Aviv."[87]

Two attacks followed al-Abed's killing, which, according to Islamic Jihad, were revenge attacks. Eight days after the death of al-Abed, suicide bomber Hisham Isma'il Muhammad blew himself up on a bicycle at an IDF outpost in Netzarim. Three Israeli officers were killed. Then, in February 1995, Anwar Suqar and Salah Shakal, both members of Islamic Jihad, blew themselves up near the bus station at Beit Lid Junction, killing twenty-two soldiers. An Islamic Jihad proclamation circulated in the territories after the attack in Netzarim stated that the perpetrator belonged to the Shahid Hani al-Abed cell.

On April 2, 1995, Kamal Kahil was killed in an explosion in the Sheikh Radwan neighborhood of Gaza City. His aide, Hatem Hassan, as well as a mother and her son, were also killed. Israel claimed that this was a "work accident" (a malfunction during the preparation or transportation of an explosive charge),[88] but Hamas blamed the attack on Israel and threatened to retaliate. According to Hamas, a terrorist named Wissam Farhat, who was arrested after the discovery of a truck of explosives in Tel Sheva on March 20, revealed to the ISA Kamal Kahil's hiding place in an apartment in Sheikh Radwan.[89] According to Sheikh Ahmed Bahar, Hamas operatives threatened revenge attacks against Israel, and a week after Kahil's death,[90] there were two suicide bombings in Netzarim and Kfar Darom in the Gaza Strip (one of them most likely carried out by Hamas), during which seven soldiers and a tourist from the United States were killed.

On June 22, 1995, Mahmoud al-Hawajah was shot to death by three masked men near his home in Gaza. The chief of the Palestinian police accused Israel of assassinating the man, saying that the way al-Hawajah was shot, with weapons with silencers, implied that Israel was behind it.[91] Hamas also blamed Israel and threatened to retaliate.

One of the most widely known targeted killings during this period (though Israel never officially took responsibility for it) was elimination of Palestinian Islamic Jihad leader Fathi Shaqaqi in Malta on October 28, 1995. According to *Der Spiegel*, Shaqaqi's assassination was the work of the Israeli Mossad by personal order by Prime Minister Rabin in February after the suicide bombing at Beit Lid Junction.[92] A few days after the killing, on November 2, two suicide attacks were carried out in Gush Katif in which fourteen Israelis were injured. Palestinian Islamic Jihad claimed responsibility for the attack.

The fact that in many cases Israel did not take responsibility for the targeted killings did not prevent the boomerang effect that occurred when revenge attacks (defined as such, at any rate, by the terrorist organizations) were instigated against Israel following the killings, as just described. The most striking example of the boomerang effect was the killing of the Engineer, Yihye Ayyash, and the subsequent suicide attacks against Israelis. Ayyash had topped Israel's most-wanted list due to his pivotal roles in numerous suicide bombings. "There was a substantial difference between Ayyash and the rest" of the top terrorists, in that he was the first to execute such attacks in Israeli territory and was involved in almost every suicide attack carried out by Hamas until his death.[93] He personally prepared explosives, planned attacks, instructed the terrorists, and trained others to carry out the suicide attacks. Ayyash was killed in Gaza by a booby-trapped cell phone that was apparently given to him by ISA agents.

Ayyash's killing took place following approximately six months in which no suicide bombing attacks occurred in Israel (although security forces claimed that several attacks were foiled during this period). The absence of suicide attacks during this period can be attributed, among other things, to a temporary agreement that was reached between Hamas and the Palestinian Authority to refrain from such attacks. After that agreement, Ayyash fled to Gaza in fear for his life.[94] About fifty days after the killing of the Engineer, and breaking the relative calm that had prevailed for the previous six months, four severe terrorist attacks took place in Israel over the course of a week, three of them suicide bombings in Jerusalem and Tel Aviv, in which dozens of people were killed and hundreds were injured.

Peres objected to the claim that these four major attacks were a boomerang response to the killing of Ayyash:

> I think it's nonsense because we knew that the Engineer was going to execute more attacks. Say we hadn't hit him and he would have carried out the attacks, what would they have said then? "You could have prevented it." It's all descriptions of the press. I know the truth; I know that he was about to carry out more attacks.[95]

Defensive and Security Action

The mass-casuality terrorist attacks during this period necessitated the search for an appropriate defensive response. The need to strengthen Israel's system of defense against terrorist attacks stemmed both the need to both thwart the attacks and take demonstrative steps to calm the public and ease their anxiety. However, as noted, defensive action to prevent terrorism, and suicide attacks in particular, is a difficult and complex task—sometimes even an impossible one. Defense is the last link in the chain of counterterrorism actions (the first and central link is intelligence). But when the rest of the links fail to prevent terrorism, the final link is immeasurably important. Even if it fails to thwart the attack, it might reduce the resulting damage.

An example of this type of achievement in defensive security during this period was the suicide bombing at Dizengoff Center in 1996. The attack, which took place during the Purim holiday, was intended to occur inside the closed shopping center. If this had been accomplished, the number of casualties would have been ten times greater. However, the suicide bomber decided to change his course of action and blow himself up on the street outside of the shopping center, apparently because the security guards stationed at the entrance to the center were checking the bags of all who entered.

The limitations of routine security measures given Israel's topography—and especially the fluidity of the dividing line between Israel within the

Green Line and the territories—can be understood from the words of Prime Minister Rabin after the murder of a resident of Afula by an axe-wielding terrorist in December 1994.

> We have to investigate how the terrorist got to Afula. . . . He crossed through the checkpoint with an axe with the intention of harming Jews. We have to check how he managed to get through. . . . If only we had more road-blocks, better roadblocks . . . but even with effective roadblocks it is difficult to identify a lone killer. Traffic there is heavy, and there are also many Jews passing through, so it is difficult to identify cars, especially since thousands of residents of East Jerusalem have vehicles with license plates like ours, and opponents of peace use these types of vehicles.[96]

In addition to the roadblocks, patrols, and physical defense of sensitive buildings, security forces employed a number of new defense initiatives during this period. These included armored buses for the transport of students and civilians on sensitive bus lines in the West Bank and Gaza, the instillation of panic buttons in vehicles of civilians living in these territories (in order to locate and assist them in case of emergency), the establishment of a bus security unit whose goal was to demonstrate the presence of security on buses and bus stations and to try to identify terrorists and explosive devices, and increased security in schools by special units. (The latter were later dismantled and their duties transferred to the police, who received specialized specifications and measures to carry out this task.)

Closures

The most prominent feature of Israel's defensive action during this period was the attempt to maximize the separation between the Israeli and Palestinian populations living in the territories, which aimed at preventing terrorist infiltration into Israel. This policy was reflected throughout the entire period in the repeated imposition of closures on residents of the territories (especially after mass-casualty attacks in Israel), and subsequently in preparations for the implementation of a comprehensive physical separation between Israel and the Palestinians in the territories.

In general, the closures imposed by Israel a this time can be classified into four categories: (a) closure for a limited period determined in advance, around a specific remembrance date; (b) closure for a limited period, due to an intelligence warning of a concrete attack; (c) closure on the territories following a multi-victim attack intended, among other things, to strengthen Israeli citizens' sense of personal security; and (d) closure intended to pressure the Palestinian Authority to adopt a certain security measure, such as the arrest of a wanted terrorist.[97] The rationale behind closures was not, as many claimed, to punish Palestinian residents for attacks, although supporters of this action maintained that the damage caused to residents' sources of income would put pressure on the terrorist organizations to refrain from continuing the attacks. Rather, first and foremost, closures were intended to place obstacles for terrorists who were on their way to the site of an attack and to make it easier for Israeli security forces to locate a terrorist's movement in Israel. Therefore, Israeli security officials and decision makers initially believed that closures could be an appropriate solution to the terrorist attacks originating from the territories.

In an April 1993 speech to the Knesset, Rabin hailed closures, saying that they "restore personal security to 99.5 percent of Israel's residents, and solve our worst social problem—unemployment. . . . Today there are opportunities to connect the two—both personal security and the return to being the builders of the country."[98] Rabin did not view closures as a complete or single solution to the problem of terrorism, and he stressed his belief that the combination of closures, force reinforcement, and deportations provided the most appropriate solution to the challenge of terrorism.[99]

But there was a fly in the ointment. Closures might have improved Israeli citizens' sense of security and in some cases even prevented or postponed the execution of terrorist attacks. But at the same time, they damaged the livelihoods of many Palestinians, which, over time, was bound to lead to unrest, the strengthening of the terrorist organizations, and an escalation of violence in the territories and even within the Green Line. This, at least, is what Arafat claimed to Rabin during their meeting in Casablanca in October 1994: "you impose a closure and the workers run out of money. Hamas has money, which means that instead of punishing them, you are punishing us." Rabin replied, "when 22 people are killed in Tel Aviv, it is more of a problem for Israelis."[100] But despite his determined position, Rabin was also aware of the shortcomings of closures. He therefore instructed that steps be taken to create jobs for Palestinians in the territories in order to prevent economic hardship.

Rabin highlighted the dilemma inherent in the decision to lift the closure in February 1995 as follows.

> I am torn between two problems: how to ensure security for Israelis and how to help the Palestinians. I tried in this decision [to lift the closure] to take a risk and help the Palestinians. In the long run, I prefer to reach a situation in which there will be investments in the territories and the Palestinians will work there, and we will begin to separate. Our policy is to create two entities.[101]

Meanwhile, the decision regarding lifting the closure on the territories was difficult and involved security risks. Rabin informed Arafat that Israel would allow the entry of 15,000 Palestinian workers. He declared that his decision was contrary to Israel's security interests and was intended to prevent tension that could increase terrorism in the territories and reduce Palestinian trust in the peace process.[102]

Moreover, following a prolonged closure, international organizations were often called on to condemn Israel for what they called the "starvation policy" regarding residents of the territories. These claims reflected international public opinion on this issue. However, public opinion in Israel demanded that the closure be continued as long as there was danger of terrorist attacks within the Green Line. This was expressed in the words of the Knesset member Hagai Merom:

> Past experience shows that every time we lifted a closure, the Israeli public was exposed to terrorist attacks, and the less strict the closure, the greater the ability of the terrorist organizations to strike inside the State of Israel.... Those who would lift the closure today assume a very heavy responsibility for the next attack.[103]

As a possible solution to the dilemma of imposing closures, Rabin declared that lifting the closure would depend on the extent of the PA's action against Palestinian terrorist organizations. "There is a clear correlation between Arafat's efforts to thwart terrorism and the Israeli response in terms of easing the closure."[104]

An examination of the suicide bombings throughout this era reveals that some of them were carried out even when a complete closure was imposed on the territories, though in some cases the attack occurred shortly after the closure was lifted. (An example is the number 18 bus attack in Jerusalem on February 25, 1996, which was carried out forty-eight hours after the prime minister, against the ISA's recommendation, decided to lift the closure in the West Bank.)[105] As noted, one of the security problems involved in imposition of the closure was that even in the best-case scenario, in which the closure actually fulfilled its goal, it did not prevent the planned attack but at most caused it to occur another time or place. Rabin claimed, for example, that the imposition of a closure on the territories sometimes led to the redirecting of hostile terrorist activity to Israeli targets and settlers in the territories themselves.[106]

The partial effectiveness of the closure, even when it was imposed, reinforced Rabin's conclusion to seek the fullest possible separation between the Palestinian population in the territories and the Israeli population in order to achieve a sufficient level of security and prevent terror. He determined that the situation created during this period reflected "a reality in which the most favorable conditions for terror against the State of Israel exist" because of the lack of separation, the fact that both Israelis and Palestinians shared the same roads, and the ongoing contact between Israeli citizens and residents of the territories.[107] The greater the wave of suicide attacks, the stronger Rabin felt that there was a need for a physical separation between the two populations. In January 1995, after the attack in Beit Lid, the Israeli government decided that it intended to achieve a "practical separation" between Israelis in the "sovereign State of Israel" and the residents of the West Bank and Gaza.[108] Thus, once again, terror attacks became the main motive for the Israeli government to formulate policy and set strategic objectives for the medium and long terms.

THE RELEASING OF PALESTINIAN CONVICTED TERRORISTS WITHIN THE FRAMEWORK OF PEACE NEGOTIATIONS

During his term as prime minister, Rabin had to deal with two extortion terrorist attacks involving the abduction of border police officer Nissim Toledano and soldier Nachshon Waxman. In both cases, he refused to free convicted terrorists from jail in return for the release of the hostages.

The Toledano Affair

First Sergeant Toledano was kidnapped on December 13, 1992, in the early hours of the morning near his home by a cell that later turned out to be inspired by Hamas but was not an integral part of the movement's military wing. In exchange for Toledano's release, the cell posed a theoretically realistic demand: the release of the movement's jailed leader, Sheikh Yassin.[109] The Israeli government convened to discuss the terrorists' demands, decided not to accept the ultimatum, and ordered security forces to launch a major search operation for the border police officer.[110] At the same time, a television interview with Sheikh Yassin was broadcasted from prison in which he called on the cell members not to hurt the kidnapped soldier. Israeli security forces launched an unprecedented three-day search that led to the arrest of some 1,600 Hamas activists. Shortly afterward, Toledano's body was found.[111]

The Waxman Affair

In early October 1994, soldier Nachshon Waxman was kidnapped by a Hamas cell when he hitched a ride in the center of the country. The cell relayed a long list of demands to the Israeli government via a foreign news agency in Gaza, including a request for the release of 200 Palestinian prisoners.[112] Israel determined that Waxman was being held in Gaza, and the prime minister announced that he considered Arafat and the Palestinian Authority responsible for the soldier's life.[113] Rabin also warned that if Waxman was not handed over to Israel alive and well, it would "have a very serious impact on the future of Israel's relations with the Palestinian Authority and the continuation of the peace process with the Palestinians."[114] At the same time, Rabin suspended the peace talks that were being held in Cairo between the Israelis and the Palestinians.

After a week or so, during which attempts were made to negotiate with the terrorists via several channels (the PA, Arab Israeli activists, and others), Israel obtained intelligence that Waxman was being held in a building in Bir Nabala, near Ramallah. Based on this information, Rabin ordered a military operation to free the abducted soldier. During the operation, Waxman was killed by his abductors before they were eliminated by IDF forces. One Israeli soldier was also killed, and a number were wounded. The prime minister explained, "there was no choice other than the operation."[115] He claimed that the government had no real leverage for negotiating: it was not possible to call the kidnappers, the ultimatum had run out, and the murder was imminent. Rabin added that the cell members had announced that they would negotiate over a corpse if necessary.[116]

The prime minister's decision to initiate a military operation and not comply with the terrorists' demands or Arafat's compromise proposal to release Sheikh Yassin was in line with the Israeli governments' long-stated policy. When a military option is available, it is preferred over giving in to the demands of the terrorists. However, this principle becomes problematic considering that when, in parallel with the decision to take a tough stand against hostage takers, Israel was willing to release thousands of terrorists but not because of an ultimatum or the danger to hostages' lives, including those belonging to fundamentalist Islamic movements, some of whom were personally involved in initiating, planning, and carrying out attacks in Israel, all within the framework of peace negotiations. Indeed, from the time that the Oslo Accords were signed and in the period discussed here, Israel released thousands of terrorists in a number of rounds, disregarding, one by one, "red lines" that the government had set for itself.

In summary, during the period reviewed here, Prime Minister Rabin changed his assessment of the threat of terrorism, shifting the definition from a tactical to a strategic threat to Israel (due to terrorism's damage to morale and its influence on political processes in general and on the peace process in particular). The change in Rabin's assessment reflected, among other things, growth in the phenomenon of suicide attacks. The unusual characteristics of this wave of attacks, the high frequency of the bombings and their occurrence in crowded centers on the Israeli home front, and the relatively large number of casualties caused by these attacks created an unprecedented sense of anxiety, to the point that citizens were afraid to go into the streets and to crowded areas or even to ride in buses. Israelis, who expected that the peace process with the Palestinians and Israel's willingness to compromise on territory, the release of Palestinian prisoners, and other areas, would lead to calm—first and foremost with regard to terrorism— were proven wrong. Ehud Sprinzak described Israeli society's wake-up call during this period as a very difficult jolt. Israeli citizens, he said, entered a mental bunker of anxiety, and public support for the government plunged to an unprecedented degree.[117]

In February 1995, minister of construction and housing and retired IDF Brigadier General Benjamin Ben-Eliezer described the public mood: "Israel's personal security has dropped to zero, making it difficult to move to the next stage of talks with the Palestinians. The people have lost confidence in the process and we look very bad on the ground."[118] This trend was reflected in public opinion polls. A survey conducted by the Dahaf Institute in January 1995 showed that the main issue causing public disappointment with the government's performance (36 percent of respondents) was "the continuation of Arab terrorism."[119] In light of the terrorist attacks that continued to take place in Israel, the public was not optimistic about the future, and they believed that the attacks would continue even if peace agreements were signed with all of the Arab countries. In the peace index survey conducted by Modi'in Ezrahi for the Tami Steinmetz Center for Peace Research in October 1994, 47.5 percent of the respondents said that even in times of peace, terrorism would continue at its current rate or even increase, and 40.9 percent believed that terrorism would decrease but not stop, compared with 7.2 percent who believed that terrorism would come to a halt.

The direct impact of the scope of terrorism on the degree of public support for the peace process stemmed not only from the sense that the process was not fulfilling its main aspiration—preventing terror and strengthening personal security—but, beyond that, from the Israeli public's belief that Arafat was duplicitous and did nothing at all to fight terrorism, never mind not doing everything within his efforts. Of the survey's respondents, 67.3 percent said they believed that the Palestinian Authority made no effort, or hardly any, to prevent terrorism; 31.1 percent believed that the PA was making a degree of effort to prevent terror; and only 1 percent thought it was making a great effort.[120]

Yitzhak Rabin saw the erosion of public support for his policy as a temporary setback, characteristic of the stage at which the process stood, but by his assessment, the public's sense of security would change in the future and, with it, support for his policy. In September 1995, Rabin said,

> Among the claims made against the government, the public's main complaint is the fear for their personal security. The issue of Israeli control over the territories is less important for the majority of the public. We have an interest in reaching an agreement that will ensure the security of Israelis wherever they live.[121]

Rabin did not ignore the public's feelings of anxiety and even saw them as a sign of the ongoing erosion of the resilience of Israelis in general and with regard to terrorism in particular. But his conclusion was the opposite of what the public demanded: not to delay or halt the peace process but to accelerate it. Efraim Inbar maintained that Rabin, like other leaders, felt that Israeli society was showing signs of fatigue and was less and less prepared to bear the consequences of the long war with the Arabs. Israelis, in Rabin's estimation, had lost some of their determination and strength; this assessment that Israeli society had gone soft, in Rabin's mind, hastened the need to successfully complete the peace process.[122]

On November 5, 1995, at the end of a pro-peace demonstration in Tel Aviv, Prime Minister Rabin was assassinated by a Jewish Israeli terrorist who opposed the peace process with the Palestinians. Shimon Peres was appointed as his successor and led the government until the elections that were held in June 1996.

The most striking expression of the moral-psychological impact of terrorism on political events and processes in the period under review actually came at the end of this era, with the political upheaval in the Knesset elections. A few months before the elections, public support for the right-wing parties reached an all-time low following Rabin's assassination. However, this trend shifted and even reversed altogether after the renewal of suicide bombings in February-March 1996. An analysis of public opinion polls and voting patterns shows that compared with of all the other election campaigns—in which terrorism and counterterrorism policy also influenced voting trends—in the 1996 elections, the issue of terrorism during the peace process was the decisive factor that led to a political upheaval.[123]

THE YITZHAK RABIN ADMINISTRATION'S COUNTERTERRORISM POLICY IN LIGHT OF THE COUNTERTERRORISM DILEMMAS MODEL

Two administrations governed Israel during the period under discussion, the main one being that of Yitzhak Rabin, and the second of Shimon Peres, which served for a short time following Rabin's assassination but which did not succeed in winning the next elections. In many respects, the Rabin government's security and diplomatic policies differed from, and even stood in direct opposition to, that of its predecessor, Yitzhak Shamir. Rabin came to power on the promise that in light of the geopolitical changes that followed the intifada and Gulf War, as well as the fruitless negotiations between Israel and the Arab states in Madrid and between Israel and the Palestinians in Washington, Rabin and his government would strive to advance negotiations and peace with the Palestinians. In other words, Rabin assured the public that he would soften Israel's positions in these negotiating channels, but as is so often the case in the Middle East, intention is one thing and reality is another.

Shortly after he was appointed prime minister, Rabin was forced to deal with a shocking terrorist attack in which border police officer Nissim Toledano was kidnapped and murdered. This attack led Rabin to carry out the largest deportation in the history of Israeli counterterrorism; 415 Palestinian terrorist operatives were expelled from the territories into Lebanon. However, this specific event (despite its strategic implications, which led to, among other things, the direct negotiating channel between Israel and the PLO in Oslo), did not typify Israel's counterterrorism policy at the time, which, as mentioned, was characterized by a marked departure from the policies of the previous governments.

More than anything else, the event that distinguished this period and shaped Israeli counterterrorism policy was the direct political process that began between Israel and the PLO in Oslo. From its inception, this process was accompanied by unprecedented waves of terror in Israel and the advent of the new and dangerous phenomenon of suicide bombings carried out in the heart of major Israeli cities by the Palestinian Islamist terrorist organizations that opposed the peace process.

The Rabin administration's counterterrorism policy is reflected in the Counterterrorism Dilemmas Conceptual Model (figure 7.1) as having a tendency toward a more restrained and less efficient, value-driven policy compared with that of other governments. As discussed, the Rabin government came to the strategic decision to give the political process with the Palestinians precedence over any other consideration, in effect making even security considerations a second priority. (This approach was based on the assumption that completion of the peace process with the Palestinians would lead to the decline and perhaps elimination of Palestinian terrorism.) This policy was accompanied by the declaration, "We will fight terrorism as if there is no peace process, and pursue peace as if there is no terrorism." This statement actually had no basis in reality, due to the

Democratic dilemma
Efficiency

Internal
influence
(Less restraint)

External
influence
(Restraint)

Restraint dilemma

Rabin 2

Values

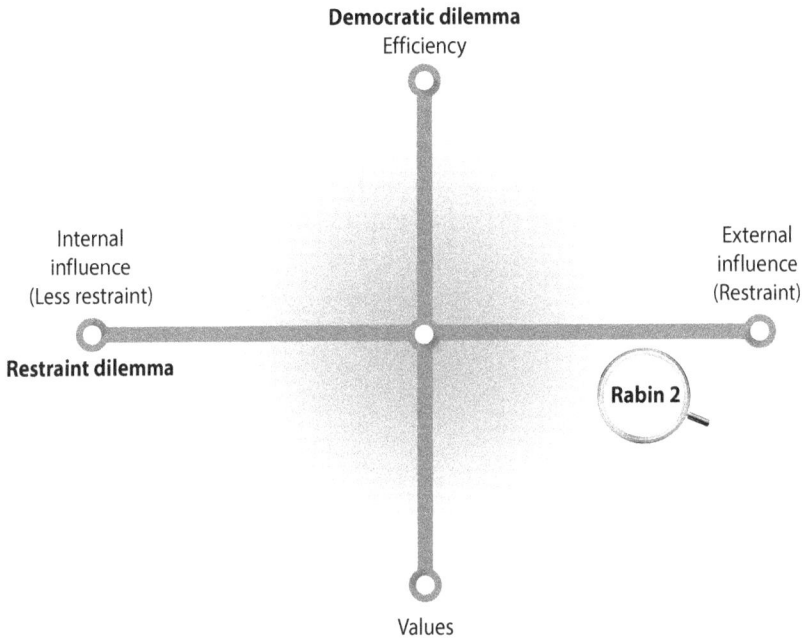

FIGURE 7.1. Counterterrorism Dilemmas Conceptual Model—Rabin administration (1992-96)

constraints that the peace agreements imposed on Israel's counterterrorism activities. The measures that the Israeli government was able to take were primarily defensive and protective, including curfews and closures in the territories that were imposed in the wake of terrorist attacks or on the basis of intelligence information that an attack was about to occur. Israel also acted to bolster the separation barriers between itself and the territories within the Green Line (the 1967 borders) and around the Israeli settlements in the territories.

The policy of the Rabin government received praise and support from the international community, which viewed positively the attempt to finally reach a resolution to the bloody Middle East conflict. On the other hand, the dissonance between the Israeli public's expectation of calm in the wake of the peace process (especially given what Israel perceived as far-reaching concessions: the relinquishing of territory, recognition of the PLO, release of Palestinian terrorists from prison, and more), and the wave of suicide bombings in major Israeli cities that resulted in unprecedented numbers of dead and wounded, brought heavy pressure on the government to do everything possible to restore security in the streets. Harsh criticism from the right-wing, Likud-led opposition and the sense among those who opposed the peace process that the government and its leaders were detached from their concerns brought political tension in Israel to a peak that eventually led to the assassination of the prime minister on November 4, 1995.

A PRIME MINISTER'S ASSASSINATION AND SHIFTING COUNTERTERRORISM STRATEGIES

The Benjamin Netanyahu Administration (1996-99)

THE FUTURE OF THE PEACE PLAN

Following the June 1996 Israeli elections and the Likud's rise to power, and in light of the right's declared opposition to the Oslo Accords and negotiations with the PLO headed by Arafat, the main question troubling the Palestinians, the countries of the region, the international community, and many Israelis was what the policy of the new government would be with regard to the peace process. Representatives of the Arab states and the Palestinian Authority met in Cairo for discussions on June 21, 1996, immediately after the elections, and declared that the new Israeli government must honor all commitments to the PA or its relations with Arab states would suffer.[1] And even U.S. officials were scared that Netanyahu "would not prove eager to make peace."[2] Netanyahu was aware of the need to reassure the public and the international community. Immediately after the elections, he reiterated his commitment to the agreements that had been signed by previous governments. In the speech presenting his government to the Knesset on June 18, Netanyahu stressed, "I want to call today to our neighbors in the Palestinian Authority and say to them: on the basis of ensuring security, we are ready to start a real partnership with you for peace, cooperation and good, neighborly relations."[3] In this speech and his address to the U.S. Congress a few days later, Netanyahu also chose to emphasize that the Israeli-Palestinian conflict did not reflect an inter-religious conflict between Judaism and Islam, and that he saw a need for dialogue with the other countries and people of the Middle East.[4] However, along with his reassuring messages immediately after his rise to power, Netanyahu repeatedly emphasized the different approach, compared with that of his predecessor, that his government would take with regard to the peace process. This approach made attaining the immediate and tangible security of Israeli citizens the government's primary goal, from which its policy regarding the peace process would be derived. In his Knesset speech, Netanyahu declared,

> The essence of peace agreements is first and foremost security, and we will not compromise on the security of Israel's citizens. . . . We will have to wage a continuous battle against terror. . . . The participants in terror should know that they will encounter a harsh response. I refer not only to the terrorists themselves but to their patrons and dispatchers, their operators and collaborators.[5]

When Netanyahu began his term as prime minister, he placed terrorism at the heart of his political agenda, as he had during his time in the opposition and throughout the election campaign, and built his policy on the relationship with the Palestinians accordingly. If the Rabin government's policy could be summed up with the sentence "fight terrorism as if there is no peace process; pursue peace as if there is no terrorism,"[6] Netanyahu's policy at the beginning of his term could be described as making peace only if there is no terror, and fighting terror as if there is no peace.

In his speech to the two houses of the U.S. Congress, Netanyahu emphasized in illustrative terms the need to test the thwarting of terrorism in order to advance the peace process:

> What we are saying here today is as simple as it is elementary. Peace means the absence of violence. Peace means not fearing for your children every time they board a bus. Peace means walking the streets of your town without the fearful shriek of Katyusha rockets overhead. . . .
>
> Peace without personal safety is a contradiction in terms. It is a hoax. It will not stand. . . . This means that our negotiating partners, and indeed all the regimes of the region, must make a strategic choice: either follow

the option of terror as an instrument of policy, of diplomacy, or follow the option of peace. They cannot have it both ways. This choice means that the Palestinian Authority must live up to the obligations it has solemnly undertaken to prevent terrorist attacks against Israel. . . . This means that the fight against terror cannot be episodic. It cannot be conditional. It must become the mainstay of a relationship of trust between Israel and its Arab partners.[7]

Two months later, Netanyahu added,

We demand actions, not just statements. Take, for example, the foolish notion of the previous government that the peace process should continue as if there is no terror and that terror should be fought as if there is no peace process. Our policy is very clear: If there is terrorism we will not continue the diplomatic process. And not only will it not be continued, but we also reserve the right to respond in other ways. These things must be said time after time, until Arafat understands them.[8]

The prime minister was soon forced to substantiate his declarations and try to develop a new policy that would encourage the Palestinian Authority to deter attacks in Israel but that at the same time would not halt the peace process and a lead to a dangerous deterioration into violence in the region. Netanyahu's first test regarding the Palestinians was approaching the question of meeting with Arafat. Netanyahu did everything in his power to postpone the meeting, though he knew that he could not avoid it. He sent Arafat emissaries from various levels within the Israeli government and evaded any request by Arafat, the United States, and others to hold the meeting. Nevertheless, during his first meeting with Egyptian president Hosni Mubarak on July 18, 1996, Netanyahu said that he was aware that "Arafat is my partner for the next four years. I have no other partner."[9]

However, all efforts to hold a meeting between Netanyahu and Arafat failed. For example, when Terje Rød-Larsen, the Norwegian emissary who was close to Arafat, told Netanyahu that Arafat was eager to meet him and that in exchange for his consent to the meeting, Netanyahu could achieve a number of goals, the prime minister replied that the time was not yet ripe for a direct meeting.[10] After some time passed, the Israeli government said it was prepared to hold a first meeting in secret, away from the media spotlight, but Arafat insisted that the meeting be public and refused to hold it on Israeli territory.[11] Not until September 4, 1996, after Arafat acceded to Netanyahu's demand that he apologize for the scathing statements made in the Palestinian press comparing Netanyahu with Hitler, did the first meeting between Netanyahu and Arafat finally take place at the Erez checkpoint.[12] Despite a joint communiqué summarizing the meeting, no breakthrough was achieved between Israel and the Palestinians, nor was there a breaking down of the personal barriers between Netanyahu and Arafat. It was a brief late-night meeting that produced no result beyond the value of the encounter itself.

A few days after the meeting at the Erez checkpoint, Netanyahu was asked in a newspaper interview, "Do you still see Arafat as someone who wants to destroy Israel?" He replied,

> I cannot see what cannot be seen, I cannot see his heart's intentions. . . . I can only see what he is doing. He has only recently begun to work hard against terrorism. . . . He has not yet dismantled the infrastructure of these organizations. He is still releasing prisoners who should not be released. There are things that he must do. . . . My approach toward Arafat is practical, first and foremost: if he carries out his commitments, we will carry out our commitments. The test is still open. We follow this process closely. This principle of reciprocity differentiates us from the previous government.[13]

Thus, Netanyahu laid out one of the basic principles of his policy toward the Palestinians, the principle of reciprocity. The election slogan that helped bring Netanyahu to power, "if they give, they will receive, if they do not give, they will not receive," has become a foundation of Israeli policy toward the Palestinians.[14] The "giving" was measured mainly in terms of prevention of terrorist attacks against Israel.

In the first months of the Likud government, it seemed that the Palestinians were careful not to give Netanyahu an excuse, in the form of a major attack in Israel, that would allow him to halt the peace process and perhaps even refrain from carrying out the previous government's commitments.[15] Netanyahu made every effort to convey threatening messages to the Palestinian public—and especially to the PA—that he intended to take a heavy hand in both the diplomatic and military sphere should terrorist attacks in Israel be renewed. In light of these warnings, and true to his worldview regarding the war on terror, the prime minister instructed the

Israeli security establishment to reexamine Israel's defense doctrine in the field of counterterrorism. He instructed the heads of the ISA and Mossad to be more proactive with regard to their organizations' counterterrorism activities.[16]

However, it soon appeared that Israel's tough stance toward Arafat and the PA was likely to provoke an outbreak of Palestinian violence. A few months into establishment of the Netanyahu government, no progress had been made, even only for appearance's sake, in the diplomatic process between Israel and the Palestinians. The prime minister's emissaries did meet with Palestinian representatives, but the latter's demands that Israel accept its proposed dates for the implementation of the commitment to redeploy in Hebron, release Palestinian prisoners, and operate a safe passage between Gaza and the West Bank (commitments that had been made by the previous government but not yet carried out) were refused.

The continued restrictions imposed on the entry of Palestinians into Israel also aggravated the general situation in the territories; Arafat expressed his frustration with threats to request international arbitration. Security sources warned the prime minister that Arafat's power in the territories was weakening due to the economic situation there and lack of progress in the peace process. The Israeli public also expressed a lack of confidence in the seriousness of the government's intentions to advance the peace process. In the peace index, a public opinion poll conducted by the Tami Steinmetz Center at Tel Aviv University at the end of August 1996, 47.7 percent of respondents believed that Israel was not fulfilling its promises to the Palestinians (a month earlier it had been only 33.3 percent). The survey also found that 37.6 percent of respondents believed that negotiations with the Palestinians were proceeding too slowly, and 24.1 percent thought that they had stopped.[17]

OPENING OF THE WESTERN WALL TUNNELS

Fire was imminent, and the spark that lit it was the opening of the Western Wall tunnel. On the last night of the Yom Kippur holiday, September 24, 1996, the government ordered the opening of the wall that blocked the ancient tunnel under the Western Wall to allow worshipers and tourists to visit. The tunnel opening led to riots by young Palestinians, first in Jerusalem and later in the West Bank. The PA made no effort to stop the riots, and

Palestinian police officers soon joined the rioters and fired their weapons at IDF soldiers. Exchanges of fire ensued for several days and claimed the lives of sixteen soldiers.

The sense of crisis that accompanied these difficult events in the territories cast doubt on continuation of the entire peace process. The Israeli government blamed the riots and escalation of the situation on the ground on the PA and its leader, Yasser Arafat. The government rejected Arafat's claim that he had not initiated the events and had no control over what was happening. The assessment was that the events in the territories were aimed at creating international, primarily American, pressure on Israel to speed up redeployment in Hebron and negotiations with the Palestinians over the next withdrawals from areas controlled by the IDF in the West Bank.[18] Netanyahu told Arafat in a telephone conversation during the crisis, "You will not see political fruits from this affair, and if you continue with the incitement of the Palestinian street, the entire process is liable to collapse."[19]

The outbreak of Palestinian violence did not occur in a vacuum. Palestinians understood that the new Israeli government would not advance the peace process amid violence and terror; in this regard, Netanyahu's message was comprehended. However, after three months of tense anticipation, during which terrorist attacks were deterred, the lack of progress in Israeli contact led the Palestinians to believe that the Netanyahu government had made up its mind not to advance the process in any case and that the terrorist attacks merely served as an excuse. Under these conditions, it was only a matter of time before violence was used against Israel, and the opening of the Western Wall tunnel provided a suitable pretext. Shortly after the outbreak of the riots, Arafat managed to reverse the situation, and instead of chasing Netanyahu and being rejected, he turned his back on the prime minister and stopped responding to the many Israeli inquiries he received.[20]

At the beginning of October 1996, the prime minister appeared on television and radio broadcasts and addressed Palestinian viewers and listeners directly, in Arabic, with a call to cease the violence and hostility and allow for the possibility of achieving peace.

> You are not dealing with someone who wishes to stop the peace process, but rather with someone who truly wishes to advance, along with you, while holding in mutual respect this peace, which is the hope and salvation of both

people. . . . If we fight and return to the blood-filled riots, we will both be los-
ers. If we walk together in the peace process, abiding by the saying "no more
war, no more bloodshed," then we will both be winners. I am convinced that
we can overcome the animosity, triumph over the violence, achieve peace.
This is my hope and my prayer for both Jews and Arabs. . . . Therefore, I am
asking you, don't lose hope.[21]

The Western Wall tunnel events ended in early October 1996 when the
Americans invited Arafat and Netanyahu to Washington, D.C., for diplomatic talks. At the meeting, it was decided to end the violence and quickly
return to negotiations. Netanyahu understood the problematic nature of
reaching diplomatic agreements and understandings in the wake of violent events (especially as such agreements had not been reached prior to
the outbreak of violence in the territories). Referring to the discussions in
Washington, Netanyahu said, "The whole world is watching us very closely,
and the degree of pressure on us is the same as the degree to which we
ourselves feel pressured. . . . What is important is that the Palestinians have
failed in their attempt to reap political gains from the tunnel crisis."[22]

That was not the way the Palestinians saw it. In a public opinion poll
conducted on the eve of the Washington summit, 58 percent of West Bank
residents said they believed that the PA would achieve much politically as
a result of the recent events in the West Bank and Gaza Strip, 53 percent
believed that Arafat's status had been strengthened following these events,
and 62 percent felt that the reason the riots had broken out was that Palestinians were disappointed with the results of the peace process and the
arrogance of the Israeli government. In that survey, 83 percent said they
believed that Israel was not working seriously toward peace, and 53 percent
supported the renewal of terrorist attacks against Israel (compared with 24
percent who had supported terrorist attacks a month earlier).[23]

Indeed, at the end of the summit in Washington, it was decided to vigorously pursue diplomatic action, including implementation of the commitment to redeploy in Hebron. The outcome of the summit reinforced the
sense that Palestinian violence was useful in advancing Palestinians' political interests. However, Israeli decision makers felt otherwise. Whether or
not the Israeli government achieved anything from the Western Wall incidents, the first diplomatic challenge it had to deal with in the Palestinian arena was the Hebron Agreement. Netanyahu found himself trapped

between his commitment to honor the agreements signed by the previous government and demands by his electorate to stop the withdrawal from Hebron. Netanyahu sought and found a way to market the Israeli withdrawal from Hebron to his constituents, saying that Israel was not disengaging from Hebron, merely redeploying. He added that he was working "to preserve the lives of the Jews of Hebron and our continued hold on our holy places in the city."[24]

RESURGENCE OF VIOLENCE

After the Washington summit, and in the wake of the Western Wall tunnel incidents, Israeli delegations began negotiations with their Palestinian counterparts out of fear of a renewed outbreak of riots in the territories.[25] In early 1997, after an IDF soldier opened fire at Gross Square in Hebron and wounded seven Palestinians before being stopped by his comrades, Israel and the Palestinians reached an agreement on the new redeployment in Hebron. The first agreement between the Likud government and the Palestinian Authority was approved by the government on January 15, 1997. It established the principle of reciprocity in the obligations of both parties. The Palestinians undertook to complete the amendment of the Palestinian National Charter in a manner that would recognize Israel's existence, take practical steps to combat terrorism and prevent incitement, collect illegal weapons, reduce the size of the Palestinian police force, and refrain from governmental activity in areas controlled by Israel.[26] In late January 1997, after signing the amended Hebron Agreement, Israel completed the redeployment of its forces in Hebron.

For a brief time, it seemed as if the peace process was on track and that all of the disputes between the sides would be resolved. But shortly after redeployment in Hebron was completed, the peace process again came to a standstill. The Israeli government decided in February 1997 to build a residential Jewish neighborhood in Har Homa on the outskirts of Jerusalem, which aroused the wrath of the Palestinians. At the same time, the Israeli position maintained that in the first phase of further redeployments, Israel would not withdraw from more than 7.1 percent of Area B (territories under Israeli security control) and approximately 2 percent of Area C (territories under exclusive Israeli control).[27] This position was based on a letter of agreement from U.S. secretary of state Warren Christopher that Israel would decide the pace of further redeployments on its own.[28] The Palestinians threatened that construction at Har Homa would provoke a violent response, and, indeed, immediately after work began on the project in March 1997, riots broke out in the territories. In reference to the new outbreak of violence, Netanyahu emphasized the need to take a tough stance regarding sovereignty over Jerusalem and its environs: "If you give in once, there is no end to it. If we give in on Jerusalem, what will we not give in on? We have to think about the overall national account. If we do not face down threats, this process will chase us to the Green Line and beyond."[29]

In light of the construction at Har Homa, the halt in the peace process, and the outbreak of violence in the territories, Israeli security sources warned that Arafat had given a green light to terrorist organizations for attacks in Israel. These sources explained that this green light was not a direct order to carry out attacks but, rather, expressed in indirect messages that were inferred from speeches or actions (such as the release of prisoners from these organizations). The prime minister explained it as follows.

> There were discussions between Hamas and the Palestinian Authority, and also between Islamic Jihad and the Palestinian Authority. These organizations interpreted what was said to them as a green light. . . . Secondly, there were releases of key operatives . . . among them the head of Hamas's military wing.

Netanyahu added a warning to the Palestinians:

> We certainly cannot continue the process . . . under a campaign of terror. I distinguish between terrorist attacks that cannot be controlled and those that are orchestrated. We do not expect the result to be 100 percent, but that the effort be 100 percent. But when the Palestinian Authority opens the gates of the prison and releases terrorist leaders who themselves declare that they intend to renew the terrorist attacks, it is clear that we will consider the PA responsible for the attacks that such people carry out, and we will respond accordingly.[30]

Netanyahu thereby adopted the position of the previous government. Despite his seemingly tough stance toward the Palestinians regarding terrorist attacks in Israel, he left Arafat with an outlet to evade responsibility for the attacks by returning to the use of the scale of "effort" to prevent terror rather than success in thwarting attacks. Netanyahu tried to prevent attacks by renewing contact with Arafat, but Arafat again chose to ignore Netanyahu's calls.

Netanyahu even complemented his efforts with unilateral gestures toward Arafat and the Palestinian Authority. For example, he was willing to allow Arafat's plane to take off from and land in Dahaniya airport[31] (even though a month and a half earlier, cartons of arms and ammunition smuggled from Egypt had been discovered in Arafat's helicopter), and he declared that at that stage, Israel was already prepared to open direct final status negotiations.[32] On March 21, 1997, only days after these gestures, a Hamas suicide bomber blew himself up at Café Apropo in Tel Aviv. Three women were killed and forty-seven people were wounded.[33] The previous day, Arafat had rejected the offer to hold permanent status talks, claiming that it was a trick by Netanyahu.[34] Arafat also would not accept the Israeli gesture that allowed him to fly freely to and from Dahaniya airport.

In the wake of the attack at Apropo, an open dispute emerged between Israeli and Palestinian security officials regarding the extent of the PA's responsibility for terrorist attacks. Discussing the suicide bombing, then head of Military Intelligence, Major General Moshe Ya'alon, made the following statement:

> The understanding was reached over the past few days, after a series of meetings between the heads of the terrorist organizations and Arafat, after Arafat returned from the United States. There is no doubt that they understand that times have changed. Up until that point, they had understood that they were forbidden from carrying out terrorist attacks. It had been clear to Hamas that if it executed an attack, it was liable to clash with the Palestinian Authority. . . . The PA has the ability to deal with terrorist organizations, as they did in February and March of last year, but for this to happen, an order from Arafat is required, and such a directive has not yet been given.[35]

Ya'alon also claimed that for the first time, terrorism was being carried out with the approval of the Palestinian Authority.[36] In contrast, Muhammad Dahlan, head of the Palestinian security service in Gaza, blamed the situation on the Israeli government and attributed the escalation to its decision to build at Har Homa and the limited extent of the first stage of withdrawals.

Dahlan expressed bitterness over what he saw as Israel's lack of gratitude for the decisive steps taken by the PA in its fight against terrorism.

> We carried out arrests of Hamas leaders and immediately complied with every Israeli demand in the realm of security. But the Israeli government was not satisfied, even when we prevented dozens of terrorist attacks in Hebron and the Gaza Strip. And then we hear that Arafat is the one sending people to carry out suicide bombings. . . . It is impossible to prevent every suicide bomber from blowing himself up in Israel. To this day, we have made efforts to prevent this, but from now on we will no longer do so.[37]

Jibril Rajoub, head of the Palestinian security services in the West Bank, also came to Arafat's defense, saying, "I personally attended a meeting in Gaza on March 9 with Hamas and the opposition organizations, and I tell you that there was almost complete consensus that terrorist attacks harm the Palestinian Authority, and do not help achieve our political goal."[38]

Rajoub noted that at this meeting, it was decided not to embarrass the Palestinian Authority. The phrase "embarrass the Palestinian Authority" was reserved only for terrorist attacks carried out in Area A (the territory that, under the agreements, was transferred to the PA's exclusive control) or attacks whose perpetrators set out directly from this area. In other words, attacks that did not embarrass the PA—that is, those carried out in Areas B and C (under Israeli security control) and in Israel proper—were not prohibited by the meeting's participants. Approximately one year later, in an interview on Al-Jazeera TV, Rajoub said in reference to the Hamas attacks that "aside from the 3 percent of the West Bank under full Palestinian control, they can do what they want. . . . My top priority is the Israeli occupation, not Hamas. . . . We are not interested in making arrests."[39] Rajoub also noted,

> You know very well that Kafr Tzurif [where the cell behind the Café Apropo attack in March 1997 came from—BG] is not under the control of the Palestinian Authority. And not every Hamas adherent is under the control of the moderate leadership of Hamas.[40]

As part of the Palestinian effort to pressure Israeli decision-makers to halt construction at Har Homa and adopt a more flexible stance toward the Palestinians, the Palestinians stopped their security cooperation with Israel.[41]

The Palestinians, in effect deliberately causing an escalation, were expressing their disappointment and anger over the Israeli government's unwillingness to transfer territory to them within the framework of the next round of redeployments and to advance the peace process in general. The danger of slipping into uncontrolled violence was becoming palpable. If, in the days of the Rabin government, the PA had no interest in stopping the attacks (given that, according to the government's policy, the attacks did not jeopardize the progress of the peace process, and sometimes even hastened it), the Netanyahu government's policy also created a situation in which the PA had no interest in thwarting terrorism and expressions of violence against Israel.

AMERICAN INVOLVEMENT IN THE PEACE PROCESS

The Rabin government determined that the terrorist attacks would not stop the peace process, but the Netanyahu government gave the opposite impression, that the peace process would not advance even in the absence of terrorist attacks. This feeling was especially dangerous because it meant that the attacks did not endanger Palestinian national interests, which were not being achieved in any case. However, the expected deterioration and outbreak of terrorist attacks did not take place, because the Palestinians' loss of faith in the Israeli government, along with their ability to advance their national interests by violent means, coincided with the development of a new Palestinian national interest alongside the two existing ones (the removal of Israel from the territories and the establishment of a Palestinian state). This new Palestinian national interest was the establishment of strategic ties between U.S. president Bill Clinton, the American administration, and the CIA and Arafat and the PA's security services. During his visits to the United States, Arafat was given the status of both a head of state and an ally, as were his security chiefs and senior Palestinian officials, who cooperated with their American counterparts. They soon realized that a wave of terrorist attacks in Israel could jeopardize these evolving strategic ties with the Americans.[42] The Clinton administration thus filled the void left by the Netanyahu government in its relations with the Palestinians.

The extent of the United States's growing importance in the Israeli-Palestinian arena can be understood from the address of the head of the Counter-Terrorism Bureau at the time, Major General Meir Dagan. At a conference of the International Institute for Counter-Terrorism (ICT) at the Interdisciplinary Center (IDC) Herzliya in March 1997, Dagan said,

> Only heavy pressure by Israeli and international elements on the Palestinian Authority may motivate the PA chairman . . . to fight resolutely and persistently against terrorism. When I refer to international elements, I'm talking mainly about the United States. In my opinion, the price of using terror has not yet been made clear to the Palestinian Authority. It must be made clear to the PA that it is endangering its political achievements and perhaps even threatening its very survival.[43]

Military intelligence head Ya'alon also explained the limited actions by the Palestinian Authority against fundamentalist organizations within the framework of its relations with the Americans, saying, "The cooperation today is meant only to win points with the American arbitrator . . . but I do not see a Palestinian Authority war on terrorist infrastructure. On this issue, like on other issues, the Americans are trying to win over Arafat out of their interest in continuing the peace process."[44]

Although the United States refrained from taking a critical stance against the Palestinians, which was liable to endanger continuation of the peace process, U.S. secretary of state Madeleine Albright did made it clear that the United States expected the PA to make increased efforts to prevent attacks. "We attach great importance to Arafat giving a red light to terrorist activities. . . . Arafat must make a 100 percent effort to try to stop the violence," she said.[45]

American involvement was not only in areas that were visible for all to see but also in a complex network of intelligence ties developed by the Americans with the security forces of both sides under the direction of the CIA. As the intelligence arm of the United States, the CIA was called on to act as a side observer to oversee fulfillment of the obligations of both sides in the framework of the signed agreements. However, the CIA quickly found itself evolving from an outside observer to a player involved in deterring terrorism, initiating and directing the two sides (especially the Palestinians) regarding the actions necessary for preventing terrorism based on existing intelligence information. (In this context, in March 1996, immediately after the Sharm el-Sheikh summit, a system of coordination between American intelligence and the three security forces led by the CIA also provided courses for Palestinian security personnel, trained them, and assisted in providing appropriate equipment for their missions.)

At a later stage, the CIA became a vital link between the two sides. When there was a rupture, or sometimes even a complete split, between the intelligence and security apparatuses on each side (due to political disputes or delays in implementation of the agreements), a link was necessary to act as a two-way pipeline to convey security and intelligence communications. The existence of this link made intelligence cooperation easier for the Palestinians, because they did not perceive the exchange of information and assessments with the Americans as cooperation with Israel. For example, immediately after the attack at Café Apropo in Tel Aviv, CIA representatives in the region quickly reached the Palestinians, and in a meeting held in March 1997 with security officials in Gaza, they demanded that the Palestinians prevent a reversion to violence against Israel. The CIA also established an independent intelligence apparatus in the autonomous Palestinian territories, in an attempt to obtain early information on terrorist attacks and thwart them before they took place. The Americans reached an agreement with Arafat on the establishment of an American veto mechanism that would ensure that Palestinians arrested or imprisoned by the PA for security offenses would be released only following American approval, but this mechanism did not actually function.[46]

STALLED PEACE PROCESS

Despite American mediation efforts, the peace process did not get back on track. Netanyahu tried to minimize as much as possible the amount of territory that would be transferred to Palestinian control in the framework of the next agreement. He tried to divert the main effort from reaching additional interim agreements to going directly to a final status agreement. In this context, Netanyahu proposed a plan whereby at the end of the process, Israel would continue to control greater Jerusalem and the Etzion Bloc, the Jordan Valley and its water sources, the areas along both sides of the "seam zone," and major settlement blocs in the West Bank and their access routes.[47] Arafat refused to discuss the final status agreement at this stage and in the framework of the next midterm agreement, demanded an increase in the size of the area that would be transferred to his control. Arafat also warned that "there is a limit to the Palestinians' patience," and that "feelings of despair lead to acts of despair."[48]

Arafat's warning reflected the strategy of exploiting violence to advance diplomatic goals; indeed, such an "act of despair" was not long in coming. On the night of July 14, security forces arrested a cell of three Palestinian terrorists on their way to launch an attack in the settlement of Har Bracha, near Nablus. It soon became apparent that the men, who had been involved in shooting attacks only a few days earlier, were Palestinian police officers who had been sent on their mission by their commanders in the Palestinian police with the knowledge of the police chief, Ghazi Jabali.[49]

Despite the revelation of a direct link between the PA chairman and terrorist attacks, only a few days later, ISA head Ami Ayalon went to a meeting with Arafat. Afterward, Israeli newspapers published headlines such as "The Israeli ISA warns: Arafat is losing control of his people." This was a concrete expression of the approach that had prevailed in the ISA since the Oslo Accords, one that stemmed from erosion of the agency's intelligence-gathering capabilities following the IDF's withdrawal from Palestinian cities in the territories, the dependence it developed on its Palestinian counterparts, and counter-espionage measures taken by Palestinian intelligence to expose ISA sources. The prime minister tried to reiterate the rules of the game, that violence harmed the peace process, but he quickly discovered that his threats carried no weight, because the Palestinians already believed that the peace process was stalled and that the Israeli government did not intend to advance it. Moreover, from the Western Wall tunnel incidents, Arafat had learned that his only chance of advancing the process was to use violence to pressure Israeli decision makers. Military intelligence head Ya'alon claimed,

The lesson that Arafat learned from the events of September is that, at this stage at least, he is not at risk. Even in the current crisis [Har Homa] he does not feel threatened. From his perspective, he achieved something in the September events. It was clear to the world that Arafat initiated the violent crisis, and despite this, he didn't pay anything for it. So he also opted for a violent move now, in the wake of the Har Homa events.[50]

In August 1997, a suicide bombing was carried out in the Mahane Yehuda market in Jerusalem. After the attack, the PA tried to evade responsibility for it, claiming that the terrorists had come to Israel from Lebanon or Syria, and certainly not from the area under its control.[51] The Israeli government did not accept the PA's claims and placed direct responsibility for the attack on its shoulders. The security cabinet convened in Jerusalem for an emergency session, during which it was decided to initiate action against the terrorist organizations. Thus, the signal was given to plan an operation to kill the head of Hamas's political arm, Khaled Mashal, who operated from Amman, several months later.[52] At the cabinet meeting, proposals were made to step up activity against the Palestinians, including the use of helicopter gunships against Hamas targets in the territories, but these were rejected at the recommendation of the prime minister and defense minister. It appeared that Netanyahu the opposition leader, who claimed that Israel should take the initiative when it came to counterterrorism activities, lost out to Netanyahu the leader, who recognized that under the conditions that had been created, the burden lay with the Palestinian Authority. The defense minister said, "We will continue to fight terror with all the means at our disposal—diplomatic, economic, organizational and military—and we will exert pressure on the Palestinian Authority to use all the means at its disposal against terror."[53]

At the same time, the prime minister instructed the heads of the defense establishment to perform the administrative work that would enable the creation of a barrier between Palestinians in the territories and Israel by increasing Israeli control over border crossings. Within a few days, however, the security services, led by the ISA, began to criticize the policy adopted by Israel. In an August 3 security briefing to the government, Ami Avalon stated that the "Palestinian Authority is not doing enough to deal with terrorist infrastructure. There is a lot less anger among the Palestinian public toward the perpetrators of terrorist attacks than there was during the wave of attacks last year."[54] During this briefing, criticism was subtly expressed that Israel's actions were only fanning the flames of hatred on the Palestinian street and, as a result, increasing Palestinian support for terrorism. The officials added that if the Israeli government continued to punish the Palestinian Authority, the PA would collapse, organizationally and economically, within a matter of weeks.[55]

For its part, at that time, the Palestinian Authority was working on unifying the Palestinians, and on August 20 it convened the National Unity Congress in cooperation with Hamas and Palestinian Islamic Jihad, with the goal of "facing up to the challenges facing the Palestinians."[56] Major General Ya'alon interpreted the rapprochement between the PA and the fundamentalist organizations as an attempt to create a threat of seemingly spontaneous and popular violence against Israel. He added, "Yasser Arafat did not give up, even for one day, terrorism and violence as a legitimate means of achieving Palestinian national goals, even though he signed the Oslo Accords."[57]

The violence that security officials had voiced materialized only a few days later. On September 4, three Hamas suicide bombers blew themselves up on the Ben Yehuda pedestrian mall in Jerusalem. Five people were killed and 166 were wounded.[58] U.S. secretary of state Madeleine Albright arrived in Israel a few days after the attack. Her visit brought the conflict between Israel and the United States to a peak after Netanyahu reprimanded Albright for demanding that Israel issue a time-out in settlement activity. However, despite the attacks, most Israelis continued to support the Oslo process. In a Gallup poll published about a week after the attack, 47 percent of respondents said they supported the continuation of the peace process, and 33 percent opposed it; 42 percent thought that Netanyahu intended to continue the Oslo process (vs. 38 percent who did not), but the majority of the public (55 percent) were not satisfied with Netanyahu's policy (as opposed to 40 percent who were).[59]

Toward the end of September 1997, it appeared that Israeli-American pressure exerted on Arafat was beginning to bear fruit. The PA began arresting activists of fundamentalist Islamic organizations. Palestinian intelligence and police forces raided the offices of charitable institutions in the Gaza Strip and ordered their closure. This operation began at the Islamic Society Institute and took place in front of the television cameras of international networks. As a result of these measures, the Israeli government decided to release funds intended for the Palestinians that had been frozen, but the government stressed that these measures should be consistent and long term.[60] The Palestinian news agency accompanied the PA's steps with the announcement that "from today, there will be no place for those who are trying to harm the national goals that we have set for ourselves, no matter how much support they receive from the public."[61]

THE MASHAL AFFAIR

This period was marked by an increase in measures against terror actors, including the use of targeted killings by Israel. One of the most prominent targeted killings during this period was one that failed, with Israel's responsibility for the botched operation publicly revealed. This was the attempt to kill Khaled Mashal, head of Hamas's political bureau. An examination of this affair reveals many details regarding the characteristics of the killings carried out by Israel, decision-making processes, and preparation and execution of such actions.

During the operation, planned for September 25, 1997, in Amman, a cell of Mossad agents intended to kill Mashal by injecting him with poison. The killing was thwarted after his personal driver and security guard intervened. The security guard stopped a passing car and began pursuing the agents, who did not notice that he was following them. After about three hundred meters, the Mossad agents stopped the car and got out. The security guard followed and accosted them and, with the help of a plainclothes police officer who was on the scene, managed to overcome and arrest them. When Israel learned of the agents' arrest, the head of the Mossad went to Jordan with an antidote to treat Mashal. In the negotiations with Jordan, it was agreed that the agents would be released in exchange for the release of Hamas's leader, Sheikh Yassin, and a number of other detainees.[62]

The swap between Israel and Jordan in the wake of the Mashal affair consisted of three stages. In the first stage, on October 5, 1997, Sheikh Yassin was released to Jordan. Two days later, the second stage involved transferring Yassin from Jordan to Gaza, along with twenty other prisoners who were released (nine of them, Jordanian nationals, were transferred to Jordan, and another eleven were transferred to the Palestinian Authority). On October 13, the third stage was carried out with the release and transfer to Jordan of eight terrorists and a prisoner convicted of a federal offense.

Ronen Bergman argues in *Rise and Kill First* that blundered operations such as the Mashal affair are discussed as acts that served to "enhance the Mossad's aggressive and merciless reputation," which is a positive thing "when the goal of deterrence is as important as the goal of preempting specific hostile acts."[63] When news of the botched operation became public, Israelis began asking tough questions. They wondered why had it been decided to strike Khaled Mashal, who, on the face of it, was a political activist in Hamas. Why was Jordan the location of the planned killing? Why was the killing attempt carried out at that time? Why was this unusual weapon used? And why did the operation ultimately fail?

Regarding the first question, Israeli security officials and decision makers emphasized that although Khaled Mashal was indeed the head of the political bureau, his hands were not clean when it came to involvement in terrorist activity. From his residence in Jordan, Mashal was involved in instigating numerous terrorist attacks against Israel, organizing with the perpetrators of the attacks, and transferring funds to finance their activities. According to the head of military intelligence,

> Mashal is certainly not "small fry." . . . There is a clear connection between Hamas's political echelon and the terrorist attacks on the ground, even though Khaled Mashal did not personally plan the attack on the pedestrian mall in Ben Yehuda. The political leadership of Hamas, which is based in Jordan outside of the Territories, is who determines the policy of attacks, and at the political level, Khaled Mashal is the first among equals, and certainly not exempt from responsibility.[64]

Netanyahu said, in reference to the choice of Mashal as a target for killing, "I definitely wanted to kill Khaled Mashal. I felt that Jordanian terrorism was a center of the agitation in Judea, Samaria, and Gaza. I wanted to do this regardless of the terrorist attacks."[65] Although Netanyahu tried to downplay the impact of the terrorist attacks on the decision to carry out the killing, former Mossad chief Danny Yatom stated: "It was important for me to stop the series of terrorist attacks when it became known that the orders to carry them out came from Hamas headquarters in Jordan."[66]

Jordan was chosen as the location for the killing due to the fact that Mashal's permanent residence was in Amman. In addition, perhaps it was chosen because of the desire to convey to terrorist operatives that there was nowhere in the world that would serve as a haven for them—that Israel's long arm would reach them anywhere.

Choice of the date of the killing was likely the result of the long planning and preparation processes required preceding such an operation. As mentioned, the decision to kill senior Hamas activists was made at a meeting of the security cabinet that took place shortly after the attack in Mahane Yehuda in Jerusalem in July 1997. The recommendation to kill Mashal came from the Mossad and was approved by Prime Minister Netanyahu. The weapon chosen for this purpose was a syringe that would inject the poison through Mashal's ear. This special method was chosen in order to conceal Israel's fingerprints and make the cause of death appear to be natural causes. Had the operation been executed as planned, Israel's responsibility for the killing would not have been exposed. In fact, it would not have been revealed as a killing at all, and thus no damage would have been caused to Israeli-Jordanian relations. According to the Ciechanover Committee, established on October 6, 1997, to examine the fiasco in Jordan, the mission had been assigned to an elite unit of the Mossad.

The stinging failure in Amman marked the beginning of a process of internal and external critical investigation in Israel, dealing not only with the incident itself and the decision-making process that preceded it but also with management of the crisis following the failure of the operation, exposure of the special methods that had been used and how this information was transmitted to Jordan, how Mashal was treated and his life saved, and exposure of the political echelon's responsibility for the affair. Regarding the decision to give the Jordanians the antidote that would enable them to save Mashal's life, former Mossad chief Danny Yatom explains that, after he learned of the failure of the operation,

> I proposed that I go to Jordan to meet with the king in an attempt to minimize the damage. In fact, the suggestion to offer Jordan an antidote that would bring Mashal back to life was Netanyahu's. . . . Someone said that this was the first time in history that we killed a man and then brought him back to life. It was clear to me that if Mashal survived, the problem between Jordan and us could be solved relatively easily.[67]

The Ciechanover Committee held forty-seven meetings, heard from thirty-five witnesses, and reviewed hundreds of exhibits and documents. The commission held all of its meetings behind closed doors. In the public portion of its report, the commission placed primary blame for the operation's failure on the "conceptual fixation" prevailing in the Mossad at people at the various levels involved in planning, approving, and carrying out the operation, who believed that they had the weapons and methods to ensure an almost completely risk-free "quiet operation" (that is, involving a silent weapon and an immediate result with no discernible damage). This perception of a quiet operation, coupled with the assumption of a minimal chance of failure, hardly took into account the possibility that the operation would fail, for whatever reason, and become "noisy."

Concurrent with the Ciechanover Committee, the Knesset Foreign Affairs and Defense Committee's Subcommittee on Intelligence and Secret Services also began to look into the failure in Amman.[68] The committee held twenty-seven meetings and heard from twenty-eight witnesses. The findings of this committee are highly relevant for the purposes of this book, if only because they determined that for many years, Israeli governments had not formulated a policy to combat terrorist organizations "based on organized thinking and a logical, continuous and consistent line."[69] The commission determined that "in the absence of a systematic approach to counter-terrorism activity, the element of response to attacks has received considerable and detrimental weight." In this regard, the committee criticized the practice of initiating offensive activity, especially after mass-casualty attacks, as opposed to acting on a regular basis or according to actual needs created in the field.[70]

The complications and diplomatic damage in the wake of Mashal's bungled killing attempt went far beyond Israel's relations with Jordan. For example, the Canadian government accused Israel of violating a commitment that it would not use Canadian passports and documents while conducting intelligence missions. Following the revelation that the Mossad agents had been using Canadian passports, the Canadian ambassador to Israel was summoned to his country for consultations.[71]

The Mashal affair clearly illustrates the problematic nature of targeted killings in general, and actions taken in the territory of a foreign country in particular, even more so in an Arab state that is maintaining a sensitive peace agreement with Israel. The case emphasized the need to weigh all possible risks in the event of the worst possible scenario before undertaking any action. On the face of it, in the Mashal case, it appears that the cost component in the cost-benefit analysis was not taken into account sufficiently during the planning of the operation. This, as the Ciechanover Committee found, was due to the overly optimistic assessment of the chances of a quiet operation that would not have Israel's fingerprints on it. Another question regarding the logic behind the decision to specifically target Mashal stemmed from the fact that a few months prior to the assassination attempt, Israel had withdrawn the request it had made to the United

States to extradite Mashal's predecessor, Mussa Abu Marzuk, whom it had arrested and who was about to be extradited to Israel.

THE WYE RIVER AGREEMENT

Throughout 1998, Netanyahu was under intense pressure from the U.S. administration to implement another midterm agreement with the Palestinians, to include withdrawals from more areas in the West Bank. The Americans did not deny Israel's right to unilaterally determine the extent of Israel's withdrawal from the territories, in accordance with an early agreement between Israel and the United States, but they argued that it would be inconceivable that the withdrawal be less than 10 percent. The Palestinians, who recognized this shift in the American position from supporting Israel's stance to taking on the role of an objective mediator exerting pressure on both sides, wanted to demonstrate to the Americans that they were fulfilling their obligations and working to prevent violence and terror.

In cooperation with Israeli security forces, on January 13, 1998, in Nablus, the Palestinians uncovered the largest Hamas explosives laboratory ever discovered in the territories.[72] The revelation served only to illustrate Hamas's ability to carry out mass-casualty terrorist attacks in Israel, and it was no coincidence that the discovery took place four days before the prime minister had set out for a meeting with President Clinton in Washington, D.C. On the eve of this meeting, the government formulated a document detailing the violations of the Oslo Accords by the Palestinian Authority, dubbed the "Naveh Document," and gave it to the Palestinians. The document called for the convening of the Palestinian National Council's legal committee and its approval of the repeal of a series of articles in the Palestinian National Charter calling for the destruction of the state of Israel and the use of the term "armed struggle." The document also contained a demand that the PA stop incitements against Israel, extradite thirty-four wanted persons to Israel, confiscate illegal weapons throughout the PA, adjust the size of the Palestinian police to the number agreed on (reducing the number from 46,000 to 24,000), and refrain from governmental activity outside of Area A and east Jerusalem.[73]

The Palestinians strongly criticized Prime Minister Netanyahu's actions and accused him of trying to destroy the peace process.[74] But in an effort to prevent renewed rapprochement between the Americans and Israel, they made sure to claim that they were fulfilling their obligations and preventing terror against Israel. This claim was accompanied by a number of demonstrative steps.[75] The tension between the sides reached a new peak in October 1998, ahead of the convening of the Israeli-American-Palestinian summit at the Wye River Plantation, the aim of which was to reach an agreement on the extent and characteristics of the next phase of withdrawals and resolve disputes between the two sides. On the eve of the Wye conference, Cabinet Secretary Danny Naveh was asked,

"What lies between us and an agreement with the Palestinians?"

He replied: "In one word: security. In two words: fighting terror."

"Can we understand, then, that all of the other problems have been resolved?"

"No, there are a number of things that have not yet been finalized, but the main issue that bothers us, without which there will be no agreement, is security and the war on terror."

"Are we waiting for an OK from Ami Ayalon [head of the ISA] and Meir Dagan [head the counterterrorism bureau at the prime minister's office]?"

"We are waiting for our security personnel to be able to confirm that the Palestinians have a clear, systematic, ongoing, and appropriate course of action to fight terror, that it's not just empty words."[76]

Instead of using the peace process as leverage to pressure Arafat to thwart terror attacks against Israel, the Netanyahu government used security claims as a way to prevent progress in the peace process. However, after massive American pressure and the confining of the two sides' delegations to the Wye Plantation for few days, which was accompanied by several breakdowns, the parties reached an agreement and signed the Wye River Memorandum. It stipulated that the next phase of withdrawals would be 13 percent of the West Bank.

A number of letters of assurance were attached to the agreement, in which the United States made commitments to both sides regarding several issues of concern. Thus, for example, Israel received letters stating that the United States would

1. publicly oppose any unauthorized release of detainees on charges of terrorist activity,

2. oppose unilateral declarations and support the demand to reaffirm the Palestinian National Charter,

3. refrain from expressing any position on the extent and nature of the third phase of withdrawals,

4. ensure that they receive from the Palestinians a list of officers serving in the Palestinian police, and

5. accept the principle of reciprocity as a basis for resolving the breakdown of trust between the parties.[77]

The signing of the Wye River Memorandum greatly improved the sensitive relationship between the American administration and the Netanyahu government.

In a public opinion poll held in Israel immediately after the signing of the agreement, 75 percent of respondents said that they supported the agreement, and only 15 percent opposed it;[78] 47 percent believed that Israel had succeeded in securing a Palestinian war on terror through the agreement, and 4 percent felt that Israel had not succeeded in this mission.[79]

Not long after the signing of the Wye memorandum, the Islamic Jihad attacked a bus carrying children in Gush Katif (a settlement in the Gaza Strip). The Palestinian Authority launched a campaign of arrests among the organization's operatives, and the head of the Palestinian General Security Service in the Gaza Strip, Muhammad Dahlan, explained that the movement had deviated from the accepted agreements by launching the attack from Area A.[80] Shortly thereafter, Islamic Jihad carried out another attack, this time a suicide car bombing near the Mahane Yehuda market in the heart of Jerusalem. The two Palestinian terrorists who were in the car were killed, and twenty-seven Israeli citizens were injured. The Israeli response was not long in coming. The prime minister halted the government's discussions on the Wye memorandum. The Palestinians, for their part, made sure to demonstrate that they were fulfilling their obligations under the accord. The PLO's Executive Committee ratified Arafat's January 22 letter to President Clinton announcing the annulment and revision of the clauses in the Palestinian National Charter that denied Israel's right to exist. The PA also put pressure on Palestinian Islamic Jihad in the wake of the attacks, and the Palestinian police raided the Islamic Women's Association, a charitable institution run by Ataf Alian, a former administrative detainee in Israel and a member of Islamic Jihad.[81] However, the Israeli government (which had finally ratified the Wye River Memorandum) again announced that it would suspend the agreement's implementation at the beginning of December 1998, following the near-lynching of two Israeli soldiers who had lost their way and ended up in Area A. Israel made implementation of the agreement conditional on the PA's fulfilling three conditions:

1. clarifying that it was committed to the agreement reached at Wye, whereby prisoners with blood on their hands or Hamas members would not be released;
2. announcing that it was abandoning its intention to unilaterally declare a Palestinian state; and
3. declaring its commitment to continuing negotiations until a final status agreement was reached. Israel also demanded that the PA immediately stop incitement and violence and punish those responsible for committing such acts.[82]

INCREASED ATTACKS, INCREASED SECURITY

The Netanyahu government, established shortly after the trauma of the wave of suicide bombings in February and March 1996, instituted a large and expensive security system (beyond the military and police frameworks) designed to protect the borders, roads, and specific installations. This included dedicated security units that were set up to provide a solution for Israel's "soft underbelly" on the home front, the public transport security unit, and the school security unit. Responsibility for securing educational institutions was removed from the Ministry of Education as it had been since the days of the Peres government, and the amount allocated for school security was reduced over the years (from ILS 120 million in 1995 to ILS 90 million, and to 60 million in 1996).[83] The system was supposed to be changed from one of security only at the school gates to one of perimeter security (by patrols of police cars around the schools), but in the end, only one security point at the front gate remained. Shortly after formation of the new Netanyahu government, the Knesset Education Committee passed a resolution obligating the government to ensure full funding for security in all educational institutions.[84] A similar process took place in the field of public transportation security. At first, the unit encountered difficulty recruiting security guards (despite the relatively high salaries offered). In May 1995, the government decided to dismantle the public transport security unit, and responsibility for security was transferred to the Israel Police, which allocated additional human resources and funding (about ILS 20 million per year).[85]

The Netanyahu government resolved to provide security to another sector of transportation: taxis. In August 1997, the government decided to offer taxi drivers a "safety basket" that would include a satellite positioning system for drivers in distress, transparent barriers to separate the driver from passengers, self-defense courses, and personal weapons.[86] Around the same time, it was made public that the cost of security for the national airline, El Al, was approximately $80 million a year, and that around 75 percent of this budget was funded by the government.[87] During this period, security continued to be a central element in the field of counterterrorism, with the government allocating very large budgets to its implementation.[88]

In a cabinet meeting held on the eve of the 1999 elections, Counter-Terrorism Bureau head Meir Dagan described Netanyahu's achievements in the field of counterterrorism. In contrast to the twenty-one suicide bombings that took place during the previous government's term, only three suicide attacks were carried out from the time the Netanyahu government came to power, and the number of shooting, grenade, and bombing attacks dropped from about 1,000 during the Rabin-Peres government to 250 during the Netanyahu government. The number of Israelis killed in attacks dropped from 245 to 70. Dagan attributed improvement in the security situation in the field of terrorism to the Palestinian Authority's motivation to prevent attacks as a result of pressure exerted on it by Israel, which included threats regarding political achievements, economic sanctions, and a demand for reciprocity. The prime minister concluded the meeting by saying, "the difference between 1996 and today cries out to the heavens. This is the fruit of proper policy, proper work, and an uncompromising demand from the Palestinians that we will not accept 'victims of peace.' "[89] Netanyahu laid out two layers of his government's counterterrorism policy. "The first is our activism, which has been very effective; the second is the clear message to Arafat that there will be no progress in the peace process if he does not fight terrorism."[90]

Prime Minister Netanyahu attributed the difference in the scope of attacks to the determination shown by his government and the condition that the peace process would continue to advance only if there was security, in addition to Israel's operational activities. There is a question regarding whether Netanyahu was correct in crediting his government's policy alone for the period of limited terrorist attacks against Israel. His critics claim that the decline in terror was not the result of a successful policy but, rather, a lack of interest on the part of fundamentalist Islamic terrorists to carry out attacks. These organizations understood that the peace process had run aground in any case, and therefore there was no need for a terrorist effort on their part. Former ISA chief Carmi Gillon said,

> It is no coincidence that during . . . Netanyahu's time there were almost no attacks by Hamas. Netanyahu attributed this to his activity, his government, and the defense establishment. I am not saying that all of these do not deserve credit, but at the core of the matter stands something completely different: Hamas had no interest in carrying out terrorist attacks during Netanyahu's term, because the diplomatic process had been curbed. Only when there was a diplomatic process, for example, in the wake of the Hebron Agreement, did the Hamas attacks resume. Luckily, the "engineer" was no longer around to plan and execute them.[91]

Another former Shin-Bet head, Yaakov Perry, supports this assessment,

> Ironically, the decline of the peace process led to a relative calm in terrorism. The attacks . . . decreased and the damage they caused decreased. The reason for this was that Hamas, Islamic Jihad, and the various rejectionist organizations were motivated to carry out attacks to neutralize, disrupt, and destroy the peace process and to mobilize Israeli public opinion against reconciliation with the Palestinians, as long as there was such a process. . . . Therefore, when there is no peace process, there is no need for terrorism either, since the object of the opponents of peace is achieved without bloodshed and especially without unnecessary entanglement with the Palestinian security apparatuses.[92]

It seems that due to its enthusiasm and desire to influence the PA to exercise its ability to thwart terrorist attacks, the Netanyahu government chose to use only the stick component of the carrot-and-stick policy that, ostensibly, it formally adopted with regard to the Palestinian Authority. The vacuum created by the absence of diplomatic progress between the Palestinians and

Israel was quickly filled by the United States, as discussed, which established strategic cooperation with Arafat and his administration and made it clear to the Palestinians that these ties would be in danger should terrorist attacks against Israel resume.

As to the question of whether the terrorist attacks were the result of advancement or halting of the peace process with the Palestinians, there is no single answer. A review of the major attacks since the signing of the Oslo Accords reveals that in the past, terrorist attacks occurred both when negotiations were progressing and when they stalled. Arafat's explanations and claims regarding the reasons underlying terrorism also changed depending on the period in accordance with the PA's interests. During the Rabin government's term, Arafat claimed that the reason for terrorism was the fundamentalist organizations' desire to stop the peace process. And during the period of the Netanyahu government, he claimed that the attacks reflected the Palestinian people's despair over stagnation of the peace process.[93]

The signing of the Wye River Memorandum saw Netanyahu facing strong opposition to his leadership from within his ruling party, the Likud. On the other hand, Netanyahu's approval in public opinion polls improved, and it appeared that Israelis supported his policy. In an attempt to translate this support into an electoral victory and strengthen his position both within and outside the Likud, Netanyahu decided to call early elections. On the eve of the 1999 elections, the issue at the heart of the dispute between the two main candidates, Benjamin Netanyahu and former IDF chief of staff Ehud Barak, was whether or not to withdraw IDF forces from Lebanon. On February 23, 1999, forces from an elite unit of the paratroopers encountered terrorists in Lebanon, and three of the unit's officers were killed. This incident led to increased criticism of the government's policy from lobby groups and various segments of the Israeli public, who demanded an immediate withdrawal from Lebanon. Barak publicly pledged that within a year of his election, he would undertake to withdraw the IDF from Lebanon.

In the months leading up to the elections, support for Netanyahu consistently declined, and his attempts to take steps to improve his chances of being elected were unsuccessful. In the elections of May 17, his rival, Ehud Barak, was elected as Israel's tenth prime minister.

THE FIRST BENJAMIN NETANYAHU ADMINISTRATION'S COUNTERTERRORISM POLICY IN LIGHT OF THE COUNTERTERRORISM DILEMMAS MODEL

During this period, Israel was led by the first Netanyahu administration. Once in power, Netanyahu, who, for many years had been the main oppositionist to the Rabin administration and to the entire Oslo process, was obliged to uphold the agreements that had been signed with the Palestinians by previous governments. In fact, he even signed additional agreements with them: the Hebron Agreement in January 1997 and the Wye River Memorandum in October 1998. On the other hand, in contrast to his predecessors Rabin and Peres, Netanyahu placed responsibility for the terrorist attacks against Israel on the shoulders of Palestinian Authority leader Yasser Arafat. The Netanyahu government adopted an indirect strategy to combat terrorism, the crux of which was to exert pressure on the PA to prevent attacks. This was based on the claim that Arafat was able to thwart terrorism but simply had no interest in doing so.

Throughout his term, Netanyahu faced international pressure from Western countries that feared that he would try to torpedo the Oslo process. In order to soothe these fears, Netanyahu held meetings with Israel's friends around the world and delivered speeches in which he declared that he was not against the peace process in and of itself but opposed political progress while terrorist attacks were taking place. Thus, the Netanyahu government's central message to the Palestinians was that terrorism did not advance Palestinian national interests. On the contrary, if there was terrorism, the peace process would not advance.

At the same time, the Netanyahu government continued to tighten security at the crossings between Israel and the West Bank and Gaza Strip within the Green Line. It also renewed targeted killings and even carried out a failed operation in Amman against the head of Hamas's political wing, Khaled Mashal.

The change in Israeli policy seemed to lead to a change in the policy of the Palestinian Authority and its leader; there was a significant decrease in the number of terrorist attacks against Israel during this period.

Turning to the Counterterrorism Dilemmas Conceptual Model (figure 8.1), we can determine that during the period under review, the Netanyahu

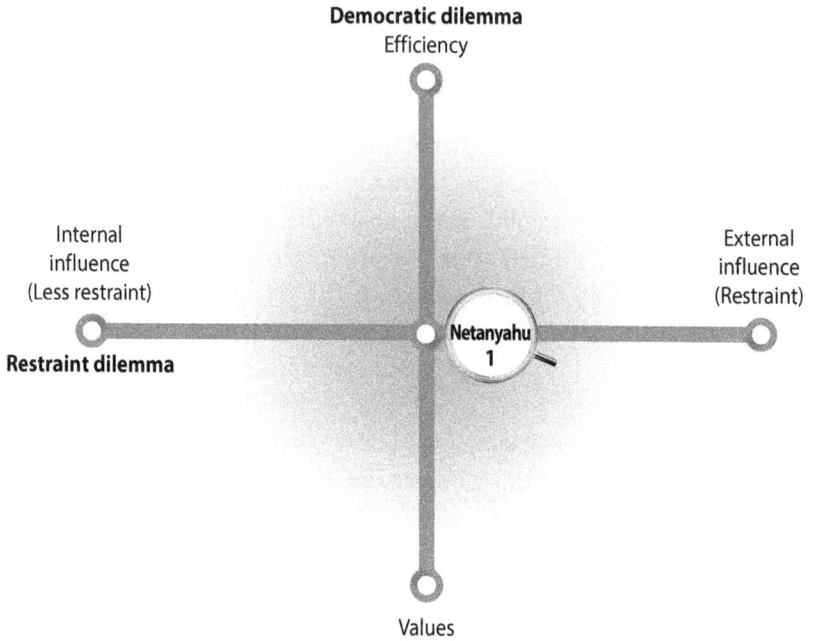

Democratic dilemma
Efficiency

Internal
influence
(Less restraint)

External
influence
(Restraint)

Netanyahu
1

Restraint dilemma

Values

FIGURE 8.1. Counterterrorism Dilemmas Conceptual Model—Netanyahu administration (1996-99)

government did not have to deal with significant domestic pressures, and that the desire to be in line with decision makers in the international arena, especially the United States, had a great impact on counterterrorism policy. With the exception of the use of targeted killings, most of the Netanyahu government's counterterrorism efforts focused on increasing security while exerting economic and other pressure on the Palestinian Authority to prevent Palestinian terrorism. Therefore, on the democratic dilemma axis, it appears that Israeli counterterrorism operations were more balanced than those of most other Israeli governments.

Chapter Nine

CONFRONTING THE AL-AQSA INTIFADA

The Ehud Barak and Ariel Sharon Administrations
(1999-2004)

After taking office in July 1999, Ehud Barak was committed to upholding the promise he made to his electorate and the Israeli public to withdraw the IDF from the security zone in southern Lebanon. Barak set a rigid time-table for the withdrawal: it was to be completed by July 2000. About a year after he was elected as Israel's tenth prime minister, Barak fulfilled his promise, and in May 2000, the IDF completed its withdrawal from all of Lebanon.

Barak's decision, and especially publication of the expected timetable for the withdrawal, led to a wave of desertions from the South Lebanon Army (which used to be allied with Israel) to Hezbollah, even before the departure of the IDF forces.[1] The final stage of the withdrawal was con-ducted quickly in order to prevent Hezbollah forces from attacking IDF soldiers as they left. Images of the IDF withdrawal from Lebanon (which Hezbollah presented as a hasty flight) and, to an even greater extent, images of the South Lebanon Army (SLA) fighters (who were accused by Hez-bollah of being collaborators with Israel) fleeing toward the Israeli bor-der and abandoning their property, cars, and sometimes even their family members in southern Lebanon seriously damaged Israel's deterrent image and the morale of the Israeli public. On the one hand, the public was glad to welcome the IDF soldiers home, but on the other hand, Israelis feared what was to come with Hezbollah now able to operate from the border fence between Israel and Lebanon. At the time, Hezbollah leader Hassan Nasrallah compared the resilience of Israeli society, especially its capacity to absorb the injury and death of its citizens, to that of a spider web. The IDF's rapid withdrawal from Lebanon again revealed, in Nasrallah's eyes, Israel's soft underbelly—the sensitivity of the Israeli public to civilian and military casualties.

In the Palestinian arena, the security and political reality in the months following Barak's election was one of calm while negotiations were being conducted with the Palestinian leadership. Joint Israeli-Palestinian patrols were held, the IDF refrained from entering Area A, the signed agreements were largely respected by the parties, and Israeli and Palestinian security forces cooperated with regard to intelligence. Terrorist attacks were still carried out in Israel but in very low numbers.

During the summer of 2000, the Barak government maintained feverish contact with Palestinian leaders in an attempt to reach an agreement on a comprehensive permanent settlement that would end the conflict between Israel and the Palestinians. The culmination of these contacts was a meeting held under the auspices of President Bill Clinton at Camp David in July 2000, in which the parties were to discuss the characteristics of a final status agreement that would bring an end to the conflict and peaceful relations. At Camp David, Arafat was offered far-reaching proposals that no Israeli government had ever before proposed. This included Palestinian control over 97 percent of the West Bank and Gaza Strip (including the evacuation of many Jewish settlements), suitable territorial compensation for areas that Israel would retain in a different area (possibly near the Gaza Strip), and the handing over of Arab neighborhoods in Jerusalem to the Palestinians, including Muslim neighborhoods in the Old City, effectively dividing the city. The proposal also included a component of compensation for Palestinian refugees outside the territories, even including the return of a symbolic number of refugees. Arafat refused the Israeli proposals, and the Camp David summit ended as a stinging failure.

In early 2000, a few months before the Camp David summit, the IDF intelligence department warned Israeli decision makers that Arafat was looking for a way to break away from his commitment to the Oslo Accords. According to Military Intelligence's assessment, Arafat had changed his mind and was unwilling to be remembered in the pages of Palestinian history as someone who had signed the plan to divide Israel-Palestine between two peoples. Thus, no matter what the results of the summit were, Arafat was determined to find an appropriate reason to dismantle the agreements at any price. On the basis of this warning, the IDF prepared for a deterioration in security in the territories and in Israel. (To this end, even before the outbreak of riots, the IDF received NIS 1.3 billion to reinforce its inventory in preparation for a possible conflict.)[2]

Between 1994 and 2000, the Israeli public hoped that the peace process would lead to the end of the conflict, security, and economic prosperity. They were disappointed by the continued Palestinian violence and terrorist attacks that accompanied the peace process, but they generally accepted Arafat's claims and explanations that he was not responsible for the attacks that were carried out by the Islamic terrorist organizations Hamas and PIJ, and that he was doing everything in his power to prevent them. Israelis accepted the division that Arafat presented to the world between so-called good Palestinians, supporters of the peace process headed by the chairperson himself, and bad Palestinians, the Islamist terrorist organizations. This division allowed Arafat time and time again throughout the Oslo process to wash his hands of all responsibility for terrorist attacks and to demand concessions from Israel that would supposedly strengthen his position among Palestinians against the violent opposition bloc.

As great as the Israeli public's expectations were, such was their disappointment after the failure of the Camp David summit. Arafat's refusal of what Israelis saw as far-reaching proposals by Prime Minister Barak severely damaged the support of most Israelis for the peace process and reinforced the position of its opponents, who had argued that from the beginning of the Oslo process, Arafat had not been interested in a peaceful solution to the Israeli-Palestinian conflict, and that this fraudulence had been exposed at Camp David. This assessment of a growing number of people in Israel was reinforced by the outbreak of Palestinian violence and what appeared to be a tacit agreement with regard to, if not the remote direction of, terrorism by Arafat and his people.

THE START OF THE AL-AQSA INTIFADA

Shortly after the return of Barak and his delegation from Camp David, opposition leader Ariel Sharon paid a visit to the Temple Mount with representatives of the Israel Antiquities Authority. Their aim was to observe at first hand the activities of the Waqf and its excavations at Solomon's Stables, which had caused damage to the historical antiquities in the area. The heavy criticism directed at Barak for the concessions he was willing to make at Camp David prevented his stopping Sharon's visit to the Temple Mount, despite the fear of disturbances and riots that were likely to occur as a result of the visit. Barak did not want to be portrayed as the one who prevented the head of the opposition from visiting the holy site.[3] Sharon's visit to the Temple Mount took place at a highly sensitive time, and he ignored the enormous tension that had followed the failure of Camp David.

The visit was exploited by Palestinian instigators, who provoked riots during the Friday prayers of September 29, 2000, on the Temple Mount and called on the faithful to defend the sanctity of Islam.[4] That morning, an IDF Border Police officer was murdered by his Palestinian counterparts during a joint patrol of Qalqiliya, making him the first Israeli victim of the al-Aqsa Intifada. That afternoon, following Sheikh Hassan Adrisi's sermon, a riot began in the Temple Mount plaza. Seven Palestinians were killed and a number of Israeli police officers were injured in the incident. The riots quickly spread to other Palestinian cities. These events involved outbursts of rage the likes of which had not been witnessed in the territories. The Palestinian security forces did not prevent the riots but, rather, took part in and even led the events at many points of conflict. Palestinian radio, controlled by Arafat, began to broadcast in a military and inflammatory style, calling on the Palestinian people to go out and defend al-Aqsa and the holy sites of Islam.

The next day, seven more Palestinians were killed in the West Bank. On Saturday night, the French television network France 2 screened a video showing a father and his son, Muhammad al-Dura, huddled by the outer wall of a storeroom at Netzarim junction. The two, who faced what appeared to be crossfire between IDF soldiers and Palestinian policemen, hid behind a sewage pipe but were hurt in the exchange of fire in front of the television cameras. These images, broadcast around the world, drew a huge wave of criticism against Israel for what was defined as its responsibility for killing Muhammad al-Dura and wounding his father. Israel investigated the incident, analyzing the videotapes and reconstructing the angles of the shooting and aerial photographs. The IDF's findings were conclusive: it was impossible that IDF soldiers' fire had hit Muhammad and his father; Muhammad had been killed by Palestinian fire.[5] That Sunday, the Jewish New Year, riots spread throughout the country. In the wake of the Palestinian riots in the

West Bank, Israeli Arabs (Palestinian citizens of Israel living within its territory; that is, within the Green Line) also began violent demonstrations, which resulted in the death of thirteen rioters from police gunfire.

Another Jewish Israeli was killed by a stone thrown at his car from a bridge near the Arab village of Jisr az-Zarqa on the "coastal road" in the heart of Israel (a fast central route connecting Tel Aviv and Haifa). On October 1, Palestinian terrorists took over a Jewish prayer site near Joseph's Tomb in Nablus, where border police soldiers were present. During the takeover, a Druze police officer, Madhat Yosef, was seriously wounded. IDF forces circled the site and the armed men inside, and rather than break in, they conducted negotiations with the Palestinian security forces, during which the IDF soldier died. The publicizing of the affair as it occurred dealt a severe blow to Israeli morale, both because of the conduct of the Palestinian police and because of what many in Israel described as the deserting of an injured soldier in the field.[6] With the outbreak of the riots, Barak sent a harsh message to Arafat:

> If we do not see a change in the patterns of violence in the next two days, we will see in this the cessation of the diplomatic negotiations on Arafat's part, this being his responsibility and at his initiative, and the IDF and the security forces will be instructed to act with all the means at their disposal to halt the violence.[7]

The IDF was prepared for the outbreak of violence. The Palestinians found it difficult to inflict casualties on the IDF and suffered heavy losses. However, these losses fanned the flames and turned the conflict into a self-perpetuating cycle: riots, fatalities, funerals that turned into clashes with the IDF, leading to more fatalities, more funerals, and so on. The unrelenting violent events led to frantic efforts by Israel to enlist Arafat and his people to take action to end the riots. When talks between the two sides failed to bear fruit, Israeli and Palestinian delegates held a conference in Paris in early October, but that proved futile as well.

Hezbollah added fuel to the fire with an ambush on an IDF patrol in the Har Dov area, at Israel's northern border, on October 7, in which they kidnapped three soldiers. Each violent incident was followed by another. On October 12, five days after the kidnapping, two IDF soldiers, Private Vadim Nurzhitz and Corporal Yosef Avrahami, accidentally drove their private vehicle into a crowded area of Ramallah in the West Bank. When their identity was revealed, they were lynched by a frenzied Palestinian mob in front of the cameras of the foreign press, and their bodies were mutilated and thrown into the street from the building in which they were being held. These events, at the start of the intifada, deeply shocked the Israeli public and shattered hopes for peace with the Palestinians.

It soon became clear to Israeli decision makers that the Second Intifada (or the al-Aqsa Intifada, as the Palestinians referred to the riots that began in October 2000 and continued until 2005) was fundamentally different from the first intifada (1987–91). Whereas the first was an authentic popular uprising of the Palestinians in the territories, manifested in waves of protests and violent demonstrations by large groups using cold weapons and throwing stones and Molotov cocktails, the Second Intifada included many shooting incidents by Palestinians and a severe escalation in terrorist attacks against Israel.

During the Second Intifada, 1,080 Israelis were killed in 25,375 attacks, including 146 suicide bombings.[8] In addition to the suicide attacks, many other types of terrorist actions occurred in Israel and the territories. These included ambushes and shooting attacks, drive-by shootings, infiltrations of settlements to murder residents, infiltrations of army bases to kill soldiers, the throwing or planting of explosives, "cold" attacks such as stabbings and vehicle rammings, tunnel digging and rigging, the firing of antitank missiles, and launching of high-trajectory fire (mortar shells, Qassam rockets, and even Katyushas). Some of these attacks were directed against civilians and others against soldiers.

In the conflict, 3,405 Palestinians were killed. In 2002, the bloodiest year for both sides, 1,033 Palestinians and 450 Israelis were killed.[9] Israel, for its part, responded with great force to the outbreak of riots. Then head of Military Intelligence, Amos Malka, estimated that about a month after the outbreak of the riots, Israeli soldiers fired about 1,200,000 bullets from light weapons.[10]

SHARM EL-SHEIKH SUMMIT

On October 17, a summit was held in Sharm el-Sheikh in Sinai led by Bill Clinton with the participation of President Mubarak, Ehud Barak, and Yasser Arafat, as well as the king of Jordan, the UN secretary-general, and other heads of state from the European Union. The conference did not succeed in ending the wave of violence, but one of its outcomes was the decision to establish a fact-finding committee to look into the outbreak of violent incidents in order to prevent their recurrence. The committee was established on November 7 and chaired by former Democratic Senator George Mitchell. It held several meetings and gathered facts from both sides, and its report, published in late April 2001, began with the following statement:

> Some Israelis appear not to comprehend the humiliation and frustration that Palestinians must endure every day as a result of living with the continuing effects of occupation, sustained by the presence of Israeli military forces and settlements in their midst, or the determination of the Palestinians to achieve independence and genuine self-determination. Some Palestinians appear not to comprehend the extent to which terrorism creates fear among the Israeli people and undermines their belief in the possibility of co-existence, or the determination of the government of Israel to do whatever is necessary to protect its people. . . . There is a growing sense of futility and despair, and a growing resort to violence.[11]

Although the committee stated in the report that it was not a tribunal, the section that examined the events preceding the outbreak of the Intifada stated,

> Mr. Sharon made the visit on September 28 accompanied by over 1,000 Israeli police officers. Although Israelis viewed the visit in an internal political context, Palestinians saw it as highly provocative to them. On the following day, in the same place, a large number of unarmed Palestinian demonstrators and a large Israeli police contingent confronted each other. According to the U.S. Department of State . . . "Police used rubber-coated metal bullets and live ammunition to disperse the demonstrators, killing 4 persons and injuring about 200." According to the GOI, 14 Israeli policemen were injured. Similar demonstrations took place over the following several days. Thus began what has become known as the "Al-Aqsa Intifada."[12]

In addition,

> The GOI asserts that the immediate catalyst for the violence was the breakdown of the Camp David negotiations on July 25, 2000 and the "widespread

appreciation in the international community of Palestinian responsibility for the impasse." In this view, Palestinian violence was planned by the PA leadership. The PLO denies the allegation that the intifada was planned. . . . From the perspective of the PLO, Israel responded to the disturbances with excessive and illegal use of deadly force against demonstrators. . . . From the perspective of the government of Israel, the demonstrations were organized and directed by the Palestinian leadership to create sympathy for their cause around the world by provoking Israeli security forces to fire upon demonstrators. For Israelis, the lynching of two military reservists in Ramallah on October 12 reflected a deep-seated Palestinian hatred of Israel and Jews.[13]

The Mitchell Committee summarized the dispute by saying,

We were provided with no persuasive evidence that the Sharon visit was anything other than an internal political act; neither were we provided with persuasive evidence that the PA planned the uprising. . . . However, there is also no evidence on which to conclude that the PA made a consistent effort to contain the demonstrations and control the violence once it began; or that the government of Israel made a consistent effort to use non-lethal means to control demonstrations of unarmed Palestinians. . . . The Sharon visit did not cause the "al-Aqsa Intifada". But it was poorly timed and the provocative effect should have been foreseen. . . . More significant were the events that followed: the decision of the Israeli police on September 29 to use lethal means against the Palestinian demonstrators; and the subsequent failure, as noted above, of either party to exercise restraint.[14]

The committee's recommendations included calling on both sides to act decisively to stop the violence and immediately afterward act to restore trust and return to the negotiating table. Israel and the Palestinians were called on to honor their previously signed agreements and commitments, prevent and condemn incitement, and renew security cooperation. The PA was called on to make "100 percent effort" to prevent acts of terrorism and punish their perpetrators, conduct security checks on Palestinians working in Israel, and prevent gunmen from using populated Palestinian areas to fire into Israel. The government of Israel was requested to "consider withdrawing" to positions held before September 28, 2000, ensure the adoption of nonlethal responses to unarmed demonstrators, lift the closure and transfer to the PA all tax revenues owed, "refrain from the destruction of homes and roads, as well as trees and other agricultural property," and ensure that the response to any gunfire emanating from Palestinian populated areas minimize the danger to the lives and property of Palestinian civilians. Above all, based on the assumption that the diplomatic freeze would lead to further violence, the committee requested that both to renew negotiations.[15]

In light of the extent and frequency of violent incidents in the first months of the al-Aqsa Intifada, a few weeks after its outbreak, Israel proclaimed the crisis an "armed conflict short of war." In practice, this declaration regulated more permissive firing procedures than during a state of calm. The Mitchell Committee believed that the Israeli definition of the situation was too broad and called for its elimination in order to "help mitigate deadly violence and help rebuild mutual confidence."[16] However, the violence did not stop after the publication of the Mitchell report, it only escalated.

THE SUICIDE BOMBING PHENOMENON

On November 9, Israel killed Hasin Abyat, one of the Hamas leaders in the West Bank, in a targeted operation. It was the first killing that Israel carried out in the course of the al-Aqsa Intifada, with many more to follow. That same month, a suicide bombing took place in Hadera. A month later, on December 9, in light of the deteriorating security situation, Prime Minister Barak called for special elections for prime minister. A short time later, a series of suicide attacks were launched inside Israel, with the Palestinian terrorist organizations (in the first stage by Islamist organizations Hamas and PIJ, and, later, Fatah as well) doing everything they could to carry out as many suicide bombings as possible, even if this increased effort impaired the "quality" of the attacks.

In the first wave of suicide bombings in Israel that took place during the Oslo process (1993–2000), Palestinian terrorist organizations maintained a high level of compartmentalization and avoided recruiting terrorists who volunteered for the mission. They preferred to identify attackers themselves (fearing infiltration by Israeli intelligence agents) and initiate the offer to carry out a suicide attack. During this period, the organizations invested considerable effort in conducting operational and psychological training for the suicide bombers, allowing them to leave for their mission only after they had completed all stages of planning, preparation, and training(a process that could last many days and sometimes weeks from the time of the suicide bomber's recruitment). However, in the second wave of suicide attacks that began with the Second Intifada, the Palestinian terrorist organizations ignored all the red lines they had previously set up for themselves and recruited suicide bombers indiscriminately, including volunteers and, later, women. The organizations sent them to carry out suicide bombings without appropriate training, sometimes within hours or days of recruitment.

During the al-Aqsa Intifada, 146 suicide bombings occurred, killing 518 Israelis and wounding 3,350 people, not including those suffering from shock and trauma.[17] However, this enormous number of attacks does not reflect the entire terrorist effort, as dozens of suicide attacks were foiled by Israeli security forces, and in some cases, the attacks were thwarted due to technical malfunctions resulting from poor physical and mental training of the suicide bombers, some of whom even surrendered before the attacks.

On December 22, a suicide attack was carried out at the Mehola rest stop in the Jordan Valley. A suicide bomber tailed a bus carrying soldiers and parked outside the rest stop. Three IDF soldiers were killed. The next day, the White House issued a proposal for the outline of a final status agreement, but in the heat of the events and with casualties on both sides, no attention was paid to the American initiative, and it evaporated, as had the many other initiatives that preceded it. In late December 2000, Israel conducted the targeted killing of the senior Fatah operative Thabet Thabet, head of the Tanzim in Tulkarm, who was involved, in addition to his involvement in terrorism, in initiatives to promote the peace process and had even fostered personal relationships with many Israeli peace activists. The response was not long in coming. Thabet's nephew, Fatah activist Raed Karmi, avenged his uncle's death on January 23, 2001. He kidnapped and murdered two Israeli restaurateurs, Etgar Zeitouni and Motti Dayan.[18]

Thabet's elimination marked a change in Israel's counterterrorism policy. Before this killing, Israeli decision makers limited targeted killings only to those terrorists defined as "ticking bombs" (that is, those who had reached the operational stage of the attacks they were planning). However, from that point on, targeted killings were also aimed at those who were defined as part of the "ticking infrastructure," operatives generally involved in the chain of command and execution of terrorist attacks even if they were not involved in carrying out concrete attacks at that time.[19]

The use of targeted killing operations also helped to boost the Israeli public's morale, which was severely damaged due to the collapse of the Oslo process and the horrific terrorist attacks that regularly occurred in Israel.[20] Israel's successes in eradicating terrorists through targeted killings were, among other things, a result of a change in its method of operation and professionalization. The IDF and ISA began to work in short cycles, whereby within a short period, they managed to gather the required operational intelligence, process it, and then plan and conduct a military operation on the basis of that information. In some cases, this process could take minutes or even hours from obtaining intelligence information to the operation itself, overcoming organizational barriers and even ego considerations. According to former prime minister Ehud Olmert:

> We have developed capabilities that no other country in the world has, and I say this with certainty. Not the United States or Russia, and certainly not any other country. The capabilities we developed broke the backbone of the main terrorist efforts after the year 2000. We developed the ability to gather intelligence through advanced technological means of locating—we can locate people who are cell leaders or senior commanders. We can find out where they are and where they are moving, we can hit them, follow them, and all from a distance and without personal contact. All of these things created a sense of tremendous achievement for Israel, and sowed fear on the other side that Israel would ultimately reach each and every of them.[21]

However, Israeli success in the operational arena did not translate into a decrease in the number of terrorist attacks, as new operatives and leaders soon replaced the terrorists who were liquidated.[22]

ARAFAT'S INVOLVEMENT IN INCITING VIOLENCE

On February 6, 2001, elections were held in Israel, with Ariel Sharon defeating Ehud Barak by a wide margin of 25 percent of the votes. The Israeli public, as well as decision makers and the heads of the security establishment, were busy dealing with the issue of the extent of Arafat's involvement in initiating and directing the Second Intifada. Two general schools of thought were formed at the time. One was headed by past and present Military Intelligence Directorate chiefs who claimed that Arafat had initiated the deterioration after the failure of the Camp David summit and that should he wish, he would be able to control the flames of or bring an end to the intifada. The second school, led by the ISA[23] and supported by a number of IDF officers, claimed that Arafat did not initiate the intifada, nor did he control it, and that he was being dragged along by Palestinian public sentiment.

The "Arafat in control" school based its assessment on Arafat's centralized system of authority, which held all powers, including veto power, in the administration of the PA, the PLO, and the Fatah movement. Arafat ran the PA's affairs, as well as negotiations with Israel, in a manner that defined limited areas of activity for his subordinates, and he took meticulous care that none of his deputies and aides stood out from the others or attempted to take over political or military powers. According to adherents of this school of thought, throughout the Oslo Accords, Arafat played a double game whereby he would broadcast to the world messages of peace and reconciliation with Israel in English and at the same time convey contradictory messages through actions, insinuations, and ambiguous statements in Arabic that sometimes encouraged violence and terrorism against Israel. However, even at the height of this activity, Arafat never de facto fought the Palestinian terrorist organizations. He tried to reduce the organizations' motivation to carry out attacks in Israel but did not take steps to eliminate their military capabilities. He did not destroy the terrorist laboratories, nor did he arrest, sentence, or imprison terrorists. He did not destroy illegal weapons and did not convey to his people messages of support for peace and acceptance of the state of Israel as a sovereign Jewish political entity. Instead, Arafat chose to turn a blind eye to the military buildup of these organizations and to continue to incite his people against Israel through state media, school textbooks, and any other means possible. According to this school of thought, if Arafat was genuinely interested in preventing terrorism during the al-Aqsa Intifada, there were steps he could have taken. He could have arrested Hamas and PIJ operatives and struck their facilities; alternatively, he could have used the Palestinian media (which was under his control) to publicly (in Arabic) call on the organizations to halt terrorist activity and violence. Arafat did not do so, however, and the Palestinian media encouraged and incited the continuation and even escalation of the intifada.

In addition, the Palestinian security and intelligence apparatuses had a very good intelligence picture of what was happening in Palestinian society in the territories. Their understanding was even better than that of the Israeli intelligence agencies, due to their foothold on the ground and the fact that they belonged to the same population within which the terrorists operated. In many cases, this enabled the PA to find out about Hamas and PIJ intentions in advance, or at the very least to locate the perpetrators shortly after the attacks. But the PA, once again, refrained from doing so. Arafat, according to this approach, was looking for a crisis after the Camp David summit failed, and so he used the pretext of Ariel Sharon's visit to the Temple Mount and the subsequent riots. If not for this particular event, the intifada would have broken out under some other pretext. Arafat could not allow himself to be seen by the Palestinian public as someone who was making strategic concessions to Israel and signing an agreement with it when, only a few months earlier, Hezbollah had succeeded in making Israel "flee" Lebanon. Whether Arafat initiated the deterioration, or even if he was only riding the wave of the riots, according to this school of thought, Arafat was the problem and not part of the solution.

In contrast, voices from the ISA maintained that the intifada was the result of an unprompted outbreak of popular anger that emanated from the bottom up, without the PA's control and direction. Adherents to this theory claimed that the PA tried to stop the riots but was unable to do so. In response to the claim that Arafat was using codes that encouraged the intifada by releasing Hamas and PIJ prisoners, the ISA responded that Arafat did so only because he had been dragged along by the mood on the Palestinian street and had never been one to swim against the current or take a stand against authentic waves of anger. The conclusion of this school of thought was clear: Israeli harm to PA targets would not lead to a change in levels of violence, in part due to the fact that the PA's structures and mechanisms had collapsed, and it was therefore unable to take responsibility and restore calm.[24]

These conceptual disagreements soon turned into personal rivalries when the followers of the "Arafat in control" school claimed that the ISA's assessments stemmed from its close relations with the heads of the Palestinian security services and was based on intelligence from them (given that the ISA had lost some of its intelligence-gathering capabilities following Israel's withdrawal from West Bank cities under the Oslo Accords). They pointed to the perhaps too-close relationship between some of the heads of the ISA and the Palestinians.[25] Proponents of the "not in control" school argued that Israel had no conclusive evidence of Arafat's involvement and control of the violent events, nor was any such evidence ever presented to the public, and that the opposing school was driven by political motives.

The dispute between the ISA and Military Intelligence regarding Arafat's responsibility for the riots that characterized the first months of the intifada came to a formal end (though even today, the heads of these organizations are at odds over this issue) after Sharon's rise to power. At this point, the ISA began withholding claims that Arafat was not in control on the ground. Prime Minister Sharon said that he was not interested in dealing with historical, anachronistic issues about which school of thought was right, because the dispute no longer existed now that "there is a prime minister who understands intelligence."[26]

The debate that took place between various experts in the defense establishment and academia during the period of the Barak government regarding Arafat's degree of responsibility and control over the events of the Second Intifada had immediate implications for Israel's response policy following terrorist attacks in its territory. Israel chose to retaliate against specific Palestinian Authority targets—bases, headquarters, and operatives of the PA's security and intelligence apparatus—in order to pressure Arafat to take the initiative for ending violent activity against Israel. However, most of the Israeli actions proved insignificant and were at most a signal to the PA and its operatives and a demonstration of Israel's military capabilities while still attempting to minimize the number of casualties on the Palestinian side as part of the notion of "containing the conflict" out of a desire to end it and return to the negotiating table.

Immediately following Ariel Sharon's victory in the February 2001 elections, a series of major terrorist attacks were launched in Israel. Three days before the new government was sworn in, on March 4, Hamas carried out a suicide bombing in Netanya, killing three civilians. Three weeks later, the Israeli public was shocked by the murder of a ten-month-old baby girl, Shalhevet Pass, by a Palestinian sniper in Hebron. Then, two days later, a suicide bombing occurred in Neveh Yamin near Kfar Saba, which killed two civilians and wounded four. Once again, Hamas took responsibility for the events.

These attacks led to harsh reactions from senior officials in the new government and drove Prime Minister Sharon to instruct the National Security

Council to prepare work on the "seam zone"—this was the start of preparation of a plan to build a ground barrier between Israel and the Arab communities in the West Bank—the security fence, which began construction approximately one year later. On April 22, another suicide bombing took place in Kfar Sava that resulted in the death of a civilian and injury to sixty-one others. A small organization close to Fatah, the Return Brigades, took responsibility for the attack. Sharon placed the blame for the bombing on the Palestinian Authority, claiming that the PA was not acting in accordance with the agreements obligating it to prevent terrorism against Israel.[27]

In May 2001, the Israeli navy intercepted the ship *Santorini* off Israel's western coast. The ship was carrying a large number of weapons being smuggled in by Hezbollah from Lebanon to the Palestinian Authority in the Gaza Strip. The shipment included four Strela antiaircraft missiles, twenty RPG launchers, dozens of Kalashnikov rifles, about 100 mortar rounds, and about 13,000 bullets.[28] In the weeks that followed, several more severe suicide bombings were carried out in Israel. On May 18, a Hamas terrorist blew himself up at the main entrance to the Sharon shopping mall in Netanya, killing six people and injuring more than seventy. On the same day, another suicide bombing occurred at the central bus station in Hadera, causing some sixty casualties.[29] A government spokesperson blamed the PA and Yasser Arafat, claiming that the attacks were the result of the PA's ongoing incitement and propaganda campaign and the release of Hamas terrorists by Arafat from PA prisons.

In response to the attacks, the Israeli air force, for the first time since the Six-Day War (1967), bombed Palestinian targets in the West Bank—in Ramallah, Nablus, Tulkarm, and Jenin—as well as in the Gaza Strip. Among other targets, the Palestinian police compound and the prison inside it were shelled, in addition to a building used by the Special Forces. In Ramallah, Israel bombed a Force 17 building and a Palestinian naval base in Sudan. Israel officially declared that from that point forward, it regarded the PA's security forces as legitimate targets for IDF attacks following terrorist attacks, which represented a significant escalation and a further deterioration of the relationship between Israel and the Palestinian Authority. It was not, however, sufficient to end the wave of attacks. July 1, 2001, witnessed one of the most horrific suicide bombings to occur in Israel. On that Friday evening, a Hamas suicide bomber entered a youth dance club called the Dolphinarium, located in Tel Aviv, and blew himself up in the club, which was full of partygoers, killing 21 teenagers and wounding 120.[30] The attack shook the Israeli public, who called for an escalation against the Palestinians. The Israeli government's political security cabinet made the following announcement at the end of a special meeting convened after the attack:

> The Government of Israel has determined that the Palestinian Authority (PA) and Chairman Arafat are engaged in terrorist activity, encourage it and are inciting to hatred and violence. The PA has not only violated all the obligations and agreements to fight the terrorist and incitement infrastructure, but its members are themselves engaged in terrorism and incitement. . . . Israel holds the PA responsible for the deterioration.[31]

The attack seemed to have changed the policy that had been adopted until that point by the Palestinian Authority and Arafat, who announced a ceasefire the day after the bombing. Israeli intelligence sources reported that Arafat was indeed working on the ground to prevent attacks and that, perhaps for the first time since the outbreak of the intifada, he was trying to bring calm and draw other organizations into the ceasefire.[32] However, Israeli decision makers claimed that despite having adopted the terms of the Mitchell Report and declared a ceasefire, more than 140 attacks had been carried out against it. Thus, Israeli spokespeople were not satisfied with Arafat's declaration and demanded an absolute halt to the attacks and to incitement to terrorism, as well as the arrest of all the terrorists who had been released from Palestinian prisons.[33]

ESCALATION OF SUICIDE BOMBINGS

About two weeks later, on July 16, a suicide bomber blew himself up at a bus stop near the train station in Binyamina, leaving two dead and eleven wounded.[34] A few hours after the attack, Israeli tanks opened fire on Palestinian police stations in Jenin and Tulkarm. Sharon even noted that the movement of Israeli forces was part of a plan to reoccupy parts of the West Bank that was under Palestinian control. The attack and the Israeli response marked the end of the ceasefire that had been declared by CIA Director George Tenet a month before these events took place.

On July 31, an attack was launched against Hamas headquarters in Samaria, which resulted in the liquidation of some of the organization's

211

CONFRONTING THE AL-AQSA INTIFADA

senior commanders. On August 9, a Hamas terrorist carried out a suicide attack at the Sbarro restaurant in Jerusalem, killing 15 people and injuring 130.[35] In response, Israel continued to strike Palestinian police and security forces. According to then foreign minister Shimon Peres, the terrorist who carried out the attack at Sbarro had appeared on the wanted list that Israel had given Arafat in order for him to make arrests, but Arafat had refused.[36] On August 27, 2001, PLFP secretary-general Abu Ali Mustafa was killed, and on September 9, Hamas instigated another suicide bombing, this time near the Nahariya train station, killing three and wounding ninety.[37]

Two days later, the world changed, and with it the Middle East, when the largest suicide attack in history took place in the United States. The attacks of September 11 shook the international public, altering opinions and indirectly affecting the policies of the United States, Israel, and even the Palestinians in the local arena. The United States had become the victim of the type of suicidal terrorism that had been reserved for remote areas such as the Middle East. Alongside the shocking images of the attack, the media showed images of Israeli citizens mourning the American victims along with the rest of the Western world, in stark contrast to many in the Arab world, including Palestinians in the West Bank and Gaza, who danced in the streets and distributed sweets to passersby to celebrate the event. These images influenced many, including the American administration.

Israeli citizens and decision makers believed that the shared experience of the United States and Israel as victims of suicide terrorism would strengthen America support for Israel with regard to the Palestinians. But they were disappointed to discover that after the attack, American pressure on Israel to hold a meeting with Arafat increased (the same Arafat who the government of Israel saw as being largely responsible for the wave of suicide attacks since the outbreak of the intifada). This pressure bore fruit, and on February 23, Sharon announced that he accepted the principle of a Palestinian state. Four days later, Peres held a meeting with Arafat in which a ceasefire was once again agreed on. But American pressure on Israel also led to Sharon's unprecedented public statements against U.S. policy in the Middle East. On October 5, he demanded that the United States cease trying to appease the Arabs at Israel's expense. "Israel will not be Czechoslovakia," Sharon said, insinuating that the situation created after the September 11 attacks was similar to the situation that preceded the signing of the agreement with the Nazis to divide Czechoslovakia before World War II.[38] After agreement on the ceasefire was reach, the number of attacks and incidents in the territories declined, but the calm was quickly disrupted on October 7, when a PIJ suicide bomber exploded at the entrance to Kibbutz Shluhot in the Beit Shean Valley, killing one Israeli and wounding several others. In the wake of the attack, Defense Minister Ben-Eliezer said, "The key to quiet is in Arafat's hands, and in the meantime he is not bringing about the silencing of terrorism even though he is able to."[39]

On October 16, an event took place that stunned the Israeli public: Tourism Minister Rehavam Ze'evi, known as a hawk with a wealth of security experience, was murdered by a PFLP operative while making his way to his hotel room in Jerusalem. The group claimed that it was a revenge attack for the killing of their leader, Abu Ali Mustafa.

Over the following months, the wave of suicide attacks in Israel intensified and the Israeli response escalated. On November 29, 2001, a PIJ suicide bomber detonated his car next to the number 823 bus in Wadi Ara, killing three civilians and wounding nine. On December 1, a double suicide bombing was carried out in the Jerusalem pedestrian mall during which two Hamas terrorists blew themselves up in the midst of a crowd of passersby, killing 11 people and wounding 188. The attack took place during the prime minister's visit to the United States, where he was meeting with President Bush. The following day, Hamas carried out a suicide bombing on the number 16 bus in Haifa, killing 15 Israelis and injuring 60. Three days later, a PIJ terrorist blew himself up on King David Street in Jerusalem, wounding eight Israelis. And four days later, on December 9, a PIJ suicide bomber carried out yet another attack on a bus in Haifa, injuring a number of passengers.

At this stage, the Israeli cabinet declared the PA a terrorist-sponsoring entity and refused the ceasefire proposed by various Palestinian organizations on the occasion of the Muslim holy month of Ramadan.[40] In Israel, the understanding was that underlying the escalation in attacks was the Palestinians' assessment that Israel would refrain from significant retaliatory activity against the PA and the reoccupation of PA-controlled territories in order to avoid harming the coalition formed by the United States at the time to fight Saddam Hussein in Iraq, which included various Arab countries. However, the wave of suicide attacks severely damaged Arafat's international support and status. Israel defined Arafat as "irrelevant" and therefore as someone who could not be a negotiating partner. Moreover, at that point he had lost the sympathy of the American administration, and

European countries were no longer standing by him either. Against this backdrop, Arafat made a speech on Palestinian television calling for an end to the intifada and to violent activity. This was the first time that he had made such a call in Arabic and in the Palestinian media. The speech was also accompanied by instructions to his people to take action to stop the violence. And, indeed, the number of violent incidents dropped sharply. A Palestinian public opinion poll published at the end of December showed that 60 percent of the public supported Arafat's call for a cessation of violence, and 71 percent supported a return to the negotiating table.[41]

Israeli and international pressure on Arafat proved tha the had had the ability all along to control the flames of the intifada but had decided to use this capability by that point. He prohibited suicide attacks and mortar fire within the Green Line. Palestinian terrorists, members of Fatah and the Palestinian police, Islamic Jihad, and Hamas complied. Some of them protested, and others publicly stated that they did not intend to submit to Arafat's orders, but even they ultimately obeyed his commands. Arafat was not even required to use force in order to implement the ceasefire. He did not fight terrorism—he did not take action to destroy the operational infrastructure of Hamas and Islamic Jihad, and he did not systematically destroy the headquarters, bases, explosives laboratories, and ammunition depots of these organizations (aside from a few isolated acts for the television cameras). Arafat did not arrest wanted terrorists and put them on trial, with the exception of a number of arrests of "small fry" operatives, once again for propaganda purposes. He did not collect and destroy the huge quantities of illegal weapons held by the terrorist organizations in the territories, and neither did he begin to educate his people to strive for peace and for solving the conflict through nonviolent means.

Although Arafat did none of these things, he did prevent attacks against Israel during this period. In fact, he returned to the modus operandi he had used throughout the years of the Oslo Accords; that is, a strategy of threat and persuasion, in which he persuaded terrorists that carrying out attacks at the time in question would endanger Palestinian national interests. He threatened that should they ignore his instructions, he might use his military forces against them, which could degenerate into a civil war in the Palestinian territories, something all sides wished to avoid.

Arafat's decision to ban suicide bombings and mortar fire in Israel was not the result of a strategic preference to return to the path of negotiations for peace. Rather, it was the result of a lack of choice that stemmed from a combination of Israeli military, political, and economic pressure and strong pressure from the United States, the European community, and moderate Arab states, all of which forced Arafat to declare and implement the ceasefire.

On January 4, 2002, the Israeli navy seized the *Karin A* ship in the Red Sea. The ship was carrying large quantities of arms and ammunition sent by Iran and Hezbollah to the Palestinians. The direct involvement of Arafat and his people in acquisition of the weapons and their transport was quickly exposed. Arafat's attempt to deny his involvement in the weapons purchase by means of a letter he sent to the White House, despite the solid evidence presented by Israel, severely damaged the channels of dialogue between Arafat and his people with the American administration.[42]

On January 14, 2002, Israel killed Fatah's most senior operative in Tulkarm and one of the symbols of the Second Intifada: Ra'ad Karmi. Karmi, who was personally responsible for the murder of twelve Israelis in shooting attacks and detonation of explosive charges—among them Etgar Zeitouni, Motti Dayan, and Zvika Shelef—had been a key target for elimination for a long time and had actually escaped previous unsuccessful attempts on his life. Karmi's killing reversed the trend of relative calm that had preceded the operation, added fuel to the fire of the intifada, and pushed Fatah activists to take part in the campaign of suicide bombings in Israel. Until the killing of Karmi, the vast majority of suicide attacks were carried out by the Islamic terrorist organizations Hamas and Palestinian Islamic Jihad.[43] Three days after the killing, an operative of Fatah's al-Aqsa Brigades launched a shooting attack at an event hall in Hadera during a bar mitzvah celebration, killing six. A short time after, Fatah executed the first suicide attack using a female suicide bomber, Wafa Idris, who blew herself up in Jerusalem.[44] The decision to kill Ra'ad Karmi thus seriously undermined the support Israel had achieved in the international community and the pressure that Israel had finally succeeded in exerting on Arafat.

OPERATION DEFENSIVE SHIELD

February and March 2002 marked an unprecedented deterioration in Israel's security situation. On January 25, PIJ carried out a suicide bombing at Tel Aviv's central bus station, injuring twenty-six people. On February 19, six IDF soldiers were killed at the Ein Ariq checkpoint, and in response, the

IDF launched a massive operation against Palestinian police officers, killing about fifty of them. On March 2, a suicide attack occurred in the Beit Yisrael neighborhood of Jerusalem, and the next day, Palestinian snipers killed ten Israelis (including seven soldiers) at a checkpoint near Ofra in the West Bank. The following day, on March 4, there was a suicide bombing at the Seafood Market restaurant in Tel Aviv, and the same day, IDF soldiers killed ten Palestinians in the West Bank. On March 7, a terrorist infiltrated the settlement of Atzmona in the West Bank and killed four Israelis. Over the next eight days, suicide bombings were carried out in Netanya (killing two) and at Café Moment in Jerusalem (killing eleven). On the Palestinian side, approximately forty Palestinians were killed in IDF operations.

The event that perhaps marked the climax of the al-Aqsa Intifada took place on the night of the Passover seder on March 27, 2002, when a suicide bomber infiltrated the Park Hotel in Netanya while people were celebrating the festive holiday meal and blew himself up, killing thirty of the seder participants and wounding many others.[45] This was the straw that broke the government of Israel's back. The horrible scenes of murdered and wounded Israelis on seder night left the public reeling and the government with no alternative but to embark on a comprehensive ground incursion against the Palestinian Authority and terrorist organizations.

The grim wave of terror attacks that struck Israel in the first months of 2002 challenged the worldview held by Ariel Sharon that had characterized his entire military and political career, according to which, in dealing with its enemies, Israel should prefer a strategy based on deterrence. Despite Israeli military activity, which included targeted killings of terrorist operatives and their leaders and many reprisals directed against PA targets, the attacks did not abate. On the contrary, they only intensified. Sharon tried to reduce the terrorist organizations' and PA's motivation to continue to attack Israel by increasing the military and diplomatic pressure on Arafat and by changing his cost-benefit balance. However, this strategy did not seem to achieve the desired goals, in part because Arafat liked to take risks and walk on the brink of the abyss.

Israeli decision makers' rationale was different from that of the Palestinians, as were their cost-benefit calculations. In the near absence of a limit on the Palestinians' ability to carry out attacks in Israel, it seems that Israeli military pressure only increased their motivation and resulted in additional attacks. The February and March 2002 attacks brought about a conceptual and strategic transformation. Instead of trying to exert pressure on Arafat and the PA to prevent their continuing their attacks, instead of trying to deal with the motivation of Palestinian terror, Israel realized that it must act to significantly reduce Palestinian terrorist organizations' ability to continue carrying out attacks. The military terrorist infrastructure of the organizations and the PA had to be destroyed, explosives laboratories demolished, weapons confiscated, and terrorists arrested. All of this necessitated the reoccupation of PA territory, those areas that had been transferred to the PA by Israel under the Oslo Accords. This was necessary whether for the purpose of a permanent Israeli presence in the entire West Bank (with an assumption that only direct control of the population would allow for the military action and intelligence required to counter terror) or only as a temporary move that would last several months (a necessary precondition for the implementation of an agreed-on or unilateral diplomatic solution).

Following the terrorist attacks in Israel, foremost being the suicide bombing at the Park Hotel, and after Israel suffered 135 casualties from terrorist attacks, the majority of which were from suicide bombings over the course of one month (March 2002), the cabinet approved calling up 20,000 reservists, and Israel launched Operation Defensive Shield. During the operation, IDF soldiers entered city centers and occupied refugee camps. Soldiers fought from house to house, often encountering booby traps that had been planted with explosive devices. Progress was slow but calculated in areas suspected of being booby trapped. Sometimes, within the refugee camps, soldiers advanced through the walls of adjacent houses by creating holes to pass from one to the other, rather than traveling booby-trapped streets, thus greatly reducing the number of casualties. Operation Defensive Shield was fundamentally different from previous operations against Palestinian terrorist organizations. It was intended to change the rules of the game and return to Israel control over the areas used by terrorist organizations to prepare and embark on attacks from Area A (those territories transferred to Palestinian Authority control during the Oslo process in the 1990s).

When the operation began, Hezbollah attempted to open an additional front in Lebanon, carrying out an ambush near Kibbutz Matzuva that killed six civilians and firing short-range rockets for thirteen days in order to prompt Israel to respond to these provocations and entangle the IDF in a multifront war. Israel conveyed a message to Hezbollah that it

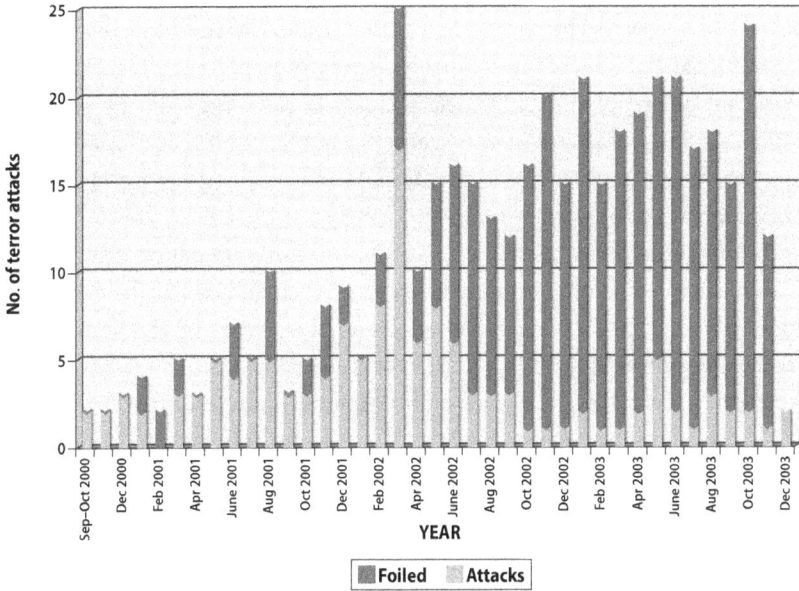

FIGURE 9.1. Foiled and realized suicide attacks in Israel (2000-2003)

was mobilizing reserves to send to the northern front, but it avoided being dragged into exchanges of fire with Hezbollah.[46]

Even the unprecedented Defensive Shield operation was not able to eliminate terrorist attacks, certainly not immediately. The motivation to attack Israel did not decline, and it even increased, although the terrorist organizations' capabilities did gradually decrease (figure 9.1).[47]

On March 31, another suicide bombing occurred, this time at the restaurant Matza in Haifa, killing fifteen Israeli citizens. The suicide bomber was a Palestinian resident of Israel (from within the 1967 borders).[48] In May 2002, fifteen people were killed in a terrorist attack at a club in Rishon Letzion, and in early June, a suicide bomber exploded next to a bus near the Megiddo junction, killing seventeen people and injuring many others. These attacks led to public pressure to accelerate construction of the security fence to separate the West Bank from Israel, at least the part of the fence bordering the center of the country. Indeed, construction of the fence began on June 22, 2002. The initial route approved by the government annexed approximately 900 kilometers, about 16 percent of the West Bank.

On June 30, 2004, the High Court of Justice ruled that the route of the security fence should be changed so as to minimize harm to the lives of the Palestinians. The updated route included only 360 square kilometers, about 6 percent of the West Bank.[49] The security fence being built by Israel in order to stop suicide terrorism became the subject of international debate and was even brought to the International Court of Justice in the Hague for discussion at the beginning of 2004.[50]

In July 2002, Israel carried out a targeted killing operation against one of Hamas's most prominent figures: Salah Shehadeh, head of the organization's military wing in Gaza. Shehadeh had been involved in a long series of terrorist attacks against Israel. He was killed while visiting his home, and in order to ensure his death, a bomb weighing 1,000 kilograms was used. This large amount of explosives in such a densely populated area naturally led to a significant number of civilian casualties— Palestinians were killed, including eleven children, which led to harsh criticism of Israel. The head of Military Intelligence at the time, Aharon Ze'evi Farkash, explained the Israeli defense establishment's considerations prior to approval of the targeted killing. Farkash stated that the defense establishment concluded that it was impossible to prevent attacks against civilians inside Israel without getting to Shehadeh, who planned the attacks and dispatched the terrorists.

> We had information that within two to three weeks, Hamas, under Shehadeh's direct responsibility, was planning to carry out one of the most severe terrorist attacks ever to take place in Israel, using operatives it recruited in the north of the country. They were going to explode 10 or 12 car bombs simultaneously in Haifa and Tel Aviv. In my own considerations, as head of the intelligence division, regarding whether or not to recommend the targeted killing, I said: I do not want mothers in Gaza to cry, but I prefer for mothers in Haifa not to cry. It was also clear to us that there was no other way to thwart the planned mega-attack aside from striking Shehadeh.[51]

Regarding collateral damage, Ze'evi Farkash noted,

> We assumed that civilians around him would be harmed, so we set out clear rules regarding collateral damage and its dimensions. The decision was not taken easily or casually. We had very good intelligence about the man, his actions and movements, and the house in which he lived. We also knew that there were not many civilians in the house itself, aside from Shehadeh's

family. . . . There were tin shacks near the building . . . and indeed, most of the civilians killed were in the tin shacks surrounding it.[52]

Inside the Palestinian arena, it seemed that Arafat's power was beginning to fade. In September 2002, the Palestinian parliament convened to discuss the approval of Arafat's new government, but Arafat was defeated, and his government did not receive parliamentary approval.[53] On October 21, another suicide bombing was carried out, this time at the Karkur junction, killing fourteen civilians. Nine days later, the Israeli national unity government disbanded, but Sharon continued to serve as head of the transitional government after appointing Mofaz as defense minister and Netanyahu as foreign minister.

THE MIDDLE EAST ROADMAP

In April 2003, President Bush presented his Middle East Roadmap, in which declarative and practical demands were set out for both sides. According to the document, the PA was supposed to declare clearly and unambiguously its recognition of the state of Israel and its commitment to end the violence and act effectively against terrorism. The PA was also required to implement political reform and governmental democratization. Israel was required to declare its commitment to the vision of two states, withdraw to the pre-intifada lines, freeze construction in the settlements, and dismantle the outposts established after March 2001. Israel was obligated to stop acts that could harm civilians, including house demolitions and deportation; help the Palestinians with rehabilitation; and provide humanitarian assistance to the Palestinians. The responsibility for monitoring the implementation of these measures by both sides was given to the leaders of the Quartet countries (the United States, European Union, United Nations, and Russia), and the parties were committed to meeting a set timetable. Although both Arafat and Sharon announced that they accepted the roadmap, neither saw the document as a binding order, and it ended up in the dustbin of history.[54]

CEASEFIRE

On November 15, 2002, a severe attack was carried out in Hebron. A cell of three PIJ terrorists ambushed Jewish worshipers who were making their way from their homes in Kiryat Arba to the Tomb of the Patriarchs. Twelve

Israelis were killed and fourteen injured before the cell was liquidated. In early 2003 (January 28), Israeli elections were held, and once again, Ariel Sharon was elected prime minister by a large majority. In March, the United States launched the Iraq War and found itself entangled in the Middle East for the next several years. That same month, Abu Mazen (Mahmoud Abbas) was appointed Palestinian prime minister. Abu Mazen's appointment was actually imposed on Arafat. At a summit meeting held in Aqaba, Jordan, in June 2003 with the participation of President Bush, Yasser Arafat, and Ariel Sharon, Abu Mazen delivered a conciliatory speech the likes of which had never been heard from Arafat and the contents of which had in fact been coordinated with the Americans beforehand. During the summit, Sharon agreed to a ceasefire (or *hudna*, meaning "quiet" or "truce") as a result of American pressure.[55]

In July 2003, about two weeks after the ceasefire was announced, the IDF intelligence directorate presented to the government the implications of the new reality created by the conflict with the Palestinians. According to Military Intelligence, the Palestinians had "captured the heart" of the U.S. administration, which was doing all it could to strengthen and encourage the new government. MI claimed that the Palestinians had given the Americans the impression that they had taken much more significant security action than they actually had, and it was on this basis that the Palestinian government received so much praise from the White House. In actuality, Abu Mazen had not taken the necessary counterterrorism measures in accordance with the ninety-day plan set out by the head of Palestinian security in Gaza, Dahlan. The PA failed to arrest the perpetrators of terrorist attacks and bring them to justice and refrained from declaring a ban on carrying weapons and from collecting illegal weapons. MI also assessed that the Palestinian terrorist organizations saw the ceasefire only as a tactical step to allow them to prepare for the next round of violence, and that they were waiting for the opportunity to launch a new series of terror attacks.

Arafat, for his part, did everything in his power to interfere with Abu Mazen's initiatives and minimize his achievements. In August 2003, Arafat was told that if he did not cooperate with Abu Mazen and subordinate the Palestinian security apparatuses to Abu Mazen's authority, the United States was liable to support Israeli steps against him, including his expulsion from the West Bank. Israel's fear was that the Palestinians would succeed in passing the first phase of the roadmap, which committed them to prove success in their war on terrorism without any real and thorough treatment of the issue of terrorism.[56]

In the weeks following the summit, Abu Mazen found himself caught in the cross fire between Arafat, who disliked the fact that his prime minister allowed the Americans and the Israelis to go over his, head, and Israel, which was not pleased that instead of fighting Hamas and the Palestinian organizations, Abu Mazen was trying to reach agreements and a *hudna* with them. In September 2003, Abu Mazen resigned following an incitement campaign against him from within the Palestinian Authority and after the collapse of the *hudna* between Israel and the Palestinians. The ceasefire collapsed on August 19 when a Hamas suicide bomber blew up the number 2 bus in which worshipers were being driven from the Western Wall to the center of Jerusalem. In the bombing, 23 civilians were killed, including 7 children, and 130 were wounded. On October 4, another suicide bombing was carried out, this time at the Maxim restaurant in Haifa. The female suicide bomber, Hanadi Jaradat, set out for the attack from Jenin. The bombing killed 21 Israelis and injured dozens.

INCREASED SECURITY

The year 2003 witnessed a growing trend of Hezbollah involvement in the Palestinian arena and with Palestinian terrorist organizations, especially Fatah/Tanzim, Palestinian Islamic Jihad, and Hamas. Hezbollah leader Hassan Nasrallah even admitted publicly for the first time that Hezbollah had a special unit that dealt with this activity along with the Palestinians.[57] The physical barrier and increasing difficulty in carrying out attacks within Israel led the Hamas movement to gradually develop the capability to launch high-trajectory fire toward Israel from the Gaza Strip. To this end, with the help of Hezbollah, Hamas began to produce primitive Qassam rockets in the Gaza Strip, which were made of iron pipes and signposts filled with explosives with no guidance system. These rockets were fired into Israeli territory from the northern Gaza Strip and, in some cases, from Samaria. In 2001, seven rockets were fired into Israel, some into the Gaza Strip, and others into Israeli territory. In 2002, 42 rockets were fired; in 2003, 105; and in 2004, 159; in the latter case, 37 of the rockets were fired into the Gaza Strip and 111 into Israeli territory within the Green Line.[58]

Another strategy that Hamas adopted from Hezbollah that was intended to enable terrorists to overcome the obstacle of the perimeter fence surrounding the Gaza Strip and carry out attacks in Israel was the digging of tunnels. These attack tunnels were dug from the Gaza Strip to IDF positions in Israeli territory along the fence and were used to hide explosives and attack positions from underground. For example, on September 26, 2001, terrorists detonated a powerful explosive device under the Termit outpost (near Rafah on the Egyptian border).

Following the explosion, the terrorists opened massive fire at the outpost and threw grenades, wounding four soldiers. On December 17, 2003, a half-ton bomb planted in a tunnel under an outpost near Rafah on the Egyptian border was detonated. On February 26, 2004, an IDF soldier was killed in a gunfire and grenade attack by Fatah/Tanzim terrorists on the IDF's post at Erez crossing; they had arrived at the site through a tunnel dug for this purpose. On June 27, Hamas blew up a tunnel under the Orhan outpost, killing one IDF soldier and wounding five. The length of the tunnels reached hundreds of meters, and their depth ranged from six to ten meters. For the longer tunnels, ventilation shafts were dug, and they were sometimes installed with ventilation compressors and lighting cables. The entrances to the tunnels were usually concealed inside buildings or hidden areas within the Gaza Strip.

Targeted Killings

On September 6, 2003, an Israeli attempt to kill Hamas leader Ahmad Yassin failed after the 250-kilogram bomb that was dropped on the building in which the Hamas leadership had gathered failed to penetrate the building's floors and strike the Hamas operatives, who were on the bottom floor. The mission was completed a few months later, however, on March 22—Yassin, Hamas's founder and leader, was killed by helicopter gunship fire as he was leaving a mosque in Gaza. Two of his guards and six civilians were also killed in the operation. On April 17, 2004, Yassin's successor, Abd al-Aziz Rantisi, another Hamas founder, was also killed—about a month after he was appointed to lead Hamas and serve as leader of its domestic headquarters. On August 31, 2004, Hamas's military wing carried out a double suicide bombing on two bus lines in Be'er Sheva within a few minutes of each other, in retaliation for the killings of

Yassin and Rantisi. Sixteen civilians were killed and more than 100 were wounded in the attack.

Israel continued to use targeted killings as a main tool to attack Hamas and Islamic Jihad operatives, even toward the end of the Second Intifada. In addition to the killings of Hamas leaders, on April 29, 2003, a senior PFLP operative, Nidal Salameh, was killed in Gaza. Salameh had been released from prison in Israel in 1999 as part of agreements with the Palestinian Authority. On August 21, senior Hamas figure Ismail Abu Shanab was killed in Gaza; though the Palestinians claimed he had been involved only in political matters, according to IDF sources, he had been a member of the group of senior officials who determined the policy of Hamas attacks and one of those responsible for rebuilding the organization's military infrastructure in Gaza and the West Bank. That same month, Muhammad Sider was also killed; he was a senior member of PIJ in Hebron who was released from Israeli prison in June 2000 and who was responsible for many attacks in the area, including the suicide attack on Jewish worshipers in Kiryat Arba in 2002.

Throughout the years of the al-Aqsa Intifada (October 2000–May 2004), Israel killed 237 terrorist operatives in targeted operations and wounded seven. In these operations, 125 uninvolved persons were killed and 585 injured.[59]

Administrative Detentions

Another means of punishment and methods to thwart attacks that Israel used extensively throughout the intifada was administrative detention. In December 2000, 12 terrorist operatives were held in administrative detention; in December 2001, there were 34 detainees; in December 2002, 960; and in January 2004, 638.[60] In late 2003, Military Intelligence indicated that great discontent among the Palestinian population resulted from Israeli actions that they regarded as "collective punishment" for terrorism, such as general closures, sieges, the cutting off of the Gaza Strip, restrictions on movement, and prevention from working in Israel. This realization led to the conclusion that continued pressure on the entire Palestinian population over a long period, rather than being focused on an active group of terrorist elements, harmed Israel's interests, as it increased despair and distress among the Palestinian population and amplified hatred of Israel and desire for revenge, which was expressed in support for the continuation of terrorist attacks.[61]

War on Financing

One of the areas of counterterrorism in which Israel was particularly active in 2004 was the war on the funding of terror. The method of drying up terrorist organizations' financial sources began to spread throughout the world, led by American efforts, after the September 11 attacks. Ariel Sharon stated that the campaign against terrorist funding was essential, as "Money is flowing from the United States and Great Britain. Money is flowing through the banking system. We must put an end to this."[62] In February 2004, Israeli security forces carried out an operation to confiscate terrorist funds deposited in banks in the territories. Money was seized from associations that were outlawed because of their links with terrorist organizations, including accounts belonging to groups affiliated with Hamas and PIJ. Also confiscated was money transferred to the territories the origin of which was foreign funds that had been outlawed in their own countries, money transferred by Hezbollah and terrorist headquarters abroad, and funds transferred from terrorist organizations to known terrorists and wanted persons in the West Bank and Gaza Strip. The funds were confiscated from branches of the Arab Bank in Ramallah and the Bank of Cairo based on intelligence information collected by Israeli intelligence sources.[63]

Operations in the Gaza Strip

During 2004, Israel carried out two large-scale military operations in the Gaza Strip. Operation Rainbow took place between May 18 and 25 in the Rafah area and on the Philadelphi Route situated along the border between the Gaza Strip and the Egyptian Sinai. The operation was intended to find and destroy the smuggling tunnels that had been dug by operatives from Palestinian organizations in order to smuggle weapons from Egypt into the Gaza Strip. Operation Rainbow also aimed to locate the terrorists who murdered the Hatuel family on May 2 (a mother and four children who were ambushed in their vehicle by terrorists who first fired at the car and then continued to shoot the family to death at close range). The IDF also sought another cell that, on May 11, fired an antitank missile at an engineering armored personnel carrier, killing five soldiers. During the operation, IDF forces also entered other villages in the southern Gaza Strip in order to find and eliminate Hamas headquarters and bases and to weaken the organization's power there. According to IDF sources, during the week-long operation, forty-one terrorists and twelve civilians were killed, fifty-six houses were destroyed (including the house of the terrorist who murdered the Hatuel family), and three smuggling tunnels were uncovered.[64] On May 19, the UN Security Council adopted Resolution 1544, which condemned the IDF's actions in Rafah and particularly the destruction of houses.

Between September 30 and October 15, 2004, Operation Days of Penitence was implemented in the Gaza Strip. This time the operation focused on the northern Gaza Strip and was aimed at locating and neutralizing sites used to launch Qassam rockets at the city of Sderot and nearby communities.[65] The operation began after two children were killed by Qassam rocket fire in Sderot. Over the course of the operation, more than 100 Palestinians were killed, among them about 60 terrorists and approximately 20 children. In addition, 77 houses were destroyed and a large number were damaged during the fighting. The Engineering Corps worked to expose areas with dense vegetation and facilities that served as hiding places for Qassam launchers.

DECREASE IN CASUALTIES

Comparison of the data on terrorist attacks in 2002 and 2003 indicates a significant decrease in 2003 and the beginning of a change of direction in the intifada. In 2003, there were 3,838 attacks against Israeli targets, in which 213 Israelis were killed, among them 50 members of the security forces and 163 civilians. In comparison, in 2002, there were 5,301 attacks during which 451 Israeli soldiers and civilians were killed. Thus, 2003 saw a 30 percent reduction in the number of attacks and a 50 percent reduction in the number of fatalities.[66]

From the end of 2003, the IDF and the ISA began to succeed in stopping Palestinian terrorism. The combination of control over the area, which disrupted the terrorist cells' ability to organize, along with the security fence, which made it difficult for cells to penetrate Israel, and the improved quality of Israeli intelligence gradually led to the end of the Second Intifada.[67] At IDC's Herzliya Conference on December 16, 2003, ISA Director Avi Dichter concluded,

In the last three and a quarter years of the conflict with the Palestinians, 109 Israelis have been killed by Palestinian terrorism, and 6,000 have been injured. 80 percent of the casualties have been civilians.[68] 540 of the Israeli fatalities were within the Green Line and Jerusalem. I must say in all honesty that the defense establishment, and the Shin Bet within it, did not provide the Israeli people with the security they deserve. It is interesting to look at other countries, at what they would do in the case of terrorism of this magnitude. It would be interesting to see how France or England, each with a population 10 times larger than the State of Israel, would respond to 9,000 dead and 60,000 wounded, or how a superpower like the United States, more than 40 times larger than the State of Israel, would react if 36,000 of its citizens were murdered and a million of its citizens wounded in three years of terror. I suppose the answer is clear to all of us.[69]

In 2004, there was a 45 percent decrease in the number of Israelis killed in terrorist attacks compared with 2003 (117 killed in 2004 compared with 213 in 2003). Regarding the number of injured, there was a similar decrease of 41 percent. In 2004, 589 Israelis were injured in terrorist attacks compared with 1,004 in 2003.

The decline in the scope of terrorism was also reflected in a significant reduction in the number of suicide bombings. Whereas in 2003 there were twenty-six suicide attacks, in 2004 there were only fifteen.[70] However, in 2004, there appeared to be an increase in the involvement of PA/Tanzim operatives in carrying out terrorist attacks in general and suicide attacks in particular. These terrorists were involved in, among other things, suicide bombings in Jerusalem (on January 29 and February 22), the Ashdod port (in March 2004), and the Erez industrial zone near the Gaza Strip (on February 26 and March 6). Some of these actions were directed by control mechanisms outside the territories through Hezbollah and Iranian elements.[71]

The security fence that was built as a barrier between the West Bank and Israel had a significant impact on the decrease in the number of attacks inside Israel. For example, in the thirty-four months spanning from the beginning of the conflict in September 2000 until establishment of the buffer zone, terrorist organizations in Samaria carried out seventy-three mass killing attacks in Israel (suicide bombings, shootings, or car bombings), in which 293 Israelis were killed and 1,950 were injured. Between the beginning of August 2003 and August 2004, when the security fence was at least partially built, terrorist elements in Samaria were able to carry out only five mass-murder attacks in Israel, in which twenty-eight Israeli civilians were killed and eighty-one injured.[72]

In view of the Palestinian terrorist organizations' increasing difficulty in conducting attacks in the years 2003 and 2004, there was a strengthening of the operational cooperation among the Palestinian terrorist organizations, and sometimes even between rival organizations that had previously fought each other. This cooperation, which occurred both in the West Bank and Gaza Strip, was reflected in, among other things, joint cells, the execution of joint terrorist attacks, and the transfer of weapons and intelligence from one organization to another. Sometimes the initiative for interorganizational coordination came from outside the West Bank and Gaza Strip, from Iran and Hezbollah.

The large number of terrorist attacks during the years of the al-Aqsa Intifada had a negative effect on morale among the Israeli public. According to the so-called Fear Index of the National Security Studies Center at the University of Haifa, anxiety levels among the Jewish population in Israel during the intifada were high, ranging from 4.9 to 5.21 (on a scale of 1–9).[73] At the end of 2004, 11.2 percent of Israelis claimed that they had been directly exposed to terrorism, and another 20.2 percent claimed that they had been indirectly exposed to terrorism through relatives or friends.[74] With regard to the mood of the Israeli public throughout the intifada, there was a significant difference between the first and second half. During the first two years, more than half of the respondents reported a bad or fairly bad mood, in comparison with 2003–2004, when more than three-quarters of the public reported a good or fairly good mood.[75] As for the "democratic dilemma of counter-terrorism" (finding a balance between preserving the liberal democratic values of the state and the need to fight terrorism effectively), the growing challenges of terrorism during the intifada seemed to reduce some Israelis' confidence in the ability of theie democracy to defend itself. In 2003, only 77 percent of the Jewish public in Israel believed that "democracy is the best form of government" (compared with 90 percent in 1999). That year, 56 percent of Israelis expressed support for the statement, "Some strong leaders can benefit the state more than all the debates and laws."[76]

In November 2004, there were reports of a significant deterioration in Arafat's health. Arafat was flown to Paris and lost consciousness and on November 10 was cut off from life support. On January 9, 2005, Abu Mazen was appointed chairman of the Palestinian Authority, and on February 8, he met with Ariel Sharon at a summit meeting in Sharm el-Sheikh with the participation of President Mubarak and King Abdullah. Immediately after the summit, the IDF stopped almost all of its military activity in the West Bank and Gaza Strip.[77] The silence that prevailed testified to the fact that the Second Intifada—the al-Aqsa Intifada—had come to an end.[78]

THE BARAK AND SHARON ADMINISTRATIONS' COUNTERTERRORISM POLICIES IN LIGHT OF THE COUNTERTERRORISM DILEMMAS MODEL

Over the course of the period under discussion, three governments were in power. The first was that of Ehud Barak, which served for a relatively short time, and the last two were administrations headed by Prime Minister Ariel Sharon. During these governments' terms, significant changes took place in the magnitude and characteristics of terrorism and in the security challenges facing the state of Israel in general.

The early part of this period, during Barak's term, witnessed a relative lull in terrorist activity. Israel and the Palestinians returned to the negotiating table and even met in Camp David in July 2000 under the auspices of the U.S. president to discuss a final settlement between the two sides. However, after the failure of the Camp David summit, and against the backdrop of opposition leader Ariel Sharon's decision to make a well-publicized visit to the Temple Mount, there was a severe deterioration in the security situation, dubbed the Second Intifada. In contrast to the First Intifada, this wave of violence involved an unprecedented number of terrorist attacks in general and suicide attacks in particular, resulting in a large number of Israeli casualties. The magnitude of the attacks and the number of victims they claimed so soon after the outbreak of this wave of terror led to the fall of the Barak government shortly after the intifada began, and to the subsequent election of Sharon as prime minister. This marked the beginning of the second phase of the period under discussion.

The suicide bombings that took place in city centers undermined Israelis' sense of personal security, and the collapse of the peace process only added to the public's frustration and despondency. This translated into domestic pressure on the Sharon government, with the public demanding that the government use all of the measures at its disposal in order to stop the unparalleled wave of terror. In the first year of his term, Sharon resisted this pressure and

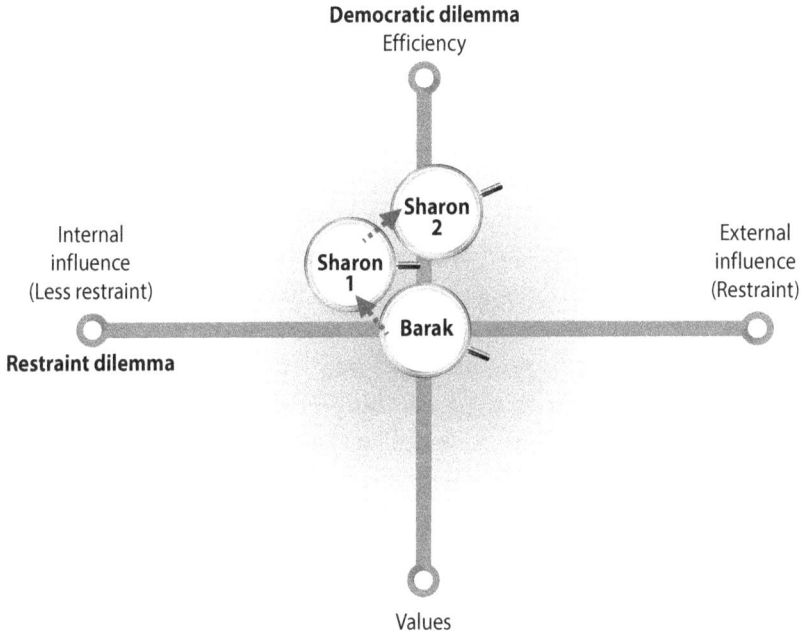

FIGURE 9.2. Counterterrorism Dilemmas Conceptual Model—Barak and Sharon administrations

refrained from initiating an escalation in counterterrorism operations. (In any case, operations were already intensive at this point and focused on carrying out targeted killings of the heads of Palestinian terrorist organizations and senior operatives, as well as on widespread administrative detentions and closures on the territories.) However, when the wave of terror reached its peak following the Passover massacre in Netanya in March 2002, Sharon removed his gloves and ordered the IDF to launch an "operation of accountability" to restore Israeli control over territories in the West Bank. This decision marked the third and final part of the period under discussion, during which Israel carried out unprecedented military operations in the territories. At the same time, the government decided to establish a physical barrier between Israel and the territories and began building the separation fence. These measures led to a dramatic decrease in the number of attacks and helped to restore the Israeli public's sense of security.

With regard to the Counterterrorism Dilemmas Conceptual Model (figure 9.2) during this period, it seems that as the terrorism threats in

Israel grew from government to government, the Barak and Sharon administrations leaned toward reaching more efficiency in the continuum of the democratic dilemma compared with previous governments. As for international pressure, during the majority of its term, Barak's government—representing the first part of this period—acted in harmony with Israel's friends in the rest of the world, primarily the United States. This cooperation was intended to advance a permanent status agreement with the Palestinians. In contrast, the first Sharon government (in power during the second part of the period under discussion) found itself in conflict with friendly countries and even reached a crisis point with the U.S. government when the latter tried to pressure Israel into returning to the negotiating table with Arafat. In the third part of this period, Sharon's second administration and President Bush were realigned after the president completely lost faith in Arafat's credibility and effectively adopted the official Israeli position, which was that Arafat was a negative force and irrelevant.

Chapter Ten

DISENGAGEMENT FROM GAZA AND ITS RAMIFICATIONS

The End of the Sharon Administration and the Ehud
Olmert Administration (2005-2008)

DISENGAGEMENT FROM THE GAZA STRIP

On December 18, 2003, Prime Minister Ariel Sharon delivered a keynote speech at IDC Herzliya's Herzliya Conference. It was a doctrinal speech that marked a fundamental change in the Israeli government's policy concerning the relationship between Israel and the Palestinians in general, and especially with regard to the future of the Gaza Strip.

> Seven months ago, my Government approved the Roadmap to peace, based on President George Bush's June 2002 speech. This is a balanced program for phased progress toward peace, to which both Israel and the Palestinians committed themselves. A full and genuine implementation of the program is the best way to achieve true peace. The Roadmap is the only political plan accepted by Israel, the Palestinians, the Americans and a majority of the international community. We are willing to proceed toward its implementation: two states—Israel and a Palestinian State—living side by side in tranquility, security and peace. The Roadmap is a clear and reasonable plan, and it is therefore possible and imperative to implement it. The concept behind this plan is that only security will lead to peace. And in that sequence. Without the achievement of full security within the framework of which terror organizations will be dismantled, it will not be possible to

achieve genuine peace, a peace for generations. This is the essence of the Roadmap. The opposite perception, according to which the very signing of a peace agreement will produce security out of thin air, has already been tried in the past and failed miserably. And such will be the fate of any other plan which promotes this concept. These plans deceive the public and create false hope. There will be no peace before the eradication of terror. The government under my leadership will not compromise on the realization of all phases of the Roadmap. It is incumbent upon the Palestinians to uproot the terrorist groups and to create a law-abiding society that fights against violence and incitement. Peace and terror cannot coexist. The world is currently united in its unequivocal demand from the Palestinians to act toward the cessation of terrorism and the implementation of reforms. . . . We began the implementation of the Roadmap at Aqaba, but the terrorist organizations joined with Yasser Arafat and sabotaged the process with a series of the most brutal terror attacks we have ever known.[1]

At that point, Sharon made a surprising declaration, which had never before been heard from him or any previous head of the Likud party:

We hope that the Palestinian Authority will carry out its part. However, if in a few months the Palestinians still continue to disregard their part in implementing the Roadmap then Israel will initiate the unilateral security step of disengagement from the Palestinians. The purpose of the Disengagement Plan is to reduce terror as much as possible, and grant Israeli citizens the maximum level of security. The process of disengagement will lead to an improvement in the quality of life, and will help strengthen the Israeli economy. . . . The Disengagement Plan is meant to grant maximum security and minimize friction between Israelis and Palestinians. We are interested in conducting direct negotiations, but do not intend to hold Israeli society hostage in the hands of the Palestinians. I have already said we will not wait for them indefinitely.

The Disengagement Plan will include the redeployment of IDF forces along new security lines and a change in the deployment of settlements, which will reduce as much as possible the number of Israelis located in the heart of the Palestinian population. We will draw provisional security lines and the IDF will be deployed along them. Security will be provided by IDF deployment, the security fence and other physical obstacles. . . . In the framework of the Disengagement Plan, Israel will strengthen its control over those same areas in the Land of Israel which will constitute an inseparable part of the State of Israel in any future agreement. . . . Israel will greatly accelerate the construction of the security fence. Today we can already see it taking shape. The rapid completion of the security fence will enable the IDF to remove roadblocks and ease the daily lives of the Palestinian population not involved in terror. . . . I would like to emphasize: the Disengagement Plan is a security measure and not a political one. The steps which will be taken will not change the political reality between Israel and the Palestinians, and will not prevent the possibility of returning to the implementation of the Roadmap and reaching an agreed settlement. . . . Obviously, through the Disengagement Plan the Palestinians will receive much less than they would have received through direct negotiations as set out in the Roadmap.[2]

This was the opening move in Israel's disengagement from the Gaza Strip. It was a process that led to a deep rift in Israeli society. Disengagement led to a strategic change in the Israeli military and civilian deployment in the Gaza Strip that influenced—and continues to affect—the characteristics of Palestinian terrorism even today. Ariel Sharon presented his initiative as punishment of the Palestinians for choosing violence and terrorism rather than diplomacy and peace. However, opponents of the Disengagement Plan argued that Sharon would not have initiated disengagement had it not been for the police investigations against him and his sons, and that a unilateral withdrawal by Israel would be a victory for terror and encourage an escalation of terrorist activity against Israel.[3]

The decision to initiate and carry out the disengagement was Prime Minister Sharon's, and it was the responsibility of the heads of the IDF and security agencies to inject the plan with operative content while trying to minimize its damage. Following publication of the Disengagement Plan at the end of 2003, the government and security apparatuses began to work diligently to prepare a detailed plan to disengage from the Gaza Strip. In February 2004, the first discussion of the plan among the top ranks of the IDF took place. At that meeting, IDF Chief of Staff Ya'alon expressed his strong opposition to a unilateral move.[4] According to Yossi Kuperwasser, then head of research at the Military Intelligence Directorate, "the army was not asked and did not deal with the question of whether or not it was right to carry out the disengagement, only the question of how to implement it.

On this subject, the heads of the army presented the prime minister with the disengagement's implications."[5]

The Disengagement Plan took about a year and a half to prepare, but turning the idea into reality was not a simple process. It encountered great resistance and was beset by political, governmental, social, security, domestic, and international crises. These crises were reflected within the various political parties and Israeli society and in the Knesset, defense establishment, and army. Ministers who opposed the plan were dismissed from the government, petitions against the evacuations were submitted to the High Court of Justice, and the phenomenon of conscientious objection within the army began to spread. The waves of protest that swept the country adopted the color orange, which became the symbol of resistance to the disengagement.

Mass demonstrations and protests, sometimes including hundreds of thousands of people, were organized in various places around the country. It seemed that the rift that was created between members of the religious Zionist camp and the rest of Israeli society in the wake of the disengagement could not be mended. The societal crisis reached its peak during evacuation of the settlements from the Gaza Strip in the last quarter of 2005 and intensified with the difficult scenes of the forceful uprooting of Israeli citizens from their homes and property. Passive and mostly nonviolent resistance sometimes deteriorated into violent incidents that saw fierce struggles by the settlers against IDF soldiers and the Israeli police. Preparations for the disengagement also brought about some heinous acts by Israeli extremists. On August 4, 2005, IDF deserter Eden Natan-Zada murdered four passengers and wounded nine others on the number 165 bus in the Druze neighborhood of Shfaram.[6] The murderer was arrested but was lynched by the angry crowd. About two weeks later, Asher Wiesgan snatched the weapon off a security guard in the industrial zone of Shilo and opened fire on the Palestinian workers who were in the area. Four workers were killed and one wounded. On that day, Yelena Bosinova set herself on fire to protest the disengagement, and on August 31, Baruch Ben-Menachem did the same.

On April 14, President George W. Bush gave his support to the Israeli Disengagement Plan in the form of a letter of commitment that was ratified by both houses of Congress. The letter stated that the large Israeli settlement blocs in the West Bank would remain under Israeli sovereignty in a future agreement with the Palestinians and that no return of Palestinian refugees to Israeli territory would be permitted under such an agreement. Dov Weisglass, who served as Prime Minister Sharon's political advisor, defined the presidential commitment as the greatest diplomatic achievement in the history of the state of Israel.[7] However, in contrast to the support given by the United States and European countries for the far-reaching Israeli move, the Disengagement Plan was met with increasing criticism and opposition from within the prime minister's home base—the Likud party.

In an attempt to bypass opposition to the Disengagement Plan within his party, Sharon announced that he would hold a referendum among all party members and that if he lost, he would resign. About 60 percent of the referendum members voted on May 2, 2004, against the Disengagement Plan. Contrary to his promise, not only did Sharon not resign, he decided to transfer the decision to the government and fired the ministers who opposed disengagement. On June 6, the Disengagement Plan was approved by the government, and on February 16, 2005, the Knesset passed the law to implement the plan, with a majority of fifty-nine votes in favor, forty votes against, and five abstentions. In response to criticism that the process of approval for the disengagement was made abruptly and undemocratically, Weisglass and Sharon's son Omri said that Sharon was not only the chairman of the Likud; he was also, and perhaps more important, the Israeli prime minister. The good of the Likud was important, but the good of the country took precedence. The High Court of Justice approved the dismissal of the ministers, saying that in those circumstances, such moves were legitimate, as they did not take place in secret but, rather, over two years of deliberations and voting in various forums.[8]

On August 15, 2005, implementation of the Disengagement Plan began in Gush Katif and a number of isolated settlements in northern Samaria. Two days later, the phase of forced evacuation of the settlers who had refused the orders to leave began, marked by difficult confrontations between the settlers who had barricaded themselves in their homes and the police officers and soldiers who had to evacuate them. On September 12, the Disengagement Plan was completed, and the Israeli settlements in the Gaza Strip were evacuated and destroyed. IDF forces left strip after thirty-eight years and redeployed along the 1967 Green Line. During the disengagement, Israel also evacuated four isolated settlements in northern Samaria (Ganim, Kadim, Homesh, and Sa-Nur).

About two weeks before the plan was rolled out, most of the Jewish Israeli public (57 percent) supported it, and 36 percent opposed it. The main reasons given by those who opposed disengagement were fears that the Palestinians would interpret it as flight by Israel and that the withdrawal from Gaza would increase terror from that area and constitute a strategic threat to the country's security. The main explanation given by those who supported disengagement was that the Israeli presence in Gaza only reinforced the motivation for terrorism and exacted too high a price in casualties, and that Gaza was not part of the historic land of Israel/Palestine.[9]

One of the main arguments against Israel's disengagement from the Gaza Strip concerned the unilateral nature of the move, which was not coordinated with the Palestinians. Some of the plan's opponents argued that the move should have been coordinated with the Palestinians, whereas others argued that Israel should have received compensation from the Palestinians for evacuating the area. Brigadier General Eival Giladi, one of the architects of the disengagement in the IDF, argued that Israel's compensation should be measured in terms not of Israeli-Palestinian relations but of Israeli-U.S. relations, in light of President Bush's letter of commitment, as well as Israel's relations with European countries, which improved in the wake of the move.[10]

As mentioned, Prime Minister Sharon presented the move as the result of Israel's disappointment with Palestinian's unwillingness to make progress in the peace process in accordance with the roadmap and as a response to the diplomatic deadlock. Despite the public image that disengagement was a unilateral move, Weisglass claimed that following Arafat's death and Abu Mazen's appointment as chairman of the Palestinian Authority at the beginning of 2005, the entire disengagement process was coordinated with Abu Mazen. According to Weisglass, the hope was that the newly evacuated Gaza Strip would become a model of economic success, as the Palestinians promised.[11] This hope quickly proved to be unfounded. The optimistic vision was shattered when reality hit. After the IDF and the Israeli settlers left the Gaza Strip, the evacuated areas were seized by Hamas activists, who ousted the Palestinian police officers, Fatah activists, and Palestinian Authority representatives.

Israelis' hopes for improvement resulting from disengagement and their desire to improve the security situation and allow the Palestinians to conduct their affairs in the strip with minimal ties to Israel, proved to be unrealistic. About two weeks after completion of the disengagement and departure of the last IDF soldier from the Gaza Strip, Israel found itself under attack from dozens of rockets fired at the communities surrounding the Gaza Strip and the city of Sderot. This was following the explosion of Qassam rockets that fell from a vehicle in the midst of a Hamas military parade in the Jabalya refugee camp. About twenty Palestinians were killed and about eighty injured, and Palestinians placed the blame on Israel.[12] The dozens of rockets fired into Israel during one night in particular led to a two-week Israeli military operation in late September 2005, dubbed "First Rain." The operation consisted mainly of retaliatory fire by the Israeli air force and artillery corps against the terrorist organizations and infrastructure targets in the Gaza Strip.[13] The IDF operation was accompanied by closure of the strip and a series of targeted killings of terrorist operatives, along with continued Qassam fire from the Gaza Strip into Israel.

The Palestinian public attributed the "achievement" of Israel's unilateral withdrawal from the Gaza Strip to Israeli fear of Hamas attacks, and not to the peace process led on the Palestinian side by Abu Mazen. The change that began to take place in the Palestinian political system was first reflected in the success of Hamas candidates in local elections in 2005, after which Hamas participated in Palestinian parliamentary elections for the first time. In January 2006, Hamas won these elections and established a government headed by Ismail Haniyeh.[14] The elections were postponed from September 2005 due to Abu Mazen's fear that Hamas would strengthen in the wake of disengagement from Gaza. In that same month, Sharon suffered a severe stroke, and his powers as prime minister were transferred to his deputy, Ehud Olmert.

OPERATION BRINGING HOME THE GOODS

At the beginning of March, Israel learned that the new Hamas government intended to release the murderers of Minister Rehavam Ze'evi, including the secretary-general of the Popular Front for the Liberation of Palestine, Ahmed Sa'adat, who were under the supervision of British monitors in the Jericho prison. The IDF was deployed to the area, and when the British inspectors left the prison, Operation Bringing Home the Goods was launched. IDF soldiers surrounded the prison and demanded that the murderers turn themselves in. When they refused, the IDF began to demolish the building until the terrorists surrendered.[15] During the operation, mass demonstrations were held throughout the West Bank, and in an attempt to force Israel to retreat and release the murderers, fourteen foreign nationals were kidnapped, and their abductors threatened to harm them. However, due to international pressure exerted on the Palestinians, the hostages were released unharmed.

At the end of the month, elections were held, and Ehud Olmert was appointed the twelfth prime minister of Israel. Shortly after the elections, a suicide bombing was carried out near the settlement of Kedumim in the West Bank. A terrorist hitched a ride and blew himself up in the car, killing its four passengers.[16] On April 17, another suicide bombing occurred, this time at the restaurant Rosh Ha'ir at Tel Aviv's central bus station. The attack killed nine civilians and injured sixty-six others.[17] For its part, Israel continued to carry out targeted killings of terrorist operatives. Olmert explained the rationale behind this counterterrorism measure:

> Against whom do we carry out targeted killings? In general, they are divided into two groups: operatives who are about to fire/launch rockets, when there is a reasonably high probability that these rockets will hit and kill someone. In these cases you say "if someone comes to kill you, rise up and kill him first." That is to say, it is an action of self-defense in the classic sense of the word. The UAV sees someone who is going to install a rocket for launch and shoots him to kill, like on the battlefield. . . . Then there is the other group [senior terrorist operatives], someone like Imad Mughniyeh.[18] He was the man who gave the orders and set the rules of conduct and was responsible for the killing of 241 U.S. Marines. He was responsible for the attack in Tyre, in which more than 90 Israelis were killed. . . . We have to be careful, moderate and focused, and only target those whose elimination substantially assists the war on terror. . . . In this context, President Bush used a definition that I agreed with. He used to ask representatives of the American agencies: This particular person that we want to target—if we do not eliminate him and he continues to live, is there a real danger that people will die as a result? Yes or No? If there is no real danger then there is no justification for the death penalty, but if there is a real danger that innocent people will be killed, then it is actually an act of self-defense. . . . There is no country in the world that does not use targeted killings against terrorists. The world is just divided between those who do it without apologizing for it and those who do it and do apologize for it, and moreover criticize others who do it.[19]

On June 9, the head of the Popular Resistance Committees, Jamal Abu Samhadana, and three of his operatives were killed in the Gaza Strip. According to the commander of the Southern Command Yoav Galant, Samhadana had been overseeing the training of a cell to infiltrate Israel in order to launch a large-scale suicide attack.[20] On the same day, a Palestinian family was killed in an explosion on the northern shore of the Gaza Strip.[21] The Palestinians accused Israel, saying that its artillery fire caused the death of the family. Despite Israeli's denial, over the following days, numerous Qassam rockets were fired at Sderot and the communities surrounding the Gaza Strip, and the IDF continued to foil the launch of rockets by shooting down the launching cells from the air.

In 2006, 24 Israelis were killed in terrorist attacks, compared with 50 in 2005, 109 in 2004, 199 in 2003, and 426 in 2002.[22] Thus, the number of Israeli victims of Palestinian terror after Operation Defensive Shield continued to decline, partly due to a decrease in the number of suicide bombings in Israel, from 60 in 2002, to 26 in 2003, 15 in 2004, 8 in 2005, and 6 in 2006. The growing difficulty that terrorist organizations faced in infiltrating Israel, both from the Gaza Strip after disengagement and from the West Bank in light of progress in construction of the land barrier (the security fence between Israel and the West Bank), led to a change in the organizations' preferred methods of terrorist attacks, specifically to an emphasis on high-trajectory fire. In comparison with the 401 rockets that hit Israel in 2005, in 2006, 1,722 rockets were fired.[23]

HAMAS TAKEOVER AND CONSOLIDATION OF THE GAZA STRIP

Shortly after completion of Israel's withdrawal from the Gaza Strip, clashes broke out between the Hamas-led Palestinian terrorist organizations and Fatah and the Palestinian police officers under Abu Mazen's authority. The PA chairman refrained from taking steps to disarm the organizations, and his men encountered severe violence from Hamas activists in the Gaza Strip. In the years that followed, Hamas sought to consolidate its rule in Gaza and turn it into a religious Islamic state by imposing Islamic rules of conduct on the population and eliminating its opponents in the area. On the one hand, control of the territory and responsibility for the well-being of the Palestinian population forced Hamas to organize itself to provide basic services to residents. Hamas's charitable infrastructure replaced the PA's dismantled apparatuses and relatively quickly facilitated the provision of educational and welfare services, which brought Hamas much approval.

On the other hand, Hamas did not abandon its involvement in terrorism, via its operatives living in the West Bank and those in the Gaza Strip, thereby becoming a hybrid terrorist organization, with one arm engaged in terror and another engaged in pseudo-legitimate *Da'wa* activities (provision of education, welfare, and religious services): a hybrid terrorist organization that controls both territory and population and is embedded within the civilian society, which is under its control.

Israel's withdrawal from the Gaza Strip during the disengagement and closure that Israel imposed on the strip after the Hamas takeover reduced the Palestinians' terrorist organizations in Gaza to enter Israel and carry out attacks on its territory. As a result, Hamas, with the assistance of Hezbollah and Iran, began a massive buildup of rockets for high-trajectory firing on Israel. Hamas and the other terrorist organizations invested considerable funds and efforts in the construction of lathes and manufacturing facilities for Qassam rockets in the Gaza Strip, while constantly trying to improve the quality of rocket fire and increase the rockets' range. At the same time, the organizations, led by Hamas, worked to dig tunnels and develop the underground infrastructure, in the Gaza Strip and via cross-border tunnels; these were both smuggling tunnels from Sinai (Egypt) into the Gaza Strip and attack tunnels into Israeli territory. In the framework of these excavations, Hamas established an underground rocket-launching system inside the Gaza Strip and built a system of bunkers that served as hiding places, weapons storage areas, situation rooms, and tunnels linking various underground facilities.[24]

ABDUCTION OF GILAD SHALIT

The tunnel system dug between the Gaza Strip and the Sinai was used to smuggle equipment and other civilian goods into the strip alongside weapons (such as Grad rockets, thousands of kilograms of explosives, antitank launchers, small arms, and more). These tunnels were also used to smuggle terrorists between the areas, as well as to bring Iranian experts, engineers, and trainers into Gaza to provide military training and direction and supervision of the rocket-manufacturing industry.[25] The Gaza Strip's sandy soil allowed terrorist operatives to dig tunnels relatively easily and use them for border crossings and infiltration into Israel to carry out attacks.

One of the most widely known such attack was the abduction near Kerem Shalom on June 25, 2006, during which Israeli soldier Gilad Shalit was captured and brought to the Gaza Strip. The attack killed two other soldiers and wounded four. A joint cell of Hamas, the Popular Resistance Committees, and the Army of Islam infiltrated into Israel through a tunnel and attacked an Israeli Merkava tank that was set up to guard the perimeter fence. In response, Israel launched an air strike against terrorist targets in the Gaza Strip, leading to rocket fire from Gaza into Israel and further Israeli air strikes in the area. A few days after the kidnapping, Shalit's captors demanded the release of 1,000 Palestinian prisoners who had been convicted of terrorist activity and were serving sentences in Israeli jails. Israel rejected these demands and announced that it would not agree to a prisoner exchange in return for the kidnapped soldier's release.[26] Despite this refusal, and perhaps in light of the determination of the prime minister, who opposed a prisoner exchange deal with Hamas, on July 20, Israel decided to release 255 Palestinian prisoners, all Fatah members, as a gesture to PA chairman Mahmoud Abbas.

In the wake of Shalit's abduction and escalation on the southern border, Israel launched a ground operation in the northern and central Gaza Strip, dubbed "Operation Summer Rains." It lasted about four months, during which Israel uncovered and destroyed tunnels, demolished rocket launcher infrastructure and weapons warehouses, and carried out arrests and targeted assassinations. As part of the Summer Rains operation, numerous military actions were conducted in various areas of the Gaza Strip. On November 26, a bilateral ceasefire was declared. The IDF withdrew its forces from Gaza, and the Palestinian terrorist organizations pledged to hold their fire. Israel failed to secure the release of Shalit during the operation, and negotiations between Israel and Hamas began, with Egyptian mediation, for a deal to free the soldier in exchange for the release of terrorists imprisoned in Israel.

In view of the deterioration of security along the southern border and the abduction of Shalit, the majority of the Israeli public changed its position on the disengagement and withdrawal from the Gaza Strip, with many concluding that Israel's decision to disengage was a mistake. Supporters of peace in Israel who had hoped that the Gaza Strip would become a model of prosperity, moderation, and the building of trust between the two sides, and that it would constitute an important step toward the establishment of Israeli-Palestinian peace, were dismayed to discover that within a short time after the Israeli withdrawal from the Gaza Strip, Hamas had taken control of the evacuated area, built up an infrastructure of terror, turned it into a huge arsenal of thousands of rockets, and deployed hundreds of launchers throughout the strip while being shielded by the Palestinian population. Even Israeli citizens who supported the disengagement on the assumption that the move would strengthen Israel's security, as it would be free to carry out preventive and retaliatory military action against any terrorist threat originating from the Gaza Strip without fear of causing harm to the settlers living there, soon discovered that this hope had no basis in reality.

Other supporters of the disengagement, on the other hand, emphasized that the use of rocket fire against Israel began not with the disengagement but years earlier, after Israel withdrew from densely populated Palestinian areas in the Gaza Strip in the framework of the Oslo Accords. At that time, rockets and mortars were fired at Israeli settlements in the Gaza Strip and at nearby Israeli communities, and from there they poured into Israel. According to Prime Minister Ariel Sharon's advisor Dov Weisglass, the increase in rocket range was not the result of the presence or absence of 8,000 Israelis in the Gaza Strip but, rather, was due to the improvement in Hamas's technological capabilities.[27] The head of research at Military Intelligence at the time, Brigadier General Yossi Kuperwasser, added that the decision to relinquish control over vital areas in the Gaza Strip within the framework of the Oslo Accords sowed the seeds for the high-trajectory fire following a "period of ripening." He claimed, however, that without Israel's withdrawal from the Gaza Strip, it would have been difficult for the Palestinians to reach the capabilities they did in the years that followed. Moreover, Kuperwasser argued that despite the claim that in the absence of Israeli citizens in the Gaza Strip, it would be easier for the IDF to operate against Hamas and respond to provocations and attacks, following the withdrawal, when the IDF suggested launching ground operations against Hamas in Gaza, the political echelon repeatedly said that "we did not leave Gaza in order to return there."[28] Thus, in effect, after the disengagement, Israel became much more limited than it had been in the past with regard to its proactive preventive capabilities.

THE SECOND LEBANON WAR

On July 19, 2005, the IDF's intelligence directorate published an assessment of the changes that had taken place in Lebanon following the assassination of Lebanese President Rafik Hariri on February 14, 2005, and the withdrawal of the Syrian army from Lebanon. The intelligence assessment described the strengthening of Hezbollah's status in Lebanon.[29] In December 2005, head of Military Intelligence Ze'evi-Farkash noted in a letter to the prime minister that Israel had lost its deterrent capability vis-à-vis Hezbollah and that because of this,

> the organization would continue to try to kidnap soldiers in 2006, as this is its only way to fight for its political and military existence in Lebanon. Hezbollah attempted to kidnap soldiers three times in 2005 and failed; there is a chance that its fourth or fifth or sixth attempt could succeed, and we will find ourselves in a strategic political mess in Lebanon as we will not stand by—we will have to respond firmly.[30]

In late 2005, the directorate presented the government with an intelligence warning about Hezbollah and the Lebanese arena. The warning did not exactly predict the kidnapping that took place several months later, but it did foresee the escalation that would come in the summer of 2006 following the potential kidnapping of an IDF soldier by Hezbollah.[31]

On the morning of July 12, Hezbollah began shelling Israeli northern communities. It was a diversion that marked the beginning of a long-planned abduction by Hezbollah that was carried out at the same time in the Zar'it area of northern Israel. A Hezbollah cell ambushed an IDF patrol of two military vehicles with antitank missiles. Three soldiers were killed in the attack. At the same time, another Hezbollah cell entered Israel and kidnapped two IDF soldiers who were injured in the ambush—Ehud Goldwasser and Eldad Regev. Rescue forces summoned to the area encountered landmines that had been dispersed by Hezbollah, delaying the rescue of the wounded.

The abduction attack in the north, which took place shortly after Shalit's kidnapping in the south, forced the government to respond harshly in order to restore Israel's deterrence against its enemies. However, Israel seemingly launched the campaign in Lebanon without clear goals and objectives and without formulating action plans to achieve these goals. Policy was improvised as the fighting developed. In one media interview, the prime minister stated that the goal was to release the abducted soldiers. In another interview, a senior minister said that the goal was to change the rules of the game vis-à-vis Hezbollah. Thus, different objectives and goals were hastily formulated. Although Israel did not choose the date of the conflict but was dragged into it following abduction of the soldiers in the north, such a kidnapping had been Israel's main reference scenario with regard Hezbollah for a few years before the outbreak of the Second Lebanon War. Nasrallah had not concealed his intentions and attempts to kidnap IDF soldiers. Despite this, immediately after the abduction, Israel acted in what appeared to be an instinctive offensive move that lacked an organized military plan.

The campaign in Lebanon lasted approximately one month, with both sides employing massive firepower. The IDF's senior command at the time was composed of former members of the Air Force: IDF Chief of Staff Dan Halutz; former Air Force commander and head of Military Intelligence Amos Yadlin, also a former senior officer; and commander Eliezer Shkedi. The composition of this group might have been the reason for the misconception that Hezbollah could be defeated from the air without the need for a significant ground maneuver in southern Lebanon. The political echelon at that time lacked military and operational experience and knowledge. The prime minister and defense minister (as opposed to those in previous governments) were not former senior military officers and therefore did not have a basis on which to challenge the assessments of the IDF commanders. One of Israel's most serious mistakes during the Second Lebanon War was thus the failure to appreciate the limits of air power in crippling Hezbollah's rocket-launching capability. However, even decision makers lacking military experience should have known that the air force had not succeeded in stopping rocket attacks on Israel in 1981, 1982, 1992, and 1996,[32] and that there was no reason for it to succeed in the current mission.

The writing was on the wall, but it might have been dimmed by another mistaken strategic assumption, that Israel would be able to create pressure on Hezbollah among the Lebanese public and government to stop the attacks. Here, too, one could have learned from history. In previous operations in Lebanon—"Accountability" (1993) and "Grapes of Wrath" (1996)—this strategy proved to be a failure. Theoretically, Israel might have been able to apply pressure on Hezbollah through the Lebanese people, but it either could not or would not pay the moral and international price involved in implementing such a strategy. Not every policy that might be suitable for a superpower like the United States is necessarily suitable for a country like Israel. It is interesting to note that another former Air Force officer, Ido Nehushtan, who was to be appointed head of the IDF's Planning Directorate after the war, challenged the misconception that was prevalent in the IDF during the war, recommending that the chief of staff "tell the government honestly that without a broad ground operation, we cannot remove the threat of Katyusha rockets. If the government does not approve this, we have to recommend that the operation be stopped now. . . . We have to tell the political echelon that we cannot reduce the firing of the Katyusha rockets unless we take the area up to the Litani River."[33]

In the Second Lebanon War, Israel essentially fell into a trap that Hezbollah had set. Although it is reasonable to assume that Hezbollah was surprised by the scope of the Israeli response, it was the organization that determined the time, place, and even conduct of the conflict. There was little room for criticism to be leveled against Israeli intelligence, as the extent of Hezbollah's armament was largely known: the quality and quantity of Katyushas in their possession, their range, the support and aid that Hezbollah received from Syria and Iran, their entrenchments and fortifications, and even their method of warfare. All of these things were known to the Israeli intelligence community and had been presented to decision makers over the years. The few intelligence surprises were mainly tactical, such as the existence of an advanced naval missile in the possession of Hezbollah. The main intelligence failure seemed to be the fact that since the withdrawal from Lebanon in 2000, senior officials had not stood firm against their prime ministers and continued to fulfill their role as Israel's national assessors, even when they understood the growing danger on the northern border as a result of hesitancy on the part of the political echelon.

The intelligence that was in Israel's hands only highlights the government's hasty decision to carry out large-scale reactionary actions in Lebanon as a result of having been dragged into a provocation by Hezbollah. Israel did indeed have to change the rules of the game against Hezbollah at the time, but the question is whether the timing of the launching of the offensive—immediately after the soldiers were abducted—was right. Although a large-scale Israeli operation against Hezbollah a week or a month after the soldiers were kidnapped would have been met with harsh international criticism even though immediate action was accepted by the international community, it would have been preferable for Israel to wait for more favorable conditions for launching the campaign and maintaining the element of surprise, to formulate clear objectives, and to engage in detailed planning and all the preparations necessary before conducting such a military operation. In any case, international support tends to erode the longer a campaign continues, making a shorter and more effective campaign preferable.

Over the course of the Second Lebanon War, Hezbollah fired some 3,990 short-, medium-, and long-range rockets into Israel (from an arsenal of about 14,000 rockets). The rocket fire killed 49 Israeli civilians and 121 soldiers.[34] In addition to the loss of life, significant financial damage occurred, in particular to the residents of the north, as well as damage to the morale and sense of security of the millions of civilians who were forced to spend long periods in shelters.[35] The rocket fire caused about a third of the residents of the north to leave their homes for the center and south of the country. Many volunteers were quick to assist in organizing the evacuees' movement and host them in public buildings and private homes. However, the state's institutions seemed unable to cope with the challenge of orderly evacuation of the northern population to the center and south of the country.

On the other side, Hezbollah was seriously hit during the month of fighting. More than 10 percent of its operatives in southern Lebanon were killed. Its rocket-launching system was impaired for the medium to long term. Hezbollah lost its network of observation and firing positions along the border with Israel, and the organization faced harsh criticism from Lebanese citizens for the destruction caused by the abduction of the IDF soldiers.[36] In light of these consequences, one can understand Nasrallah's declaration in an interview with Lebanese television on August 27, 2006: "the capture was carried out because we did not think that Israel would go to war against us, and had we estimated, even 1 percent, that Israel would go to war, we would not have carried out the operation."[37]

On August 12, 2006, the UN Security Council adopted Resolution 1701 calling for a ceasefire between the two sides. Two days later, the ceasefire went into effect, and UNIFIL forces began to enter the areas vacated by the IDF.[38] In the wake of the Second Lebanon War, a state commission of inquiry was established, headed by retired judge Aharon Winograd. Defense Minister Amir Peretz and IDF chief of staff Halutz resigned from their posts.

THE LULL IN THE GAZA STRIP AND OPERATION CAST LEAD

Despite the rounds of fighting between Israel and Hamas and the Palestinian organizations following the disengagement from the Gaza Strip, and despite the fact that Israel's aerial activity and ground operations caused many casualties among these organizations' activists and the Palestinian population, Hamas and the other terrorist organizations did not cease efforts to arm themselves and improve their military infrastructure, rocket-launching system, and underground tunnels.

In August 2006, Israel foiled a major attack when it uncovered an attack tunnel near the Karni crossing, one of the main crossings from Israel through which vital goods are transferred to the Gaza Strip. The Palestinians intended to plant dozens of powerful explosive devices at the end of the tunnel, just below the IDF administration building at the border crossing. The explosion was intended to cause a large number of casualties.[39]

The ceasefire reached after Operation Summer Rains in November 2006 did not end the high-trajectory fire from the Gaza Strip into Israel. The new alignment of forces in the strip and Hamas's policy led to confrontations with Israel from time to time, whether initiated by terrorist operatives not affiliated with Hamas or initiated and directed by Hamas. Although the organization's control over the Gaza Strip was undisputed, the movement's leaders allowed other fundamentalist terrorist organizations—such as PIJ, the Popular Resistance Committees, the Al-Aqsa Brigades, and Salafist-Jihadist groups (Jaljalat)—to continue operating in the strip. In its conduct with these organizations, Hamas chose to establish its control through negotiations, persuasion, and, when necessary, even threats and local clashes. However, Hamas did not take steps to neutralize these organizations' military capabilities or disarm them (despite the fact that from time to time, their members challenged Hamas's hegemony and acted in opposition to its policies and perhaps even to its interests by firing at Israel sporadically).

Israel, for its part, continued to take action to prevent rocket fire and terrorist attacks through aerial assaults and targeted killings. In 2006, there was a 100 percent increase in the number of rocket attacks against Israel compared with the previous year: in 2006, 1,247 rockets and mortar shells were fired from the Gaza Strip into Israel, whereas in 2005, only 286 were launched. In 2007, there were 938 launches; in 2008, 1,270.[40]

On January 29, 2007, Palestinian Islamic Jihad carried out a suicide attack in the southern city of Eilat in which three Israelis were killed. The terrorist had departed from the Gaza Strip and continued to Egyptian territory in Sinai, and from there, he then returned to the Israeli border near Eilat and infiltrated the Israeli resort town to execute the attack.[41] In February that year, Hamas leaders met with Abu Mazen under the auspices of King Abdullah of Saudi Arabia and agreed to establish a Palestinian unity government and end all hostilities between the various organizations.[42] However, this agreement was short-lived. The violent confrontations between Hamas and Fatah in the Gaza Strip soon resumed and even escalated, leading to the dismantling of the unity government. Hamas had the upper hand, and it completed its takeover of the Gaza Strip in mid-2007, expelling PA officials and Abu Mazen loyalists.

Israel continued its offensive activity in Gaza in order to thwart terrorist attacks and the firing of rockets and to cause damage to the terrorist organizations. In most cases, these counterterrorism activities were carried out by air, sea, or artillery fire, and in a small number of cases, offensive activity also included incursions by small numbers of infantry forces, armored forces, or engineering corps forces. Some of these actions were aimed at capturing Hamas operatives and gathering intelligence to help locate the kidnapped soldier, Gilad Shalit. In light of these actions, at the beginning of September, the Palestinians claimed that Israel had captured a senior Hamas operative, Abu Khaled, who had been involved in Shalit's abduction and knew where he was being held.[43] At the same time, rocket fire continued into Israel, and on September 11, sixty-nine soldiers were injured when Qassam rockets hit a basic training base in Zikim, near the Gaza Strip. The escalating rocket fire from Gaza prompted the Israeli government to declare the strip a "hostile entity," thereby separating it from the West Bank under Abu Mazen's control.[44]

At the end of November, an Israeli-Palestinian conference was held at the U.S. Naval Academy in Annapolis, Maryland, under the auspices of President Bush, to promote the stalled peace process. Although the conference, which included the participation of delegations from some forty countries (including Arab states), ended seven years of political stalemate and closed with a joint statement by Abu Mazen and Ehud Olmert on the opening of negotiations and commitment to the roadmap in order to attain a final status agreement, it did not bring about a real renewal of the peace process. After a few months, each sides blamed the other for not fulfilling its obligations.[45]

In early 2008, a number of severe terrorist attacks were perpetrated against Israelis. On January 24, Palestinian terrorists infiltrated Kfar Etzion in the West Bank and stabbed three yeshiva students. On the same day, another Palestinian opened fire at Israeli police near Shuafat, killing an officer and injuring a policewoman. On February 4, Hamas carried out a suicide bombing at a shopping center in Dimona, in which a woman was killed and nine people were wounded. Following an Israeli targeted killing operation on February 27, 2008, in which five Hamas operatives were killed after having returned from training in Iran, Hamas fired dozens of rockets at Israel, and a civilian was killed when a rocket hit Sderot's Sapir College.

The escalation of rocket fire into Israel led to another Israeli ground operation in the Gaza Strip in February 2008, Operation Hot Winter. During the forty-eight-hour operation, infantry forces entered the northern Gaza Strip near the neighborhood of Shejaia with the aim of exposing infrastructures built by the terrorist organizations near the border fence in order to launch attacks. The IDF ground incursion was followed by the firing of dozens of Qassam rockets at communities in the south of the country—those surrounding Gaza, the western Negev communities, and the cities of Sderot and Ashkelon.[46] Two IDF soldiers were killed during the operation, and eight were injured. On the Palestinian side, some 120 people were killed. (The Palestinians claimed that most of these were civilians, but the IDF claimed that most of them were armed and that civilians were sometimes injured by unintentional fire from the Palestinians.). The Palestinians sustained severe damage but continued to fire Qassams at Israel throughout the operation. Afterward, Hamas began indirect talks with Israel via Egyptian mediation in order to achieve a ceasefire, or *tahadiya* ("lull").[47] These talks, led by the Ministry of Defense under Ehud Barak, conflicted with the positions of Foreign Minister Tzipi Livni and ISA Director Avi Diskin, who feared the talks would strengthen Hamas at the expense of PA Chairman Abu Mazen.[48]

On March 6, 2008, a Palestinian terrorist from east Jerusalem entered the Mercaz Harav Yeshiva in Jerusalem and opened fire. Eight students were killed and eleven were wounded in the attack. That same day, two IDF soldiers were killed by a roadside bomb planted by terrorists near the Gaza perimeter fence. On April 9, two Israeli civilians were killed at the

Karni crossing in a shooting attack carried out by Islamic Jihad operatives together with the Resistance Committees. On April 16, three IDF soldiers were killed in combat in the Gaza Strip, and on April 19, Hamas conducted a coordinated attack on an IDF post near the Kerem Shalom crossing, during which mortar shells were fired at the outpost, as well as fire from armored vehicles, while three suicide bombers entered Israel from the Gaza Strip and detonated two car bombs. The attacks wounded thirteen Israeli soldiers.

Throughout this period, the terrorist organizations continued to fire rockets at Israeli communities in the vicinity of Gaza. Three Israeli civilians were killed by rocket fire in May 2008, and in June, an Israeli man was killed and four others were wounded by mortar shells that landed near Kibbutz Nir Oz. In light of the escalation in the south and progress in the negotiations with Hamas toward achieving a truce, on June 11, 2008, the Israeli government decided to prepare for a large-scale ground operation in the Gaza Strip but to first give the negotiations a chance to be completed.[49] Egypt's mediation efforts bore fruit, and on June 19, 2008, a lull was declared between Israel and Hamas and the Palestinian organizations in Gaza. The agreement included the opening of the crossings into Gaza and progress in the negotiations for the release of Gilad Shalit. It significantly reduced the number of rocket attacks and attempted terrorist attacks by the organizations, but it also marked the beginning of a wave of self-initiated attacks carried out by Palestinian lone wolves who did not belong to any particular terrorist organization and from which they did not get any operational support (though they were generally inspired and incited by those organizations). At the beginning of July, a Palestinian resident of east Jerusalem attacked passersby on a central street in Jerusalem with a shovel, killing three people and injuring thirty-six. And on September 22, an east Jerusalem Palestinian rammed his car into a group of soldiers, injuring nineteen of them.

Even after the lull began, the Palestinian organizations, especially PIJ and other so-called rogue groups, continued to fire rockets at Israel sporadically. They, as well as Hamas, also took advantage of the lull to continue to build up their high-trajectory fire capability and dig tunnels both within Gaza as well as attack tunnels into Israel. In early November, Israel carried out an operation to destroy a booby-trapped house and an attack tunnel dug by Hamas in Gaza strip 300 meters from the border with Israel. Six terrorists were killed during the operation. This action and the response that followed, which included massive rocket fire at the communities surrounding the Gaza Strip and Ashkelon, ended the lull, and in the following days and throughout the month of November, the rocket fire continued. In response, Israel once again closed the crossings for the movement of people and goods into the Gaza Strip.[50]

The exchange of fire escalated in early December 2008, which led to hundreds of thousands of Israeli citizens spending long periods in shelters, under the heavy barrage of rockets from the Gaza Strip. On December 18, a day before the lull was meant to end, and after a discussion among the Palestinian organizations in Gaza, the Palestinians, led by Hamas, announced the end of the lull.[51] In the following days, Hamas spokesmen declared that they were interested in renewing the truce, but this was not reflected in a reduction in rocket fire into Israel. From the beginning of the lull and until the occurrence of another large-scale operation conducted in the Gaza Strip, 361 rockets and 303 mortar shells were fired into Israel.[52]

In view of Hamas's announcement declaring the end of the lull, as far as Israel was concerned, conditions were ripe for a long-planned large-scale military operation in the Gaza Strip. Operation Cast Lead began with a wide-ranging attack by the Israeli Air Force on December 27. Its purpose was to take action against the Hamas infrastructure in the Gaza Strip and stop the rocket fire into Israel.[53] On the eve of the operation, the prime minister held a discussion with the heads of the secret services, in which it was decided that the operation would begin only when intelligence indicated that Hamas operatives and leaders would be present at the targets chosen for attack. The aerial operation that launched Cast Lead thus included the simultaneous attack by about sixty Israeli fighter jets of approximately seventy targets that included ammunition stockpiles, rocket-manufacturing facilities, Hamas bases and those of the other Palestinian terrorist organizations, as well as the closing ceremony of the Hamas police officers' course.[54] Hamas and the Palestinian organizations suffered heavy damages from the air strikes but did not actually bear a strategic loss; most of the key operatives and force commanders hid in the underground tunnels under civilian buildings in densely populated areas, thus surviving the attack.[55] During the first week of the operation, the weather prevented the IDF from launching a ground maneuver, as there were heavy clouds over the Gaza Strip.

With the beginning of the ground operation, there was a significant change in the use of Israeli forces as a result of the directive of ISA's head to provide the IDF with all of the organization's intelligence capabilities throughout the operation. The ISA also decided to use all the intelligence means at its disposal to help the operation, even at the risk of exposing intelligence sources. This unprecedented decision enabled the combat forces in Gaza to access up-to-date intelligence on the area in which they were fighting.[56] However, during the operation, the Palestinian terrorist organizations executed Palestinians who were suspected of collaborating with Israel. Hamas also launched false accusations of cooperation with Israel in order to eliminate its opponents, including many Fatah activists.

The IDF forces, advancing along various routes in the Gaza Strip, encountered many booby traps—explosive charges hidden in homes, public institutions, and mosques as well as tunnels. Terrorist operatives tried their best to kidnap soldiers. However, the terrorists generally avoided direct confrontations with IDF soldiers, preferring to hide among the civilian population. After completion of the first ground phase of the sectioning of the Strip into three parts, Prime Minister Ehud Olmert was interested in moving on to the next stage, in which the IDF would take over the southern Gaza Strip and rid the city of Rafah of terrorist elements. However, the prime minister's plan was met with opposition from Foreign Minister Tzipi Livni and Defense Minister Ehud Barak due to the operation's proximity to the Israeli elections, which were supposed to take place about three weeks later. In September 2008, Olmert was forced to resign due to criminal allegations against him and criticism from within his party, and he announced that early elections would be held on February 10, 2009.

In light of increasing international pressure, as well as UN Security Council Resolution 1860, which called for an immediate ceasefire between Israel and Hamas followed by a full Israeli withdrawal from the Gaza Strip, the government ultimately decided to withdraw most of its ground forces from Gaza, leaving only five battalions to secure the areas controlled by the IDF. However, due to a mistake in transferring the order to the field, all of the forces ended up withdrawing, and Operation Cast Lead was brought to a close on January 17, 2009, with a unilateral Israeli ceasefire, ending three weeks of fighting.[57]

Over the course of the operation, 1,300 Palestinians and 13 Israelis, both civilians and soldiers, were killed. Israeli and Palestinian sources differ in their estimates of the number of Palestinian casualties and the number of terrorist operatives who were among the casualties. According to then-GOC Southern Command Yoav Galant, the operation marked a change in the IDF's combat doctrine:

> In the past, every Hamas commander built a three-story house, with the basement serving as a weapons storehouse, the main floor as his headquarters, and the third floor being the place where his family lived. Over the years, they understood that the IDF would not harm the house due to the family being there. The moment we changed the concept by making contact with the family and firing a single bomb, with the building being destroyed afterwards, the commander was left troubled by the fact that he had no headquarters and no home for his family.[58]

Galant was referring to a plan of action whereby warning messages were transmitted to the occupants of a building that was marked as a target via text messages to their cell phones and the "knock on the roof" procedure. This procedure involved the firing of a device with a small amount of explosives to the roof of a building, which was not intend to cause any damage but, rather, make a noise to convey to those in the building that it was going to be hit within a short time and that they must evacuate.

Despite this warning, and in light of the ratio of Palestinians to Israelis injured in the operation, Operation Cast Lead provoked considerable criticism of Israel, which was accused by various parties of acting with disproportionate force and causing environmental damage in contravention of the laws of war. UN Secretary-General Ban Ki-moon, who visited the Gaza Strip after the operation, said he was shocked by the extent of the destruction he saw and criticized what he called an "excessive use of force." At the same time, he also criticized Hamas for firing rockets at Israel.[59]

In an article responding to this criticism of Israel, Israeli ethics expert Asa Kasher stated that in Operation Cast Lead, Israel had stood the test of "legitimate self-defense" in embarking on a military operation, as the state's intention was to protect its citizens against terrorist organizations' ongoing practice of employing massive and sustained rocket fire. Deterrence, he claimed, was not a main objective of the operation but only a side effect that accompanied the goal of self-defense and an improvement in the security situation by stopping or reducing the fire into Israel. According to Kasher, the principle of proportionality does not include a demand for numerical equivalence in the number of casualties on both sides; rather, it calls for comparison of, on the one hand, the protection that the IDF provided Israeli citizens through the operation (in relation to assessment of the existing threats) and the measures that had to be taken in order to avert these threats, with, on the other hand, the suffering and destruction caused to the other side as a result of the operation. Kasher rejects the claim that Israel used excessive force in Operation Cast Lead, explaining that this claim can be justified only when it is possible to identify alternatives that are both available and effective, that would provide the necessary protection against the threat, and in which the use of force would be reduced.[60]

Prior to the operation's launch, the IDF's International Law Department attached a legal appendix to the order that detailed the principles of international law, clarified which acts constituted war crimes, and demanded that any suspected cases of such crimes be investigated. The appendix instructed operation commanders to exercise extra caution in the use of cluster bombs, "incendiary weapons" (including white phosphorous), anti-personnel mines, and booby traps. The appendix stated that these weapons could be used, the Military Advocate General's Office must render its specific judgment on the individual case. It also stated that "to the extent possible under the circumstances, the civilian population located near a legitimate target must be warned ahead of an attack," as long as this did not endanger the operation or the military forces themselves. The legal advice given by international law experts during the planning stage of the operation and during its implementation was comprehensive. They received the relevant intelligence and operational material in advance and gave their input during discussions led by the head of the IDF's Operations Division and its High Command and Southern Command.[61]

In the wake of Operation Cast Lead, Venezuela, Bolivia, Mauritania, and Qatar severed diplomatic relations with Israel. In Turkey, anti-Israel sentiment was fueled by the Erdogan regime, which also canceled a joint military exercise with Israel. The attempt by Turkish and other elements to put Israeli officials on trial for alleged war crimes failed, and the various claims made against Israel were dropped.

On September 15, the UN Human Rights Council Commission of Inquiry, headed by South African judge Richard Goldstone, published its findings on the conduct of Operation Cast Lead. Israel refused to cooperate with the commission. The report was clearly biased against Israel and even recommended that the findings be submitted to the International Criminal Court in The Hague, though it also accused Hamas leaders of violating international law. Approximately two years after release of the report, on April 11, 2011, Judge Goldstone published an article in *The Washington Post* titled "Reconsidering the Goldstone Report on Israel and War Crimes." He wrote that if he "had known then what I know now," and if Israel had cooperated with his committee, the conclusions of the report would have been different. He noted that the UN Human Rights Council was biased against Israel and stressed that Israel had investigated its actions and drawn the necessary conclusions, whereas Hamas had not.[62]

After Operation Cast Lead, Israeli military and political analysts claimed that it had been a tactical and operative success but a strategic failure, as Hamas had not been significantly damaged during the operation. Its underground military and operational infrastructure had not been hit, and the operation did not advance a deal for the release of kidnapped Israeli soldier Gilad Shalit. The high-trajectory firing of rockets and mortar shells into Israel did not stop in the wake of Cast Lead, but the number of weapons fired did drop significantly in the years following the operation. Whereas in 2008, 1,270 rockets were fired into Israel, in 2009, after the operation, only 158 rockets entered Israel, and 103 rockets were fired in 2010.[63]

Even after Operation Cast Lead, terrorist attacks in the south of Israel continued. On January 27, 2009, a roadside bomb was detonated when a military vehicle passed by it in the area of Kissufim, killing one soldier and injuring three others. The Tawhid and Jihad Brigades claimed responsibility for the attack, declaring itself a group linked to Al-Qaeda.[64] At the same time, rogue organizations continued to launch sporadic but limited rocket fire at Israel. This activity was met with retaliatory Israeli air assaults. Hamas and the other organizations continued their efforts to arm and establish themselves in the Gaza Strip. On March 28, 2009, ISA Director Diskin informed the government that since the end of Operation Cast Lead, forty-five tons of raw materials for the manufacture of weapons, twenty-two tons of explosives, dozens of rockets, hundreds of mortar shells, and dozens of antitank missiles had been smuggled into the Gaza Strip. These weapons likely came from Iran via the Persian Gulf to Yemen and from there to Sudan, Egypt, and through Sinai via tunnels to the Gaza Strip.[65] In light of this activity, one can understand the American CBS network's report that in January 2009, the Israeli Air Force attacked a convoy of seventeen trucks in Sudan that were carrying weapons for Hamas in Gaza. According to the report, thirty-nine of the convoy's passengers were killed in the attempt to stop the transfer of advanced weapons and long-range missiles. It should be noted that two days before the end of Operation Cast Lead, Israeli foreign minister Tzipi Livni and U.S. Secretary of State Condoleezza Rice signed a security intelligence memorandum of understanding regarding the war on arms-smuggling from Iran through the Persian Gulf and Sudan to the Gaza Strip. This memorandum was apparently one of the Israeli conditions for the ceasefire; it stated that Iran was the source of the smuggling of arms into Gaza and outlined the commitment of the United States and European countries to help monitor the smuggling routes and exchange intelligence information on the issue.[66]

On March 26, 2009, Prime Minister Olmert said in a speech at IDC Herzliya, "We take action wherever we can strike terrorist infrastructures, in nearby places and places that are less near. Wherever we can hit the terrorist infrastructure, we do. Those who need to know that there is no place that the State of Israel cannot take action. There is no such place."[67] This statement was apparently a reference to the action in Sudan. Olmert's view of the war against terror can be summed up with the following words:

> There is no situation in which terrorism can be prevented completely. In Gaza as well—we strike and for a certain period we are successful in stopping terror, and then the shooting starts again. . . . We always have to let the terror gain some momentum [before we attack—BG] because in the war against terror, the army represents proven strength, and it is fighting against people who are seemingly successful in fostering a sense of discrimination in the consciousness of some of the public. And then the power of the state is in fact perceived as a detriment in the public consciousness. So I did not respond to every missile, I only reacted when the level of rocket fire reached some kind of momentum, at which point counteraction seemed justified. Not daily actions . . . I am in favor of continuing targeted actions that lead to the destruction of the terrorists' infrastructure—both the human infrastructure and the logistical infrastructure. . . . I directed the various systems to carry out this type of activity, which requires the integration of the security services and the special units of the army. There is no doubt that it is possible to deter terror, but it is impossible to make the political or ideological

movements that produce the terrorist acts or the terrorists disappear. . . . Total deterrence is, in my opinion, impossible. We are not able to do it in Israel, and the Americans are not able do it in Pakistan, Afghanistan, Iran, Iraq, and elsewhere.[68]

Olmert strengthened this point by saying, "The State of Israel has never had more powerful deterrence than that that it has created in recent years."[69] On March 31, 2009, the term of the thirty-first government of Israel came to an end, and Benjamin Netanyahu entered the post of prime minister.

THE END OF THE SHARON ADMINISTRATION AND THE EHUD OLMERT ADMINISTRATION'S COUNTERTERRORISM POLICIES IN LIGHT OF THE COUNTERTERRORISM DILEMMAS MODEL

In summary, this period witnessed two governments but can actually be divided into three subperiods. The first was the end of the second Sharon administration—a period that was cut abruptly short in January 2006 when Sharon suffered a stroke and became incapacitated and all his powers were transferred to his deputy, Ehud Olmert. In the second subperiod, Olmert replaced Sharon and was appointed acting prime minister (hereafter this is referred to as the first Olmert government, which was a direct continuation of the second Sharon government). The third subperiod began in May 2006, when Olmert won the general elections and served as Israel's thirty-first prime minister (hereafter referred to as the second Olmert government).

The period examined here, which began after the end of the Second Intifada, was characterized by low-level and sporadic terrorist activity against Israel alongside an intensification of rocket fire from the Gaza Strip. The aforementioned Israeli governments continued to initiate counterterrorism operations in the West Bank, including targeted killings, and carried out extensive military operations in the Gaza Strip in order to prevent the firing of rockets into Israeli territory. These governments also continued to build the barrier intended to separate Israel from the West Bank and prevent the entry of terrorists and unauthorized Palestinians.

The main strategic change that occurred during the period under discussion stemmed from the second Sharon government's decision to unilaterally disengage from the Gaza Strip, evacuating the settlers living there and demolishing their houses. Sharon's controversial decision, which received the support of most of the Israeli people, caused a major rift between supporters of the right and supporters of the center and left. It led the prime minister to resign from his political home, the right-wing Likud party, and establish the new centrist party, Kadima, in November 2005. Sharon's policy generated intense social and political tension in Israel and led to mass demonstrations of hundreds of thousands of right-wing supporters.

In the meantime, Israel's disengagement from the Gaza Strip enabled Hamas to take over the evacuated territory and violently oust Fatah and Palestinian Authority. Hamas quickly turned the Gaza Strip into a hive of violent activity against Israel. The organization built up an arsenal of Qassam rockets and used them to attack the southern Israeli communities in the vicinity of Gaza. Hamas also began digging attack tunnels to penetrate into Israel and even used one of them to attack an IDF outpost and kidnap soldier Gilad Shalit. This kidnapping led to a large-scale military campaign in the Gaza Strip, which was followed by a ceasefire that led to a lull in the Qassam fire into Israel.

However, after a brief period, the rocket fire resumed, and the IDF was forced to recommence operations in the Gaza Strip in order to prevent the firing of rockets and to deter the Palestinian terrorist organizations. On the northern border, following an attack on an IDF patrol and the abduction of two reserve soldiers, the IDF launched a sweeping military operation, the Second Lebanon War, which ended only after a month of massive exchanges of fire as well as a UN resolution to create a buffer between Israel and Hezbollah and to prevent the arming of Hezbollah in southern Lebanon.

Toward the end of the Olmert administration, Israel carried out two major operations; one occurred in Syria in September 2007, in which Israel destroyed the atomic reactor that Syria had secretly built with the assistance of North Korea, and the second was another extensive operation in Gaza, Operation Cast Lead, which consisted of numerous air strikes and artillery fire intended to once again stop the firing of Qassams into Israeli territory.

On the domestic front, the Israeli government paid a heavy price, with intense criticism from the right accusing Sharon of implementing a policy that allowed Hamas to harm Israel. In the international arena, however, Sharon's government won sweeping support from Israel's friends around the world, especially the United States. This was reflected in, among other

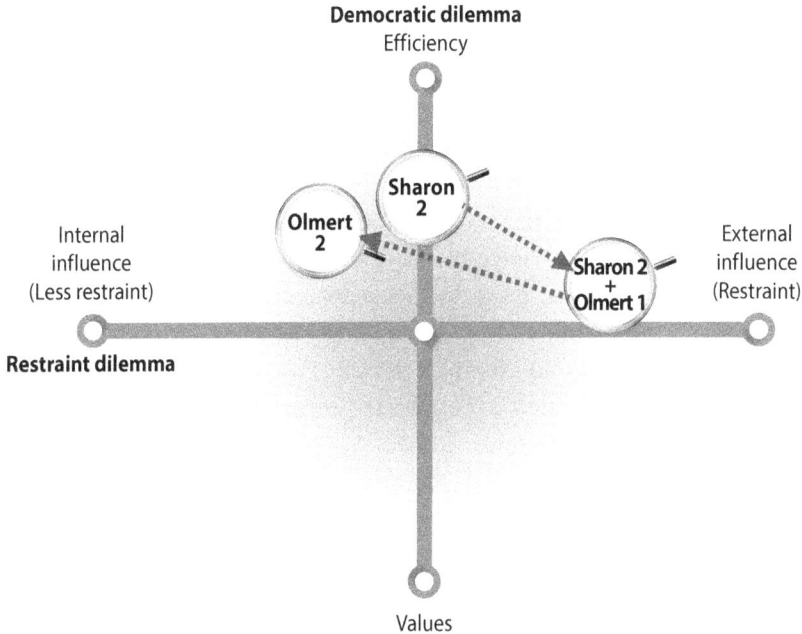

FIGURE 10.1. Counterterrorism Dilemmas Conceptual Model—Sharon and Olmert administrations

things, in the presidential letter given to Sharon by President Bush and approved by Congress, which expressed support for Israel's strategic interests in the West Bank. But the international support that Israel enjoyed during the first two parts of the period under discussion waned and was even replaced with harsh criticism in light of the operations Israel carried out in the Gaza Strip to stop the rocket fire into its territory, which caused many Palestinian casualties. This condemnation, which claimed that Israel was reacting disproportionately, reached its peak with publication of the Goldstone Report, which accused Israel of committing war crimes. In fact, though, the IDF's advisors on international law had given the combat forces instructions that in many cases limited their actions in order to avoid exactly these types of claims against the IDF.

An examination of the policies of the Israeli governments during the period under review using the Counterterrorism Dilemmas Conceptual Model (figure 10.1) shows that in the first and second subperiods, the governments chose to ignore heavy domestic pressure in favor of advancing the strategy of disengagement from the Gaza Strip with the support of the international community. In the third subperiod however, the Olmert government changed its policy significantly and acted as it thought the Israeli public expected it to, carrying out large-scale military operations in Gaza in order to stop the rocket threat to Israel. The extensive collateral damage these caused dealt a significant blow to Israel's status in the international community, to the point that the state's diplomatic relations with several countries were severed. As for the democratic dilemma throughout the period being examined here, the different Israeli governments continued to undertake various counterterrorism measures, including targeted killings that they considered effective in preventing terrorism and deterring the terrorist organizations.

Chapter Eleven

CHANGES IN THE GREATER MIDDLE EAST

The Netanyahu Administration (2009–18)

NETANYAHU'S REELECTION

After the elections for the eighteenth Knesset, in March 2009, Benjamin Netanyahu was again elected prime minister of Israel's thirty-second government. He was elected twice more after that and served as the prime minister of Israel's thirty-third and thirty-fourth governments. As chair of the Likud party, Netanyahu led his governments to more hawkish positions than those held by predecessors Olmert and Sharon with regard to negotiations with the Palestinians and the peace process.

About two months after the establishment of his government, on June 14, Netanyahu laid out his political doctrine and strategic worldview in an address at Bar-Ilan University. In his speech, Netanyahu emphasized what he called the greatest danger to Israel, the Middle East and the entire world: the Iranian threat, which represented the combining of radical Islam with nuclear weapons. Netanyahu named the advancement of peace as one of the three most important challenges facing the State of Israel. He stated that he supported U.S. president Barack Obama's idea of regional peace and called on Arab leaders and states to meet with him to talk and make peace. On this point, Netanyahu stressed the importance of developing regional economic initiatives, which he dubbed "economic peace."

Netanyahu declared that his government was committed to international agreements and called on the leadership of the Palestinian Authority to begin negotiations immediately and without preconditions. Netanyahu explained to his audience that peace was still out of reach despite Israel's outstretched hand, because the heart of the conflict lay with the continued refusal to recognize the right of the Jewish people to a state of its own in its historic homeland. Netanyahu noted that Israel's withdrawals from territories (within the framework of the Oslo Accords and the Disengagement Plan) had been met with large waves of suicide terrorism and thousands of missiles.

Netanyahu surprised listeners in his Bar-Ilan speech when he stressed that Israel was not interested in ruling the Palestinians, running their lives, or forcing the Israeli flag and culture on them. He noted that in his vision of peace, in this small land at the heart of the conflict, there would be "two free peoples living side by side, with good neighborly relations and mutual respect, each with its flag, anthem and government, with neither one threatening its neighbor's security and existence."[1] Netanyahu stressed the importance of the demilitarization of Palestinian territory in any future peace agreement, because without demilitarization, "there is a real fear that there will be an armed Palestinian state which will become a terrorist base against Israel, as happened in Gaza."[2] He continued,

> We do not want Qassams on Petah Tikva, Grads on Tel Aviv, or missiles on Ben-Gurion International Airport. To ensure peace we need to make sure that the Palestinians are not able to bring into their territory missiles or rockets, or have an army, or control of airspace that is closed to us, or make treaties with countries like Iran, or Hezbollah . . . above all, the Palestinians must decide between the path of peace and the path of Hamas. The Palestinian Authority must establish law and order in the Gaza Strip, and they must overcome Hamas.[3]

In his Bar-Ilan speech, Netanyahu publicly accepted the two-state solution, in contrast to the extreme right in Israel. However, he did distinguish himself from the Israeli center bloc in Israel, previously led by Sharon and Olmert, by requiring negotiations with the Palestinians without preconditions and in effect releasing itself from the proposals that the previous government had made to the Palestinians at the Annapolis conference.

The Bar-Ilan speech should be understood against the background of the sensitive—even volatile—relationship that had begun to develop between newly installed President Obama and Israel's elected prime minister. President Obama's attempt to turn over a new leaf, as he defined it, with the Muslim world, and his desire to end the Israeli-Palestinian conflict brought political pressure on the Netanyahu government. A few months later, on November 25, the government approved Netanyahu's plan to temporarily freeze building in the West Bank settlements (including east Jerusalem) for a period of ten months. This plan was the result of Obama's demand to lay the groundwork for the renewal of negotiations with the Palestinians and a response to the precondition set by Abu Mazen for negotiations. Even so, the opening of negotiations was delayed due to, among other things, Abu Mazen's hesitation and the additional preconditions that he demanded. The Jerusalem District Planning and Building Committee's March 9, 2010, decision to approve 1,600 new housing units in northern Jerusalem, made during Vice President Joe Biden's visit to Israel and the Palestinian Authority, also contributed to the lack of trust between the parties. On September 2, the United States finally succeeded in launching direct talks between Israel and the Palestinians with a meeting between Benjamin Netanyahu and Abu Mazen in Washington. Three weeks later, however, the ten-month construction freeze in the West Bank came to an end, and Israel refused to extend it.

This period was characterized by a relatively low level of terrorist attacks against Israel. One that took place two days after the Bar-Ilan speech, on June 16, 2009, was an exception. A suicide bomb cell made up of ten Palestinian Salafists supporting al-Qaeda who were riding horses loaded with explosives attacked the IDF outpost at the Karni Crossing on the border with the Gaza Strip. In the exchange of fire and explosion of the bombs, four terrorists were killed without having succeeded in injuring any Israelis. High-trajectory fire against Israel also declined significantly, with only 103 rockets fired into Israel in 2010—the lowest annual amount in eight years (since 2002).[4] It appeared that the Palestinians, led by Abu Mazen, adapted the military-terrorist struggle into a diplomatic one.

THE *MAVI MARMARA* FLOTILLA

In late May 2010, after several months of preparation, a flotilla of ships organized by various nonprofit organizations headed by the Turkish IHH arrived near Israel's territorial waters. The highly publicized flotilla was intended to embarrass Israel in an attempt to penetrate its naval blockade on the Gaza Strip. The passengers aboard the ships were a mix of activists, among them peace activists from countries around the world, along with members of associations and movements supporting Hamas's rule in the Gaza Strip. On the thirty-first of the month, after a few days' sailing in the Mediterranean, Israel's Shayetet 13 naval commandos (SEALs) took command of the flotilla. One of the ships, the *Mavi Marmara*, refused to stop. When the first Shayetet commandos boarded the ship, they were severely beaten, stabbed, and thrown off the deck. In the confrontation that broke out between, nine of the passengers were killed and several Shayetet fighters were injured.

The confrontation on the ship, broadcast live worldwide by Al Jazeera photographers and other journalists who were aboard, and the large number of passengers injured during the conflict, drew international criticism of Israel's conduct in the affair. Even in Israel itself, the question was raised of whether or not the method by which the ship was taken over was the right move under the circumstances and in view of the fatal consequences. A number of investigations were initiated in Israel in order to draw conclusions from the flotilla incident. These included an internal investigation conducted by the military unit that carried out the takeover, Shayetet 13, which examined the operational aspects of the takeover; the Eiland Committee, appointed by the IDF chief of staff, which examined the army's conduct during the affair; and the public commission of inquiry headed by retired Supreme Court Justice Jacob Turkel, which was established on June 14 to probe the flotilla incident.

The lessons learned from the *Mavi Marmara* flotilla incident were vital to Israel not only because of the domestic and international criticism it faced but also due to the fact that the same organizations that carried out the flotilla, as well as others, continued to try to challenge Israel and break the blockade on Gaza with additional flotillas. Another flotilla infiltration attempt was made in July 2011, but that flotilla encountered technical and procedural problems, and only two boats reached the Gaza coast, where they were intercepted by the Israeli navy. At the same time, the navy continued to thwart repeated attempts by Hezbollah and Iran to smuggle advanced weapons into the Gaza Strip by sea. On March 15, 2011, Shayetet 13 took control of the cargo vessel *Victoria* outside Israel's territorial waters in the Mediterranean and confiscated arms and ammunition.

GILAD SHALIT'S RELEASE

During this period, there was also a turnaround in the affair of kidnapped soldier Gilad Shalit. On October 2, 2009, Israel released twenty female Palestinian prisoners who were serving sentences for their involvement in terrorist activities. The prisoners were released to Gaza in return for a videotape proving that the abducted soldier was still alive. In the two-minute and forty-two-second video, Shalit appeared, holding up an up-to-date issue of a newspaper and appealing to his family and the Israeli government to respond to the terrorists' demands for his release. This was the first stage of the process of Shalit's release, which was agreed on in negotiations between Israel and Hamas via Egyptian mediation. On October 6t, after lengthy negotiations and more than five years of the soldier's captivity, Israel signed an agreement to release 1,027 Palestinian prisoners held in Israel after being convicted of executing or being involved in terrorist attacks in exchange for the return of Shalit.[5] Of these prisoners, 477 were released immediately, including 280 terrorists who had been involved in deadly attacks and sentenced to life imprisonment. Another 550 prisoners were to be released several months later.[6] Some of those released resumed their involvement in the initiation, planning, preparation, and execution of further terror attacks; some were again arrested by the IDF and the security forces, and a few were assassinated in targeted IDF operations.

Shalit's release was made possible after a long and extensive public relations campaign led by his family with the help of a nonprofit association that was established to bring about his release, and many Israeli citizens volunteered their help for this purpose. The campaign, which had worldwide reach, was intended to put international pressure on Hamas to release the soldier, but most of the activity was aimed at pressuring the Israeli government to bring about Shalit's immediate release. Indeed, tremendous public pressure was created in Israel, first directed at the Olmert and then the Netanyahu government. Mass rallies, huge demonstrations, and public events were held, with the participation of public opinion leaders, singers, and intellectuals, as well as rallies and protest tents erected in front of the prime minister's home.

It is interesting to note that the call for Shalit's release was also heard among the growing demonstrations of young people throughout the country. These people took to the streets against the backdrop of the wave of protests in the Arab world as part of the so-called Arab Spring, and they called for economic and social justice and improvement in the economic situation of young people in Israel. At these rallies, which were attended by hundreds of thousands of demonstrators, signs and flags bearing Shalit's picture were also waved, accompanied by a demand for his immediate release. Prime ministers Olmert and Netanyahu found themselves under increasing pressure by those who saw the leaders and their governments as responsible for Shalit's prolonged captivity. Hamas had seemingly succeeded in using sophisticated psychological warfare to convince the Israeli public that Israel's refusal was preventing Shalit's release.

However, although Olmert refused to give in to Hamas's demands, and though at the beginning of his first term as prime minister, Netanyahu adopted Olmert's tough approach to negotiations with Hamas, two years later, accompanied by a sharp decline in his popularity (and assuming that Shalit's release would improve his public image), Netanyahu paid a price even higher than the one Olmert had refused to pay during his tenure.[7]

Israel's willingness to agree to the Shalit deal must be understood against the background of what has been called the "Ron Arad trauma." On October 16, 1986, as part of his reserve duty, Air Force navigator Arad was flying a Phantom jet on a mission to attack terrorist targets in the Sidon area of Lebanon. A technical problem forced the pilot, Yishai Aviram, and Arad to eject. Aviram was rescued immediately, but Arad was captured by the Amal Movement. The organization demanded $3 million and the release of 200 Lebanese prisoners and 450 Palestinian terrorists in return for Arad's release. But the political echelon, perhaps influenced by criticism over the price paid in the Jibril Deal, refused to comply.[8] The negotiations were halted in 1988 after Arad was taken from Amal and his trail was lost.[9] Arad's disappearance and the rumors that he had been transferred to Hezbollah and from there most likely to Iran, where he might have been murdered by his captors, turned the Arad trauma into a model that pressure groups in Israeli society used to demand that Israeli governments give in and pay the extortionate prices demanded by terrorist organizations for the release of prisoners.

Prime Minister Netanyahu's decision to accede to the terrorists' demands received support and sympathy from a large portion of the Israeli public, but many others criticized it as a capitulation to terrorism. This was especially the case in light of the fact that over the years, before he was appointed prime minister, Netanyahu had repeatedly emphasized in writings and interviews the importance of never giving in to terrorists' demands and refraining from releasing imprisoned terrorists in exchange for hostages. Netanyahu described the situation of hostage-taking as "a classic terrorist act,"[10] and he praised the virtue of "resolve" against the terrorists' demands to release their comrades in return for hostages. In this context, Netanyahu made the following statement:

> The release of convicted terrorists . . . seems like an easy and tempting way of defusing blackmail situations in which innocent people may lose their lives. But its utility is momentary at best. Prisoner releases only embolden terrorists by giving them the feeling that even if they are caught, their punishment will be brief.[11]

In Netanyahu's opinion, history shows that a consistent refusal to capitulate to terrorists' demands in hostage-taking situations ultimately led to a reduction in the number of such attacks, thus "the only sensible policy is a refusal to yield and a readiness to apply force."[12]

In the decade prior to his election as prime minister in 1996, Netanyahu was disappointed with Israel's position on this issue. He reiterated that Israel, once the world's leader in counterterrorism policy, continually repeated the mistake of exchanging prisoners for hostages. Netanyahu did not hide his criticism of past governments in this matter. In his various roles, he openly protested against any exchange deal with terrorist organizations, first and foremost against the deals to release jailed terrorists in return for soldiers held by Fatah and the Jibril Front in 1983 and 1985. While serving as Israel's ambassador to the UN, Netanyahu also recommended this policy to U.S. Secretary of State George Schultz when a Trans World Airlines (TWA) plane to Beirut was hijacked in 1985. In this case, it was known that the terrorists had scattered the hostages throughout Beirut and threaten to kill them if their demands were not met. Netanyahu writes that he recommended to Schultz that he persevere in his tough approach to the terrorists. He recommended that Schultz "issue[s] a counter-threat" to "make it clear to the terrorists that if they so much as touch a hair on any of the hostages' heads, the United States will not rest until every last one of them has been hunted down and wiped out."[13]

Thus, despite Netanyahu's tough stance in his public statements, writings, and advice to decision makers in Israel and around the world, in practice, in a case of terrorist blackmail, Netanyahu's policy as prime minister was no different from—and perhaps even worse than—that of those leaders whose policies he had previously criticized.

In the wake of the criticism voiced in Israel for the enormous price paid for Shalit's release, the government set up a committee headed by retired Supreme Court Justice Meir Shamgar to recommend the necessary Israeli policy in the event of similar cases in the future. On January 5, 2012, the committee published a few of its recommendations (most of the report remains confidential), including that in future negotiations for the exchange of prisoners, a reasonable ratio be maintained between the number of prisoners released and the number of hostages; only a small number of prisoners should be released in exchange for a single captive.

During the period under discussion, a number of attacks were carried out in Israel and the West Bank. On March 11, 2011, two terrorists infiltrated a house in the West Bank settlement of Itamar, stabbing five members of a family (two parents and three children) to death. About two weeks later, a bomb exploded at a bus stop in central Jerusalem, killing a tourist and injuring thirty-nine people.[14] On May 15, 2011, a truck driver from Kfar Kassem carried out a ramming attack in Tel Aviv's Hatikva neighborhood, killing a man and injuring many others. Another ramming attack occurred on August 29, during which a Nablus terrorist drove his taxi into a border police checkpoint in Tel Aviv, exited the car, and began stabbing passersby. Eight people were injured in the incident.[15] These attacks marked a rise in the trend of self-initiated lone wolf attacks, which included ramming attacks using cars, trucks, and tractors and cold-weapon attacks in which terrorists attempted to stab passersby with knives, axes, or other weapons.

THE USE OF THE SINAI FOR TERROR PURPOSES

One of the most severe attacks of this period took place on August 18, 2011. A terrorist cell belonging to the Popular Resistance Committees infiltrated Israeli territory from the Sinai and fired small arms and antitank missiles at passing vehicles on Highway 12 near Israel's southern border. In addition to firing at the passing vehicles, the terrorists detonated a suicide vest. In the attack and the ensuing clashes with IDF forces (who arrived on the scene to assist civilians), eight Israelis were killed and dozens were injured.[16]

This assault set a dangerous new trend in which the north of the Sinai Peninsula, which was returned to Egypt as part of the peace treaty signed in 1977, became a fertile ground for terrorism, a preferred arena for the terrorist organizations, and a base for attacks on southern Israel. These terrorist organizations were composed mainly of al-Qaeda–affiliated Salafi operatives from among the Bedouin population or Palestinians who had moved their bases from Gaza to the northern Sinai. A particularly worrisome trend began to emerge among young Sinai-born Bedouins. Whereas in the past these operatives had earned their living by smuggling goods and people into Israeli territory, helping the terrorist organizations operating in Sinai to cross the border into Israel, and sometimes even participating in carrying out attacks for financial gain, this period saw a change in the number of Bedouin terrorists who were taking part in attacks on their own initiative. The economic motive became secondary; many Bedouin terrorists began acting on Salafi-Jihadist ideology. The terrorist activity from Sinai was also a sign of the weakening of the Egyptian military forces there, and in particular an indication of the significant damage done to the Egyptian security forces' intelligence capabilities with regard to the Bedouin population in the Sinai. This drift toward Egyptian governmental failure in the Sinai intensified after Hosni Mubarak was ousted and the Muslim Brotherhood took over in the framework of the Arab Spring revolutions. The Egyptian revolution led to, among other things, the opening of many of the country's prison gates and release of many dangerous terrorists, most of whom moved to the Sinai Peninsula, which led to the further deterioration of the situation.

In order to disrupt the supply of energy to Israel and Jordan, on September 27, terrorists blew up the pipeline supplying Egyptian natural gas to those countries, causing a temporary halt in the supply of gas. This action was repeated several more times over the months that followed, causing significant financial damage to Egypt, Israel, and Jordan. During the same period, terrorist operatives belonging to the global jihad movements also launched a campaign against the Egyptian army, police, and government and attempted or carried out several attacks on these targets.

In response to the grave assault in the south of the country, Israel conducted targeted killings of leaders of the Popular Resistance Committees in the Gaza Strip. Abu Oud al-Nirab, commander of the organization's military wing, and Khaled Shaath, a senior member of the organization, were killed in an air strike in Rafah. The Palestinian terrorist organizations responded with massive rocket fire from the Gaza Strip, including rockets directed at Ashkelon and Be'er Sheva, and those attacks were followed by several days of exchanges of fire between Israel and the organizations in the Gaza Strip. The number of rockets fired at Israel over approximately ten days was the largest since the conclusion of Operation Cast Lead in 2008. Although Iron Dome (Israel's rocket interception system) operated successfully and intercepted a large number of rockets, some landed in populated communities in Israel. They caused the death of three civilians and injured dozens of others in Ashdod and Be'er Sheva.

About six months later, on March 9, 2012, Israel launched an air strike against the secretary-general of the Popular Resistance Committees, Zuhair al-Qaisi, in the Gaza Strip, which resulted in his death. According to the IDF, at the time of his death, Qaisi, who was one of the planners of the attack on Highway 12, was involved in the final preparation stages for another terrorist attack in Israel.[17] Additional members of the organization were killed in the operation, and in its wake, the organizations renewed massive rocket fire into Israeli territory. Three days of rocket fire ended with a ceasefire brokered by Egypt. Israel dubbed this round of fighting "Operation Returning Echo." Even after the ceasefire agreement, sporadic rocket fire into Israel from the Gaza Strip continued; on April 5, a Grad rocket was fired from Sinai into Eilat without causing casualties or damage, and on June 15, rockets were fired from Sinai into the communities of Uvda and Mitzpeh Ramon in the south of the country.

In the following months, Sinai became the main arena for terrorism against Israel. On June 18, 2012, three terrorists infiltrated Israel from Sinai and attacked a passing vehicle with antitank missiles, small arms, and roadside bombs. One of the passengers in the vehicle was killed before two members of the cell were eliminated and the others fled into Egyptian territory. About two months later, another attack was carried out from Sinai, this time a complex and multistage assault. On August 5, a joint cell of Palestinian terrorists from Gaza and Salafist operatives from Sinai attacked an Egyptian military position, killing fifteen soldiers and taking control of their armored personal carriers, with which they broke through Israel's border fence near the Kerem Shalom crossing. The attack was accompanied by rocket fire into Israel but was eventually thwarted by IDF forces without Israeli casualties. On September 21, an IDF soldier was killed and another wounded in a clash with terrorists on the border fence between Sinai and Israel. On November 10, an antitank missile was fired at an IDF jeep, wounding four soldiers. At the same time, three Israeli civilians were injured by a Qassam rocket that was fired at a factory in Sderot.

Thus, Israel's southern region did not enjoy calm even after Operation Returning Echo, and IDF forces continued to encounter roadside bombs, ambushes, and exchanges of fire, while sporadic rocket fire was launched from the Gaza Strip into Israel. In early November 2012, the security situation deteriorated further. On November 6, three soldiers were wounded by a roadside bomb that had been planted along the border fence. Two days later, terrorists blew up a tunnel that penetrated into Israel, injuring a soldier, and on the tenth of the month, four soldiers were injured after their vehicle was hit by antitank fire near the fence bordering the Gaza Strip. The intensification of terrorist attacks in the south was accompanied by an increase in high-trajectory fire from Gaza into Israeli territory. Over a period of three days, from November 10 to 12, more than 170 rockets and mortar shells were fired into Israel.[18]

OPERATION PILLAR OF DEFENSE

As a result of the escalation of terrorism, on November 13, the government decided to launch a military operation in the Gaza Strip, Operation Pillar of Defense. Defense Minister Ehud Barak defined the goals of the operation as strengthening Israeli deterrence, severely damaging Hamas and the Palestinian organizations' rocket arsenal, crippling Hamas and the terrorist organizations, and minimizing harm to the Israeli home front.[19] The government and heads of the defense establishment decided to launch the operation with a severe blow that would surprise Hamas and instantly cause the organization serious damage. To this end, a plan was devised to deceive Hamas regarding Israel's offensive intentions. Members of the government gave media interviews in which they rejected the possibility of military action in Gaza in the wake of the upsurge in violence, while the prime minister and defense minister went on a publicized military tour in the north of the country, on the front with Syria.[20] Then, on November 14, Operation Pillar of Defense commenced with a large number of air strikes against Hamas targets, including their headquarters, bases, launch pads, rocket and artillery warehouses, and terrorist operatives. The main air strike was directed against Ahmed Jabari, head of Hamas's military wing. Jabari, who was also responsible for the kidnapping of Gilad Shalit, was killed while riding in his car in the Gaza Strip.

During the eight-day operation, Hamas and Islamic Jihad fired approximately 1,506 rockets from the Gaza Strip into Israel. (About half of them were short-range rockets, with a range of up to twenty kilometers, and the rest were medium range, reaching between twenty and sixty kilometers.) Seven rockets were fired at Tel Aviv and two at Jerusalem. More than a quarter of the rockets (421) were intercepted by Iron Dome.[21] Over the course of the operation, six Israelis, four civilians, and two soldiers were killed. The IDF refrained from launching a ground incursion into the Gaza Strip, choosing instead to focus on air strikes, in which 1,500 targets in the Gaza Strip were hit.[22] These included the organizations' rocket systems (such as launch facilities and weapons depots), tunnels (some were assault tunnels leading into Israeli territory, and others were smuggling tunnels along the Gaza-Sinai border), military industrial facilities (including those used in the manufacturing and development of drones), headquarters and homes of senior commanders of Hamas's military wing, and Hamas government centers.[23] According to the Intelligence and Terrorism Information Center, 178 Palestinians were killed in these attacks; of these, 101 were active members of terrorist organizations, 68 were uninvolved civilians who were killed unintentionally (some as a result of being used by Hamas as human shields), and nine whose identity is unknown.[24]

On November 21, 2012, the ceasefire went into effect. A few hours before, a bomb exploded on a bus in Tel Aviv, wounding twenty-nine people.[25] Hamas and Islamic Jihad terrorists were arrested within a few hours. As part of the understanding between Hamas and Israel at the end of the fighting, Israel agreed to double the permitted fishing zone for Gaza fishermen and allowed Palestinian farmers to work their plots that were adjacent to the security fence with Israel.[26] On November 29, the UN General Assembly decided, by a majority of 138 countries with 9 opposing and 41 abstaining, to include the Palestinian Authority as an observer state.[27]

Although the operation ended without a military victory for either side, the occupation of territory in the Gaza Strip, or the removal of Hamas from power in Gaza, it appeared to have succeeded—at least temporarily—in deterring Hamas from launching high-trajectory fire at Israel. It also forced Hamas to prevent other organizations from carrying out such activities. In the year following Pillar of Defense, there was a drastic decrease in the number of rockets and mortar shells fired into Israeli territory. In 2013, only 63 rockets and 11 mortar shells entered Israel from Gaza, compared with 2012, during which 280 rockets were launched (excluding the rockets launched in Operation Pillar of Defense); and 2011, when 419 rockets were fired.[28]

Hamas refrained from launching high-trajectory fire toward Israel, but it worked vigorously to rehabilitate its military infrastructure after the operation and continued digging tunnels of various types. Some tunnels were located in the Gaza Strip (for the purposes of launching rockets, storing weapons, maintaining communications and control channels, and operating underground command centers), some were attack tunnels used to infiltrate Israel, and others were smuggling tunnels into Sinai. Hamas made special efforts to strengthen its rocket arsenal, which was severely damaged during Operation Pillar of Defense. In June 2014, the head of Military Intelligence's Research Division, Itai Brun, estimated that after the end of the operation, Hamas doubled the number of rockets and upgraded their capabilities.[29]

At the same time, Hamas suffered a severe blow in another arena: Syria. With the outbreak of the Syrian civil war in mid-2011, and against the backdrop of Hamas's support for the Syrian Muslim Brotherhood's rebellion against Bashar al-Assad, the organization's leaders found themselves forced out of their homes and headquarters in Damascus and sent into exile in Lebanon, Turkey, and the Gulf states. The disconnection and hostility created between the Assad regime and the Hamas movement seriously harmed one of Hamas's most important sources of support and led to a decline in the status of the organization's "international leadership," headed by Khaled Mashaal.[30]

The rift between Hamas and the Assad regime also led to the cooling of the relationship between Hamas and its Iranian patron and its Lebanese branch, Hezbollah. Until the outbreak of the civil war in Syria, and despite the ethnic differences between Hamas and Iran/Hezbollah (Shiite versus Sunni), Hamas greatly benefited—economically, militarily, and operationally—from Iran and Hezbollah. Hamas obtained its weapons arsenal in Gaza largely from its Shiite patrons, and it obtained its knowledge regarding development of the Gaza Strip's arms manufacturing industry, underground tunnel warfare, and methods of warfare against Israel from Iran and Hezbollah. Throughout Hamas's existence, its leaders had maintained its independence in decision-making and did not accept Iranian authority, but they did enjoy a wide variety of benefits. Iranian aid to Hamas did not end altogether after outbreak of the civil war in Syria, but it decreased in scope. Compensation for this loss came from another source: Egypt.

Following the overthrow of President Mubarak in early 2011 as part of the events of the Arab Spring, the Muslim Brotherhood took control of Egypt. The movement, which, until that point, had been part Islamist social movement and part vocal opposition seeking to undermine the legitimacy of Mubarak's regime, was legally sanctioned following referendums and the January 2012 elections, in which its members won nearly 50 percent of the seats in the Egyptian parliament.[31] The Egyptian Muslim Brotherhood movement is the mother organization of the Palestinian Muslim Brotherhood and its military wing, Hamas. Although the new Egyptian regime did not annul the peace treaty with Israel, the relationship between the two countries, frosty even before the change in the Egyptian government, cooled even further. At the same time, Hamas and the new Egyptian regime grew closer.

Israel adopted a neutral stance with regard to the civil war in Syria, with the understanding that any victory in the war, be it by the Assad regime supported by Iran and Hezbollah or the rebels led by the jihadist Islamist terrorist organizations ISIS and Jabhat al-Nusra, would not advance Israel's interests in the region. Thus, with the exception of providing some medical assistance to wounded Syrians who reached its borders, Israel maintained a policy of noninterference. Israeli spokespeople made it clear that the state would stick to this policy as long as the situation in Syria was not used to transfer strategic weapons to Hezbollah (such as long-range missiles, advanced surface-to-air and antiship missiles, and chemical weapons). In light of this policy, in the years that followed, Israel carried out a number of air strikes in Syrian territory against weapons depots and convoys attempting to smuggle weapons of this type from Syria into Lebanon.[32]

At the beginning of 2013, elections were held in Israel. Netanyahu presented his new government in March, with Defense Minister Ehud Barak replaced by Moshe (Bogey) Ya'alon. Although the border between Israel and Gaza was generally quiet, the southern border was sometimes confronted by the Salafist-Jihadist terrorist organizations located in the Sinai Peninsula. Among the attackers were terrorists who had fled Egyptian prisons after the overthrow of Mubarak, along with the area's Bedouin residents and foreign fighters who had volunteered to join the jihad arena in the Sinai. On August 13, Iron Dome intercepted a rocket sent by these elements from Sinai for the first time. Several months later, in April 2014, rockets were again fired from Sinai, landing in open areas near Eilat and on the Jordanian side of the border.

During this period, Israel focused on dealing with the danger of the Iranian nuclear program. Israel's efforts were concentrated on the international arena in an attempt to pressure its allies, especially European countries and the United States, to take a tough stance in negotiations with Iran and even expand the sanctions on Iran until it would be forced to dismantle the technology that enabled the construction of nuclear weapons. In his speech to the UN General Assembly in October 2013, Prime Minister Netanyahu stated,

> Today our hope for the future is challenged by a nuclear-armed Iran that seeks our destruction. . . . A nuclear-armed Iran would have a choke hold on the world's main energy supplies. It would trigger nuclear proliferation throughout the Middle East, turning the most unstable part of the planet into a nuclear tinderbox. And for the first time in history, it would make the specter of nuclear terrorism a clear and present danger. . . . Israel will never acquiesce to nuclear arms in the hands of a rogue regime that repeatedly promises to wipe us off the map. Against such a threat, Israel will have no choice but to defend itself.[33]

At the same time, though, Netanyahu found himself under mounting pressure from the United States and European countries to open negotiations aimed at reaching an agreement with the Palestinians, after three years of a complete diplomatic deadlock. Following the establishment of Netanyahu's new government, direct talks between Israel and the Palestinians opened in Washington, D.C., on July 20. As a gesture of goodwill, after the meeting, Israel released twenty-six Palestinian terrorists from prison, most of whom were convicted of murder or attempted murder and who were serving sentences in Israeli jails.[34] About three months later, Netanyahu declared,

> Israel continues to seek an historic compromise with our Palestinian neighbors, one that ends our conflict once and for all. We want peace based on security

and mutual recognition, in which a demilitarized Palestinian state recognizes the Jewish state of Israel. . . . Twenty years ago, the peace process between Israel and the Palestinians began. Six Israeli prime ministers, myself included, have not succeeded in achieving peace with the Palestinians. My predecessors were prepared to make painful concessions. So am I. But so far the Palestinian leaders haven't been prepared to offer the painful concessions they must make in order to end the conflict. For peace to be achieved, the Palestinians must finally recognize the Jewish state, and Israel's security needs must be met.[35]

Over the following months, several rounds of talks were held, mainly mediated by U.S. Secretary of State John Kerry, who shuttled between Jerusalem and Ramallah. During one of Kerry's visits in December 2013, Netanyahu said,

> On the Palestinian issue, I want to say that Israel is ready for historic peace, and it's a peace based on two states for two peoples. It's a peace in which Israel can and must be able to defend itself, by itself, with our own forces against any foreseeable threat. I would also stress that Israel continues to honor all understandings reached in prior negotiations. If this process is going to continue, we're going to have to have a continual negotiation.[36]

Indeed, it appeared that the main obstacle in these rounds of talks, rather than any territorial dispute, focused on the security arrangements demanded by Israel, which the Palestinians refused to provide. In an attempt to move the stalled diplomatic process forward, Kerry enlisted the help of General John Allen, who was supposed to propose technological solutions and alternative security arrangements that would satisfy Israel's demands and be acceptable to the Palestinians. During his visit to Israel on December 5, 2013, Kerry announced,

> Israel's security is fundamental to these negotiations. General John Allen, who is one of the very best military minds in the United States, one of our most experienced military leaders, who has been spending months now analyzing the security challenges with respect to this process—President Obama has designated him to play a very special role in assessing the potential threats to Israel, to the region, and ensuring that the security arrangements that we might contemplate in the context of this process will provide for greater security for Israel.[37]

A few days later, Netanyahu declared,

> We insist upon security. Without security, there can be no agreement. Peace
> that cannot be defended is not peace. I will not accept trickles of missiles,
> rockets or terrorists. When that starts, a response will come immediately.
> One thing is clear: If we want a peace that will last, security must remain in
> our hands. Israel must defend itself, with its own forces, against any threat,
> and this is true everywhere and in the face of any threat. I cannot promise
> that an agreement will be reached—it is not dependent only on us.[38]

At the start of a cabinet meeting on December 20, 2013, Netanyahu said,

> The State of Israel, I believe, has a strategic interest in diplomatic negotiations
> aimed at reaching an agreement that will end the conflict. . . . A diplomatic
> agreement will be signed only if these vital interests are secured, first and
> foremost our security and their demilitarization. Only if Israel is recognized
> as the nation-state of the Jewish people, and only if the Palestinians give up
> on the dream of return and the rest of their demands on the territory of the
> Jewish state, will we reach an agreement.[39]

Throughout the period of negotiations, which moved at a sluggish pace,
Israel claimed that despite Abu Mazen's denials, the PA chairman was working to promote the boycott of Israel in international organizations.[40] At the
same time, Israel continued to publish tenders for construction in East
Jerusalem and the West Bank.[41] The rounds of talks between Israel and the
Palestinians ended officially in April 2014, when both sides took unilateral
steps that contradicted the initial understandings. After three rounds of
releasing Palestinian terrorists from Israeli jails (twenty-six prisoners each
time), Israel refused to carry out the fourth round, scheduled for early
April, because the Palestinians refused to extend the designated period
for negotiations and placed conditions on their continuation. In response,
Netanyahu said on April 6,

> To my regret, as we reached the moment before agreeing on the continua-
> tion of the talks, the Palestinian leadership hastened to unilaterally request
> to accede to 14 international treaties. Thus the Palestinians substantially vio-
> lated the understandings that were reached with American involvement. The
> Palestinians' threats to appeal to the UN will not affect us. The Palestinians

have much to lose by this unilateral move. They will achieve a state only by direct negotiations, not by empty statements and not by unilateral moves. These will only push a peace agreement farther away and unilateral steps on their part will be met with unilateral steps on our part.[42]

The final blow to the talks came after the Palestinian Authority announced at the end of April that a reconciliation agreement had been reached between Fatah and Hamas, which led to Israel's suspension of negotiations and imposition of economic sanctions on the PA.[43]

The political process that took place between Israel and the Palestinians was accompanied by sporadic terrorist activity. In September 2013, IDF soldier Tomer Hazan was kidnapped for the purpose of extortion, but his body was soon discovered in a water cistern. In the same month, another soldier, Gal Kobi, was killed by a Palestinian sniper near the Tomb of the Patriarchs in Hebron. At the beginning of October, Colonel Sariya Ofer was murdered in the northern Jordan Valley, and at the end of the month, five combat engineering fighters were injured during an operation to clear terror tunnels along the Gaza Strip border. Besides these organized terrorist attacks, self-initiated attacks were carried out in Israel during this period, in which Palestinian lone wolves attempted to murder Jews using cold weapons. In one case, for example, a soldier was murdered in a stabbing attack in Afula on November 13. However, the relatively low level of terror at that time was presented by the prime minister as one his government's achievements. In his remarks at the start of the cabinet meeting on March 18, 2014, Netanyahu said,

> In the past year and over the last five years, there has been a low level of terrorism. Last year, it was the lowest in a decade, both in terms of victims and in the launching of missiles and rockets. From time to time we must take vigorous action, as we are now doing, so that this quiet may continue. This vigorous policy is what is responsible for maintaining Israel's security and that of its citizens. Relative to the Middle East as a whole, which is undergoing profound turmoil, Israel is the most stable and secure place in the entire region.[44]

However, in 2014, the Gaza front began to heat up again. On January 16, five rockets were fired into Ashkelon but were intercepted by Iron Dome.

On March 5, 1,500 kilometers from the Israeli coast, the navy seized an Iranian ship carrying weapons and rockets to Hamas and the terrorist organizations in the Gaza Strip.[45] A week later, it was clear that all the understandings reached after Operation Pillar of Defense were no longer relevant when, on March 12, Palestinian terrorist organizations, headed by Islamic Jihad, fired more than seventy rockets at Israeli communities surrounding the strip. This mass firing took place after an Islamic Jihad cell fired mortar shells at IDF forces on the border, and in response, the Israeli Air Force killed three of the organization's operatives.[46] On April 21, during the Passover holiday, terrorist organizations fired about ten rockets from Gaza at the communities surrounding the strip. At the end of May, Border Police officers apprehended a Palestinian terrorist wearing an explosive belt on his way to carry out a suicide bombing in Israel.[47] On June 12, three students were abducted as they were making their way home from their yeshiva in the West Bank. The IDF launched a large-scale search operation to locate the students, dubbed "Bring Back Our Brothers." Eighteen days after the kidnapping, the bodies of the three youths were discovered near the town of Halhul in the West Bank. This led to a change in the operation's objectives, which, from that point on, focused on severely damaging Hamas's military and civilian infrastructure in the West Bank, making arrests, confiscating funds and equipment, and more. On June 22, the prime minister said:

> We are focusing on returning the abductees, on finding the kidnappers and on striking at the organization to which they belong. We have unequivocal proof that this is Hamas. . . . I think that at that time Abu Mazen's remarks in Saudi Arabia will be put to the test in practice . . . his willingness to dissolve the unity government with Hamas, which abducted the youths and calls for the destruction of Israel.[48]

Five days later, Netanyahu further elucidated his worldview regarding the security challenges and threats posed to Israel in the Middle East arena:

> Anyone observing what is going on in the Middle East can see clearly how the violence is spreading like wildfire. In Syria, Iraq, and in other countries, Shi'ites and Sunnis are fighting each other with murderous fury, as well as anyone within range. The images of mass slaughter in cold blood recall dark

scenes in human history. . . . Today it is clearer than ever why I insist that security of the State of Israel begin at the Jordanian line. We also look east and north from there at what was once known as the "Fertile Crescent" and today is a "bleeding crescent" of fanaticism and terror that knows no bounds. Our ability to defend ourselves and deal effectively with dangers is not only a cornerstone of the Zionist vision; it is an existential necessity that remains constant regardless of what changes happen over time.[49]

Following exposure of the perpetrators' identity and their affiliation with Hamas, Netanyahu reiterated the demand that Abu Mazen cancel the reconciliation agreement with Hamas.[50] On July 2, Jewish terrorists kidnapped and murdered a sixteen-year-old Palestinian boy, Muhammad Abu Khadir. The autopsy showed that the boy had been burned to death while he was still alive, a revelation that led to violent riots in east Jerusalem, which then spread to other parts of the West Bank and Arab Israeli towns.[51]

OPERATION PROTECTIVE EDGE

With the abduction of the teenagers on June 12, and against the backdrop of the severe blows dealt to Hamas and the Islamist organizations in the West Bank, action escalated on the southern border, with dozens of rockets fired at Israel from the Gaza Strip each day. Hamas, which for months had refrained from using the vast rocket infrastructure it had built in the Gaza Strip (on the eve of the operation, about 10,000 rockets that could cover the majority of Israeli territory), began indiscriminately firing dozens of rockets into Israeli territory day after day, attempting to hit civilian areas. In light of this severe escalation of rocket fire into Israel from the Gaza Strip by the Palestinian terrorist organizations led by Hamas, Israel launched Operation Protective Edge on July 8, 2014.

From the outset of the operation, many in Israel deliberated over what motivated Hamas to change its policy. Was the organization unintentionally dragged into this activity by the other fractional Palestinian terrorist organizations? Did Hamas choose to adopt this policy as a deliberate escalation in response to the damage caused to the organization's infrastructure in the West Bank after the kidnapping and murder of the three Israeli teenagers? Or perhaps was it an outburst to protest the organization's economic crisis and its inability to pay the salaries to its members? Whether or not

Hamas entered the campaign in a planned or accidental manner, during its early stages, Hamas spokespersons defined their goal publicly and clearly: the lifting of the blockade on the Gaza Strip. Hamas made it clear that it was seeking to build a seaport and airport and to open the land crossings between Israel and the Gaza Strip and the Rafah crossing to Egypt.

Israel found itself dragged into a battle that it was not interested in and for which it had not prepared. In the first days of the operation, Israeli decision makers did not correctly assess the nature of the campaign or Hamas's goals, and therefore they did not set clear aims for the IDF. During the first month of fighting, different Israeli spokespeople presented various goals as forming the basis of the campaign, including restoring quiet and calm, severely damaging Hamas's military infrastructure, neutralizing the Palestinian organizations' rockets systems, destroying the attack tunnels penetrating Israel, and demilitarizing the Gaza Strip. Despite the variety of targets tossed about by these spokespeople, most agreed that Israel should not set as a campaign goal the toppling of the Hamas regime in the Gaza Strip.

In contrast to the range of goals stated by various Israeli representatives, Prime Minister Netanyahu consistently presented a single goal throughout the entire operation: "restoring quiet and security for all Israeli citizens, especially to the residents of the south."[52] On the face of it, this consistent stance should have countered the lack of clarity regarding Israel's operational objectives in Operation Protective Edge. But, in fact, the goal that was defined was a passive one, return to the status quo. Such a goal might be achieved in various ways, including negotiating with Hamas and reaching an agreement, preventing Hamas from continuing to fire at Israel, and neutralizing Hamas's military capabilities. The dangerous combination of the lack of understanding of the enemy's strategic objective and the vague definition of Israel's own strategic objective led the IDF to take hesitant steps during the first weeks of the fighting, based on the repeatedly discredited assumption that Hamas would hold its fire and agree to a ceasefire within a short time.

The decision to refrain from defining the stated goal of Operation Protective Edge as the toppling of Hamas essentially dictated a strategic goal that was designed to achieve a settlement with Hamas rather than its defeat. The defeat of a military campaign is achieved by delivering a severe blow to the enemy's military infrastructure and destroying its fighting capability. A settlement, on the other hand, should be achieved by neutralizing the enemy's motivation to continue fighting even if it still has residual fighting capability. A settlement can be reached in one of three ways: coercion, compromise, or surrender. The type of settlement is determined by the ability to deter the enemy from continuing to fight. For instance, when the state succeeds in causing significant damage and demonstrating its military and intelligence superiority, it might be able to deter the enemy from continued fighting and achieve a coerced settlement in which the state imposes its conditions on the enemy. When the state is unable to cause significant damage to the enemy and its military and intelligence superiority is not reflected in military success, or when the enemy succeeds in causing severe and sustained damage to the state, a situation might develop in which the enemy is the one that deters the state from continuing to fight and is the one to dictate the terms of surrender. When both sides are unable to neutralize the enemy's motivation to continue fighting, or when both sides equally deter and are deterred, then the settlement achieved is one of compromise, in which neither side is able to dictate the terms of the settlement.

From the outset of Operation Protective Edge, Israel decided not to make the defeat of Hamas its strategic objective. This forced Israel to achieve a high level of deterrence in order to bring Hamas to a coerced settlement, or at least to one of compromise, in which it would be Israel that dictates terms to Hamas. However, it is difficult for a liberal-democratic state such as Israel, with its moral and legal restraints, to achieve a high level of deterrence when it is dealing with a hybrid terrorist organization such as Hamas, which controls territory and population and deliberately embeds its operatives, bases, headquarters, and defenses into the civilian population and uses citizens as human shields. Moreover, the cost-benefit analysis of a terrorist organization like Hamas is essentially different from the cost-benefit considerations of a liberal-democratic Western state like Israel. Costs that are considered intolerable for a state are certainly tolerable for a terrorist organization.

Whereas a state undertakes military operations with the goal of protecting its citizens, a terrorist organization embeds itself within the civilian population in order to protect its military infrastructure, facilities, and leadership. In order for a terrorist organization to be deterred from continuing to fight, the state must force the organization to pay a heavy price in terms of the cost-benefit considerations that guide the organization and its leaders. When the terrorist organization manages to preserve its senior chain of command and military infrastructure located within or beneath dense civilian centers and protected sites such as hospitals, mosques, and UNRWA buildings, the state has almost no chance of forcing the organization to pay a price high enough to deter it from continued fighting due to the state's concern about causing disproportionate collateral damage. In other words, according to the conditions described earlier, the ability to deter a terrorist organization is inversely related to a restrained military policy. On the one hand, a lack of restraint that would lead to significant collateral damage to civilians (even when attacking legitimate military targets) is likely to provoke severe international criticism, a delegitimization campaign against the state, and internal protests within the state.

Thus, during Operation Protective Edge, Israel found itself facing an impossible paradox. Its erroneous assessment of Hamas's objectives and the nature of the campaign led Israel, during the first ten days of the operation prior to the ground incursion, to be overly meticulous in trying to avoid collateral damage to civilians. Its restrained air strikes might have lent it support and international legitimacy in its justified war against Hamas, but these attacks were virtually useless because they did not significantly damage Hamas's military infrastructure, headquarters, launchers, or commanders, who were entrenched within and near densely populated civilian areas.

These attacks, which damaged structures used by Hamas in the Gaza Strip, did not actually affect the organization's cost-benefit balance and certainly did not achieve the desired deterrent effect. Israel's policy of restraint essentially led to prolonging the operation to fifty days of fighting, and it did not prompt Hamas to seek a quick settlement. Even after the government instructed the IDF, on July 17, to carry out ground maneuvers in the Gaza Strip after a Hamas cell infiltrated Israeli territory via an attack tunnel, Israel did not change the strategic objective of the campaign or its policy of restraint. The numerous Palestinian casualties during the ground operation were the result of entanglements of ground forces in ambushes planned by Hamas that occurred on the outskirts of civilian neighborhoods and the return fire used to extricate IDF troops and casualties. Moreover, the Hamas leadership, which felt secure and protected in underground tunnels in civilian areas, was not deterred from repeatedly violating ceasefires and humanitarian pauses in the fighting. (During the fifty days of the fighting, there were attempts to maintain twelve ceasefires, most of which were accepted by Israel but violated by Hamas and the Palestinian organizations.)

Thus, when the discussions in Egypt on a settlement deteriorated after it became clear to Israel that it would not succeed in dictating a coerced settlement on Hamas (by adding a section about the demilitarization of the Gaza Strip from rockets and weapons), and after Hamas failed in its attempts to force Israel to accept a settlement through surrender (by forcing it to agree to the establishment of a seaport and airport in the Gaza Strip), the Palestinians again violated the ceasefire. In response to this violation, Israel carried out targeted killings of leaders of Hamas's military wing in the Gaza Strip in a way that demonstrated its military and intelligence superiority. This was perhaps the first time in more than forty days of fighting that Hamas was forced to pay a strategically significant price for its insistence on continuing the fighting. Hamas's immediate response to the attack on its leadership was to launch an unprecedented number of rockets in an attempt to demonstrate to Israel that neither its rocket-launching capability nor its motivation had been damaged. However, after the boomerang effect (an increase in the terrorist organization's motivation as a result of significant damage to its operational capability) ended, and after Israel succeeded in showing Hamas that it could force the organization to pay a heavy strategic price while simultaneously absorbing about 100 rockets a day, most of which were intercepted by Iron Dome, the deterrent effect was achieved and Hamas was forced to return to the Egyptian negotiating table and accept a settlement with conditions favorable to Israel.

As noted earlier, Operation Protective Edge ended after fifty days of fighting. The cost of the operation was estimated at $9 billion.[53] During the operation, 4,594 rockets and mortar shells were fired at Israel, with 735 intercepted by Iron Dome.[54] The IDF struck 6,231 terrorist targets in the Gaza Strip, destroying thirty-four terrorist tunnels, of which fourteen were attack tunnels penetrating Israel. Over the course of the operation, 64 Israeli soldiers and 7 civilians were killed, and on the Palestinian side, approximately 2,200 were killed, of whom 1,400 were terrorists. More than 10,000 buildings in the Gaza Strip were destroyed by bombs, and the number of homeless people in the Gaza Strip in the wake of the operation increased to between 300,000 and 500,000.[55]

THE LONE WOLF CHALLENGE

Following Operation Protective Edge, there was a lull in rocket fire from the Gaza Strip. In addition to its severe economic crisis and loss of support in the Arab world, Hamas faced growing criticism from the residents of Gaza in light of the new reality created in the area after the operation and the lack of achievements by Hamas and the other organizations. The calm in the south of the country, however, was offset by a deterioration in security in the country's center, especially in Jerusalem and its environs, due to a wave of cold-weapon and stabbing attacks by Palestinian lone wolves who were incited by Hamas and other terrorist organizations.

At the beginning of August, a Palestinian carried out a ramming attack with a tractor in Jerusalem, killing an Israeli civilian and injuring six others. On October 22, another Palestinian killed an infant and another Israeli and injured several pedestrians in a ramming attack in Jerusalem using his car. About two weeks later, yet another ramming attack caused the death of two Israelis and the wounding of several others. On November 10, a soldier was murdered in a stabbing assault in Tel Aviv, and on the same day, a girl was murdered and two were wounded in a stabbing attack in Alon Shvut in the West Bank. In early December, a Palestinian minor carried out a knife attack in a Ma'aleh Adumim supermarket, injuring two customers. About ten days later, a Palestinian terrorist poured acid on a family in Gush Etzion and tried to stab them with a screwdriver. Five were injured in the attack. The next day, the prime minister declared,

> We are in the midst of a campaign of incitement and terrorism directed against the State of Israel and its citizens. This campaign has continued since the foundation of the state and even before then. We have defeated terrorism until today and we will defeat it this time as well.[56]

Netanyahu detailed the new counterterrorism measures that his government intended to employ in order to stop this wave of terrorism and deter lone wolves:

> These steps include increasing forces on the ground throughout the country in order to boost your security, citizens of Israel, the demolition of terrorists' homes, a strong hand and more severe punishment of those who throw

stones, bottles, fireworks and firebombs, fines for the parents of children and young people who throw stones, the outlawing of those elements that are stirring up unrest in Jerusalem, and other measures. . . . We are determined to take all possible action against incitement and escalation; we will take vigorous action against the terrorists.[57]

On November 18, 2014, a murderous attack took place in a Jerusalem synagogue. It was carried out by two members of the Popular Front for the Liberation of Palestine who infiltrated the synagogue during morning prayers and opened fire on worshippers. Four people were killed and eight were wounded. On January 18, the ISA arrested seven Palestinian residents of Israel who had established an ISIS cell and planned to carry out attacks.[58]

After another election season in Israel, Netanyahu was reelected for a third consecutive term and was appointed Israel's thirty-fourth prime minister on May 14, 2015. Following the establishment of the new government, there was renewed firing of rockets at Ashkelon and the southern communities around the Gaza Strip, along with retaliatory Israeli air attacks. During that period, it became known that in two separate incidents, Israeli civilians had crossed the border into the Gaza Strip and were apparently in the hands of Hamas. One was Avera Mengistu, a twenty-eight-year-old from Ashkelon, and the other was a Bedouin man who had apparently tried to cross the border into Gaza several times before succeeding.[59]

The cold-weapon and ramming attacks by lone wolves continued and even intensified in the second half of 2015, becoming an unprecedented wave. These attacks stemmed from nationalist and mainly religious motives, against the backdrop of incitement in which Israel was accused of attempting to desecrate the Al-Aqsa Mosque and of changing the status quo on the Temple Mount. These messages of incitement had been voiced for a long time by Palestinian terrorist organizations, mainly Hamas and Islamic Jihad spokesmen, but they caught a tailwind when senior PA officials and other leaders joined the chorus, urging Israel not to "contaminate" the Temple Mount.[60] These calls were a catalyst that drove young insurgents into the streets and take the law into their own hands, randomly injuring and killing Israelis.

The wave of self-initiated attacks began as a series of terrorist attacks carried out mostly by incited lone wolves using cold weapons such as knives, axes, and vehicles. But a cost-benefit analysis seemed to show that the wave failed. Most of the attacks resulted in the death, injury, or capture of the assailant after he or she succeeded in causing limited damage, usually the injury of a small number of Israelis. As a result, Palestinian terrorist organizations, led by Hamas, increased their incitement activities on the internet and on social media, issuing guidelines instructing terrorists how to be more effective in their attacks. These guidelines were often accompanied by video clips that demonstrated what kind of knives lone wolves should use, where to strike the victim, from which angle to attack, and so on. In some cases, the terrorist organizations recommended that pairs or groups of attackers initiate action, and that the victim's weapon be seized and used to open fire in the area.

However, the organizations' institutionalized incitement and training of terrorists via the internet reflected only one aspect of the growing importance of social media in the so-called Knife Intifada. These networks, especially Facebook and Twitter, served in many cases as a platform to convey the terrorists' thoughts, feelings, and political messages prior to their departure to launch the attack. Some of the terrorists chose this medium to put their suicidal actions into a desired context, to emphasize the sacrifice and altruism in their actions, and to leave a kind of spiritual last will and testament, guiding friends and family on how to act after their deaths. These messages were intended to preserve and glorify the terrorists' image among their peers and in Palestinian society as a whole. Thus, social media enabled the lone wolves to be glorified in the wake of their terrorist acts. Spurred on by terrorist organizations and their supporters, the social networks encouraged others to follow in their friends' footsteps and carry out attacks. One attack thus fueled the next one, becoming a model for emulation by others, in a process creating a kind of terrorist epidemic.

During these years, Israel was challenged by a range of terrorist attacks, some of them organized attacks; that is, initiated, planned, prepared, and executed by Palestinian terrorist organizations (such as kidnappings, murder using firearms, and suicide bombings). Others self-initiated (such as stabbings, ramming attacks, and the throwing of Molotov cocktails) by lone wolves who had no operational links with the organizations but were for the most part inspired by incitement by leaders of the Palestinian terrorist organizations. Throughout this period, these organizations, headed by Hamas, sought to abduct Israeli soldiers or civilians. On the basis of Israel's policy over the years and the price that Israel had been prepared to pay, for instance, for the return of Gilad Shalit, taking an Israeli hostage was seen by the organizations as a strategic goal that could bring about tangible achievements. Most of the attempted abductions occurred in the West Bank, and a few within Israel proper.

From mid-2015 throught 2017, a number of lone wolf attacks with various types of cold weapons were carried out in Israel and the West Bank. In recent years, there has been a significant increase in these types of attacks, which reached an unprecedented peak in the second half of 2015. Between September 14, when the wave of stabbing attacks began, and the middle of November, 24 people were killed and 185 injured. According to the findings of the International Institute for Counter-Terrorism (ICT), the profile of most of the terrorists who took part in this wave was that of a young man (in 85 percent of cases), with an average age of 22.[61] Most of these terrorists did not belong to any organization, conducting their attacks alone after making a spontaneous decision and without organizational assistance. The perpetrators' motivations were a combination of personal considerations stemming from their own frustrations, the desire to gain fame as a martyr, revenge for the death of friends and relatives, and especially exposure to extreme incitement in the Palestinian media, combined with national and religious motivations. With the continuation of this wave of attacks, an epidemiological effect was created, which was transmitted through, among other means, social networks and contributed to the motivation for carrying out further attacks.[62]

In the following years, the number of terrorist attacks in Israel decreased: 163 in 2015, 108 in 2016; and the number declined to 54 in 2017.[63] ISA director attributed this decrease to, among other measures, the growing use of big data, artificial intelligence (AI), and machine learning in Israel's counterterrorism policy.[64]

The unique characteristics of lone wolf attacks include that they usually do not involve other individuals in preparing or executing the attack, they do not require lengthy preparations, and, in some cases, the attacks are spontaneous. Challenging traditional intelligence-gathering methods such as human intelligence (HUMINT) and communications intelligence (COMINT), the lone wolf phenomenon forced the Israeli intelligence and security services (as well as others around the world) to rely more on open source intelligence (OSINT) and Web-based intelligence (WEBINT).

Once again, the terrorism challenge posed to Israel led to new and innovative counterterrorism strategies and technologies, which, by their very essence, brought new dilemmas and challenges.

In the second half of Netanyahu's fourth term, in January 2017, his friend and ally Donald Trump was elected as the forty-fifth president of the United States. Netanyahu and Trump shared a similar view of the Iranian threat, both in the nuclear realm and with regard to the Iranian regime's support for terrorist organizations, chief among these Hezbollah. The two were also coordinated with regard to Israel's fundamental interests in the Israeli-Palestinian conflict. In contrast to the murky relationship that characterized the Netanyahu administration's interactions with President Obama, the Israeli government enjoyed a warm and close relationship with the Trump administration.

THE NETANYAHU ADMINISTRATIONS' COUNTERTERRORISM POLICY IN LIGHT OF THE COUNTERTERRORISM DILEMMAS MODEL

The period under discussion consisted of three governments headed by Netanyahu. The thirty-second government (Netanyahu's second) served until March 2013. This term was characterized by deep tension between the Israeli government and the administrations of friendly countries, most notably the United States under the leadership of President Obama, who demanded that Netanyahu freeze settlement construction in the West Bank in order to advance negotiations with the Palestinians. In addition, Israel was also accused by various countries of killing a senior Hamas official, Mahmoud al-Mabhouh, in Dubai, using passports from foreign countries. During this period, Turkish supporters of Hamas tried to break the naval blockade imposed by Israel on the Gaza Strip and trigger international criticism of Israel by organizing flotillas of Turkish and other ships. These flotillas were stopped by the Israeli navy, and the violent clashes that broke out between IDF soldiers and activists on the ships led to casualties on both sides and deterioration in Israeli-Turkish relations.

The magnitude of terrorist attacks against Israel during this government's term was generally low in comparison with other periods. However, Israel was forced to deal with shooting attacks that were carried out mainly in the West Bank, rocket fire from the Gaza Strip, and attacks launched on its territory from Sinai by Palestinian cells with the help of global jihadi activists from among the Bedouin tribes living in the area. In light of these attacks, the Netanyahu government continued with its counterterrorism policies, which included targeted killings using air strikes in the Gaza Strip. These actions led to the launching of rockets into Israel, and in June 2012, the deterioration in the situation led Israel to launch a major military operation in the Gaza Strip, Operation Pillar of Defense, toward the end of the year.

The third Netanyahu government (the thirty-third Israeli government) served until May 2015. It observed the geopolitical changes taking place in the region intently, including security challenges stemming from the Arab Spring and the civil war in Syria. However, it identified Iran's nuclear activity as the main threat to Israel, one that had the potential to become an existential threat should the Iranians develop a nuclear bomb. Israel's uncompromising opposition to the nuclear agreement that was being formulated between Iran, the United States, European, and other countries put the Netanyahu government on a collision course with the Obama administration and with some of its other allies in the world. The government faced a lot of pressure from attempts by the United States to advance negotiations between Israel and the Palestinians, but these attempts quickly fell flat. The gradual deterioration in the area as well as the escalation of rocket fire from the beginning of 2014 culminated in another large-scale military operation in Gaza in the summer of 2014, which lasted about fifty days and involved massive exchanges of fire from both sides.

Toward the end of the third Netanyahu government in 2015, a new wave of terror erupted involving cold-weapon attacks (such as stabbings and vehicle rammings) and, rarely, firearms. These assaults were conducted by Palestinian terrorists who were acting independently without the operational assistance of any terrorist organization. This wave of lone wolf attacks, which was encouraged by aggressive incitement by Palestinian terrorist organizations through the media and social networks, seemed to wane after the Israeli security forces began using big data and AI technology in order to identify these terrorists' intentions.

An examination of Israel's counterterrorism policy during the period under review using the Counterterrorism Dilemmas Conceptual Model (figure 11.1) demonstrates that most of the time, Netanyahu's governments were subjected to international pressure regarding their policy vis-à-vis the

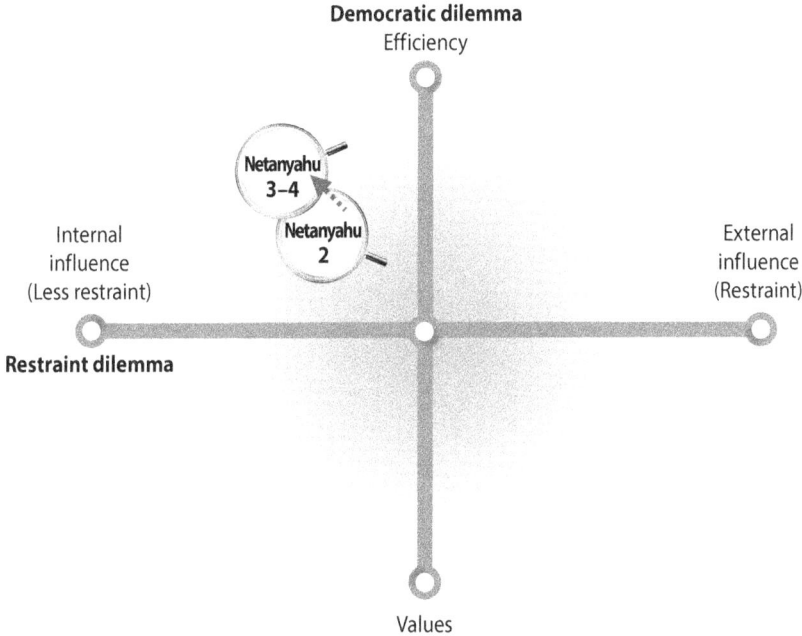

FIGURE 11.1. Counterterrorism Dilemmas Conceptual Model—Netanyahu administration (2009-18)

Palestinians (in both the diplomatic and the security contexts, which in many cases were intertwined). But Netanyahu preferred to adhere to the concerns of his own political base and domestic pressure, especially with regard to the increase in rocket attacks from Gaza Strip toward Israeli cities and villages. Israeli counterterrorism activity was aimed at curbing the rocket fire into Israel, which included a number of operations in the Gaza Strip, continuation of the naval blockade of Gaza, and targeted killings in the territories and possibly abroad. These moves only intensified the tension that already existed within the international community. Netanyahu did not hesitate to use the means that he and his government considered to be effective in dealing with terrorism, despite the fact that they were likely to increase international criticism of Israel. On the Israeli domestic front, the government received widespread support, which was reflected in the repeated election of Benjamin Netanyahu as prime minister, largely on the basis of the image he presented to the voters as being "Mr. Security."

Chapter Twelve

ISRAEL'S COUNTERTERRORISM POLICY FROM THE PERSPECTIVE OF ISRAELI DECISION MAKERS

As has been discussed in various chapters of this book, the objectives and policies of Israel's counterterrorism strategy have changed over time depending on the scope and characteristics of the threat, international and local processes and events, Israeli leaders' worldview, its foreign relations and bilateral and multilateral relationships with other countries, the state of the relationship and negotiation processes with the Palestinians and Arab states, domestic political pressures and considerations, external pressure and criticism, and the recommendations of Israeli security agencies.

The Counterterrorism Dilemmas Conceptual Model presented in the first chapter enables us to compare the policies of the various governments with regard to the democratic dilemma axis and the axis of restraint. A long-term examination of Israeli government policy on the democratic dilemma axis demonstrates that almost all of the administrations prioritized considerations relating to the degree of effectiveness of various counterterrorism measures even when they sometimes came at the expense of liberal democratic considerations (figure 12.1). Most of the governments tended to respond to internal pressures, which led to less restraint in their counterterrorism policies, even if their actions sometimes contradicted the expectations and demands of international actors who urged Israel to exercise more restraint. Moreover, looking at the counterterrorism policies of the various governments on the model's axes indicates that, with

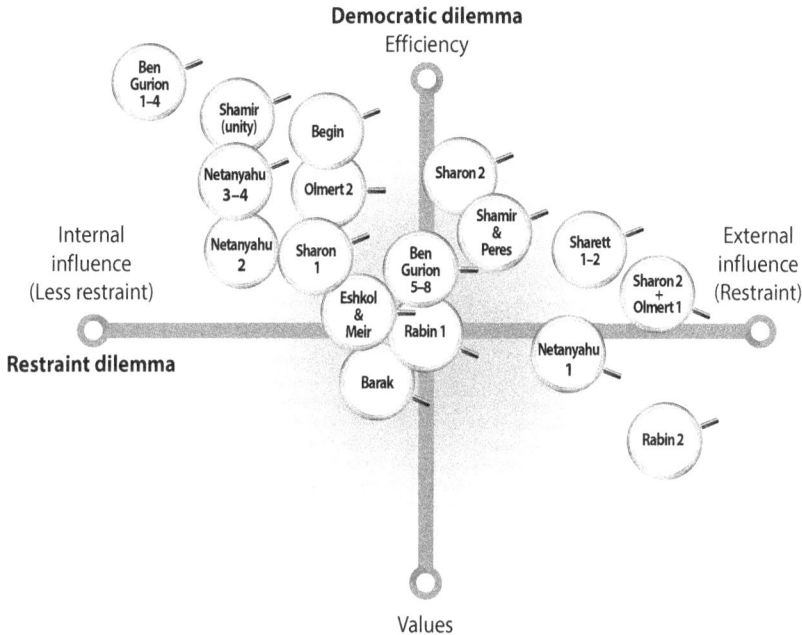

FIGURE 12.1. Counterterrorism Dilemmas Conceptual Model—various governments

only a few exceptions (the second Sharon and the first Netanyahu governments), the policies of most Israeli governments of the last twenty years
fall into the model's upper-left quadrant. This reflects a lesser degree of
restraint in counterterrorism, the prioritization given to responding to
domestic pressure, and the adoption of measures that are perceived as
being more effective, with liberal and democratic considerations being
secondary.

The Counterterrorism Dilemmas Model shows how Israel's counterterrorism policies have changed and transitioned from period to period and
government to government (figures 12.2–12.4). The inclusion on the timeline of major events that have occurred over the years (wars, peace agreements, waves of terror, and military operations) can help us to understand
the constraints and causes of change in Israeli policy.

The various administrations decided whether to increase or reduce their
use of different counterterrorism measures and whether or not to adapt
their policy in the struggle against terrorism by contemplating the tensions

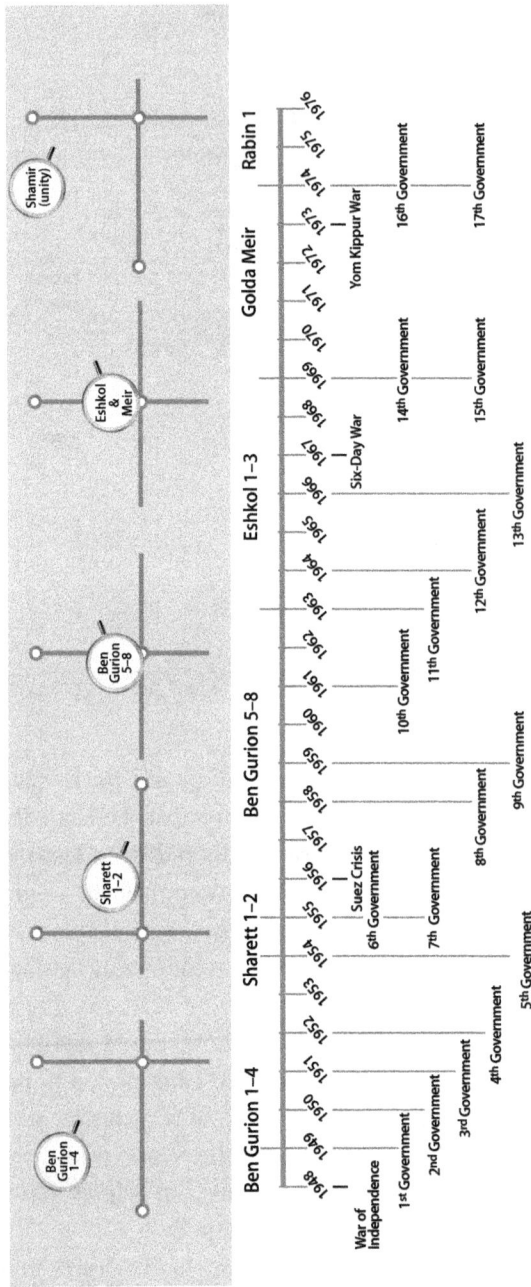

FIGURE 12.2. Timeline of major events: 1948–76

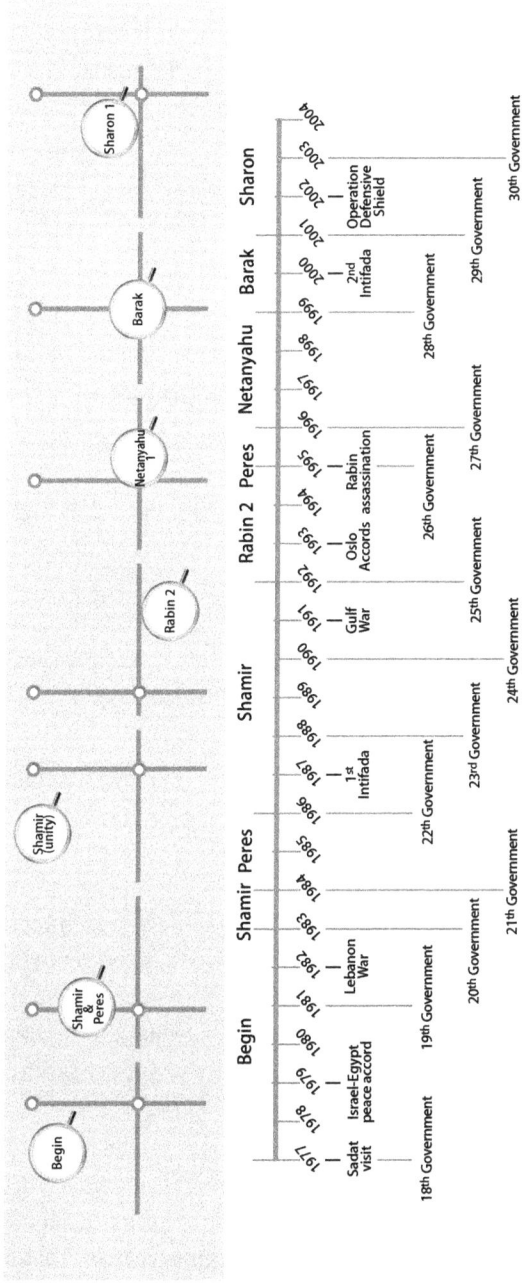

FIGURE 12.3. Timeline of major events: 1977–2004

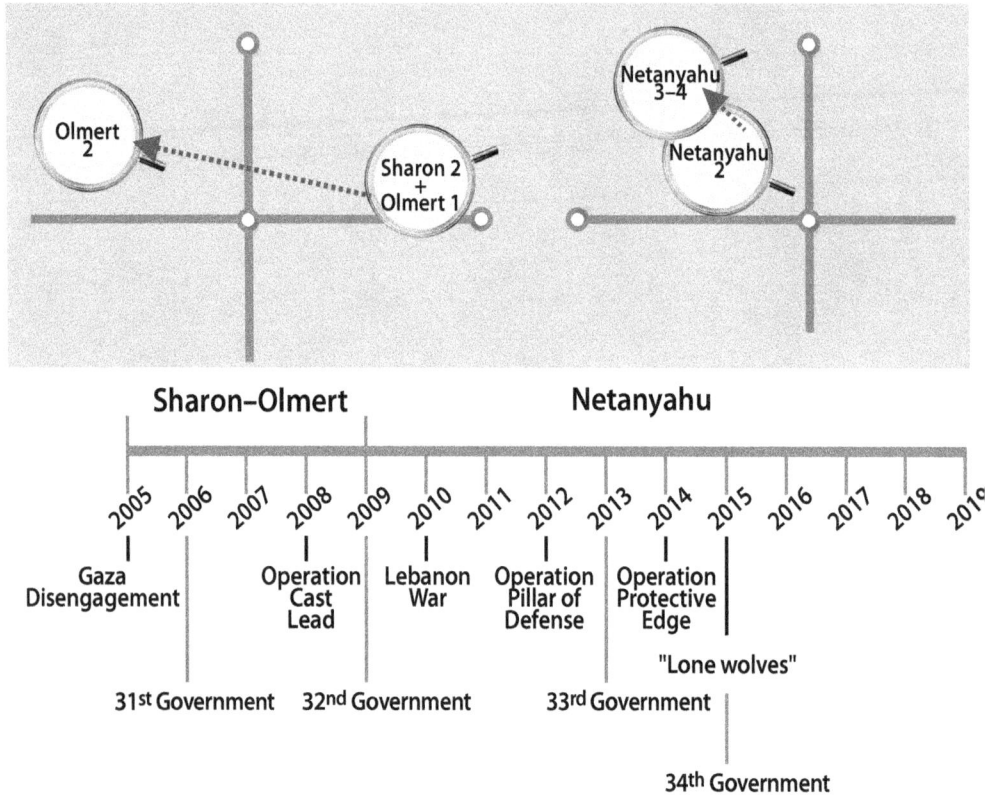

FIGURE 12.4. Timeline of major events: 2005–19

between practical and moral considerations and between internal political pressures and external international criticism. As noted by Byman,

> Counterterrorism, even as its most impressive, comes with trade-offs, and most of the time effectiveness simply means fewer attacks or less deadly ones rather than a complete end to violence. As Israel's experience shows, government must often choose among bad options: the least bad is often the most to hope for. Realistic expectations of what democratic government can and cannot accomplish is vital. Such realism enables leaders to fight or not fight, spend or not spend, and ultimately make sensible decisions about blood and treasure, knowing that citizens understand there are no easy answers.[1]

The state of Israel, established in 1948, grew, developed, and became a regional military and economic power—a kind of modern Goliath. However, when this Goliath was constantly confronted with the threat of terror, he found himself handcuffed and shackled by the chains of moral and ethical considerations, Israeli and international law, and criticisms and pressure from international bodies, friendly countries, international tribunals, and world public opinion. These shackles prevented the Goliath that is Israeli from exhausting all of its military and other capabilities in its struggle against terrorist organizations and operatives. The Israeli public, for its part, expected its leaders (especially during periods of frequent terrorist attacks) to ignore these constraints and limitations, demanding that they provide citizens with maximum personal and national security.

Despite the (sometimes extreme) differences between the policies of each Israeli government in dealing with terrorism, most governments seem to have acted with a common ethos dictating that the state, army, and Israeli security forces provide citizens with the protection and sense of security that they deserve. This was the case even if counterterrorism activities were likely to exact high physical prices and exposed Israel to international pressure, possibly even harming diplomatic relations with other countries.

Against this background, it is interesting to examine what Israeli decision makers believe its counterterrorism goals should be. In order to answer this and other questions, this summarizing chapter includes testimonies compiled through personal interviews with twenty-two decision makers who, over the last fifty years, have served in the most senior positions in the Israeli security establishment—the decision makers who have shaped Israeli policy on how to deal with terror. These prime ministers; defense ministers; IDF chiefs of staff; heads of the Mossad, ISA, and the Military Intelligence Directorate; advisors on counterterrorism to the prime minister; and special coordinators for Israeli counterterrorism were interviewed over the course of several years, each answering the same questions. Among those interviewed were five prime ministers (Shamir, Peres, Sharon, Netanyahu, and Olmert), four defense ministers (Peres, Arens, Sharon, and Mofaz), three IDF chiefs of staff (Lipkin-Shahak, Mofaz, and Ashkenazi), three IDF heads of the intelligence directorate (Amit, Gazit, and Lipkin-Shahak), four IDF generals (Tamir, Ze'evi, Sharon, and Dagan), four ISA chiefs (Ahituv, Perry, Gillon, and Dichter), three heads of the Mossad (Amit, Shavit, and Dagan), and four advisors on counterterrorism to the prime minister or coordinators for counterterrorism (Sharon, Eitan, Pressler, and Nuriel). It should be noted that some of the interviewees held multiple positions and are therefore counted in every relevant position. These interviews provide a range of perspectives, worldviews, and ideologies from a variety of individuals serving in Israel's top security profiles.

OBJECTIVES OF ISRAELI COUNTERTERRORISM

The different goals of Israeli counterterrorism from 1948 on can be learned from those who held senior security positions at the time. Among the most important goals, many pointed out, was neutralizing terrorism's strategic impact; that is, its impact on morale and the impact of attacks on the peace process. This is because one of the strategic objectives of Palestinian terrorism with regard to Israel was to harm public morale through terrorist attacks and to translate the public's anxiety into pressure on decision makers and influence over Israel's strategic considerations. Rehavam Ze'evi, who served as commander of the Central Command in the late 1960s and was the prime minister's advisor on counterterrorism in the 1970s, believed that the role of the campaign against terror was to release Israeli decision makers from the effects and constraints of terrorism when discussing strategic and policy issues.

> My goals, which I defined for myself, were to reduce terrorism to such a low flame that it would have no influence on the decisions of the political echelon. No one in the world can totally eliminate terrorism. . . . The political leader should consider his strategic political moves, contact with the Arabs, whether to make concessions or not, free of this pressure. . . . My role is not to find a political solution, and I must not deal with political issues. I have to make sure that whoever is authorized to deal with the political solution be free from this distress and this headache [of terrorism].[2]

Conversely, Avraham Tamir, a former IDF general and senior military consultant, maintained that proper military thinking must be linked to political goals, that the military struggle is not something that stands on its own.

> The purpose of the army is to enable the achievement of political goals. They can be negative and they can be positive. . . . From this starting point, you

have to measure all military activity, from the level of the battle through the campaign and all the way to war.[3]

Shlomo Gazit (former head of Military Intelligence) also defined the supreme goal of counterterrorism as a political goal: "The goal is not to defeat the enemy. I wish I could, but I cannot defeat him, so I have to pressure him so that when we get to the negotiating table, he will want to reach an agreement from a place of weakness and attrition, not from a place of achievement."[4] Gazit's approach is essentially Clausewitzian—the war against terror, according to Gazit, is not just the continuation of policy but preparation for the next stage of policy.

Former prime minister Yitzhak Shamir did not view the goals of Israeli counterterrorism in this way. He believed that the goal is "simply to prevent and to reduce [terror attacks]. Prevention is elimination. If you are going to eliminate the terrorists, then can you not eliminate terror?" Shamir did not accept the argument that Israel's counterterrorism policy should improve its ability to realize its interests and facilitate better conditions for a future peaceful settlement with the Palestinians. He said that the opposite is true; this approach conveys dangerous weakness and in fact rewards Palestinian terrorism. Shamir maintained that terrorism's main goal is to lower morale.

> Terror and partisan war, in all its forms, all together, can damage morale and reduce it to the level of willingness to surrender. . . . As soon as morale is lowered and the victims reach the conclusion that it is impossible to stand up to terror, then they begin to compromise, to give in, to surrender. Every concession strengthens terrorism. . . . It is not true that in this war victory cannot be achieved. It can be. And any theory that has only political solutions is baseless. Capitulation to terror can be done via political means. This is not a solution but a capitulation . . . therefore, my political conclusion is that the Oslo Accords saved terrorism and prevented its elimination, because eliminating terror is made possible by an unremitting war and not by one-time acts, no matter how large and sophisticated they are. And we were there; we were very close to seeing the results of our war.[5]

Another prime minister, Ariel Sharon, also believed that the response to terrorism should not be political:

By what means can terrorism be eliminated? By political means? Where has it been eliminated using political means? . . . I would not put all of our hopes into a diplomatic solution to this matter. We should try to reach a diplomatic solution, we definitely need to reach one, but to say that it will prevent terrorism? It will not prevent terrorism. The animosity and hatred are so deep, and so is the incitement. There will always be someone willing to carry out an attack. I am not saying that it is possible to eliminate it completely [by other means]. But you can reduce it. I would definitely say that you can reduce it to a level that you can almost live with.[6]

Not surprisingly, Shimon Peres defined the objectives of counter-errorism differently from Shamir and Sharon:

For seventy years, the Palestinian political leadership claimed that terrorism was its only strategic weapon, both to defeat Israel and to keep them on the international agenda, the Arab agenda. I was always of the opinion that the war on terrorism's main challenge should be to drive a wedge between terrorism and its people. The most important thing is to enlist the terrorists in fighting terrorism. I think that Oslo's greatest success was to stop terror. I think that the cooperation between the [Israeli and Palestinian] police is the most important thing there is. The fact is that since Oslo, there has been almost no Palestinian terrorism. [Peres was referring to terrorism perpetrated by the Fatah organization.] For the first time in history, a terrorist organization agreed to disengage from terrorism and fight terrorism. In my opinion, this is the genius thing about Oslo.[7]

Peres therefore defined two operational goals of counterterrorism during his tenure as follows, "first, maintain good relations with the [Palestinian] population so that it does not support terror. Second, identify who is in charge of the terrorism and strike him."[8]

Lipkin-Shahak, who served as IDF chief of staff at that time, added,

During my term as chief of staff, Palestinian terrorism was at a very low level. Fatah had almost completely abandoned terrorism, with the exception of some on the margins that did not join the diplomatic talks. It was Hamas and Islamic Jihad who took the lead. The state of Israel's goal was first and foremost to minimize the damage as much as possible. Strike them as hard as possible and let the Palestinians understand that this path [of terrorism], when a diplomatic process is in progress, interferes with or prevents the process from achieving the desired result for both sides."[9]

Former ISA head Yaakov Perry contributed to the debate: "I do not think that any goal has ever been defined, except for a definition that we used and which is always correct—to eliminate terrorism, to eradicate it." Perry said,

> Everyone knew that the truth was that a correct and effective war would succeed only in reducing it. It is impossible to do anything totally. . . . I think that the Intifada made it very clear for the first time to the leaders and to those who headed the war on terror. . . . There is no alternative but to solve the matter diplomatically. . . . Things became a bit more realistic, a little more down-to-earth. But there is still no statesman or Shin Bet, Military Intelligence, or Mossad head that will stand up and say something other than that the goal is to eliminate them, get rid of them, and suppress them.[10]

In this context, Carmi Gillon (another former ISA head) believed that "the First Intifada succeeded for them. Terrorism did not. Terrorism, even the worst attacks, strengthened the spirit of the people rather than weakening it. . . . They did not succeed in undermining the morale of the people—on the contrary, they achieved the opposite goal."[11] Meir Dagan (former head of Mossad) added:

> The real goal in dealing with terrorism is to keep it at a level that does not affect the public agenda. As long as terrorist attacks were kept at the level of sporadic events that did not disrupt people's lives and the public agenda, I would think that we are winning the war. As soon as terrorism affects the public agenda and the heart of daily life in the state of Israel, terrorism will prevail. As such, the goal of eliminating terrorism is one that cannot be realized. . . . The goal should be very limited. I would say that thwarting acts of terror acts is the main objective.[12]

Another person who supports this approach is Rafi Eitan, former counterterrorism advisor to the prime minister. In response to the question about the objectives of Israeli counterterrorism, Eitan emphasized the importance of preventing and thwarting attacks:

First of all, prevention. This was the number one task of all of the branches—
Prevention with a capital P. The second thing was prevention by means of
counteractions. . . . When I was adviser to the prime minister, we initiated
dozens of operations . . . the main goal was to thwart the next attack. The
second was to carry out as many operations as possible, and the third was, of
course, infiltration [of the terrorist organization] using intelligence.[13]

In that regard, another former ISA head, Avi Dichter, addressed the question referring to the period of the Second Intifada (2000–2005):

It was clear to all of us what the directive was—to bring down the level of
terrorist attacks. It came up every day in discussions and talks with the prime
minister, with the cabinet, with the government, in security meetings, during
visits by American officials, in talks in Egypt, and in talks with the Palestinians. Every encounter with Yasser Arafat and his people at the time was for
the sole purpose of lowering the level of terror. Everyone was focused on it.
No one dealt with anything else.[14]

Shabtai Shavit (former head of the Mossad) described the goals of counterterrorism while distinguishing between goals that constitute aspirations
that are not necessarily attainable and those that are strategic objectives. "In
terms of an aspiration and not necessarily in terms of the formal definition
of goals, the aim was to eradicate terrorism," he said. "We realized that it is
impossible to eradicate terror, so the hope—and you can call it a strategic
goal—was to reduce the terrorists' capabilities and terrorist incidents as
much as possible."[15]

Former IDF chief of staff Gabi Ashkenazi emphasized the challenge of
dealing with terrorism as a multidimensional threat.

We understood that terrorism is multidimensional in the sense that it has a
civilian context, a political context, a regional context. This is a very complex
problem, and there are not many elements that constitute a common denom-
inator between Hamas and Hezbollah. Both are terrorist organizations, both
want to destroy us, both are extremists, but the conditions, the environment,
the impetus, the patterns of activity, are different. . . . Israel faces this multidimensional challenge periodically in repeated military rounds, whether in
the Gaza Strip or Lebanon.[16]

Ashkenazi set for IDF the goal of ending every military round in a way that would delay the next round as long as possible. "That is what I call deterrence; ending the conflict in such a way that there will be no questions as to who won and who lost and how it ended."[17] Ashkenazi defined three levels of military achievement against terrorism:

> The minimum is buying time [until the next round]; the second level is a return to acceptable "rules of the game"; and if you want to achieve a greater result, then you have to carry out operations like "Defensive Shield," occupying territory. Only then can you dismantle infrastructure, but it has a price—it takes up more time and more resources.[18]

The question of defeating and eliminating terrorism is, of course, a function of how one defines the term "defeating terror." Is it the physical destruction of the organization? of its military forces? of its organizational or political infrastructure? Is it about the eradication of political ideologies or the neutralizing of their influence on the broader public? Or is it about forcing the terrorist organization to give up its strategic goals, or at least to abandon the path of terror in favor of legitimate, nonviolent political activity? In this regard, Shaul Mofaz (former defense minister and IDF chief of staff) said,

> A terrorist organization has political goals, and it wants to achieve them through terror and violence, which is the most murderous degree of terrorism that there is, as it is willing to do anything to achieve these goals. If the organization ceases trying to achieve its goals through terrorist activity and looks for other paths, in my eyes, that is a tremendous victory [against terrorism].[19]

Mofaz emphasized that these were conditions set out by the Quartet that Israel accepted. If Hamas had accepted them as well, it would no longer be a terrorist organization.[20]

A different approach was taken by Prime Minister Netanyahu, who believed that terrorism could be eliminated through military means. Referring to a question about the military component of terrorism, he said,

> Why not? Certainly. You have to ask whether you can eliminate crime using the police, and the answer is that to a certain extent, yes, you can. No one

would consider asking such a question on criminal issues. . . . The goal was to strike as many terrorist targets as possible. I would be glad to have been able to strike them all. At a certain stage, we hit a lot terrorist leaders, and that really neutralized their military capability. Over time we have to uproot this weed.[21]

Netanyahu praised the method of targeted killings of terrorist operatives by Israel, calling it an effective means of eliminating terrorism.

Indeed, despite differences in the approaches and policies adopted by the various Israeli governments in their struggle against terrorism, it appears that all of the administrations, without exception, considered targeted killings to be one of the most effective means of combating terrorism. They did not hesitate to use this measure in accordance with the changing circumstances.

TARGETED KILLINGS

As Netanyahu pointed out in his remarks, there is no doubt that offensive action and a proactive approach have been at the foundation of Israel's policy in countering Palestinian terrorism for many years. The Israeli doctrine was based on the principle of preventing attacks by means of both preemptive attacks on terrorist targets, based on precise intelligence regarding the terrorist organizations' intentions and plans to carry out attacks, and deterring the perpetrators, their dispatchers, and their sponsors. In this context, targeted killings—strikes directed at the heads of the terrorist organizations, their military chiefs, and the initiators, planners, and perpetrators of attacks—were a central element in Israeli counterterrorism policy. This is also apparent from statements made by Israeli decision makers in the security field.

Former ISA chief Dichter described the tension that exists between the ideological and operational components of terrorism, and the advantages and limitations of using targeted killings to stamp out the phenomenon of terrorism.

In the phenomenon of terrorism, sometimes there is a particular leading figure, who is actually the center of gravity, and sometimes striking a blow at this figure can shake the structure so that the whole thing crashes.[22]

In examining the issue of targeted killings, three main questions were asked: How effective is this method of action? Is the method legal, legitimate, and moral? And what guiding principles should it be based on? These questions can also be divided into the following subquestions: On the subject of effectiveness, do targeted killings succeed in achieving their underlying goals, and what exactly are these goals? Regarding to the question of morality, can such a method of action be justified if it is likely to be seen as a form of punishment without trial—a death penalty without the accused being given the opportunity to defend himself in a fair and orderly legal process? As for the guiding principles of the targeted killings, we must ask what conditions and circumstances justify their use. Who are the targets whose killing should be allowed, and who should not be a target?

Shlomo Gazit took a critical approach to the method of targeted killings, from both a moral perspective and a practical-operational perspective:

> We ignore our input to terrorism. A series of actions that we have taken and may be taking are unacceptable and should be prohibited, from a long-term perspective. I include in this the whole issue of eliminating leaders. And I see it as twofold: First, because in the battle of the killing of leaders, we have the lower hand; their reward will be so severe and painful that we cannot bear it, be it in Israel or abroad. Not that they will succeed in carrying out an operation to liquidate [an Israeli leader] tomorrow afternoon, but they will respond with a bus bombing, or a car bomb, or an attack on a building in Buenos Aires. Second, we do not understand that we will have to make peace with these people tomorrow. So if someone tells me I can eliminate the leader of a small terrorist gang, it's not at all easy, but I'll take the risk. Shaqaqi, Abu Nidal, or someone like that, it's worth doing. . . . When you kill Abu Jihad, it's meaningless, because an organization like Fatah or the PLO is essentially a large popular political movement that is not based on one person. And such an action will only have negative effects in terms of what you produce.[23]

Gazit's criticism is therefore directed at the use of targeted killings of terrorist leaders, not necessarily against operatives and "ticking bombs."

Shavit, on the other hand, presented a contradictory position that highlights the effectiveness of the method of targeted killings in counterterrorism strategy in general and the striking of the leaders of terrorist organizations in particular.

In my opinion, this is a very effective [measure], but its effectiveness is a direct derivative of the selectivity of its use. If you use it against every crook, you will lose its effectiveness and pay a price in public opinion. If you are more selective and target only those people who are causing you the most trouble, it is more effective and more likely to be accepted in the eyes of the public. . . . The killing of terrorist leaders is never without publicity. Even if there are no headlines in the newspapers and on television, whoever needs to know will know. You can't hide it. Take, for example, Wadie Haddad. The headlines came long after he died. But the effectiveness of his disappearance was felt among his peers. In the elimination of individuals, the effect is immediate—you are neutralizing a person who has enormous potential for damage. It also has the added advantage that the entire circle of people surrounding the target, which had operated by virtue of his leadership, becomes completely paralyzed, or at least for a certain period until strength is rebuilt. There is also a deterrent effect in circles far beyond that particular organization, as well as a contribution to the morale of your own forces. Israel's policy of not taking responsibility has proven itself. It gained an advantage even when the killing was actually carried out by someone else.[24]

Perry also emphasized the need to use this method selectively: "I think that targeted killings are a tool that the state of Israel sometimes employed too vastly. When it was used in the right quantity, along with the propaganda effect, then it was an effective tool. If you do it routinely, if you have a list of names and you just cross them off one by one, it is not effective." Perry also believes that Israel's policy of not taking responsibility for such actions is correct and effective. "I think the policy of ambiguity is correct. All in all, the world understands and the world knows and the secret is revealed faster than people think, and I think that's a good thing."[25]

Thus, Shavit and Perry's only hesitation regarding the use of targeted killings has to do with selectivity in the use of this method. And what is the criterion for this selectivity? Netanyahu stated, "I have no objection [to targeted killings]. Terrorist leaders should not be immune. I was cautious about injuring people who had reached the political echelon but not about operational leaders. With regard to operational leaders, it is obvious."[26] Thus, according to Netanyahu, the restriction on the use of targeted killings should be avoidance of targeting political leaders who are not operational.

Peres presented a different approach: "In principle, I am against this measure. I am only for it only if the target is a ticking bomb. Take the case of Abu Jihad,[27] for example—I was told that he was one of their most moderate. We eliminated him. Where did that get us?"[28] Peres therefore advocated restricting the use of this measure to cases of ticking bombs';that is, to targeted killings intended to prevent concrete attacks when intelligence information in Israel's possession shows that preparations for the attack are in full swing or in the final stages, and that if Israel does not carry out the killing immediately, the planned attack will be initiated.

Prime Minister Ehud Olmert presented a clear position on the subject of targeted killings:

> I ordered targeted killings so I will not take a position that is the opposite of what I did. . . . Who are we talking about when it comes to targeted killings? . . . They are divided into two groups: one group consists of people who we see are about to fire or launch rockets, when there is a reasonably high probability of the [concrete] danger that these rockets will hit and kill someone. In these cases, you say "if someone comes to kill you, rise up and kill him first." That is to say, it is an action of self-defense in the classic sense of the word. . . . [The second group refers] to the enemy that you cannot catch and bring to trial. . . . In this context, [President Bush] would use a definition that I agree with. . . . He would ask representatives of the American agencies: This particular person that we want to target—if we do not eliminate him and he continue to live, is there a real danger that people will die as a result? If there is no real danger, then there is no justification for the death penalty, but if there is a real danger that innocent people will be killed, then it is actually an act of self-defense. . . . Maybe he is not the commander of the operation, he only prepares the forces, he prepares their weapons, he teaches them how to carry out the attack action, he dispatches them. He sits at headquarters. But he is the one who enables them to carry out the attack, and if he survives, the attack will take place.[29]

In contrast to the selective approach to the use of targeted killings, former Israeli counterterrorism coordinator Nitzan Nuriel offered a different approach based on questions that illustrate the dilemmas involved in choosing a legitimate target for targeted killings. In Nuriel's assessment, from an operational stance, targeted killings are almost always the right thing to do.

> If there is someone who is expert in producing bombs, and now you have killed him and that expertise is postponed by half a year, then it's the right thing to do. If there is someone who is an expert in transferring money, and now you have killed him and the transferring of money becomes more cumbersome, then it's the right thing to do. If there is someone who is the world champion in making operational plans [for terror attacks] and now you've eliminated him and so the planning of the next attack is careless, that's always good. In terms of prevention, [targeted killings] are very effective. They make an operational contribution.[30]

Nuriel continued,

> If you've killed not the biggest expert on money laundering but the two smallest ones, then you've done something, but I'm not sure that it's completely positive. Because you've sown hatred. . . . What is the problem with these actions? That they occur very rarely so they do not have a cumulative deterrent effect.[31]

Gillon explained the effectiveness of targeted killings as follows:

> You have to remember that a terrorist organization is not like a [military organization]. When you hit the chief of staff, there is a line of generals who will replace him. You cause damage. To say that there is no one to fill the ranks [in a terrorist organization] is nonsense. Of course there is. The ranks will always be replaced. But it's a process that takes time.[32]

Dichter emphasized that the use of targeted killings is not without problems. This method of action actually impairs the ability to gather intelligence on the terrorist organization.

> Targeted killing is the second choice and not the first. The first choice would be to make an arrest, but you can't always make arrests; you are not in Gaza, you are not in Judea and Samaria. You can't make arrests. The targeted killing is a result of having a lack of choice. What is the whole idea of

counterterrorism? Instead of having the terrorists invest ninety-five percent of their time producing terror and five percent of their time trying to survive, let's make them invest ninety-five percent of their time on survival and five percent of their time on producing terror.[33]

In examining the legitimacy of targeted killings, Dagan presented a broad approach, but he emphasized that the test of applicability should be primarily utilitarian.

I'm in favor of [targeted killings], but with a proviso. The bottom line is yes, but it must always be weighed against the benefit. . . . There are three purposes: thwarting attacks, deterrence, and punishment. These certainly seem to me to be legitimate. Then, within these definitions we must examine the cost versus the benefit. Would I target a religious personality who is not involved in terrorism but is only an authority figure? The answer is no, because it is counterproductive.[34]

In contrast to Dagan, Lipkin-Shahak challenged the deterrent benefit of targeted killings.

I do not think that this [measure] holds great deterrent value. There is a kind of "eye for an eye," or some kind of justice in the most abstract sense of the word, or revenge. . . . Knowing that if you commit such an act [of terrorism], you've crossed a line that means that in another year, or three, or five, or ten years, you will pay the price. You took part in this? You will pay the price.[35]

Ashkenazi believes that development of the model of targeted killings as a means of fighting terrorism is one of Israel's contributions to the global counterterrorism methodology. He claimed that Israel solved the moral dilemma by laying out the principle according to which whenever it is possible to catch the terrorist, Israel will choose to arrest him rather than kill him.

If you wake me up in the middle of the night and ask me what the first rule of targeted killings is, I would say that the first rule is to first see if he can be arrested. . . . Our moral dilemmas did not stem from this question, but rather from the issue of collateral damage. . . . The question is, where do you draw the line? Let's say that Shehade[36] is driving with his wife and this is probably your only chance [to kill him]. Do you decide to strike him and his wife? Or let's say that you know he lives in a certain place and now you realize that the only way to eliminate him is from the air, but it's possible that the house next to his will collapse and a wall will cave in and there are families there—do you do it or not? That's the kind of discussion we would wrestle with all the time. And I can tell you that there were many occasions when we stopped the operation because of the "one plus" ["one" being the terrorist and "plus" being uninvolved persons near him].[37]

Mofaz gives Israel high marks in its moral and legal considerations and the procedures it has taken in its use of targeted killings.

A question we asked ourselves was the question of price. I can say that there were incidents in which we decided against targeted killings because, from a cost-benefit analysis, we estimated that the conditions and the cost that would result from this action would be [too high]. The potential damage that could arise from the killing was greater than its benefit, so we usually refrained from carrying out targeted killings. . . . Our considerations were pragmatic, professional, not risk-free.[38]

Mofaz believes that targeted killing is important when dealing with suicide bombers who are ticking bombs. "It is very hard to arrest people like this." In reference to the suicide attackers' dispatchers, he said, "from the moment they realized that we could get to them wherever they were, they wanted to save their own lives more than they wanted to send others to carry out an attack."[39]

As for targeting the heads of terrorist organizations, Mofaz believes that this measure is also justified. "I maintained that a leader who engages in terrorism is a terrorist. . . . I thought that if the leadership is perceived to be a political entity but engages in terrorism, then it ceases to be political."[40]

These issues and dilemmas presented by the decision makers regarding the legitimacy, morality, and effectiveness of targeted killings have been discussed in several petitions submitted to the Israeli High Court of Justice. In its decisions in these petitions, the High Court determined the guidelines that permit the use of targeted killings in the framework of Israel's struggle against terrorism. According to the court's rulings, the use of targeted killings is permitted only as a preventive act of a concrete threat, not as an act of punishment or general deterrence. It can be used against only an active terrorist and not against those who are no longer involved in terror. In addition, the targeted killing must be proportionate and employed only in the event that there is no possibility of arresting the terrorist and bringing him to justice.[41]

But even when targeted killings are justified, legal, and legitimate, the question of whether or not they will prove beneficial must be asked. What will be the result of the targeted killing? Will these actions trigger a response in the immediate, short, medium, or long term? What will be the response of the terrorist organization, and what price will Israel pay for this action? In other words, any offensive activity against a terrorist organization—especially a targeted killingvraises the issue of the boomerang effect.

THE BOOMERANG EFFECT

One of the strongest arguments against targeted killings concerns revenge attacks that might be carried out following a targeted killing operation: the so-called boomerang effect. The basic assumption is that the more the state succeeds in harming the terrorist organization, the more motivated will the leaders and activists of the organization be to take revenge by carrying out retaliatory attacks increases. Among the cases in which it has been claimed that boomerang attacks were triggered in the wake of targeted killings by Israel was the killing of Hezbollah Secretary-General Abbas Musawi in 1992. That was followed a few weeks later by a revenge attack on the Israeli embassy in Buenos Aires and the killing of the "Engineer," Yahya Ayyash, in 1995, which was followed by four revenge attacks in Israel.

Israeli decision makers are divided among themselves with regard to the existence of the boomerang effect. Dagan rejected it:

> In my opinion, there is no boomerang phenomenon. What there is, is an understanding of terrorism as psychological warfare on the part of the other side [the terrorist organization], which leads them to create the boomerang argument. When dealing with terrorist activity, the question is one of capability.[42]

According to Dagan, the motivation to launch an attack is secondary, because a terrorist organization by its nature is interested in carrying out terror attacks. For Dagan, the declarations of vengeance and boomerangs are merely a form of psychological warfare against the state.

> The shrewdness [of the terrorist organization] was to create the boomerang argument, which created a balance of deterrence against us. Suppose I did not carry out the [counter-terrorist] operation—would the terrorist attacks still be carried out? To the best of my judgment—yes. Maybe a little differently, perhaps at a different time, on a different schedule, but would it have taken place? The answer is yes. Therefore, I am saying that there is no boomerang phenomenon. . . . In this respect, in my opinion the state of Israel should have defined the objectives of its war without taking the boomerang phenomenon into account at all.[43]

Peres referred to the boomerang phenomenon as nothing more than a "journalistic dilemma." "There's the story of the Engineer [Yihye Ayyash] with the phone.[44] In my eyes it's nonsense, because we knew that the Engineer was going to carry out more attacks [anyway]. Say we hadn't targeted him, and he would have executed the attacks—what would people say then? These are all journalistic narratives"[45] Dichter was even more extreme in his rejection of the boomerang effect principle. "This is one of the most serious mistakes I am aware of regarding the fight against terror—the development of theories that have no basis in reality, despite the fact that they sound logical. . . . It is nonsense in both a professional sense and in a normative sense, because terrorism builds itself up according to its capabilities."[46]

Netanyahu agreed with this approach and maintained that the boomerang effect should be ignored in the overall considerations of Israel's counterterrorism activities. "Those attacks will be carried out anyway, and therefore it is preferable to perform the [counterterrorist] operations. At the same time, I suggest considering making public the identity of the committer of the act [Israel's taking responsibility]. It causes humiliation among many of the terrorists, and in any case they know who did what."[47]

In contrast, Lipkin-Shahak believed that the boomerang phenomenon actually occurs. "There are such phenomena, and they have to be taken into account [before carrying out counterterrorist actions]. Definitely. In the end the considerations are always comprehensive, since you never know how to assess the damage accurately."[48] Gillon explained:

There is a cycle here that never ends. But the question you have to ask yourself is: If I absorb the blows [terrorist attacks] and do nothing beyond routine thwarting and preventive actions, does this reduce terrorism? That's the question. The answer is unequivocally no. In other words, you can't stop terror with your head down. It won't help. You have no choice. Terrorism has a goal, it has a mission, and it will continue to try to achieve it.[49]

Yigal Pressler (former counterterrorism advisor to the prime minister) also believes that concerns over the boomerang effect should be neutralized in the planning of Israel's counterterrorism activities and added that counterterrorism activities must be examined over time. "If there is a boomerang attack, we have to continue to escalate our strikes against the terrorist organizations so that we will have the last word. The war on terror must not be judged in the short term but over time. In the short term, they will always win. They target civilians, we do not. And so it should continue."[50] A similar position was expressed by Shavit:

You have to be prepared for it [the boomerang effect] and you have to be willing to escalate on your part as well, or if not escalate, then respond in a smarter and more painful way than the enemy. You also need to be prepared to be hit. If you are not willing to take a hit, then don't go to war . . . but you have to know that even if you are willing to give up, it is not a guarantee that the terror will stop. The dynamics can create the opposite process—the more you succumb to the terror, the stronger it becomes.[51]

Former defense minister Moshe Arens supports this approach:

There is a theory that says that in any case, they will do everything they were planning on doing, and we have to do everything we can do. I think this is a bit of an oversimplification. I don't know if they would have blown up our embassy [in Buenos Aires] if we hadn't killed Musawi. I think that this also reflects the fact that something like Musawi's killing [does indeed] provoke them and put them in a position in which they feel obligated to take such action, also in terms of the internal dynamics that exist there. . . . Of course, this is not to say that we should not fight them or that we should decrease our activity.

Arens argues that sporadic targeted killing operations are not effective and that counterterrorism operations should be systematic.

> I think that if we ask ourselves whether Musawi's killing weakened or diminished or changed [Hezbollah's] ability to carry out terrorist attacks, I think that the answer is no, it didn't. On the other hand, I would say that in the final calculation . . . it's almost one-nothing in their favor, as if they taught us a lesson: "friends, we are better than you at this game."[52]

Mofaz concludes:

> There is such a thing as a boomerang effect, mainly abroad [retaliatory attacks against Israeli and Jewish targets outside Israel]. Make a list of all these events, and you will see that the intensity of the effect is usually felt abroad. . . . In Israel there have been cases where the liquidation of someone brought on a wave [of attacks]. But the question here is, would this wave not have taken place anyway? It's difficult to answer. Very difficult. . . . I would not take this into consideration as something that should prevent us from fighting terrorism.[53]

Most of the decision makers who support the use of targeted killings in Israel's counterterrorism policy, even when Israel is forced to pay a price due to the boomerang effect, do so on the grounds that this measure is successful in deterring terrorists. Indeed, one of the main parallels in the policies of the various Israeli governments was the emphasis placed over the years on the need for deterrence—whether the need was to deter the countries that sponsor terrorism, the Palestinian terrorist organizations, the terrorist operatives themselves, or the populations that support them. The primacy of the component of deterrence in Israeli counterterrorism policy is likely the result of the assumption by most decision makers that terrorism cannot be defeated and therefore that the strategic prevention of terrorist attacks (as opposed to the concrete prevention of one attack or another) can be achieved only by deterrence. We can see this approach reflected in Israel's counterterrorism activities at various times since its establishment.

A prominent example are the military operations of the past decade in Gaza, against the background of the rocket threat to Israel since the disengagement in 2005. Whenever the "trickle" of rocket fire from Gaza turned into a barrage, Israel was forced once again to launch a large-scale military operation that would deter Hamas and the other organizations in Gaza from continuing to fire at Israel. Each time, the operation, which usually included massive bombing of terrorist targets from the air, sometimes accompanied by ground operations, would end with a ceasefire. The ceasefires and the Palestinian terrorist organizations' cessation of rocket fire reflected the deterrent capability that Israel had achieved in the operation. However, time after time, this deterrence was eroded, with the Palestinians resuming the fire from Gaza after a certain period.

The extent to which deterrence makes up a central component of Israel's counterterrorism policy can be learned from the interviews with Israeli decision makers.

DETERRING TERRORISTS

Questions about the boomerang effect and the effectiveness of targeted killings are only one derivative of a much larger and more complex issue: deterrence in counterterrorism. The challenges stemming from the attempt to deter states from taking military action and launching conventional and unconventional wars have been the basis of academic research for many years. However, many dilemmas remain unresolved. The complexity of the issue of deterrence between states stems from, among other things, an analysis of questions regarding the extent of the adversary's rationality and the ability to identify his weak points and apply the appropriate pressure to deter him from carrying out certain actions or to persuade him to change his course of action to a different one.

In the abstract, deterrence is the result of a red line drawn by the deterring side in front of the side to be deterred, accompanied by the threat that should this line be crossed, the deterred side will have to pay very heavy prices that far outweigh any benefit that it might gain from crossing the line. Analysis of the adversary's cost-benefit considerations and finding the right threatening message is therefore a precondition for deterrent capability. The deterring side must understand the adversary's subjective rationale—its cost and benefit scale (which does not necessarily correspond to its own scale). If this is not enough, in deterrence, the image created in the eyes of the deterred side is more important than reality. In other words, the deterred side must assess that the threatening side is capable and determined to make it pay the heavy prices it threatens in the event that the red line is crossed.

Deterrence will not bear fruit if the adversary assesses that the deterring side is either incapable or not sufficiently determined to carry out the threat (even if, in reality, it does possess the capability and intends to use it). Image is therefore more important than reality in the creation of deterrence. This is true when analyzing the issue of deterrence between states, but when dealing with the relations between a state actor and a nonstate actor—such as a terrorist organization—the situation is much more complex. The deterring side's ability to understand the enemy's rationale and cost-benefit considerations depends on its ability to analyze the terrorist organization's decision-making processes, identify its weaknesses, and formulate messages and actions that would resonate with the cost-benefit calculus of the organization and would threaten the organization and its leaders, and is imperative for achieving the desired deterrent effect.

In this context, it is interesting to examine how Israeli decision makers understood the rationale of terrorist organizations that have operated against Israel over the years, as well as Israel's ability to deter these terrorists. In response to the question regarding the state's ability to deter terrorism, Dagan said,

> The bottom line is that the answer is negative, because at the end of the day, [terrorist] operations are being carried out. But this is not accurate. I argue that there is tactical deterrence, but not on the strategic level. . . . You can't talk about strategic deterrence, because you are not facing a state. . . . One of the biggest mistakes that people make is to treat the terrorist organization like a state, that weighs decisions based on a rational process, and therefore the entire system of rules and the organizational language of the war on terror contains army motifs: force concentration, destroying the lines of communication . . . and when you look at the terrorist organizations, they do not work like that. . . . It is not that they are irrational. . . . They are rational organizations, but their rationale works differently. Their modus operandi is different, their priorities are different, and as a result you have to adjust your war to the arena in which you are fighting.[54]

Dagan added,

> If I now convince the organization that it will not succeed in blowing up buses, then it will take buses off its list of targets. If I convince it that it won't succeed in carrying out attacks on shopping malls, it will remove shopping malls from this list as well. This allows me mobility, freedom, and the concentration of my forces in the places that I choose. Must deterrence be achieved against the terrorist organization? The answer is yes. Is it possible to achieve strategic deterrence? The answer is no.[55]

Netanyahu believes that "a terrorist organization can be deterred. Most of the organizations do not want to commit suicide. The organizations are rational in their essence and take cost and benefit considerations into account."[56] Gazit also referred to terrorist organizations as rational actors, but he pointed out the gap between the rationale of the organizations' leaders and that of the operatives on the ground. "Let me start with the leadership," he said.

> I have yet to encounter an Arab leader who is irrational. I may not like his rationale, but it is not difficult for me to analyze. . . . All in all, the terrorist organizations—even those who do the dirtiest work—act rationally, and to a great extent the difference between the organizations is not in the leader's rationality, but rather in the size of the organization and its degree of responsibility for and dependence on the population. The smaller the organization, the more it engages in dirty things, in part because it is unbound by public opinion [and the effects of] Israeli countermeasures.[57]

Shaul Mofaz proposed an additional distinction between different types of organizations, whereby it is possible, in his opinion, to achieve a high level of deterrence vis-à-vis institutionalized organizations, which is not necessarily the case when it comes to terrorist networks and noninstitutionalized organizations.

> The less organized, institutionalized, and led from above the organization is, the more difficult it is to deter it. . . . The more organized and semi-military the [organization] is, the stronger its leadership and its national aspirations, the easier it is to deter it. I think we succeeded in deterring Palestinian terrorism.[58]

Lipkin-Shahak emphasized the need to understand the unique rationale of the terrorist organizations: "They have their rationale, which is not necessarily our rationale."[59] Peres also believed that the terrorist organizations have a unique rationale that differs from that of the state of Israel.

> They are rational according to their rationale. There is no objective rationale. There is a rationale that is also emotional.[60] We controlled Gaza, and no one understands why we sat there for thirty-three years like idiots. . . . Who is the rational one and who is the irrational one? Maybe we were the irrational ones?[61]

General Avraham Tamir, former commander of the IDF's planning division, explained that in relation to achievements, it is possible to examine rationale in retrospect. "If you look at the PLO as a leading terrorist organization, it was very rational relative to its achievements. From their point of view, through terrorism and the protection of Arab states, they succeeded in becoming a state-in-the-making."[62] Avraham Ahituv, former head of the ISA, also believed that the terrorist organizations' policy of attacks was generally dictated by rational cost-benefit considerations, and he warned against underestimating the cognitive skills of the organizations' leaders. "[These] are all thinking people. Their level in many cases exceeds ours. I'm not saying that this is the level of the fighters, but of their leaders."[63]

In contrast, Meir Amit (former head of Israeli Military Intelligence and of the Mossad) highlighted the impulsivity of terrorist activity, as opposed to activity that is the result of rational considerations: "In my opinion, there is also a great deal of impulsiveness in terrorism. It also helps them to defend themselves when there is compartmentalization and local initiatives, making it harder for the state to cope. . . . There is more impulsiveness than logical thinking."[64] Former ISA head Perry maintained that the rationale of the terrorist organizations operating against Israel has developed over the years.

> I think that in recent years, there has been more rationalization. . . . There were periods when it was less rational and more emotional, as a result of fewer serious discussions concerning whether to do it, how to do it, and who should do it. As the years passed, it has become more rational. . . . This is due to the maturity of the terrorist organization, changes in circumstances, the

general atmosphere, the place they are currently dwelling . . . internal struggles within the organizations, the debate within the Islamic organizations between the "domestic" (the leadership in the territories) and the "external" (the leadership of the organizations based in Arab countries) . . . and more.[65]

Most of the Israeli decision makers who were interviewed believe, then, that the terrorist adversary (at least at the level of the organizations' heads) is a rational actor who takes cost-benefit considerations into account. If this is the case, can terrorist organizations be deterred? And has Israel succeeded in this mission? On this point, Nuriel stated, "I have no doubt that all terrorism can be deterred . . . it is possible to deter terrorism . . . I think that people are willing to suffer to a certain extent (in order to achieve certain goals). If you know the extent to which they are willing to suffer and add a little more, they won't go there, at least not en masse." Nuriel gives Israel a grade of "C plus" in terms of its success in deterring the terrorist organizations. "People are replaced, and human memory doesn't always work in our favor. I think that the two operations in Gaza show that deterrence is limited. In 2008, we launched an operation, and two years later we needed another operation. It's an expired product in this sense."[66]

Nuriel believes that punishment by deportation is one of the most effective tools in the Israel's counterterrorism arsenal. "I think expulsion as a deterrent punishment is the game changer," he said.[67] Dichter emphasized the need for sustained and consistent activity in order to preserve the deterrent effect. "In the end, deterrence is to what extent those who instigate terrorism understand that they will pay a price." He explained,

The moment that Sheikh Yassin [Hamas's leader] was liquidated, they understood that we have no limits. Everyone is equal before the bullet. This is a very constitutive sentence when speaking about deterrence. . . . [You have to remember] that deterrence comes with time. . . . In deterring terrorism, you must be consistent because deterrence must be maintained. It's not a one-time deal.[68]

Tamir rejected the notion that the state has the ability to deter terrorist organizations. "No. A terrorist organization will not be deterred. A nationalist terrorist organization, like the PLO, will not be deterred so long as it has not achieved its national goals."[69] Amit also believed that a state could not deter a terrorist organization, and Gillon is skeptical about such deterrent capability.

> Deter them? Very little. . . . The weapon of the weak is the Achilles' heel of the strong. Take the great IDF, for example. The IDF doesn't know how to respond to two shepherds with a Katyusha. Or a missile. [The IDF] knows how to respond to three divisions moving from right to left, but for shepherds in the Wadi, that doesn't help.[70]

Yaakov Perry pointed out the state's limits on deterrence. In answer to the question of whether a state can deter terrorist organizations, he responded,

> That's a tough question. I think that in general, no. However, if a long list of consistent measures is adopted by the state, by the political echelon, it is possible to raise the level of deterrence. I think that if a terrorist organization has the goal of attacking, destroying, killing, damaging, then the state won't stop it, even if it's a totalitarian state like Russia. The more rigid and the more consistent the state, the more it both makes declarations and follows them through, the higher the level of deterrence can be. But in my opinion, it can't be total.[71]

In contrast, Olmert claimed,

> There is no doubt that it is possible to deter terrorism, but it is impossible to make the political or ideological movements that are generating the terrorist acts or the terrorists [themselves] disappear. You can't. You can deter Hamas to a great extent and cause damage and so on, but you can't prevent the existence of this ideological movement. . . . [Therefore], deterrence is possible, but in my opinion, absolute deterrence is impossible. We are unable to achieve it here, and the Americans are unable to do it in Pakistan, Afghanistan, Iran, Iraq, and all kinds of other places. . . . Terror cannot be stopped completely, but it can definitely be deterred for periods of time that can be significant.[72]

Ashkenazi believes that the state has deterrent capability in the war on terror.

I have no doubt that terrorism can be deterred. But what is the problem with deterrence? It's that deterrence is limited in time. The second problem is that you don't know when it's going to stop. I grew up in the north [of Israel] and I think it's unprecedented that children in the Galilee today reach the second or third grade without having to have spent one night in a shelter. You don't need to be an expert to understand that this is a dramatic achievement.[73]

Lipkin-Shahak also believed that terrorist organizations could be deterred.

Yes, of course, the question is what is the extent of the terrorists' determination and what is the extent of the state's deterrence? But yes, it is certainly possible. You can deter them [from carrying out] a certain type of action.[74]

Shavit distinguished between the theoretical ability of a state to deter terrorist organizations and the practical inability to achieve this goal due to external constraints that prevent the state from taking the necessary steps to achieve deterrence. In answer to the question of whether a state can deter a terrorist organization, Shavit responded,

Yes, if the nation is prepared to go all the way. But in today's normative world . . . The cost the nation might have to pay—and not necessarily in military or economic terms, but rather in terms of public opinion and international relations—is such that it will think twice before making any decision to ignore criticism and go all the way.[75]

In order to achieve a deterrent effect, Israel needed to demonstrate its strength, intelligence, and operational superiority over the terrorist organizations. However, one of the main assertions of this book is that in its struggle against terrorism, Israel has behaved throughout most of its history like a shackled Goliath —a regional military power that cannot allow itself to utilize the vast majority of its weapons arsenal and methods of action at its disposal to combat terrorism. The Counterterrorism Dilemmas Conceptual Model that has been used to analyze and compare Israel's counterterrorism policies in various periods illustrates this by showing the degree of restraint Israeli governments have had to exercise, as well as by referring to the democratic dilemma in counterterrorism. The Israeli leaders interviewed in this book also offered their opinions on these dilemmas and on the limitations faced by Israel in its fight against terrorism.

THE DEMOCRATIC DILEMMA IN COUNTERTERRORISM

The ability to deter terrorism is not just the result of understanding the enemy's rationality, its consideration, and the ability to construct effective and relevant threatening messages. It is also the result of the liberal state's inhibitions on the use of force against the terrorist organization. As a rule, the state—every state—possesses more power than the military strength of a terrorist organization, be it the strongest terrorist organization in the world. However, when the state in question is a liberal democracy, it often finds itself in the role of the shackled Goliath, forced to fight terrorism with its hands tied behind its back. These shackles and chains holding it back are the liberal values and norms to which a liberal state is committed, to international humanitarian laws, as well as to its own code of internal law. The liberal democratic state restricts itself through of its own value-system, not only because of its commitment to international humanitarian law. Any deviation from the state's values in its struggle against terrorism will lead to harsh criticism in the international arena.

By its nature, the terrorist organization is not committed to these values and in fact sees them as its enemy's soft underbelly and Achilles' heel. These values are exploited by the terrorist organization to carry out attacks, on the one hand, and for the purpose of hiding among the civilian population behind human shields, thus preventing retaliation, on the other. Because of the state's reservations stemming from concerns over compromising its values, the terrorist organization gains a double advantage. First, the liberal state will be deterred from employing harsh and perhaps even draconian methods that might be effective against the organization, and second, if it does employ these methods, it will lose its moral legitimacy and perhaps even its status as a liberal democratic state. This "democratic dilemma" reflects the need to find the delicate balance between securing the citizens of the liberal democratic state who are facing terrorism and preserving the vast majority of the liberal democratic values in the country. Finding solutions to the democratic dilemma is therefore a central component of the art of combating terrorism.

Israel, as a liberal democratic state that has been forced to contend with terror from its inception, has found itself challenged by the democratic dilemma throughout its existence. It has dealt with waves of terrorism of different types and intensity (such as hijackings, suicide bombings, lone wolf attacks, and attacks against Israeli and Jewish targets abroad). Israeli decision makers who were responsible for security matters were thus forced to cope with the tension created by the democratic dilemma in counterterrorism and to find the best possible solutions to the challenges they faced.

Sharon explained the state's power limitations and the operative conclusions derived from them:

> In my opinion, people do not understand the dangers of terrorism. They belittle it. Israel is a [regional] power, but this does not prevent terrorism from happening. Because the state cannot use its power. It can't use everything that it has. And the Arabs, in my opinion, have learned the limitations of the use of force very well. [This] is a tough front.[76]

Arens regards the democratic dilemma in counterterrorism as follows.

> As with any other subject, the democratic system is restrictive. For every issue that you look at and ask whether you can advance it [more] effectively without the limitations of a democratic government, the answer is yes. But when you look at the whole picture, of course we would not consider giving up the great advantages of the democratic system. Therefore, we are willing to accept the limitations produced by the democratic system.[77]

Shimon Peres took a clear moral stance on the democratic dilemma: "At the end of the day, I tried as hard as I could not to deviate from moral considerations. . . . I thought that every war was conducted twice: once on the battlefield and once in the history books. I would not want to lose a battle in the history books." Peres added that the decision maker must not rely on the secrecy of the actions being taken: "You think there is secrecy, but the nature of secrecy is that it is revealed at the moment that is least suitable for you, so you should try to make decisions that won't leave a black mark on the state in the future."[78]

Shavit presented a different order of priorities in balancing the tension between the effectiveness of counterterrorism and liberal democratic values:

> Given a choice between being less democratic and surviving, and dying democratically, I prefer the first [option]. And in the intellectual discussion of the democratic dilemma, we ultimately reach this point, and we must face up to it. Mrs. Thatcher said that in order to protect democracy, you sometimes have no choice but to use undemocratic means.[79]

In an attempt to solve the democratic dilemma in counterterrorism, Gillon relied on the rulings of the High Court of Justice.

> On this issue I go by the words of Barak [president of the Supreme Court], who said, "Democracy is not a recipe for suicide." . . . You can say that democracy is the most important value in your eyes, and there is a consensus about that . . . [but you need to know] that it is possible that [the fight against terrorism] will harm the margins of democracy. . . . In another statement [of Barak's], he talked about types of judges, saying, "I hope that there won't be a naive judge who sees democracy as the be-all and end-all." On the other hand, he said, "I hope that there won't be a naive judge who sees security as the be-all and end-all, but that there will be a reasonable judge who finds a balance between the two things." We have no choice. That is what we need to do.[80]

His predecessor in the post, former ISA chief Yaakov Perry, regards the dilemma as follows.

> [This] is a very difficult question. Difficult and complicated. Personally, I have been deliberating with this question for many years. Fighting terrorism using the tools of a democratic state is almost impossible. [The dilemma is reflected] in almost every activity, from the recruitment and operation of the agent through his arrest, his interrogation, to his imprisonment. . . . It is inconceivable, for example, that eliminating individuals, or applying pressure, or deportation are things that would be associated with democracy. I think that on the whole, Israel should get positive marks in this regard. . . . It would certainly not be acceptable to many of the bleeding-heart liberals.[81]

Another former head of the ISA, Avraham Ahituv, tackled the question in a different way:

> The problem becomes smaller, but doesn't disappear, when you have to solve a tactical problem, whether it's "breaking" someone you're interrogating, or if you have to storm a house in the hills of Hebron, and you know that there are women and children living there along with an arsenal of weapons. When you know that someone is about to plant an explosive and blow it up in Dizengoff Center [a mall in Tel Aviv]. What do I mean by the problem becomes smaller? It takes on different proportions, but it does not disappear. . . . I can testify that in my time, we definitely put limitations on ourselves.[82]

Avraham Ahituv believed that, at least during his tenure as head of the ISA, the right balance was found between effective counterterrorism and the preservation of liberal democratic values, a dilemma that lay on his shoulders as the ISA chief.

> I tried to explain this to the Kahan Committee [that] was sitting in the Supreme Court, discussing the wiretapping law. Judge Kahan's question was: "Avraham, let's say I believe you, and I personally do believe you, but how can I believe that someone else won't misuse it [wiretapping]?" My answer was, "you do not believe him. You cannot believe him. You have to trust him. You chose this type or that type of person, and that's the point."[83]

Ahituv said, in response to the question of whether the security forces should sometimes take steps that are on the verge of being unlawful or even in violation of the law, and whether they should inform decision makers before or after the operation,

> It depends on who the prime minister is and on who the head of the ISA is. I never asked in advance in such cases. Never. Not once. . . . In the end, as head of the service, I always tried to think about what the prime minister's reaction would be and act accordingly. In most cases I succeeded. Not in all of them. But in most cases, I tried to adapt my responses according to the opinion of the prime minister.[84]

Netanyahu is also aware of the democratic dilemma in dealing with terrorism. "Usually you move in between these two poles [effectiveness and liberal values], and the two poles must be demarcated in accordance with events and the level of terror."[85]

Dagan did not accept the concept of the democratic dilemma in counterterrorism and the contradiction between the effectiveness of the struggle against terrorism and liberal democratic values. He argued that although there is a tension between these two ends, this tension could be bridged by special legislation.

> I think that there is no contradiction between the two things. What states need to do [is] to legislate special laws on counterterrorism, within limited time frames. If such a law is passed with no time limit, it can also be applied for other things. . . . When you are in the midst of a wave of terror, or expecting such a wave, you can enact a law whose validity will be good for one year. . . . If you've come to the conclusion that the wave is over and that there is no need for these measures anymore, you say that this law is revoked. The problem with this is that the legislative [process] is usually long. But since the life of these laws is short, it is possible to have a dialogue within the democratic system, between the legislative and executive branches, on the nature of the law. This is how to strike a balance between democracy and the desire to fight an effective war on terrorism.[86]

Shamir did not believe that the democratic dilemma really limited his room for maneuvering as prime minister, but his words indicate that he was aware of this dilemma. In response to the question, "Did you sometimes feel that the democratic system restricted you from carrying out necessary or important actions in the war on terror?" he said,

> No, no, not at all. Democracy is not a factor here. Of course you have to make some adjustments. You need to find ways to fight these organizations despite the democratic limitations, and within the limits of democracy there are interrogation methods. We dealt with these things. We can't change our democratic way of life because of these things, because that is a kind of surrender. The enemy has then achieved something. You shouldn't give him the satisfaction of achieving even such a partial goal. What is necessary is to fight within the framework of freedom of expression.[87]

Dichter presented several other detailed dilemmas involved in decision-making in the fight against terrorism:

> People have no idea how many ethical problems are involved in counterterrorism . . . [for example], ethical issues involved in deciding where to carry out targeted killings within built-up areas—and we work a lot in built-up areas. Or [if the target] is driving along the main road of Gaza, and you launch a missile from a plane that takes a few seconds until it hits the car. Do you know how many things can happen in ten to twenty seconds? You see him get out of the car and you hit just as he [leaves]. Each of these missiles has an accuracy rate of eighty-five percent. A fifteen-percent chance of missing. The dilemma is great. [Especially] in a setting brimming with innocent people, how can you ensure that they don't get hit? In attempts to rescue hostages, innocents have been killed . . . even by the gunfire of our own forces. . . . You always find yourself in dilemmas. . . . [For example], you know that in order to blow someone up you need half a kilo of TNT, but you don't know what circumstances he will be in. You can put [the explosives] in the fax machine, but it's a house and you don't know if there will be children there. . . . So you say, "let's go for a cell phone." Do you know the difference between placing a device in a fax machine and putting one in a cell phone? It's two months of work, risk, complexity, a thousand and one other things.[88]

Dichter also provided a unique glance into the democratic dilemma in reference to interrogations of terror suspects from the point of view of the head of the ISA:

> At two a.m. I get a call telling me that there is a report of a terrorist in the Tel Aviv area. [He] has placed a bomb at a bus stop [operated via] a cellular phone that is supposed to be activated from Nablus when the buses start running at six a.m. . . . you have no idea which bus stop in Tel Aviv. [You can decide] that no one can go to any bus stop. You can say that no buses are allowed to go anywhere. You [put] the whole country into a panic. You have no idea when they will activate [the explosive], who will activate it, whether or not [they] have eye contact. You launch an intelligence-collecting campaign, and within two hours, at four a.m., a Palestinian is arrested on his way to work in Petah Tikva. They arrest him [knowing] with certainty that he is connected to the explosives, because the calls were made from his cell

phone from Nablus. You begin to interrogate him. He is defined as a ticking bomb, you check with the attorney-general, confirm with the Foreign
Affairs and Defense Committee [of the Knesset], a ministerial committee on
ISA affairs. Now we have to get a set of special measures approved. . . . And
what happens when you do not get [permission], and it turns out that after
that, after the attack, he speaks and incriminates [the perpetrator]? And it
turns out that you had the [ability to prevent the] attack in your hands. You
had it [but] people were killed. People always ask me "how do you feel when
your orders cause a lot of terrorists to be killed?" I reply, "No one was killed
for no reason, barring any mishaps." I'm less worried about that. If there is
something that will torment me until my last day, it is those cases in which I
did not give the order and did not enable what should have been done, and
apparently [because of this], the attack took place. I know that these Israelis
[died]. I sometimes know their names. It's hard.[89]

Former ISA chief Gillon also referred to interrogations of ticking bombs as
a case in which the democratic dilemma is most blatantly reflected.

What is a ticking bomb? . . . If the interrogator knows that in two hours a
bomb is definitely going to explode and all he needs to know is whether it
will be at thirty-nine Rothschild [Street] or thirty-eight Rothschild Street, no
matter what the law says, the interrogator will risk going to prison. But this
is [usually] not the situation. The situation is that you have intelligence and a
suspicion that Mustafa knows that Ahmed recruited a suicide bomber whose
identity he doesn't know, and who is now preparing to become a Shahid.
That is the best intelligence you get. This is what you know. And I call this a
ticking bomb, and in the end what we knew could end up [not being true],
or perhaps Mustafa is not Mustafa and it's Ahmed who heard about Mustafa.
There are a thousand and one things that can happen. . . . Therefore; my
opinion on this matter is clear and well known. I think that the special permits have been applied to 8 percent of Hamas and Islamic Jihad suspects, and
in 90 percent of these cases, it led to results. I claim that [arguing that this is]
undermining the foundations of democracy is nothing but demagoguery.[90]

Lipkin-Shahak also addressed the issue of interrogating a ticking bomb,
but unlike Gillon, he advocated for giving the interrogators more room to
maneuver and act in the first place.

I have no doubt that a ticking bomb justifies interrogations that use [moderate] physical force if that is the only way to prevent the explosion of the ticking bomb that will kill innocent civilians. The questions are, is it a ticking bomb? When will [it explode]? How do you know if it is ticking, and if it is a bomb? Maybe it has two more months of ticking ahead of it, and so you have a month to prevent the explosion? Therefore, the dilemma is very complex. In my view at least, it is impossible to leave it up to those who are operating in the field. You can't decide to support people's decisions retroactively; rather, you need to give them freedom of action in advance, and anyone who makes a mistake because of bad judgment will have to pay [the price]. But it's not that he committed a criminal offense . . . a disciplinary hearing, demotion, imprisonment, or dismissal, but he could not be prosecuted as a criminal who broke the law of the state of Israel. That is not how you send people to operational activity, and the state owes its fighters this protection; these ISA interrogators are in fact soldiers in the interrogation rooms, and their goal is to prevent attacks on Israeli citizens.[91]

Former Mossad chief Shavit is more extreme in his approach to the ticking bomb phenomenon.

The whole argument over *tiltulim* [shaking as an interrogation technique, which was used in the eighties and nineties by the ISA in cases of ticking bomb situations] is nonsense to me. When someone wants to kill me, I do not have time to deal with inane definitions of shaking. What is the terrorist's purpose in the attack? To kill me. And I have to be noble toward him? Either he survives or I do.[92]

This shaking technique, together with other techniques involving use of moderate force in interrogations of terrorists, was forbidden by the Israeli Supreme Court in 1999.

In summary, in light of the many dilemmas involved in Israel's confrontation with terrorism, detailed in this and previous chapters, the question arises regarding the degree to which Israel has succeeded in achieving the goals it has set for itself in dealing with terrorism. This question was presented to four Israeli prime ministers, who were asked to reflect on the achievements of Israeli counterterrorism through a retrospective lens.

ACHIEVEMENTS OF ISRAELI COUNTERTERRORISM

Referring to achievements in Israeli counterterrorism, Ariel Sharon said,

> There are things we succeeded in doing and things we did not succeed in doing. The fact that we succeeded in taking an entire terrorist organization from its headquarters and expelling it from Beirut [during the First Lebanon War in 1982], that was something unprecedented. . . . I think that we would have found ourselves in difficult times and facing very serious situations if that independent terrorist empire had continued to develop in Lebanon. . . . The Gaza Strip was [also] a success. You have to think about what would have happened had it not been done. That is also a question. It's a hypothetical question that needs to be answered. I would say [that there were] successes for [defined] periods.[93]

Ehud Olmert argued:

> In terms of our policy, a distinction between two elements should be made: From the military aspect of the fight against terror, we have developed capabilities that no country in the world has, and I say this with certainty. Not the United States, nor Russia, and certainly not any other country. We developed capabilities that ultimately broke the necks of the main terrorist effort that was present in 2000. This is completely clear. Also our amazing technological capabilities. And our ability to gather intelligence . . . All of these things created a cognizance of tremendous achievement, and also sowed the fear that in the end there is no escaping Israel, as it will reach every [terrorist]. On the other hand, politically, we have succeeded in certain milieus in creating an understanding that the Palestinian issue is not an issue that has one obvious solution . . . we were successful in creating a certain degree of political understanding [of Israeli needs]. Where have we failed miserably? We failed in that we were not prepared to make an [agreement] at a time that we could have paid prices that perhaps would have been lower than we will have to pay when an agreement is reached.[94]

Benjamin Netanyahu also analyzed the success of Israeli counterterrorism during his term.

In the past three years [during his first term as prime minister], counter-terrorism policy has succeeded. . . . My goal was to make it clear to the Palestinians that terrorism would harm them. If they feel that terrorism serves their purposes and that the Jews do not have the ability to withstand it, then terrorism will increase. . . . If you show tolerance for terrorism, then it will increase. If you show tenacity and resolve, then terrorism will not increase. There is going to be terrorism here in any case, whether or not there is peace.[95]

Shimon Peres, on the other hand, believed that Israeli counterterrorism policy was not successful

because we could have done all the things we did earlier. [Peres refers to the Oslo Accords, which were signed with the Palestinians in 1993.] And we could have already had twenty-seven years without terror. We didn't have the courage to do what we did in the early ninteen nineties. If we had made the [Oslo] agreement, we would have been able to save ourselves the Intifada. . . . We wouldn't have sat in Gaza for thirty-three years like idiots, oppressing them and endangering ourselves, allowing hostility and hatred to grow rampant.[96]

Indeed, it can clearly be seen that the prime ministers' responses to the question of the success of Israeli counterterrorism policy depend on their "conception"—the product of their ideological and political worldview. In analyzing the effectiveness of counterterrorism policy, they attribute success to the policy that they adopted during their terms of office, ostensibly in comparison with the ineffectiveness of their predecessors' policies. This approach should not be seen merely as an expression of arrogance or self-satisfaction. The more accurate conclusion is that, on the one hand, Israeli counterterrorism policy is influenced to a large extent by the ideology and outlook of the person at the top of the decision-making pyramid—the prime minister. On the other hand, the assessment of the degree of the policy's success depends on the evaluator's ideological perspective and is not necessarily the result of objective variables and indices.

The words of former Mossad head Shabtai Shavit seem to summarize the Israeli narrative on this issue in the clearest possible way:

The answer to the [question] of whether the policy was correct or incorrect is that there was no other way. How do you respond to terrorism? Succumb to it? In the first stage of terrorism, are you already going to say "I'm willing to give you a Palestinian state, just don't commit acts of terror"? The saying "if someone comes to kill you, rise up and kill him first," has been true since the creation of the world, and it is still true today. Turning the other cheek is a luxury that can be afforded only by those who are very big, strong, and rich, and not by the weak. And if we disappear off the face of the earth, no one will shed a tear.[97]

CONCLUSION

The Art of Israeli Counterterrorism

Israeli decision makers remain divided on many matters related to Israel's counterterrorism policy. Nevertheless, it seems that on at least one issue, Israeli prime ministers, senior IDF officials, and former defense establishment directors are in unanimous agreement: Israel has no stated or written policy on combating terrorism. The main reason for the lack of a formulated counterterrorism doctrine, despite years of continuous struggle with terrorism, is that in its very essence, counterterrorism is a form of art. The art of fighting terrorism involves finding a balance between various action alternatives, which can sometimes appear contradictory, spanning different ideologies and worldviews, and consisting of a variety of approaches and measures.

The art of counterterrorism requires knowledge of the enemy's rationale and understanding that this rationale is different from that of the state and its leaders. This rationale is based on a cost-benefit analysis by terrorist organizations and perpetrators; it varies from one terrorist organization to another and fluctuates depending on circumstances and the changing interests of the organizations.

The art of counterterrorism requires finding the necessary balance between actions that are intended to neutralize a terrorist organization's operational capability and actions intended to neutralize the motivation that underlies acts of terrorism. Understanding the friction and contradictions between these actions and striking the correct balance is what will ensure a sound and effective fight against terrorism.

The art of counterterrorism requires decision makers to constantly engage with the public, all the while maintaining the necessary balance between calling on citizens to be alert in order to help thwart terrorist attacks and minimize the damage they cause, and calming them to prevent anxiety and irrational behavior due to the threat of terrorism.

The art of counterterrorism requires finding solutions to and balances in the various aspects of the democratic dilemma that presents itself in the fight against terror; that is, the requirement to balance the need for an effective war on terror with the protection of the liberal democratic values of the state. Democratic nations are more sensitive to the threat of terrorism. The social contract in which the state holds a monopoly on the use of force for the security of the nation that is appropriate in times of peace and calm is put to the test when that nation is facing a wave of terrorism. The reluctance of a liberal democratic government to employ all possible measures to prevent terrorism might pave the way for radical opposition elements to conduct vigilante activities and even take power through promises that they have the solutions required to restore order, security, and stability and that they are determined to employ them without reservation or hesitation. Whether this is just the appearance that terrorists have some kind of magic solution or an actual plan of action, it is likely that in the midst of a wave of terrorism, the public would prefer to hang onto these promises rather than support a leadership that is perceived as hesitant and weak. In this respect, terrorist attacks might have a significant impact on elections in democratic countries. Voting patterns might fluctuate in periods of terrorism, with citizens prioritizing security matters over economic and other considerations.

The art of counterterrorism cannot and probably should not be made into a written doctrine, but one can operate within its framework in accordance with certain guidelines. The art of combating terrorism can and should be taught. One can improve and learn to adapt to changing challenges resulting from the evolution of the phenomenon of modern terrorism. Decision makers need to understand the principles of the art of counterterrorism and develop the skills required for effectively handing terrorism. In other words, decision makers and others engaged in dealing strategically with terrorism must be artists. They must act wisely and with an artist's sensitivity in dealing with a phenomenon as complex and volatile as terrorism. They must be equipped with the appropriate toolbox to carry out the difficult tasks they face—one that includes cognitive tools, intelligence and emotional intelligence, the ability to integrate administrative and operational work, and the ability to work in cooperation as a team. They must be attentive to the people but act fearlessly, ignoring outside pressures and political considerations. Artists in the fight against terrorism must be willing to learn from others' experiences, both the successes and the failures. Although Israel does not have a written and binding counterterrorism strategy, one can conclude from examining the policies of the various governments and prime ministers over the years that Israeli policy in this area is largely determined on the basis of a model of decision-making processes, as follows.

Given the intelligence and operational information passed on to decision maker from the various security agencies, he or she must first define the nature of the counterterrorism challenge facing Israel at that particular time and the intelligence gaps he or she is required to bridge. Decision makers bring to this process their own ideological worldview, personal experience, value and belief system, and formal and informal spheres of influence (as described in chapter 1). Accurate identification of the challenge enables decision makers to determine the specific goals they want to achieve. For example, is the goal to prevent a concrete attack or a specific type of attack? Is it to damage the enemy's operational capability and thereby to reduce his capability to carry out an attack? Or is it to neutralize the motivations and reasons underlying the concrete threat of terrorism? Does the decision maker want to deter the terrorist organizations? to defeat them? Or is it merely his or her intention to reduce the damage caused by terrorism and try to save lives? It should be emphasized that distortions in the perception of the enemy or in assessment of the threat can disrupt the decision-making process and lead the decision maker to focus on an irrelevant enemy or attribute too much importance to a marginal threat. In this context, it should be remembered that Israel often must simultaneously deal with several sources of terrorism and with a variety of threats. Therefore, a decision to take action against one threat might directly or indirectly affect other threats either positively or negatively.

Once decision makers have defined the goals and objectives that they want to achieve in the face of a specific terrorist threat, they begin the process of identifying the most appropriate action methods and counterterrorism measures to achieve the desired goal. These measures can then be selected from an existing toolbox that includes methods of taking action and technological and other measures from the different areas of counterterrorism (offensive and defensive measures, punitive actions and legislation, intelligence tools, and legal procedures). The state's counterterrorism strategy is in fact the synergetic aggregate of all these methods of action and measures.

In considering the action methods and measures proposed by the security agencies in response to the challenge of terrorism, Israeli decision makers examine these measures using two parallel tests: the test of effectiveness and the test of legitimacy. In other words, the proposed measure must respond to the challenges of the democratic dilemma. Through the prism of effectiveness, the decision maker examines the cost-benefit considerations of the proposed method of action or measure against the goal defined by the decision maker. (The effectiveness of each action method and of all the counterterrorism measures must be examined under the assumption of the planned action's future success as well as in the case of failure.) Means and methods that do not pass the efficiency test are abandoned, and the decision maker has to find an alternative measure from the toolbox that might achieve the defined goal. This process continues until ultimately he or she judges that the proposed method or measure is effective and likely to achieve the defined goal.

The measures that have passed the test of effectiveness are then examined through the moral/value prism, which assesses the legality of their use and the degree to which they might infringe on the state's liberal values. Using the value prism, the decision maker examines each proposed method and measure in relation to the laws of the state, international humanitarian law, the laws of war and the Geneva Conventions, as well in relation to the subjective value system of the decision maker and the ethics practiced in the country. Measures and methods of action that do not pass the test of the value prism are abandoned, and the process begins again until an option is found that is effective and able to achieve the counterterrorism goals and does not contradict the laws or the values of the state or the decision maker's own values. These measures and action methods are added

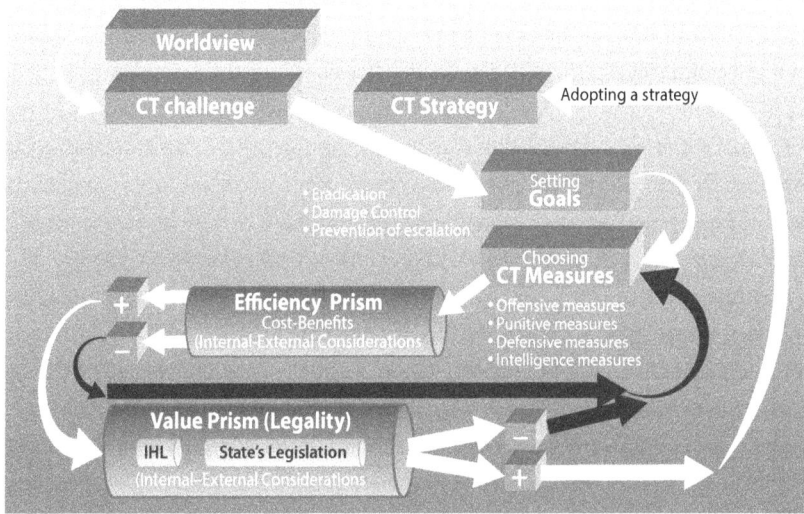

FIGURE 13.1. Aggregated Israeli counterterrorism policy

to previous ones and, together, shape the state's counterterrorism strategy during that particular period (figure 13.1).

Analysis of Israel's conduct in the face of terrorism over the years shows that there is no one way to deal with terrorism. Just as waves of terror rise, fall, and change shape, so do the measures employed to deal with it. Indeed, terrorist organizations around the world are driven by a variety of motivations and strive toward different operational goals. However, many of them share common denominators, including the Islamist-jihadist ideology that underlies their actions, their strategy of extreme violence used in order to sow fear and anxiety among their target societies, and the exploitation of modern technology, first and foremost of the internet and social networks. Despite the differences among the types of terrorism committed around the world, the challenges faced by Western countries with regard to terrorism are similar and sometimes even identical. These similarities, and the global operational links among terrorists, terrorist organizations, and networks around the world, require the states coping with this phenomenon to cooperate, help one another in dealing with terrorism, and learn from one another's experiences.

EIGHT TENETS OF ISRAEL'S COUNTERTERRORISM POLICY

A retrospective examination of Israel's counterterrorism policy points to eight tenets that form the art of Israeli counterterrorism and should be used as a guide for Western countries facing the challenge of terrorism.

1. *The central role of intelligence.* This basic component of counterterrorism is essential for preventing terrorist attacks. Intelligence is crucial in sending alerts before the attack takes place, planning and executing operative and offensive actions against terrorist organizations, increasing the effectiveness of security and prevention systems, and prosecuting the perpetrators of terrorism, their abettors, and their dispatchers. However, intelligence plays another key role in tackling terrorism: it helps to clarify the enemy's rationale. Intelligence analyzes and explains the cost-benefit analysis of terrorist organizations and perpetrators, as well as their decision-making processes and the translation of those processed into operational activities. Decision makers can then formulate counterterrorism policy effectively and develop leverage to be used against the organization.

Over the years, Israeli intelligence has proven exceptional in penetrating terrorist organizations, collecting valuable information, and adapting and translating it into counterterrorism actions. It has proven time and again that it has the ability to obtain relevant and accurate intelligence in real time based on human sources (HUMINT), communications intelligence (COMINT), and even open sources (OSINT) while monitoring the internet and especially social networks. One can learn from the Israeli use of intelligence—that intelligence gathering never ends and that one must be wary of complacency even when intelligence achievements are high. It should be remembered that the phenomenon of terrorism is dynamic, elusive, and ever-changing and that terrorist organizations are constantly learning and trying to find the soft underbelly of a nation in order to carry out devastating attacks. The art of collecting, processing, analyzing, and implementing intelligence is therefore a central element in the art of dealing with terrorism.

2. *Domestic cooperation between branches and agencies.* The ability to achieve and maintain a high level of intelligence against terrorist organizations and perpetrators is not sufficient. Intelligence in and of itself is not much use if it is not quickly converted into operational action against terrorist perpetrators, their dispatchers, and all those involved in initiating, planning, preparing, and executing attacks. The Israeli model demonstrates the need to overcome organizational (and personal) egos in order to enable full cooperation among various intelligence and

security agencies. Disputes between authorities, jealous guarding of one's intelligence sources, and competition over who takes credit are some of the dangers that security and intelligence forces must be aware of and avoid. This requires the development of mechanisms and methods to neutralize these dangers.

This can be done in many ways, including through the establishment of interagency information-sharing centers, joint operations and activities that integrate the security and intelligence branches and agencies, regular meetings to coordinate with the authorities, and, above all, the appointment of a coordinator for counterterrorist activities who will integrate intelligence and operational action concerning terrorism. This coordinator should be appointed by the top decision maker in the country (the prime minister or the president), from whom he or she will draw authority and to whom he or she will report directly. The art of counterterrorism requires harmonious, synergistic, and coordinated action by one leader.

3. *International cooperation.* Modern terrorism is an international phenomenon. Even terrorism that is seemingly local to one country is generally associated with various international elements, such as supporters and collaborators based in different countries, states that sponsor terrorism, money transfers through the international banking network, incitement based in other countries, and operational action by terrorists originating outside the territory of the country under attack.

Israel maintains diverse intelligence and operational ties with many countries on issues related to counterterrorism. In this field, cooperation prevails over political and other disputes and is a force multiplier in the fight against terrorism. The art of counterterrorism thus relies on bilateral and multilateral international cooperation.

4. *The principle of proactivity.* Over the years, Israel has employed a wide range of operative and offensive counterterrorist actions. Some have been routine actions against terrorist organizations, some were reprisals following terrorist attacks in Israel, and some actions have been proactive-preventive, designed to damage a terrorist organization's ability to launch attacks. The Israeli experience shows that—especially when dealing with suicide bombers and ticking bombs—that an effective fight against terrorism requires the state to be proactive. One of the most effective proactive measures undertaken by Israel over the years has been targeted killings aimed at terrorist masterminds, perpetrators, and dispatchers. Judging from the words of Israeli decision makers, their guidelines with regard to targeted killings were the need to find the correct "dose" of the use of this measure, the need to take into account the boomerang effect during the planning phase, and the understanding that this measure should be used only as a last resort, after all of the other tools in the toolbox have been deemed inadequate to achieve the desired result.

Operational counterterrorist action based on the principle of pre-emption is thus a prerequisite for the success of the art of counterterrorism.

5. *Public vigilance and resilience.* One of Israel's greatest achievements in confronting terrorism is its ability to harness the power of the Israeli public to multiply its efforts in thwarting attacks and preventing terrorist organizations' success. Over the years, Israeli citizens have been forced to cope with many waves of terror. One attack was followed by another, occurring on both the frontline and the home front, in cities and villages, on the roads, in the air, in the sea, and on land. There have been stabbings, shootings, suicide bombings, and hostage situations. Many civilians have been killed or wounded over the years. Despite the high price, the suffering and stress that these terrorist attacks have inflicted on Israelis, public spirit has not been diminished by terrorism. Palestinian terrorist organizations have failed in their attempts to arouse anxiety among Israelis, prevent the immigration of Jews from other countries to Israel, and harm the economy. Although at times they were successful in using their terrorist activities to achieve political and territorial gains (such as the Israeli disengagement from the Gaza Strip in 2005), the Israeli public as a whole learned to cope with the damage that terrorism caused to its psyche and morale and did not let itself be paralyzed by the fear of terror attacks.

The resilience of the Israeli public is one of the reasons behind the success of its counterterrorism policy. Another dimension of this public strength is reflected in the mobilization, both organized and spontaneous, of citizens to help Israeli security forces prevent terror attacks and minimize the damage from attacks once they occur. As part of this organized volunteerism, many citizens (especially in the 1970s), after receiving appropriate training, joined the ranks of the Civil Guard under the command of the Israel Police to assist in securing large crowds. Regarding spontaneous action, many terrorist attacks in Israel have been thwarted or curtailed due to the awareness and involvement of civilian bystanders who acted quickly and decisively against terrorists, either armed with a licensed weapon or with their bare hands. Another component of public resilience is reflected in the actions of Israeli rescue teams and municipal authorities, who have proven very effective in responding immediately at the scene of a terrorist attack while trying to return the area to "business as usual" as quickly as possible. Here, too, the Israeli public has shown maturity and stamina and made a point of visiting the places where the attacks were carried out shortly after the event, be it a shopping mall, place of entertainment, or public transportation line. Many Israelis see a quick return to normal routine following a terrorist attack as their message to terrorist organizations and perpetrators that they did not allow terrorism to succeed in damaging morale or normalcy of everyday life. In an era in which terrorist attacks occur regularly in countries around the world, the Israeli art of resilience in dealing with terrorism acts as a guiding principle for citizens across Europe and other Western countries.

6. *The "Rabin Doctrine" in hostage situations.* The Israeli experience in dealing with terrorism during which hijackers and other terrorists seized Israeli hostages either at home or abroad led to the development of a doctrine by former prime minister Yitzhak Rabin. The so-called Rabin Doctrine dictates that Israel end such events via military intervention rather than negotiation. Only in the absence of a military response would Israel enter into effective negotiations with the terrorists and their dispatchers to try to reach a deal to bring about the release of the hostages. It seems that this doctrine has correctly balanced the many dilemmas stemming from a hostage situation. On the one hand, with a preference for military interven-tion, the doctrine is intended to prevent terrorists from taking hostages. On the other hand, in the absence of a military option, the doctrine offers the government a possible way to end the crisis through negotiation while paying the most reason-able price possible. The Israeli art of managing terrorist crisis situations in general and hostage crises in particular should be studied by other countries that are coping with similar situations.

7. *The solution to counterterrorism's democratic dilemma.* As a liberal democratic country having to grapple with a large number of terrorist attacks over the years, it seems that in many cases, Israel has found the necessary balance between effective-ness in the fight against terrorism and preserving liberal democratic values. This balance was achieved largely through the Israeli legal system and primarily by the Supreme Court. Those in the Israeli justice system understood that a democratic country defending itself against the threat of terrorism has unique needs and that the legal system must enable security officials to grant citizens the maximum pos-sible protection. At the same time, however, the country has a duty to act as the guardian of liberal democracy; its job is to prevent Israeli law enforcement agencies from misusing the prerogatives at their disposal and violating human or civil rights that are protected under Israeli or international law.

8. *Dealing with terrorists' motives.* An examination of Israeli policies in dealing with terrorism over the years through the lenses of the terrorism and the coun-terterrorism equation is likely to show mixed results—a combination of successes and failures. On the one hand, it seems that Israel has been successful in dealing with the variable of the operational capacities of terrorist organizations. In the shadow of the threat of terrorism, Israel has succeeded in thwarting many attacks and limiting the fallout from terrorism, allowing its citizens to live as normally as

possible. But on the other hand, it seems that Israel has failed when it comes to the second variable of the equations: neutralizing terrorist motivations. However, it must be remembered that the terrorism perpetrated against Israel over the years had a unique and extreme goal: the eradication of the Jewish state and the establishment of a Palestinian state in its place. It is very difficult, if not impossible, to appease such a radical motive. Unlike terrorism driven by separatist, socioeconomic, or other limited motives, when the terrorists' ultimate demand is to bring about the suicide of the entity they are acting against, one cannot take steps that would serve to neutralize their motives even partially. Nevertheless, perhaps Israel could have invested more effort over the years in diminishing or neutralizing motivations, whether by promoting various political initiatives and economic reforms in the West Bank and the Gaza Strip, engaging in person-to-person efforts with the Palestinian population, or encouraging gestures on the part of Israeli decision makers toward the Palestinians.

THE RELEVANCY OF THE ISRAELI EXPERIENCE

In conclusion, the question arises as to whether the Israeli experience in counterterrorism reflects only the Israeli case or whether it is relevant to other countries around the world.

Due to the scope and unique characteristics of the terrorist threat to Israel, over the years, many in the Western world have tended to differentiate the terrorist challenges faced by Israel from those faced by the rest of the Western world. These voices claim that the uniqueness of the terrorist threat to Israel stem from, among other things, Israel's geopolitical reality, the Israeli-Palestinian conflict, and Israel's occupation of the West Bank and the Gaza Strip in 1967. Moreover, whereas other countries had to deal with domestic terrorism by extremists who were motivated by ideologies such as communism, fascism, anarchism, or Islamism (terrorism that was, at most, a nuisance to the state and its citizens), Israel was forced to deal with terrorist organizations that posed a threat to its very existence. Israel's critics have therefore argued that the scope of the threat and the danger that terrorism has posed to Israel have led it to use counterterrorism measures and action methods that are unsuitable for use in other Western countries.

The September 11, 2011, terrorist attacks and the waves of Islamist-jihadist terrorism that have struck Western countries since that time require that leaders of Western countries reconsider these basic assumptions.

In retrospect, one can see that the waves of terror that were perpetrated against Israel in the past, which at the time appeared to constitute a threat that was unique to Israel, soon became an example for other terrorist organizations to apply elsewhere in the west. This has been the case with hijackings, hostage takings, suicide bombings, and lone wolf attacks.

Furthermore, whereas in the past it appeared that the high intensity of terrorist attacks against Israel was unique to the Israeli case, the reality today is that many Western countries (especially in Europe) are forced to deal with high-intensity Islamist-jihadist terror attacks aimed at establishing an Islamic state around the world. For these reasons, Israel's handling of terrorism, with regard to both its successes and its failures, should serve as a model for European and other Western countries that find themselves facing growing threats of terrorism. On the basis of Israel's experience, these countries should train the next generation of decision makers so they can develop effective methods and doctrines to deal with terrorism that are in line with their challenges, culture, and characteristics. In other words, the art of Israeli counterterrorism should serve as a platform for different interpretations and variations by other countries as they develop their own art of counterterrorism.

APPENDIX

LIST OF INTERVIEWEES

- **Avraham Ahituv** was director of the Israeli Security Agency (ISA) from 1974 to 1980. The interview was conducted on November 17, 1999.
- **Meir Amit** is a former IDF major general, member of Knesset, minister in the Israeli government, and Mossad chief. In the late 1950s and early 1960s, he served as head of Central Command and head of military intelligence. Between 1963 and 1968, he served as head of the Mossad. The interview was conducted on November 8, 1999.
- **Moshe Arens** served as the Israeli ambassador to the United States in 1982, as minister of defense from 1983 to 1984, and as minister of foreign affairs from 1988 to 1990. The interview was conducted on November 22, 1996.
- **Gabi Ashkenazi** was the IDF's sixteenth chief of staff from 2007 to 2011. The interview was conducted on February 24, 2014.
- **Meir Dagan** is a former IDF major general. He headed the counterterrorism bureau between 1996 and 2000 and served as head of the Mossad between 2002 and 2011. The interview was conducted on December 4, 1998.
- **Avi Dichter** was head of the ISA from 2000 to 2005. He later served as a member of Knesset and as minister of public security from 2006 to 2009 in the Olmert government. The interview was conducted on March 3, 2014.

- **Rafi Eitan** is a former senior Mossad official, member of the Knesset, and minister in the Israeli government. He headed operational units in the Mossad during the 1960s and early 1970s. He was appointed as the prime minister's advisor on counterterrorism in the late 1970s, and in 1981, Eitan was appointed head of the Bureau of Scientific Relations in the Ministry of Defense. The interview was conducted on October 31, 1999.
- **Shlomo Gazit** is a former IDF major general who served as head of military intelligence from 1974 to 1979. The interview was conducted on November 7, 1999.
- **Carmi Gillon** is a former head of the ISA, serving from March 1995 to February 1996. The interview was conducted on November 24, 1999.
- **Amnon Lipkin-Shahak** was commander of the Central Command, head of military intelligence (1986–91), IDF chief of staff (1995–98), member of the Knesset, and a minister in the Israeli government. The interview was conducted on December 12, 1999.
- **Shaul Mofaz** was the IDF's sixteenth chief of staff from 1998 to 2002. He went on to serve as a member of the Knesset and as minister of defense in the Olmert government from 2002 to 2006. The interview was conducted on February 17, 2014.
- **Benjamin Netanyahu** was prime minister between 1996 and 1999 and again from 2009 to the present. The interview was conducted on December 20, 1999.
- **Nitzan Nuriel** is an IDF reserve brigadier general who served as director of the counterterrorism bureau at the National Security Council from 2007 to 2012. The interview was conducted on February 2, 2014.
- **Ehud Olmert** served as Israel's twelfth prime minister, from 2006 until 2009. The interview was conducted on February 5, 2014.
- **Reuven Paz** served as the head of research of the ISA and was the first Academic Director of ICT.
- **Shimon Peres** was a former member of the Knesset, minister of defense (1974–76), and Israel's eighth prime minister (between 1984 and 1986). He also served as president of the state of Israel from 2007 to 2014. The interview was conducted on February 11, 2000.
- **Yaakov Perry** was head of the ISA between 1988 and 1994 and later served as a member of the Knesset and minister in the Israeli government. The interview was conducted on December 4, 1998.
- **Yigal Pressler** is an IDF retired brigadier general who served as the prime minister's advisor on counterterrorism between 1992 and 1996. The interview was conducted on October 31, 1999.

- **Yitzhak Shamir** is a former senior Mossad official, member of the Knesset, and a minister. He served as Israel's seventh prime minister during various periods between 1983 and 1989. The interview was conducted in November 1996.
- **Ariel Sharon** served as IDF Commander of the Central Command in the early 1970s. He then filled the post of defense minister from 1981 to 1983 and later served as Israel's eleventh prime minister, from 2001 to 2006. The interview was conducted on September 13, 2000.
- **Shabtai Shavit** served as head of the Mossad from 1989 to 1996. The interview was conducted on November 22, 1999.
- **Avraham "Abrasha" Tamir** is a former IDF major general who served as head of the IDF Planning and Policy Directorate in the mid-1970s. In 1979, he was appointed to head the national planning division of the Ministry of Defense, and in 1981, he established the Ministry of Defense's National Security Unit. In 1984, he began serving as director-general of the Prime Minister's Office and as national security advisor, and in 1986, he was appointed director-general of the Foreign Ministry. The interview was conducted on November 27, 1999.
- **Rehavam Ze'evi** is a former IDF major general, member of the Knesset, and a minister in the Israeli government. In the late 1960s and early 1970s, he served as IDF OC Central Command. In 1974, he was appointed by Yitzhak Rabin to be his advisor on counterterrorism and intelligence affairs. In 2001, while serving as minister of tourism in the Sharon administration, he was murdered by three terrorists belonging to the Popular Front for the Liberation of Palestine in retaliation for the assassination of Abu Ali Mustafa, the organization's secretary-general. The interview was conducted on November 14, 1999.

SELECTED HEBREW-LANGUAGE NEWSPAPERS

Davar
Haaretz
Haolam Hazeh
Hatzofeh
Ma'ariv
Yediot Aharonot (also sometimes cited as Ynet)

NOTES

1. THE ISRAELI COUNTERTERRORISM STRATEGY AND DECISION-MAKING PROCESS: CONCEPTUAL MODELS

1. Boaz Ganor, *The Counter-Terrorism Puzzle: A Guide for Decision-Makers* (New Brunswick, NJ: Transaction, 2005), chap. 6.
2. Interview with Rafi Eitan, October 31, 1999. All interviews noted here were conducted by the author.
3. Interview with Gabi Ashkenazi, February 24, 2014.
4. Interview with Yitzhak Shamir, November 1996.
5. Interview with Shimon Peres, February 11, 2000.
6. Interview with Reserve Major General Avraham (Abrasha) Tamir, November 27, 1999. Tamir emphasized the strategic aspect of terrorism as a catalyst for war: "When discussing terrorism in and of itself, generals will tell you that it does not endanger the existence of Israel. The PLO does not endanger the existence of Israel, Hezbollah does not endanger the existence of Israel, but terrorism is a strategic problem because it is a factor that, since the War of Independence [1948], has deteriorated into major wars that could endanger the state of Israel. Therefore, it is a strategic threat. . . . [H]ad it not been for terrorism, we would not have deteriorated into the Sinai War in '56, we would not have deteriorated into the Six-Day War in '67, and the Yom Kippur War [1973] should be seen as a by-product of the occupations of the Six-Day War."
7. Interview with Ariel Sharon, September 13, 2000.
8. Interview with Meir Dagan, December 4, 1998.
9. Interview with Shabtai Shavit, November 22, 1999.
10. Former ISA chief Carmi Gillon examined the dimensions of the terrorist threat to Israel from a Palestinian perspective:

I see terrorism by Hamas and Islamic Jihad, as opposed to Abu Nidal's terrorism, for example, not as terrorism intended only to kill Jews simply because they are Jews. Their interest is to use the only military weapon available to them to stop the peace process . . . to destroy it. . . . Terrorism is an instrument for attaining political goals, which is exactly what a state does when it uses its army. . . . Even Rabin himself, 'Mr. Security,' admitted, "I am threatened; I see this [terrorism] as a strategic threat. I chose a path and terrorism is getting in its way." That's the problem. You can criticize it, but the fact is that what terrorism did is that it halted the [peace] process . . . so it is right to define [terrorism] as a strategic threat. I do not think it changed the face of history. It did not lead Israel to declare that it was cutting off all ties with the Palestinians, which is what Hamas wanted, but it stopped the process. It struck a blow to the pace but not to the path. Who chose terrorism as a strategic threat? The Jews did. The Israelis. The victim is the one who determines . . . the population's tolerance and what it is willing to bear is what determines the intensity of terrorism.

(Interview with Carmi Gillon, November 24, 1999)

11. Interview with Amnon Lipkin-Shahak, December 12, 1999.
12. Interview with Yigal Pressler, October 31, 1999.
13. Interview with Rehavam Ze'evi, November 14, 1999.
14. Former defense minister Moshe Arens believed terrorism could become a strategic threat "if it leads to a large part of the population living in fear and therefore being willing to do almost anything to remove this fear." Interview with Moshe Arens, November 22, 1996.
15. Interview with Meir Amit, November 8, 1999.
16. Interview with Shlomo Gazit, November 7, 1999.
17. Sharon, 2000
18. Shavit, 1999.
19. Dagan, 1998.
20. Interview with Benjamin Netanyahu, December 20, 1999.
21. Interview with Nitzan Nuriel, February 2, 2014.
22. Ashkenazi, 2014.
23. Lipkin-Shahak, 1999.
24. Dagan, 1998.
25. Interview with Yaakov Perry, December 4, 1998.
26. Dagan, 1998.
27. Shamir, 1996.
28. Ze'evi, 1999.
29. Perry, 1998.
30. Shamir, 1996.
31. Pressler, 1999.
32. Lipkin-Shahak, 1999.
33. Shavit, 1999.
34. Netanyahu, 1999.
35. Netanyahu, 1999

36. Peres, 2000.
37. Gillon, 1999.
38. Shamir, 1996.
39. Shamir, 1996.
40. Pressler, 1999.
41. Shavit, 1999.
42. These two axes are generic and reflect the tensions that typically face any (democratic) country confronting terrorism. However, due to the magnitude and characteristics of the terrorism with which the state of Israel has been forced to contend over the years, the country's small territory and population, and Israel's unique geostrategic challenges as a country surrounded by numerous enemies that do not recognize its existence, these tensions are particularly significant in the Israeli case.
43. Ganor, *The Counter-Terrorism Puzzle*, chap. 6.

2. THE "FEDAYEEN PHENOMENON": THE DAVID BEN-GURION AND MOSHE SHARETT ADMINISTRATIONS (1948-63)

1. "Armistice Lines (1949–1967)," Israel Ministry of Foreign Affairs, accessed December 7, 2020, http://mfa.gov.il/MFA/AboutIsrael/Maps/Pages/1949-1967%20Armistice%20Lines.aspx.
2. Zaki Shalom, *David Ben-Gurion, the State of Israel and the Arab World, 1949–1956* [in Hebrew] (Sde Boker, Israel: Ben-Gurion Heritage Institute, 1995), 148.
3. According to Israeli police reports, of the 7,018 registered infiltrations into Israel (and it is likely that there were more unreported infiltrations) 1,621 were defined as "non-hostile" and 5,379 as "hostile," of which 1,625 were belligerent acts that included 6 acts of espionage, 17 injuries, 39 murders, 79 shootings, 14 robberies, and 4 cases of stolen weapons and explosives. According to Morris, these data show that less than 10 percent of the infiltrations from 1949 to 1953 were violent or politically motivated. Benny Morris, *Israel's Border Wars, 1949–1956* [in Hebrew] (Tel Aviv: Am Oved/Sifriyat Ofakim, 1996), 64.
4. Morris, *Israel's Border Wars*, 44.
5. David Ben-Gurion, *The Sinai Campaign* (Tel Aviv: Am Oved, 1959), 39.
6. Morris, *Israel's Border Wars*, 443.
7. Morris, *Israel's Border Wars*, 134.
8. Morris, *Israel's Border Wars*, 123.
9. Morris, *Israel's Border Wars*, 443.
10. Morris, *Israel's Border Wars*, 440.
11. Shalom, *David Ben-Gurion*, 149.
12. Shalom, *David Ben-Gurion* 151.
13. Contrary to conventional belief, Morris claims that it is difficult to assess how much influence the Mufti had on the violent political infiltrations into Israel in the years 1949–56. According to him, attributing every attack to the Mufti actually served the interests of Jordan and often of Israel. Morris, *Israel's Border Wars*, 77.
14. According to Morris, the deepening of Egyptian involvement in the infiltrations into Israel was the result of the Israeli reprisals in Gaza in 1955. He claimed that "before the raid, Egypt's policy, with a few exceptions, was to consistently object to

infiltration. After the raid . . . the Egyptian authorities themselves initiated violent infiltrations, driven by political and military considerations." Nevertheless, Morris's book contains many examples of Egypt initiating infiltrations into Israel for the purposes of espionage, murder, and revenge. These actions were directed by the Egyptian Ministry of Military Intelligence in Gaza under the command of Mustafa Saad, even before the raid in Gaza. Morris, *Israel's Border Wars*, 100–101.

15. Morris, *Israel's Border Wars*, 51.

16. Ben-Gurion, *The Sinai Campaign*, 39–43.

17. Eliezer Ben-Rafael, *Israel-Palestine: A Guerrilla Conflict in International Politics* (Westport, CT: Greenwood Press, 1987), 99.

18. Morris, *Israel's Border Wars*, 444.

19. Hanan Alon, *Countering Palestinian Terrorism in Israel: Toward a Policy Analysis of Countermeasures* (Santa Monica, CA: Rand, 1980), 15–16.

20. Alon, *Countering Palestinian Terrorism*, 16.

21. Ian S. Lustick, "Terrorism in the Arab-Israeli Conflict: Targets and Audiences," in *Terrorism in Context*, ed. Martha Crenshaw (University Park: Pennsylvania State University Press, 1995), 528.

22. Interview with Ariel Sharon, September 13, 2000.

23. Sharon, interview.

24. Ami Pedhauzer, *The Israeli Secret Services and the Struggle Against Terrorism* (New York: Columbia University Press, 2009), 24.

25. Aryeh Avneri, *Pshitut Hatigmul*, pts. 1 and 2 [in Hebrew] (Tel Aviv: Sifriyat Madim, 1954), 251.

26. M. Barry Blechman, *The Consequences of Israeli Reprisals: An Assessment* (doctoral thesis, Georgetown University, 1971), and Alon, *Countering Palestinian Terrorism*, 17.

27. Israel Tal, *National Security: The Few vs. the Many* (Tel Aviv: Dvir, 1996), 131.

28. Sharon, interview.

29. Avneri, *Pshitut Hatigmul*, 61.

30. Avneri, *Pshitut Hatigmul*, 67.

31. Shalom, *David Ben-Gurion*, 162.

32. Morris, *Israel's Border Wars*, 201.

33. Sholomo *Aharonson* and Dan Horowitz, "The Strategy of *Controlled Retaliation*—The Israeli Experience," *State & Government* 1, no. 1 (1971): 81.

34. Aharonson and Horowitz, "The Strategy of *Controlled Retaliation*."

35. Avneri, *Pshitut Hatigmul*, 36.

36. Morris, *Israel's Border Wars*, 203.

37. Avneri, *Pshitut Hatigmul*, 32.

38. Avneri, *Pshitut Hatigmul*, 285.

39. Avneri, *Pshitut Hatigmul*, 212.

40. Ben-Gurion, *The Sinai Campaign*, 39–43.

41. Interview with Meir Amit, November 8, 1999.

42. Yoav Gelber. "Anti-Terror Warfare and Its Influence on Regular Warfare," in *Future Terrorism Trends*, ed. Yonah Alexander, Yuval Neeman, and Ely Tavin (Washington, DC: Global Affairs, 1991), 58.

43. To illustrate the ineffectiveness of Israeli reprisals, some researchers point out that the major Czech-Egyptian arms deal took place following the Israeli retaliatory raid in Gaza, which probably also contributed to the arms race in the region that greatly

enhanced the Egyptian military forces. Mordechai Bar-On, *The Gates of Gaza: Israel's Defense and Foreign Policy 1955–1957* (Tel Aviv: Am Oved, 1992), 55.

44. Morris, *Israel's Border Wars*, 107.
45. Morris, *Israel's Border Wars*, 442, 446, 447.
46. Aharonson and Horowitz, "The Strategy of Controlled Retaliation," 82.
47. Shalom, *David Ben Gurion*.
48. Avneri, *Pshitut Hatigmul*, 254.
49. Ben-Gurion, *The Sinai Campaign*, 214.
50. Noemi Gal-Or, "Tolerating Terrorism in Israel," in *Tolerating Terrorism in the West*, ed. Noemi Gal-Or (London: Routledge, 1991), 69.

3. PALESTINIAN NATIONAL TERRORISM AFTER THE SIX-DAY WAR: THE LEVI ESHKOL AND GOLDA MEIR ADMINISTRATIONS (1963-73)

1. Hanan Alon, *Countering Palestinian Terrorism in Israel: Toward a Policy Analysis of Countermeasures* (Santa Monica, CA: Rand, 1980), 39.
2. Yitzhak Rabin, *Service Book* [in Hebrew] (Tel Aviv: Sifriyat Ma'ariv, 1979), 121.
3. "Terrorism Deaths in Israel 1920–1999," Israel Ministry of Foreign Affairs, January 2000, http://www.mfa.gov.il/mfa/foreignpolicy/terrorism/palestinian/pages/terrorism%20deaths%20in%20israel%20-%201920-1999.aspx.
4. Yezid Sayigh, *Armed Struggle and the Search for State* (Oxford: Clarendon, 1997), 141.
5. Yigal Alon, *Kelim Shluvim* [in Hebrew] (Tel Aviv: Kibutz Meuhad, 1980), 71–73.
6. Alon, *Kelim Shluvim*, 74.
7. Asher Susser, *The PLO After the Lebanon War* [in Hebrew] (Tel Aviv: Hakibutz Hameuchad, 1985), 142.
8. Interview with Abraham Ahituv, November 23, 1999.
9. Ronen Bergman, *Authority Given* [in Hebrew] (Tel Aviv: Yediot Ahronot, 2002), 20, 25.
10. David Maimon, *The Terror That Was Defeated: The Suppression of Terror in the Gaza Strip, 1971–1972* [in Hebrew] (Bnei Brak, Israel: Steimatzky Publishing, 1993), 50.
11. Interview with Ariel Sharon, September 13, 2000.
12. Shlomo Gazit, "How the PLO Is Different," Special Edition—International Terrorism, *Monthly Review*, no. 7 (July 1980): 72–73.
13. Maimon, *The Terror That Was Defeated*, 19.
14. Alon, *Kelim Shluvim*, 76–77.
15. Bergman, *Authority Given*, 74.
16. Sayigh, *Armed Struggle*, 203.
17. Interview with Rehavam Ze'evi, November 29, 1999.
18. Alon, *Kelim Shluvim*, 77.
19. Amir Oren, "Debacle in the Desert," *Haaretz*, May 13, 2011, https://www.haaretz.com/israel-news/debacle-in-the-desert-1.361453.
20. Alan Hart, *Arafat: The Definitive Biography Written in Co-Operation with Yasser Arafat* (London: Sidgwick & Jackson, 1994), 224.
21. Hart, *Arafat*, 205.
22. Hart, *Arafat*, 227.

23. Sayigh, *Armed Struggle*, 179–81.
24. Yehoshafat Harkabi, *Fatah in the Arab Strategy* [in Hebrew] (Tel Aviv: Maarachot, 1969), 89.
25. Harkabi, *Fatah in the Arab Strategy*, 245.
26. See Israeli Air Force, "El Al Flight Does Not Answer," http://www.iaf.org.il/4371-37667 -he/IAF.aspx (Hebrew).
27. See Israeli Security Agency (Shin Bet), "Attack on an El Al Plane in Zurich," http:// www.shabak.gov.il/heritage/affairs/Pages/Zurich1969.aspx (Hebrew).
28. See "47 Killed in Explosion of February 21, 1970 on Swissair Plane Flying to Tel Aviv," *Haaretz*, http://www.haaretz.co.il/news/education/1.1163211 (Hebrew).
29. See "El Al Flight Does Not Answer."
30. See Yaron Druckman, "A Turntable Trapped in an El Al Plane: The Week Before" [in Hebrew], Ynet, http://www.ynet.co.il/articles/0,7340,L-4418294,00.html.
31. See "1976: Israelis Rescue Entebbe Hostages," BBC, http://news.bbc.co.uk/onthisday/hi /dates/stories/july/4/newsid_2786000/2786967.stm.
32. See Avinoam Mishnikov, "Terrorist Attacks on El Al Planes and Offices," Sky High, http://www.sky-high.co.il/%D7%94%D7%AA%D7%A7%D7%A4%D7%95%D7%AA -%D7%98%D7%A8%D7%95%D7%A8-%D7%A2%D7%9C-%D7%9E%D7 %98%D7%95%D7%A1%D7%99-%D7%95%D7%9E%D7%A9%D7%A8%D7 %93%D7%99-%D7%90%D7%9C-%D7%A2%D7%9C.html (Hebrew).
33. Ariel Merari and Shlomi Elad, *The International Dimension of Palestinian Terrorism* (Boulder, CO: Westview Press, 1987), 16.
34. Merari and Elad, *International Dimension of Palestinian Terrorism*, 26, 28, 31.
35. Sayigh, *Armed Struggle*, 215, 304, 300.
36. Aryeh Avneri, *Pshitut Hatigmul*, pts. 1 and 2 [in Hebrew] (Tel Aviv: Sifriyat Madim, 1954), 383–84.
37. Merari and Elad, *The International Dimension of Palestinian Terrorism*. 116.
38. According to Israeli sources, Black September was a code name used to conceal the fact that the attacks abroad were carried out by Fatah and Habash Front activists. The name "Black September" refers to the many losses that the Palestinians suffered during the civil war that they perpetrated in Jordan in September 1970. Black September attacks, therefore, were carried out mainly against Israeli and Jordanian targets.
39. Sayigh, *Armed Struggle*, 281.
40. Arik Rolo, *Without a Homeland: Abu-Iyad's Conversations with Eric Rolo* (Jerusalem: Mifras, 1979), 158.
41. Merari and Elad, *The International Dimension of Palestinian Terrorism*, 118.
42. Peter St. John, "Counterterrorism Policy-Making: The Case of Aircraft Hijacking, 1968–1988," in *Democratic Responses to International Terrorism*, ed. Charters A. Savid (New York: Transnational Publishers, 1991), 76.
43. Rolo, *Without a Homeland*, 166–67.
44. Rolo, *Without a Homeland*, 166–67.
45. Shmuel Stampler, "The Multilateral Fight Against Terrorism," *Monthly Review*, no. 10 (October 1972): 3.
46. Gad Barzilai, *A Democracy in Wartime: Conflict and Consensus in Israel* (Hebrew) (Merhavia, Israel: Sifriyat Hapalim, Kibbutz Haartzi, 1992), 152.
47. See Jewish Telegraphic Agency, "Gen. Aharon Yariv Dead at 74; Headed Israeli Military Intelligence," https://www.jta.org/1994/05/10/archive/gen-aharon-yariv-dead-at-74-headed -israeli-military-intelligence.

4. CROSS-BORDER TERRORISM AFTER THE YOM KIPPUR WAR: THE YITZHAK RABIN ADMINISTRATION (1974-76)

1. Lital Levin, "This Week in Haaretz, 1976/Air France Flight Hijacked to Entebbe," *Haaretz*, July 2, 2012, https://www.haaretz.com/print-edition/features/this-week-in-haaretz -1976-air-france-flight-hijacked-to-entebbe-1.299560.
2. Raffi Berg, "Entebbe: A Mother's Week of 'Indescribable Fear,' " *BBC News*, June 27, 2016, http://www.bbc.com/news/magazine-36559375.
3. Yitzhak Rabin, *Service Book* [in Hebrew] (Tel Aviv: Sifriyat Ma'ariv, 1979), 524.
4. Rabin, *Service Book*, 526.
5. Rabin, *Service Book*, 526.
6. Rabin, *Service Book*, 526.
7. Rabin, *Service Book*, 528.
8. Asher Susser, *The PLO After the Lebanon War: The Quest for Survival* [in Hebrew] (Tel Aviv: Hakibutz Hameuchad, 1985), 185.
9. Rabin, *Service Book*, 528.
10. Rabin, *Service Book*, 528.
11. Rabin, *Service Book*, 532.
12. Rabin, *Service Book*, 532.
13. Ariel Merari and Shlomi Elad, *Hostile Terror Activities Abroad: Palestinian Terrorism Outside of Israel 1968–1986* [in Hebrew] (Bnei Brak: Hakibutz Hameuchad, 1986).
14. Merari and Elad, *Hostile Terror Activities Abroad*, 134.
15. Robert Johnson, "Chronology of Terrorist Attacks in Israel Part II: 1968–1977," *Johnston Archives*, December 4, 2017, http://www.johnstonsarchive.net/terrorism/terrisrael-2.html.
16. Alan Hart, *Arafat: The Definitive Biography Written in Co-Operation with Yasser Arafat* (London: Sidgwick & Jackson, 1994), 270.
17. Hart, *Arafat*, 268.
18. Ephraim Lapid, "Black September: Arab Struggle with Terrorism," *Israel Defense*, September 9, 2014, https://www.israeldefense.co.il/he/content/%D7%A1%D7%A4%D7 %98%D7%9E%D7%91%D7%A8-%D7%94%D7%A9%D7%97%D7%95%D7%A8-%D7%9E %D7%90%D7%91%D7%A7-%D7%A2%D7%A8%D7%91%D7%99-%D7%91%D7 %98%D7%A8%D7%95%D7%A8.
19. Yezid Sayigh, *Armed Struggle and the Search for State* (Oxford: Clarendon, 1997), 267.
20. Interview with Rehavam Ze'evi, November 14, 1999.
21. Sayigh, *Armed Struggle*, 358.
22. Hanan Alon, *Countering Palestinian Terrorism in Israel: Toward a Policy Analysis of Countermeasures* (Santa Monica, CA: Rand, 1980), 83–85.
23. Terrorist Incidents Database from the International Institute for Counter-Terrorism (ICT).
24. Rabin, *Service Book*, 520.
25. Gad Barzilai, *Democracy in Wartime* [in Hebrew] (Bnei Brak, Israel: Kibbutz Poalim, 1992), 183.
26. Shlomo Gazit, *Trapped Fools: Thirty Years of Israeli Policy in the Territories* (London: Frank Cass, 2003), 69.
27. Shlomo Gazit, "How the PLO Is Different," Special Edition—International Terrorism, *Monthly Review*, no. 7 (July 1980): 83.
28. Gazit, "How the PLO Is Different," 84.

29. Eliezer Ben-Rafael, *Israel-Palestine: A Guerrilla Conflict in International Politics* (Westport CT: Greenwood, 1987), 60–61.
30. Pinhas Inbari, *A Triangle Over Jordan* [in Hebrew] (Tel Aviv: Sifriyat Maariv, 1984), 191, 194.

5. TERRORISM AGAINST THE BACKDROP OF THE LEBANON WAR: THE MENACHEM BEGIN, YITZHAK SHAMIR, AND SHIMON PERES ADMINISTRATIONS (1977-86)

1. Shlomo Gazit, "How the PLO Is Different," Special Edition—International Terrorism, *Monthly Review*, no. 7 (July 1980): 94.
2. Gazit, "How the PLO Is Different," 91.
3. Yezid Sayigh, *Armed Struggle and the Search for State* (Oxford: Clarendon, 1997), 483.
4. Yigal Carmon, "The Story of the Palestinian Village Leagues," *MEMRI*, September 13, 2016, https://www.memri.org/reports/story-palestinian-village-leagues.
5. Pinhas Inbari, *Broken Swords* (Tel Aviv: Ministry of Defense Publishing House, 1994), 60.
6. Tami Bash, Yuval Ginbar, and Eitan Felner, *Deportation of Palestinians from the Occupied Territories and the Mass Deportation of December 1992* (Jerusalem: B'Tselem—The Israeli Information Center for Human Rights in the Occupied Territories, 1993).
7. Gazit, "How the PLO Is Different," 94.
8. Inbari, *Broken Swords*, 51.
9. Inbari, *Broken Swords*, 187.
10. Rafael Eitan, *The Story of a Soldier* [in Hebrew] (Tel Aviv: Sifriyat Maariv, 1985), 192.
11. Michael Omer-Man, "This Week in History: Israel's Deadliest Terror Attack," *Jerusalem Post*, March 11, 2011, http://www.jpost.com/Features/In-Thespotlight/This-Week-in-History-Israels-deadliest-terror-attack.
12. Arye Naor, *Begin in Power: A Personal Testimony* [in Hebrew] (Tel Aviv: Yediot Aharonot, 1993), 245.
13. Naor, *Begin in Power*, 248.
14. Naor, *Begin in Power*, 253.
15. Naor, *Begin in Power*, 253.
16. Sayigh, *Armed Struggle and the Search for State*, 508–9.
17. Sayigh, *Armed Struggle and the Search for State*.
18. Sayigh, *Armed Struggle and the Search for State*, 257.
19. Raphael Israeli, *PLO in Lebanon, Selected Documents* (London: Weidenfeld & Nicolson, 1983), 26.
20. Israeli, *PLO in Lebanon*, 29.
21. Rashid Khalidi, *Under Siege: PLO Decision Making During the First Lebanon War* [in Hebrew] (Tel Aviv: Ministry of Defense, 1988): 53–54.
22. Dan Schueftan, "The PLO and the Lebanon War: An Interim Assessment," in *The Lebanon War* [in Hebrew] (Tel Aviv: Hakibbutz Hameuchad, Kav Adom, 1983), 83.
23. Interview with Shlomo Gazit, November 8, 1999.
24. Naor, *Begin in Power*, 282, 286.
25. Uri Milstein, "Terrorism as a Tool for the Arab Struggle Against Israel," [in Hebrew] *Skira Hodshit* 29, no. 10 (June 1982): 19.

26. Yitzhak Rabin, "Political Illusions and Their Price," in *The Lebanon War* [in Hebrew] (Tel Aviv: Hakibbutz Hameuchad, Kav Adom, 1983), 20.

27. Mike Eldar, *Shayetet 13: The Story of the Naval Commando* [in Hebrew] (Tel Aviv: Sifriyat Maariv, 1993), 627.

28. "The Tyre HQ Bombing—First Suicide Attack Against Israel," *Shin Bet*, November 3, 1983, https://www.shabak.gov.il/english/heritage/affairs/Pages/TheTyreHQBombing .aspx.

29. Eldar, *Shayetet 13*, 636.

30. "The Lebanon War: Operation Peace for Galilee," Israel Ministry of Foreign Affairs, http://www.mfa.gov.il/mfa/aboutisrael/history/pages/operation%20peace%20for%20galilee %20-%201982.aspx.

31. *Maariv*, October 10, 1985, 13.

32. Eitan, *The Story of a Soldier*, 331–32.

33. Ben Caspit and Ilan Kfir, *Ehud Barak* [in Hebrew] (Bnei Brak, Israel: Galei Alpha Communications, 1999), 186.

6. THE FIRST INTIFADA AND ACTIVITIES OF THE PALESTINIAN ISLAMIST ORGANIZATIONS: THE YITZHAK SHAMIR ADMINISTRATION (1987-91)

1. Interview with Reuven Paz August 20, 2000.

2. Yossi Melman, "Background/The Mother of All Prisoner Exchange Deals," *Haaretz*, January 29, 2004, https://www.haaretz.com/1.4684075.

3. Yezid Sayigh, *Armed Struggle and the Search for State* (Oxford: Clarendon Press, 1997), 626.

4. Anat Kurz, *Islamic Terrorism and Israel: Hezbollah, Palestinian Islamic Jihad and Hamas* [in Hebrew] (Tel Aviv: Papyrus, Tel Aviv University, 1993), 120.

5. Ze'ev Shiff and Ehud Ya'ari, *Intifada* [in Hebrew] (Jerusalem: Shocken, 1990), 50–51

6. Amira Hass, *Drinking the Sea at Gaza: Days and Nights in a Land Under Siege* [in Hebrew] (Tel Aviv: Kibbutz Meuhad, 1996), 79.

7. Daniel Byman, *A High Price: The Triumphs and Failures of Israeli Counterterrorism* (Oxford: Oxford University Press, 2011), 103.

8. Shiff and Ya'ari, *Intifada*, 48.

9. Kurz, *Islamic Terrorism*, 140.

10. Kurz, *Islamic Terrorism*, 140.

11. Byman, *A High Price*, 98

12. Byman, *A High Price*, 182.

13. Aviv Shabi and Roni Shaked, *Hamas: From Belief in Allah to the Road to Terrorism* [in Hebrew] (Jerusalem: Keter, 1994), 108.

14. Sayigh, *Armed Struggle*, 625.

15. Shabi and Shaked, *Hamas*, 96.

16. Pinhas Inbari, *Broken Swords* [in Hebrew] (Tel Aviv: Ministry of Defense Publishing House, 1994), 37.

17. Alan Hart, *Arafat: The Definitive Biography Written in Co-Operation with Yasser Arafat* (London: Sidgwick & Jackson, 1994), 468.

18. Gad Gilber, "Economic and Demographic Developments as Causes of the Intifada," in *In the Eye of Conflict: The Intifada* [in Hebrew], ed. Gad Gilber and Asher Susser (Tel Aviv: Hakibbutz Hameuhad, 1992), 21, 33.
19. Gilber, "Economic and Demographic Developments," 35.
20. Hillel Frisch, "From Armed Struggle to Political Mobilization: Changes in the PLO's Strategy in the Territories," in Gilber and Sasser, *In the Eye of Conflict*, 42–23.
21. Shiff and Ya'ari, *Intifada*, 76.
22. Shiff and Ya'ari, *Intifada*, 12.
23. Shaul Mishal and Reuven Aharoni, *Stones Aren't Everything: The Intifada and the Leaflet Weapon* [in Hebrew] (Tel Aviv: Hakibbutz Hameuchad, 1989), 267.
24. Paz, interview.
25. Shiff and Ya'ari, *Intifada*, 144.
26. Shiff and Ya'ari, *Intifada*, 57, 58.
27. "Intifada Begins on Gaza Strip," History.com, accessed December 27, 2020, http://www.history.com/this-day-in-history/intifada-begins-on-gaza-strip.
28. Interview with Ariel Sharon, September 13, 2000.
29. Thomas Friedman, *From Beirut to Jerusalem* (New York: Farrar, Straus & Giroux, 1989), 368.
30. Aryeh Shalev, *The Intifada: The Reasons, the Characteristics and the Implications* [in Hebrew] (Tel Aviv: Papyrus, 1990), 98–107, 114.
31. Kurz, *Islamic Terrorism*, 141.
32. Sayigh, *Armed Struggle*, 614.
33. Yitzhak Rabin, "The Clubs, the Bullets, the Words" [in Hebrew], *Yediot Aharonot*, November 11, 1990, 5.
34. Daniel Williams, "4 Israeli Soldiers Convicted of Brutality in Arab's Death," *Los Angeles Times*, May 26, 1989, http://articles.latimes.com/1989-05-26/news/mn-716_1_four-soldiers-gaza-strip-jabaliya-refugee-camp.
35. Efraim Inbar, "Yitzhak Rabin and Israeli National Security," *Middle East Security Studies* 25, no. 25 (1996): 28.
36. Yaakov Erez "Israel's Security Problems, Spring 1988" (interview with defense minister Yitzhak Rabin) [in Hebrew], *Skira Hodshit* 35, no. 5 (June 30, 1988): 8, 9.
37. Shalev, *The Intifada*, 123.
38. Shalev, *The Intifada*, 123.
39. Shalev, *The Intifada*, 151.
40. Amnon Straschnov, *Justice Under Fire* [in Hebrew] (Tel Aviv: Yediot Aharonot Press, 1994), 141.
41. Ronny Talmor, *The Use of Firearms by the Security Forces in the Occupied Territories* [in Hebrew] (Jerusalem: B'Tselem—Israeli Information Center for Human Rights in the Occupied Territories, July 1990)
42. Straschnov, *Justice Under Fire*, 145–46.
43. Ehud Sprinzak, *Between Extra-Parliamentary Protest and Terror: Political Violence in Israel* [in Hebrew] (Jerusalem: Jerusalem Institute for Israel Studies, 1995), 96.
44. Shalev, *The Intifada*, 120–21.
45. Shane Darcy, "Punitive House Demolitions, the Prohibition of Collective Punishment, and the Supreme Court of Israel," *Penn State International Law Review* 21, no. 3 (2003): 493.

46. *Human Rights Violations in the Territories, 1990–91* [in Hebrew] (Jerusalem: B'Tselem—Israeli Information Center for Human Rights in the Occupied Territories, 1991), 41.
47. Straschnov, *Justice Under Fire*, 80–81, 85.
48. Straschnov, *Justice Under Fire*, 82–85.
49. Interview with Yitzhak Shamir, November 1996.
50. *Yediot Aharonot*, October 13, 1988.
51. Straschnov, *Justice Under Fire*, 92.
52. *Demolition and Sealing of Houses as a Punitive Measure in the West Bank and Gaza Strip During the Intifada* [in Hebrew] (Jerusalem: B'Tselem—Israeli Information Center for Human Rights in the Occupied Territories, September 1989), 41.
53. Shalev, *The Intifada*, 129.
54. Interview with Rafi Eitan, October 31, 1999.
55. Interview with Yigal Pressler, October 31, 1999.
56. Interview with Shimon Peres, February 11, 2000.
57. Interview with Yaakov Perry, December 4, 1998.
58. Straschnov, *Justice Under Fire*, 66, 72.
59. Straschnov, *Justice Under Fire*, 66, 67, 70
60. Straschnov, *Justice Under Fire*, 71.
61. Straschnov, *Justice Under Fire*, 70.
62. Shalev, *The Intifada*, 119–20.
63. Straschnov, *Justice Under Fire*, 72.
64. Straschnov, *Justice Under Fire*, 73.
65. *Detained Without Trial: Administrative Detention in the Occupied Territories Since the Beginning of the Intifada* (Jerusalem: B'Tselem—Israeli Information Center for Human Rights in the Occupied Territories, October 1992), 7.
66. Interview with Moshe Arens, November 22, 1996.
67. Perry, interview.
68. Pressler, interview.
69. Peres, interview.
70. *Yediot Aharonot*, August 28, 1989, 5.
71. In November 1987, the Commander of the Southern Command issued an order to deport Abd al-Aziz Odeh, Islamic Jihad's spiritual leader in the territories.
72. Tami Bash, Yuval Ginbar, and Eitan Felner, *Deportation of Palestinians from the Occupied Territories and the Mass Deportation of December 1992* (Jerusalem: B'Tselem—The Israeli Information Center for Human Rights in the Occupied Territories, June 1993), 14.
73. "24 Hours," *Yediot Aharonot*, January 7, 1988, 17.
74. "24 Hours," 17.
75. *United Nations Security Resolution 607*, Yale Law School, Avalon Project, accessed December 27, 2020, http://avalon.law.yale.edu/20th_century/un607.asp.
76. Jonathan C.R. and al, "Behind Abu Jihad's Death," *Washington Post*, April 17, 1988, https://www.washingtonpost.com/archive/opinions/1988/04/17/behind-abu-jihads-death/9dfod092-1476-4bfd-befo-ebadbf5403fd/?utm_term=.7fb27002adeo.
77. Mike Eldar, *Shayetet 13: The Story of the Naval Commando* [in Hebrew] (Tel Aviv: Sifriyat Maariv, 1993), 654.

78. "Israelis Sink a Dinghy, Thwarting PLO Raid," *New York Times*, February 29, 1988, http://www.nytimes.com/1988/02/29/world/israelis-sink-a-dinghy-thwarting-plo-raid.html.

79. Sprinzak, *Between Extra-Parliamentary Protest and Terror*, 97.

80. UN General Assembly Security Council, Letter Dated 13 April 1988 from the Acting Chairman of the Committee on the Exercise of the Inalienable Rights of the Palestinian People addressed to the Secretary-General, https://unispal.un.org/DPA/DPR/unispal.nsf/0/2A1C633BCC465F67852561DA004EBBD3.

81. *Haaretz*, April 12, 1988, 2.

82. "Israel: Supreme Court Judgement in Cases Concerning Deportation Orders," *International Legal Materials* 29, no. 1 (1990): 139–81, http://www.jstor.org/stable/20693420.

83. UN General Assembly, "Question of Palestine: Report of the Special Committee to Investigate Israeli Practices Affecting the Human Rights of the Population of the Occupied Territories. Letter Dated 26 August 1988 from the Chargé d'affaires a.i. of the Permanent Mission of Mauritania to the United Nations Addressed to the Secretary-General, https://unispal.un.org/DPA/DPR/unispal.nsf/0/5EC5F482C9F2E8DF85256B6B006C4CBD.

84. Shalev, *The Intifada*, 130.

85. Mati Alon, *The Return to Zion* (Bloomington, IN: Trafford, 1995), 69.

86. Bash et al., *Deportation of Palestinians from the Occupied Territories*, 16.

87. Shalev, *The Intifada*, 130–31.

88. Joel Brinkley, "Israel Army Expels Eight Palestinians," *New York Times*, June 30, 1989, http://www.nytimes.com/1989/06/30/world/israel-army-expels-eight-palestinians.html.

89. Bash et al., *Deportation of Palestinians from the Occupied Territories*, 15.

90. *Yediot Aharonot*, May 22, 1989.

91. Bash et al., *Deportation of Palestinians from the Occupied Territories*, 11

92. Yehezkel Lein, *Human Rights Violations of Palestinians from the Occupied Territories Working in Israel and the Settlements* (Jerusalem: B'Tselem—The Israeli Information Center for Human Rights in the Occupied Territories, August 1999, 90).

93. Bash et al., *Deportation of Palestinians from the Occupied Territories*, 16.

94. Perry, interview.

95. Michael Sasser, *Conversations with Rehavam Gandhi Zeʾevi* (Jerusalem: Yediot Aharonot Press, 1992), 132–33.

96. *Haaretz*, February 26, 1990.

97. *Haaretz*, February 26, 1990.

98. Yaakov Havakook and Saleh Shakib, *Islamic Terrorism: Profile of the Hamas Movement* [in Hebrew] (Jerusalem: Israeli Defense Ministry, 1999), 39.

99. Avraham Sela, "Authority Without Sovereignty: The Palestinian National Movement from Armed Struggle to a Political Settlement," in *The Palestinian National Movement: From Confrontation to Reconciliation?* [in Hebrew], ed. Moshe Maoz (Tel Aviv: Maʾarachot, 1996), 401–402.

100. Hart, *Arafat*, 469.

101. Alexander Bligh, "Hussein's August Initiative and Its Impact on the Influence of Jordan and the PLO," *Monthly Review* 4, no. 9 (1988).

102. Interview with Meir Dagan, December 1998.

7. COUNTERING TERRORISM DURING THE PEACE PROCESS: THE YITZHAK RABIN ADMINISTRATION (1992–96)

1. Eytan Gilboa, "The United States and the PLO: The Path to Negotiations", [in Hebrew] *Skira Hodshit* 35, no. 12 (August 1989): 6.
2. Ze'ev Shiff and Ehud Ya'ari, *Intifada* [in Hebrew] (Jerusalem: Schocken, 1990), 307.
3. Gilboa, "United States and the PLO," 8.
4. Sylvana Foa, "Battle of Wombs," *Village Voice*, December 3, 2002, https://www.villagevoice.com/2002/12/03/battle-of-the-wombs/.
5. Anat Kurz, *Islamic Terror and the State of Israel: Hezbollah, Palestinian Islamic Jihad and Hamas* [in Hebrew] (Tel Aviv: Papyrus and the Centre for Strategic Research, 1993), 144.
6. Avraham Sela, "Authority Without Sovereignty: The Palestinian National Movement from Armed Struggle to a Political Settlement," in *The Palestinian National Movement: From Confrontation to Reconciliation?* [in Hebrew], ed. Moshe Maoz (Tel Aviv: Ma'arachot, 1996), 369.
7. Shimon Peres, "The Threat and the Response," in *International Terrorism: Challenge and Response*, ed. Benjamin Netanyahu (Abington, UK: Routledge, 1981).
8. Alan Hart, *Arafat: The Definitive Biography Written in Co-Operation with Yasser Arafat* (London: Sidgwick & Jackson, 1994), xxi.
9. Clyde Haberman, "Mideast Accord: The Secret Peace/A Special Report; How Oslo Helped Mold the Mideast Pact," *New York Times*, September 5, 1993, http://www.nytimes.com/1993/09/05/world/mideast-accord-secret-peace-special-report-oslo-helped-mold-mideast-pact.html?pagewanted=all.
10. *The Mass Deportation of 1992* (Jerusalem: B'Tselem—Israeli Information Center for Human Rights in the Occupied Territories, January 1, 2011), http://www.btselem.org/deportation/1992_mass_deportation.
11. *Ha'aretz*, March 31, 1993.
12. Kurz, *Islamic Terrorism*, 175.
13. Aviva Shabi and Roni Shaked, *Hamas: M'emuna b'Allah Lederech Hateror* [Hamas: From belief in Allah to the path of terrorism] [in Hebrew] (Jerusalem: Keter, 1994), 7.
14. *Yediot Aharonot*, December 12, 1994, 7.
15. *Human Rights Violations in the Territories, 1992–93* (Jerusalem: B'Tselem—Israeli Information Center for Human Rights in the Occupied Territories, 1993), 61–63.
16. *Ma'ariv*, February 1, 1995, 6–7.
17. Yossi Beilin, *To Touch Peace* [in Hebrew] (Rishon L'Zion, Israel: Yediot Aharonot, 1997), 103.
18. Beilin, *To Touch Peace*, 109.
19. Beilin, *To Touch Peace*, 137.
20. B'Tselem is the Israeli Information Center for Human Rights in the Occupied Territories.
21. *Yediot Aharonot*, September 3, 1993, 4.
22. Carmi Gillon, *Shabak Bein Hakraim* [in Hebrew] (Tel Aviv: Yediot Aharonot, 2000), 189.
23. *Yediot Aharonot*, October 26, 1993, 5.
24. *Yediot Aharonot*, October 27, 1993, 6.

25. "*Hoshvim*"—*The Issues at Hand* [in Hebrew], Chief Education Officer, Education and Information Branch, "There Is Something to Talk About This Week; the Gaza-Jericho Agreement First," May 1994, 113.
26. Uri Savir, *The Process: Behind the Scenes of a Historic Decision* [in Hebrew] (Tel Aviv: Yediot Aharonot, 1998), 180, 199.
27. Storer Rowley, "So Far, Arafat Maintains Balance on Shaky Tightrope," *Chicago Tribune*, April 28, 1996.
28. Barry Rubin, *The Transformation of Palestinian Politics: From Revolution to State-Building* (Cambridge, MA: Harvard University Press, 1999), 7–8.
29. Daniel Byman, *A High Price: The Triumphs and Failures of Israeli Counterterrorism* (Oxford: Oxford University Press, 2011), 82.
30. Boaz Ganor, "The Rationality of the Islamic Radical Suicide Attack Phenomenon," *ICT*, March 21, 2007, https://www.ict.org.il/Article/973/TheRationalityoftheIslamic-RadicalSuicideattackphenomenon.
31. Boaz Ganor, *Countering Suicide Terrorism: An International Conference* (Herzliya, Israel: ICT, 2001), 137–38.
32. *Maariv*, April 16, 1998, 3.
33. Boaz Ganor, *Israel Counter-Terrorism in the Shadow of Oslo* (Jerusalem: Shalem Centre, 1995).
34. *Maariv*, June 11, 1994, 2.
35. Gillon, *Shabak Bein Hakraim*, 194.
36. Ganor, "Rationality of the Islamic Radical Suicide Attack Phenomenon."
37. "Suicide and Other Bombing Attacks in Israel Since the Declaration of Principles," Israel Ministry of Foreign Affairs, 2016, http://www.mfa.gov.il/mfa/foreignpolicy/terrorism/palestinian/pages/suicide%20and%20other%20bombing%20attacks%20in%20israel%20since.aspx.
38. *Haaretz*, February 15, 1995.
39. Gillon, *Shabak Bein Hakraim*, 18.
40. *Haaretz*, April 14, 1995.
41. *Yediot Aharonot*, December 12, 1994.
42. *Haaretz*, April 12, 1994, 2a.
43. *Yediot Aharonot*, November 13, 1994, 13.
44. This section is based on Boaz Ganor, "Israeli Counterterrorism in the Shadow of Oslo," *Policy View* no. 17 (December 10, 1995).
45. Tony Karon, "Israel Peace Talks Aren't a Reward for Terror," *Time*, April 10, 2002, http://content.time.com/time/world/article/0,8599,229868,00.html.
46. Byman, *A High Price*, 80
47. *Haaretz*, April 14, 1995.
48. *Haaretz*, August 16, 1995.
49. *Davar*, April 10, 1995.
50. *HaTzofeh*, May 20, 1994.
51. *Maariv*, April 14, 1994.
52. *Yediot Aharonot*, November 30, 1993, 3.
53. *HaTzofeh*, May 20, 1994.
54. *Maariv*, April 14, 1995.
55. *Haaretz*, April 14, 1995.
56. *Haaretz*, January 24, 1995.

57. *Ha'aretz*, July 18, 1995.

58. *Ma'ariv*, November 17, 1994.

59. *Ha'aretz*, April 17, 1994.

60. *Ha'aretz*, April 17, 1994.

61. Abraham Gur, "PA: A Terror Organization Under the Guise of a Security Apparatus," *Ariel Centre for Policy Research*, no. 154 (September 1993): 10.

62. *Ha'aretz*, September 13, 1995.

63. *Ma'ariv*, February 8, 1995.

64. *Ma'ariv*, September 1, 1994.

65. This was the case in August 1994, when Israel gave Palestinian forces precise information regarding the people behind the double murders at a construction site in Ramle (*Ma'ariv*, August 29, 1994), and in February 1995, when Israel received reports of Hamas and Islamic Jihad intentions to smuggle a car bomb from Jericho into Israel to commit a terrorist attack in Jerusalem (*Ma'ariv*, February 5, 1995).

66. *Yediot Aharonot*, September 8, 1995.

67. *Yediot Aharonot*, April 12, 1995.

68. In April 1995, it was reported that Shin Bet had foiled a suicide bombing attack in Netanya and arrested the terrorist the day before the planned attack. The terrorist had been recruited by Hamas in the area in which he lived, after having been suspected of collaborating with Israel. In an attempt to clear his name, he suggested to Hamas that he carry out a suicide bombing. Five months later, Daniel Fry was murdered and his wife, who was pregnant, was seriously injured by a terrorist who wanted to rid himself of the accusation of collaborating with Israel (September 5, 1995).

69. *Yediot Aharonot*, April 10, 1995.

70. "Shortly after the murder of Haim Mizrahi, Yasser Arafat received a report from Fatah members in the territories that Fatah was responsible for the murder. According to sources in Tunis, Israeli authorities also knew that Arafat had received this information. But it was in the interest of both sides to hide this as much as possible, in order to prevent any disruption of the peace process" (Uzi Mahnaimi, *HaOlam Hazeh*, November 17, 1993).

71. *Ha'aretz*, September 13, 1993.

72. *Ha'aretz*, December 31, 1994.

73. *HaOlam Hazeh*, September 15, 1993.

74. *Ha'aretz*, August 16, 1994.

75. *Yediot Aharonot*, August 15, 1994.

76. *Ma'ariv*, August 29, 1994.

77. *Ha'aretz*, August 16, 1995.

78. Uri Savir, *The Process: Behind the Scenes of a Historic Decision* [in Hebrew] (Tel Aviv: Yediot Aharonot, 1998), 176.

79. *Yediot Aharonot*, January 24, 1995.

80. *Ha'aretz*, April 14, 1995.

81. *Yediot Aharonot*, August 1, 1994.

82. *Ha'aretz*, September 26, 1994; *Ha'aretz*, January 20, 1995.

83. *HaTzofeh*, September 19, 1994.

84. *Ha'aretz*, November 21, 1994.

85. Gillon, *Shabak Bein Hakraim*, 197.

86. *Ma'ariv*, November 3, 1994.

87. *Yediot Aharonot*, November 3, 1994, 2.
88. *Yediot Aharonot*, April 4, 1995.
89. *Ha'aretz*, April 5, 1995.
90. *Davar*, April 4, 1994.
91. *Ma'ariv*, June 25, 1995.
92. *Ha'aretz*, November 15, 1995.
93. Ronen Bergman, *Rise and Kill First* (New York: Random House, 2018), 445.
94. Orli Azoulay-Katz, *The Man Who Defeated Himself* [in Hebrew] (Tel Aviv: Yediot Aharonot, 1999), 238.
95. Interview with Shimon Peres, February 11, 2000.
96. *Ma'ariv*, December 1, 1994.
97. Amira Hass, *Drinking the Sea at Gaza: Days and Nights in a Land Under Siege* [in Hebrew] (Tel Aviv: Kibbutz Meuhad, 1996), 94.
98. *Yediot Aharonot*, April 9, 1993, 2.
99. *Ha'aretz*, June 7, 1993.
100. *Ma'ariv*, October 31, 1994, 3.
101. *Ma'ariv*, February 2, 1995.
102. *Davar*, February 20, 1995.
103. *HaTzofeh*, February 19, 1995.
104. *Davar*, February 20, 1995.
105. Ben Caspit and Ilan Kfir, *Ehud Barak* (Bnei Brak, Israel: Galei Alpha Communications, 1999), 101.
106. *Yediot Aharonot*, April 10, 1995.
107. *Ma'ariv*, April 12, 1995.
108. *Ma'ariv*, September 30, 1995, 9.
109. A statement given to the Red Cross office in the Old City of Jerusalem read: "Today, December 13, 1992, the sixth anniversary of the establishment of the Hamas movement, an officer of the occupation army was abducted. . . . The soldier is being held in a safe place. We are informing the authorities of the occupation that we demand . . . the release of Sheikh Ahmed Yassin in exchange for the release of this officer. . . . Within ten hours, no later than 9:00 PM, according to the following conditions:

   1. The timetable must be met, otherwise we will kill the officer when the time expires.
   2. The release of Sheikh Yassin will take place in the presence of a representative of the International Red Cross, the Egyptian Ambassador, the French Ambassador, the Swedish Ambassador and the Turkish Ambassador. The occupation authorities must pledge to these representatives that Sheikh Yassin will not be arrested again.
   3. We warn the occupation authorities not to harm the Sheikh. Such an attack will bring about a response on our part, and we will not let it pass in silence.
   4. We undertake to release the officer immediately after the Sheikh's release in a manner we deem appropriate.
   5. Israeli television should broadcast Sheikh Ahmed Yassin's release live, during which foreign representatives will be given the Israeli commitment that the Sheikh will not be arrested. Signed: The special unit, the Izz al-Din al-Qassam Brigades, the military wing, Hamas" (Shabi and Shaked, *Hamas*, 11–12).

110. The government's announcement read, "The Government of Israel views with great severity the abduction of a border police officer. It demands the immediate release of First Sergeant Toledano, and sees the abductors and their dispatchers as responsible for his safety and for his release. The government warns the kidnappers not to inflict any harm on First Sergeant Toledano" (Shabi and Shaked, *Hamas*).

111. Shabi and Shaked, *Hamas*.

112. Byman, *A High Price*, 84.

113. *Yediot Aharonot*, October 13, 1994, 5.

114. *Ma'ariv*, October 12, 1994, 3.

115. *Ha'aretz*, October 17, 1994.

116. *Ha'aretz*, October 17, 1994.

117. Ehud Sprinzak, *Israeli Society and the Challenge of Islamic Terrorism* [in Hebrew] (Tel Aviv: Israeli Intelligence Heritage and Commemoration, 1997), 2.

118. *Ma'ariv*, February 1, 1992, 12.

119. *Yediot Aharonot*, January 20, 1995, 3.

120. *Ha'aretz*, October 23, 1994.

121. *Yediot Aharonot*, September 24, 1995, Rosh Hashanah supplement, 2.

122. Efraim Inbar, "Yitzhak Rabin and Israeli National Security" (special memorial issue), *Mideast Security and Policy Studies*, BESA Center for Strategic Studies, Bar-Ilan University (March 1996), 33–34.

123. Caspit and Kfir, *Ehud Barak*, 102.

8. A PRIME MINISTER'S ASSASSINATION AND SHIFTING COUNTERTERRORISM STRATEGIES: THE BENJAMIN NETANYAHU ADMINISTRATION (1996-99)

1. Yaakov Havakook and Saleh Shakib, *Islamic Terrorism: Profile of the Hamas Movement* [in Hebrew] (Jerusalem: Israeli Defense Ministry, 1999), 165.

2. Daniel Byman, *A High Price: The Triumphs and Failures of Israeli Counterterrorism* (Oxford: Oxford University Press, 2011), 88.

3. "Address in the Knesset by Prime Minister-elect Netanyahu Presenting his government," Israel Ministry of Foreign Affairs, June 18, 1996, http://mfa.gov.il/MFA/For -eignPolicy/MFADocuments/Yearbook11/Pages/4%20Address%20in%20the%20 Knesset%20by%20Prime%20Minister-elect%20N.aspx.

4. In his speech to the Knesset, Netanyahu said, "We oppose the description of Islam as the enemy of Israel and the West. Along with political discussions between Israel and the countries in the region, we must add a parley between Judaism and Islam. . . . We have no conflict with Islam. We have a struggle with militant forces, who use their distorted interpretation of Islam as a tool for violence, hatred, and bloodshed" (*Ha'aretz*, June 19, 1996).

In July 1996, in his speech to a joint session of the U.S. Congress, he said, "We want peace with all our neighbors. We have no quarrel with them which cannot be resolved by peaceful means. Nor, I must say, do we have a quarrel with Islam. We do not subscribe to the idea that Islam has replaced Communism as the new rival of the West, because our conflict is specific. It is with those militant fanatics who pervert the central tenets of a great faith toward violence and world domination. Our hand is stretched out in peace to all who would grasp it" (*Ha'aretz*, July 11, 1996).

5. *Ha'aretz*, June 19, 1996.

6. Tony Karon, "Israel Peace Talks Aren't a Reward for Terror," *Time*, April 10, 2002, http://content.time.com/time/world/article/0,8599,229868,00.html.

7. "Address by Prime Minister Netanyahu to a Joint Session of the US Congress," Israel Ministry of Foreign Affairs, July 10, 1996, http://www.mfa.gov.il/mfa/foreignpolicy /mfadocuments/yearbook11/pages/14%20address%20by%20prime%20minister%20 netanyahu%20to%20a%20joint.aspx.

8. *Ma'ariv*, September 13, 1996, 2.

9. Danny Naveh, *Government Secrets* [in Hebrew] (Tel Aviv: Yediot AharonotPress, 1999), 31.

10. Naveh, *Government Secrets*, 27.

11. Naveh, *Government Secrets*, 31.

12. Marjorie Miller, "Barrier to Peace Breached as Netanyahu, Arafat Meet," *Los Angeles Times*, September 5, 1996, http://articles.latimes.com/1996-09-05/news/mn-40799_1 _arafat-meet.

13. *Ma'ariv*, September 13, 1996.

14. Shlomo Gazit, *Trapped Fools: Thirty Years of Israeli Policy in the Territories* [in Hebrew] (Tel Aviv: Zmora Bitan, 1999), 279.

15. This was also the assessment of Shin Bet chief Ami Ayalon, as expressed in a security briefing he gave at a cabinet meeting on August 2, 1996 (*Ha'aretz*, August 4, 1996).

16. *Ha'aretz*, August 12, 1996.

17. *Ha'aretz*, September 3, 1996, B3.

18. Havakook and Shakib, *Islamic Terrorism*, 166.

19. *Naveh, Government Secrets*, 37–38.

20. Ben Caspit and Ilan Kfir, *Ehud Barak* [in Hebrew] (Bnei Brak, Israel: Galei Alpha Communications, 1999), 337.

21. *Ma'ariv*, October 4, 1996, 3.

22. Naveh, *Government Secrets*, 42.

23. *Ha'aretz*, October 1, 1996, survey conducted by the Palestinian Center for Public Opinion in Beit Sahour, headed by Dr. Nabil Kukali.

24. *Ha'aretz*, November 22, 1996, 20.

25. Naveh, *Government Secrets*, 50.

26. Naveh, *Government Secrets*, 57.

27. Earl Thorpe, *The Other Truth about the Middle East Conflict* (self-pub.), lulu.com, 2006.

28. Letter from Secretary of State Warren Christopher to Benjamin Netanyahu, January 17, 1997, Israel Ministry of Foreign Affairs, http://www.israel.org/MFA/ForeignPolicy /Peace/Guide/Pages/Letter%20from%20Secretary%20of%20State%20Christopher .aspx.

29. *Ma'ariv*, March 21, 1997, 5–6.

30. *Ma'ariv*, March 21, 1997.

31. *Ma'ariv*, March 18, 1997, 2.

32. *Ha'aretz*, March 20, 1997, A3.

33. "Bomber, 3 Women Killed in Tel Aviv Blast," CNN, March 21, 1997, http://edition. cnn.com/WORLD/9703/21/israel.blast.too/index.html/.

34. Serge Schmemann, "Israelis Revive Plan to Forgo Oslo Pact Steps," *New York Times*, March 20, 1997, http://www.nytimes.com/1997/03/20/world/israelis-revive-plan-to-forgo -oslo-pact-steps.html.
35. *Ma'ariv*, March 24, 1997, 2; and *Ha'aretz*, May 11, 1997, B5.
36. *Ha'aretz*, May 11, 1997, B5.
37. *Ma'ariv*, March 25, 1997, 2.
38. *Ma'ariv*, March 25, 1997, 4.
39. *Ha'aretz*, June 4, 1998.
40. *Ma'ariv*, March 25, 1997, 4.
41. *Ha'aretz*, March 27, 1997; *Ma'ariv*, April 21, 1997.
42. Orli Katz Azoulay, *The Man Who Defeated Himself* [in Hebrew] (Tel Aviv: Yediot Aharonot-Hemed Books, 1999), 138.
43. *Ha'aretz*, March 28, 1997, A3.
44. Barry Rubin, *Conflict and Insurgency in the Contemporary Middle East* (New York: Routledge, 2010), 126.
45. Rubin, *Conflict and Insurgency*, 128.
46. Naveh, *Government Secrets*, 77.
47. *Yediot Aharonot*, June 5, 1997.
48. *Ha'aretz*, June 9, 1997.
49. IDF Spokesperson's Unit, Annual Summary of Security Events, 1997.
50. *Ha'aretz*, May 11, 1997, B5.
51. *Yediot Aharonot*, August 8, 1997, Saturday supplement, 12.
52. David Blair, "Khaled Meshaal: How Mossad Bid to Assassinate Hamas Leader Ended in Fiasco," *Telegraph*, December 7, 2012, http://www.telegraph.co.uk/news/worldnews /middleeast/palestinianauthority/9730669/Khaled-Meshaal-How-Mossad-bid-to -assassinate-Hamas-leader-ended-in-fiasco.html.
53. *Yediot Aharonot*, August 1, 1997.
54. *Ma'ariv*, August 4, 1997, 6.
55. The dispute between Military Intelligence and the Shin Bet regarding the measures and degree of pressure to be exerted on Arafat in order to spur him to act against the terrorist organizations is described in Alex Fishman's article in *Yediot Aharonot*, August 22, 1997.
56. Havakook and Shakib, *Islamic Terrorism*, 167–68.
57. *Ha'aretz*, August 20, 1997.
58. IDF Spokesperson's Unit, Annual Summary of Security Events, 1997.
59. *Ma'ariv*-Gallup poll, *Ma'ariv*, September 12, 1997, Saturday supplement.
60. *Ha'aretz*, September 28, 1997; and *Ma'ariv*, September 30, 1997.
61. *Ma'ariv*, September 30, 1997.
62. Blair, "Khaled Meshaal.
63. Ronen Bergman, *Rise and Kill First* (New York: Random House, 2018), xxiii.
64. *Ma'ariv*, October 10, 1997, 12–13.
65. Interview with Benjamin Netanyahu, December 20, 1999.
66. *Yediot Aharonot*, April 16, 1999, 34–41.
67. *Yediot Aharonot*, April 16, 1999, 34–41.
68. The six members of the committee were Yossi Sarid of Meretz, Uzi Landau, Benny Begin and Gideon Ezra of the Likud, and Uri Or and Ehud Barak of Labor. All of the committee members were united regarding the need to wage all-out war against

terrorism, but Sarid maintained that the use of targeted killings should be more selective (*Ha'aretz*, March 17, 1998, B2).

69. *Ma'ariv*, February 16, 1998.

70. *Ha'aretz*, March 17, 1998, B2.

71. Serge Schmemann, "Jordan Expecting Israel to Release More Palestinians from Jail," *New York Times*, October 5, 1997, https://mobile.nytimes.com/1997/10/05/world/jordan -expecting-israel-to-release-more-palestinians-from-jail.html.

72. Rubin, *Conflict and Insurgency*, 133.

73. Rubin, *Conflict and Insurgency*, 133.

74. Arafat said, "At his core, Netanyahu is a person who is not at all interested in peace" (*Ha'aretz*, July 11, 1998); head of the Preventive Security Service in the West Bank, Jibril Rajoub, said, "Netanyahu is bloodthirsty and a racist. He is leading his people and the region to bloodshed and killing. He is a liar—he begins to lie the moment he opens his mouth" (*Ha'aretz*, July 29, 1998).

75. For example, an intelligence document submitted to the government stated that the PA was closing Hamas institutions only for show. According to the authors of the document, at that time, sixteen Hamas institutions that, according to the PA, had been officially closed since September 1997 were operating in Gaza (*Ha'aretz*, July 7, 1998, A2).

76. Naveh, *Government Secrets*.

77. Naveh, *Government Secrets*, 134.

78. According to the Peace Index, at that time, support for the agreement stood at 70 percent, with 24 percent opposed to it (*Ha'aretz*, November 1, 1998).

79. *Ma'ariv*, October 30, 1998, 9.

80. *Ha'aretz*, November 12, 1998.

81. Rubin, *Conflict and Insurgency*, 135.

82. Rubin, *Conflict and Insurgency*, 135.

83. *Ha'aretz*, July 19, 1996.

84. *Ha'aretz*, July 19, 1996.

85. *Ha'aretz*, February 12, 1997, A2. This decision reflected the differences in approach between the former counterterrorism advisor to the Prime Minister Yigal Pressler and his successor, Meir Dagan. Pressler had prevented the dismantling of the unit and transferal of the responsibility for public transport security to the police, claiming that the police would deploy the resources within the organization, and that in the end, in both routine periods and in periods of high security alerts, police forces would not be designated to this task alone (*Yediot Aharonot*, May 11, 1997).

86. Zvi Lavi, "Transportation Minister Will Offer to Subsidize a 'Safety Basket' for Taxi Drivers at a Cost of About NIS 5,000," *Globes*, August 19, 1997, http://www.globes. co.il/news/article.aspx?did=149352.

87. The company's spending on security has increased six-fold over the last decade. Security standards are determined by the Shin Bet, with approval of the Knesset Foreign Affairs and Defense Committee. The cost of security depends on the destination and frequency of flights. Security costs on the Israel-Amman route, for example, reach $35,000, Antalya is $233,000, Barcelona is $64,000, Delhi is $38,000, St. Petersburg is $97,000, Manchester is $140,000, and Paphos is $105,000 (*Ha'aretz*, August 12, 1997).

88. The overall share of security costs in the Israeli economy is many times greater due to the many additional resources that are invested in security by the private sector.
89. *Ha'aretz*, April 19, 1999.
90. Netanyahu, interview.
91. Carmi Gillon, *Shabak Bein Hakraim* [in Hebrew] (Tel Aviv: Yediot Aharonot, 2000), 189.
92. Yaakov Perry, *Haba Lehargekha* [in Hebrew] (Tel Aviv: Keshet, 1999), 265.
93. *Yediot Aharonot*, August 8, 1997.

9. CONFRONTING THE AL-AQSA INTIFADA: THE EHUD BARAK AND ARIEL SHARON ADMINISTRATIONS (1999-2004)

1. Amir Rapaport, *Fire on Our Forces* [in Hebrew] (Tel Aviv: Ma'ariv, 2007), 68.
2. Aharon Ze'evi-Farkash and Dov Tamari, *How Will We Know? Intelligence, Operations and State Politics* [in Hebrew] (Tel Aviv: Yediot Aharonot, 2011), 87.
3. Raviv Drucker and Ofer Shelah, *Boomerang: The Failure of Leadership in the Second Intifada* [in Hebrew] (Jerusalem: Keter, 2005), 106.
4. Since 1929, the Temple Mount has historically been used by local Arab leaders as a pretext for the outbreak of riots against Jews. At that time, riots broke out over whether to allow freedom of worship for Jews next to the Western Wall.
5. Yom Tov Samia, Leadership in Moments of Truth [in Hebrew] (Tel Aviv: Conṭenṭo de Semriḵ, 2014), 400–401.
6. Samia, *Leadership in Moments of Truth*, 414–15.
7. Drucker and Shelah, *Boomerang*, 28.
8. Boaz Ganor, "Israel and the Palestinian Liberation Organization," in *The Routledge History of Terrorism*, ed. Randall D. Law (New York: Routledge), 254.
9. These numbers come from several sources, including Shin Bet, the IDF (Military Intelligence and the Spokesperson's Unit), the Intelligence and Terrorism Information Center at the C.S.S., and *The Seventh War* [in Hebrew] by journalists A. Harel and A. Issacharoff (Tel Aviv: Yediot Aharonot, 2004).
10. Drucker and Shelah, *Boomerang*, 32.
11. "The Mitchell Report," *BBC News*, November 29, 2001, http://news.bbc.co.uk/2/hi/in _depth/middle_east/2001/israel_and_the_palestinians/key_documents/1632064.stm.
12. Ahmed Qurie, *Peace Negotiations in Palestine: From the Second Intifada to the Roadmap* (London: I. B. Tauris, 2015), appendix 2.
13. Ourie, *Peace Negotiations in Palestine*, 294.
14. Ourie, *Peace Negotiations in Palestine*, appendix 2.
15. Sharm el-Sheikh Fact-Finding Committee, *Mitchell Report*, April 30, 2001, http:// eeas.europa.eu/archives/docs/mepp/docs/mitchell_report_2001_en.pdf.
16. Sharm el-Sheikh Fact-Finding Committee, *Mitchell Report*.
17. Ganor, "Israel and the Palestinian Liberation Organization," 254
18. Harel and Issacharoff, *The Seventh War*, 182.
19. In reference to Israel's policy of targeted killings, the Mitchell Report states: "Controversy has arisen between the parties over what Israel calls the 'targeting of individual enemy combatants.' The PLO describes these actions as 'extra-judicial executions,' and claims that Israel has engaged in an 'assassination policy' that is 'in clear

violation of Article 32 of the Fourth Geneva Convention.' The government of Israel states that, 'whatever action Israel has taken has been taken firmly within the bounds of the relevant and accepted principles relating to the conduct of hostilities.' "

20. Drucker and Shelah, *Boomerang*, 160–64.

21. Interview with Ehud Olmert, February 5, 2014.

22. Drucker and Shelah, *Boomerang*, 159, 165.

23. Prior to his retirement in May 2000, Shin Bet chief Ami Ayalon claimed that the Palestinians were fighting Hamas's infrastructure more than Israel was. In November 2000, his replacement claimed that Arafat was not in control of what was happening on the ground and was not necessarily capable of stopping the violence. In contrast, the heads of Military Intelligence and the IDF's research division maintained that Arafat had initiated the intifada and controlled its intensity. In retrospect (December 2003), Shin Bet head Avi Dichter stated,

> throughout the years of the conflict, Arafat has refrained from instructing his security personnel to act to prevent terrorism. It is clear to Arafat that he is the only one in the Palestinian Authority who can unite the entire security apparatus in order to act successfully against terror. Arafat knows that he is the only one who can connect Fatah to these security apparatuses in order to deal with terrorism. Arafat continues to ensure the flow of money to Fatah members, but does not instruct them to stop terrorism. In other words, I would say that Arafat is not deserving of the trust that the State of Israel gave him, nor of the trust that many countries around the world gave him, both during the seven years between Oslo and the beginning of the Intifada and in the last three years of the Intifada. His men expected to receive instructions from him to stop the terror, but he chose instead to sit back and watch what was happening from the sidelines.

Danny Naveh, a cabinet member at the time, described the dispute between the Israeli intelligence services in his book *Government Secrets*:

> There is a professional competition between Military Intelligence and the Shin Bet, a kind of "intelligence officers' envy," regarding intelligence assessments and analyses pertaining to the Palestinian Authority. There have been disagreements between the heads of MI and the Shin Bet regarding the analysis of Yasser Arafat's decisions, actions, and intentions, and I do not see this as improper. It is good that there is not a monopoly in Israel over intelligence on the Arab world. . . . It appeared that the political echelon was at peace with the substantive differences in the assessments of the two main intelligence bodies—Military Intelligence and the Shin Bet.

The book attributed this fundamental and dangerous dispute to reasonable, and perhaps even desirable, intelligence pluralism.

This was not the first time that at least one of the Israeli intelligence services held a misconception about the degree of responsibility and control that the Palestinian Authority and Arafat had over terrorism. The then head of Military Intelligence, Major General Moshe Ya'alon, said in April 1998, "Because both the Shin Bet and Military Intelligence deal with the issue of the Palestinian Authority, I think that it is only healthy that there be arguments. This is why the 'Agranat Commission' [a commission that was established after the 1973 war to investigate Israeli intelligence

failures before the war—BG] determined that there should be pluralism, which by
its very nature leads to debate between the bodies. . . . I just hope that we're arguing
over assessments and not over facts."

24. Drucker and Shelah, *Boomerang*, 52, 65.

25. Drucker and Shelah, *Boomerang*, 66.

26. Interview with Ariel Sharon, April 30, 2001.

27. "Suicide and Other Bombing Attacks in Israel Since the Declaration of Principles,"
Israel Ministry of Foreign Affairs, 2013, http://mfa.gov.il/MFA/ForeignPolicy/Terrorism
/Palestinian/Pages/Suicide%20and%20Other%20Bombing%20Attacks%20in%20
Israel%20Since.aspx.

28. "12 Year Sentence to Captain of Santorini" [in Hebrew], *Arutz 7*, March 23, 2003,
http://www.inn.co.il/News/News.aspx/47526.

29. "Suicide and Other Bombing Attacks in Israel Since the Declaration of Principles."

30. "Tel Aviv Suicide Bombing at the Dolphin Disco-1-Jun-2001," Israel Ministry of
Foreign Affairs, June 2, 2001, http://www.mfa.gov.il/MFA/MFA-Archive/2001/Pages/Tel
-Aviv%20suicide%20bombing%20at%20the%20Dolphin%20disco%20-%201-.aspx.

31. "Political Security Cabinet Communique, 2-Jun-2001," Israel Ministry of Foreign
Affairs, June 2, 2001, http://www.mfa.gov.il/MFA/Government/Communiques/2001
/Political-Security Cabinet Communique-2-Jun-2001.

32. Drucker and Shelah, *Boomerang*, 52, 65.

33. "PM Sharon Meets with German FM Fischer," Israel Ministry of Foreign Affairs, June
3, 2001, http://www.mfa.gov.il/MFA/Government/Communiques/2001/PM Sharon
meets with German FM Fischer.

34. Shaul Shai, *The Shahids: Islam and Suicide Attacks* (Piscataway, NJ: Transaction,
2004), 165.

35. Tamar Pileggi, "Top Jordan Court Denies US Bid to Extradite Jerusalem Bombing Accomplice," *Times of Israel*, March 20, 2017, https://www.timesofisrael.com/top
-jordan-court-denies-us-bid-to-extradite-jerusalem-bombing-accomplice/.

36. Clyde Haberman, "At Least 14 Dead as Suicide Bomber Strikes Jerusalem," *New
York Times*, August 10, 2001, http://www.nytimes.com/2001/08/10/world/at-least-14
-dead-as-suicide-bomber-strikes-jerusalem.html.

37. "Suicide and Other Bombing Attacks in Israel Since the Declaration of Principles."

38. Drucker and Shelah, *Boomerang*, 139–40.

39. Sharon Rofeh, "Israeli Killed in Suicide Attack in the North," Ynet, July 10, 2001,
http://www.ynet.co.il/articles/0,7340,L-1178529,FF.html.

40. "Israel Rejects Militants' Cease-Fire Offer," CNN, December 10, 2001, https://edition
.cnn.com/2001/WORLD/meast/12/09/mideast/index.html

41. Drucker and Shelah, *Boomerang*, 165–66.

42. Harel and Issacharoff, *The Seventh War*, 181.

43. Harel and Issacharoff, *The Seventh War*, 188.

44. Drucker and Shelah, *Boomerang*, 171.

45. "Passover Suicide Bombing at Park Hotel in Netanya," Israel Ministry of Foreign
Affairs, March 27, 2002,

46. Ze'evi-Farkash and Tamari, *How Will We Know?*, 85.

47. Boaz Ganor, *The Counter-Terrorism Puzzle: A Guide for Decision-Makers* (New
Brunswick, NJ: Transaction, 2005): 71

48. Arab citizens of Israel—Palestinians who have lived in Israel within the 1967 borders
since the establishment of the state—in many cases held demonstrations against IDF

operations in the territories. But generally they refrained from taking an active part in the intifada and certainly from carrying out terrorist attacks. In this respect, the attack on the Matza restaurant was exceptional.

49. "Israel Building Fence along West Bank," CNN, June 18, 2002, http://edition.cnn .com/2002/WORLD/meast/06/17/mideast/index.html.

50. Drucker and Shelah, *Boomerang*, 260, 276–78.

51. Ze'evi-Farkash and Tamari, *How Will We Know?*, 202–203.

52. Ze'evi-Farkash and Tamari, *How Will We Know?*, 202–203.

53. Drucker and Shelah, *Boomerang*, 240.

54. Drucker and Shelah, *Boomerang*, 308–309, 318.

55. Drucker and Shelah, *Boomerang*, 319, 322.

56. Ze'evi-Farkash and Tamari, *How Will We Know?*, 270.

57. Meir Amit Intelligence and Terrorism Information Centre, "Iran and Hezbollah as Generators of Terrorism in Israel and the Territories: Increasing Iranian Involvement Using Hezbollah in Palestinian Terrorism in Israel and the Territories During 2004," January 12, 2005.

58. Meir Amit Intelligence and Terrorism Information Centre, "Four Years of Confrontation Between Israel and the Palestinians—Summary," 2004, 15.

59. Drucker and Shelah, *Boomerang*, 152.

60. "Statistics on Administrative Detention in the Territories" (Jerusalem: B'Tselem—The Israeli Information Center for Human Rights in the Occupied Territories, updated November 22, 2020), http://www.btselem.org/hebrew/administrative_detention/statistics.

61. Ze'evi-Farkash and Tamari, *How Will We Know?*, 272.

62. Sharon, interview, September 13, 2000.

63. Meir Amit Intelligence and Terrorism Information Centre, "Special Information Bulletin," February 2005.

64. "The Operation in Rafiach Has Ended. The Soldiers Have Left the City"[in Hebrew], *Walla News*, May 25, 2004, http://news.walla.co.il/item/547595.

65. Ze'evi-Farkash and Tamari, *How Will We Know?*, 322.

66. "Analysis of Terror Attacks in the Last Decade" [in Hebrew], Shin Bet, 2010, https://www.shabak.gov.il/SiteCollectionImages/Hebrew/TerrorInfo/decade/DecadeSummary _he.pdf.

67. The effectiveness of the security fence that was built as a barrier between the center of Israel and the West Bank can be gleaned from the words of Shin Bet chief Avi Dichter at the Herzliya Conference on December 16, 2003:

> I can say as head of the Shin Bet that the fence that was built in Samaria has already reaped huge benefits and has literally saved human lives. One might say that the "fence saves blood," and this has already been proven. Perhaps in order to illustrate this point, I'll use [the example] of the latest terrorist attack that was planned against a school in Yokne'am. The area of northwest Samaria is already within a proper "buffer zone," of which the fence is just one component. In this zone we encounter cells that understand that crossing into Israel is becoming a problematic issue: When the Palestinian Islamic Jihad cell from Jenin wanted to attack the Yokne'am school, instead of taking a direct route of 27 km . . . the long route that the terrorists were forced to take enabled the defense establishment—the IDF, the police and the security services—to cooperate in order to catch the murderers the moment before

the attack, instead of the moment after. I think that the cooperation between these organizations is unprecedented not only in the history of the State of Israel, but also in other countries around the world. I allow myself to say that the route of the fence must be built faster.

68. In total, from September 2000 until the end of August 2005, 1,074 people were killed in terrorist attacks in Israel: 47 in 2000 (from September), 207 in 2001, 452 in 2002, 214 in 2003, 124 in 2004; and in 2005 (until August, inclusive), 30 people were killed. ("Victims of Palestinian Violence and Terrorism Since September 2000," Israel Ministry of Foreign Affairs, accessed December 31, 2020, http://www.mfa.gov .il/mfa/foreignpolicy/terrorism/palestinian/pages/victims%20of%20palestinian%20 violence%20and%20terrorism%20sinc.aspx.)

69. Avi Dichter, "Alternative Options for Resolving the Israeli-Palestinian Dispute" (presentation, 4th Annual Herzliya Conference, Herzliya, Israel, December 16, 2003).

70. "Four Years of Violent Confrontation Between Israel and the Palestinians" [in Hebrew], Meir Amit Intelligence and Terrorism Information Center, October 13, 2004, 3, http://www.terrorism-info.org.il/he/286/.

71. Meir Amit Intelligence and Terrorism Information Centre, "Iran and Hezbollah as Generators of Terrorism in Israel and the Territories."

72. "Four Years of Violent Confrontation Between Israel and the Palestinians."

73. Meir Elran, "Israel's National Resilience: The Influence of the Second Intifada on Israeli Society," memorandum no. 81 (Tel Aviv: Jaffee Center for Strategic Studies, Tel Aviv University, January 2006), 28.

74. Elran, "Israel's National Resilience," 31.

75. Elran, "Israel's National Resilience," 32.

76. Elran, "Israel's National Resilience," 50.

77. Drucker and Shelah, *Boomerang*, 397–98.

78. With Arafat's death, Abu Mazen acted, contrary to his predecessor, to fulfill his commitment to prevent Palestinian terror against Israel. However, he adopted Arafat's method whereby, in an attempt to reach an agreement with the Islamic organizations and thereby reduce their motivation to carry out attacks, at least for a limited time, he conveyed the message that the terrorist attacks would not advance—and might even harm—Palestinian national interests. Like his predecessor, Abu Mazen did not attempt to strike and neutralize the operational infrastructure of the Palestinian terrorist organizations, thereby limiting their ability to carry out attacks. He lacked Arafat's leadership quality, control, and charisma, and therefore his ability to impose his will on the Palestinian organizations was questionable. In this respect, Arafat was capable but unwilling, whereas Abu Mazen was willing but incapable.

10. DISENGAGEMENT FROM GAZA AND ITS RAMIFICATIONS: THE END OF THE SHARON ADMINISTRATION AND THE EHUD OLMERT ADMINISTRATION (2005-2008)

1. Terje Rod-Larsen, Fabrice Aidan, and Nur Laiq, *The Search for Peace in the Middle East* (London: Oxford University Press, 2014), 372–73.

2. Ariel Sharon, "The Herzliya Address" [in Hebrew] (presented at the 5th Annual Herzliya Conference, Herzliya, Israel, December 13, 2004).

3. Raviv Drucker and Ofer Shelah, *Boomerang: The Failure of Leadership in the Second Intifada* [in Hebrew] (Jerusalem: Keter, 2005), 365.

4. Amir Rapaport, *Fire on Our Forces* [in Hebrew] (Tel Aviv: Ma'ariv, 2007), 68.

5. Yossi Kuperwasser speaking at the conference Israeli Society Ten Years After the Disengagement held at IDC Herzliya, August 13, 2015.

6. Jack Khoury, "Reconstruction of Shafaram Lynch Shows Natan Zada Was Killed After Some Policemen Stepped Off Bus," *Haaretz*, August 8, 2005, https://www.haaretz .com/reconstruction-of-shfaram-lynch-shows-natan-zada-was-killed-after-some -policemen-stepped-off-bus-1.166193.

7. Dov Weisglass speaking at the conference Israeli Society Ten Years After the Disengagement held at IDC Herzliya, August 13, 2015.

8. Dov Weisglass and Omri Sharon speaking at the conference Israeli Society Ten Years After the Disengagement held at IDC Herzliya, August 13, 2015.

9. "Peace Index for July 2005" [in Hebrew], *Peace Index*, http://www.peaceindex.org /indexMonth.aspx?num=63&monthname=יולי.

10. Eival Giladi speaking at the conference Israeli Society Ten Years After the Disengagement held at IDC Herzliya, August 13, 2015.

11. Weisglass and Sharon speech at ID Herzliya.

12. Amir Bohbot and Itamar Inbari, "Qassam Rocket Fire Toward Sderot: 5 Injured" [in Hebrew], *Ma'ariv*, September 24, 2005, http://www.nrg.co.il/online/1/ART/988/022 .html.

13. Roni Sofer, "Mofaz: They Fired a Qassam? We'll Send Them A-Zhar as a Warning," Ynet, September 27, 2005, http://www.ynet.co.il/articles/0,7340,L-3148026,00.html.

14. Drucker and Shelah, *Boomerang*, 400.

15. Rapaport, *Fire on Our Forces*, 58.

16. Efrat Weiss and Ali Wakad, "Four Israelis Killed After Giving Terrorist Hitchhiker Ride" [in Hebrew], Ynet, March 31, 2006, http://www.ynet.co.il/articles/0,7340,L-3234497 ,00.html.

17. Ruti Sinai, Asaf Carmel, Anat Balint, Yoav Borovich, Yuval Azulay, and Vered Cohen, "Nine Killed in Attack on Old Tel Aviv Central Station" [in Hebrew], *Haaretz*, updated August 30, 2011, http://www.haaretz.co.il/1.1099382.

18. On February 12, 2008, one of the modern era's most dangerous terrorists was killed. Imad Mughniyeh was on the U.S. government's list of the twenty-six most-wanted terrorists, with a $5 million reward for anyone who could provide information that could help lead to his capture and trial. He was number two in Hezbollah, head of its military wing, a member of its "shura council," and the liaison between Hezbollah and the Revolutionary Guards and the Iranian regime. Mughniyeh was responsible for many attacks in Lebanon and throughout the world. He was killed in a car explosion in Damascus, and although Israel never claimed responsibility, Hezbollah attributed the act to Israel and threatened revenge attacks. Prime Minister Olmert chose to present Mughniyeh's killing as "a classic example of harming a man who had no substitute and will never have a substitute within Hezbollah," without actually taking responsibility for the operation.

19. Interview with Ehud Olmert, February 5, 2014.

20. Amos Harel, "IDF Apparently Did Not Know that Samhadana Lived in Camp Bombed in the Gaza Strip" [in Hebrew], *Haaretz*, updated August 30, 2011, http:// www.haaretz.co.il/misc/1.1111439.

21. Ali Wakad and Hanan Greenberg, "Seven Palestinians Killed by Shell Fire on Gaza Beach"[in Hebrew], Ynet, updated June 09, 2006, http://www.ynet.co.il/articles/0 ,7340,L-3260818,00.html.

22. "2006 Conclusion—Statistics and Trends in Palestinian Terror," Israeli Security Agency, 2006, 3.

23. "2006 Conclusion—Statistics and Trends in Palestinian Terror," 4.

24. "Hamas Strengthening and Force Buildup," Israeli Security Authority, November 30, 2008, 1, https://www.shabak.gov.il/SiteCollectionImages/english/TerrorInfo/hamas -report-en.pdf.

25. "Hamas Strengthening and Force Buildup," 2.

26. On July 9, a few days after Shalit's abduction, the Institute for Counter-Terrorism conducted a public opinion poll of a representative sample of Israel's adult population (502 people). Results showed that 59 percent of the public (62 percent of the sample) believed that negotiations for the release of the soldier should be conducted either directly or through a mediator (36 percent were for direct negotiations and 23 percent thought that they should be conducted only through a mediator). In addition, 50 percent of the Jewish public (and the entire sample) believed that if negotiations were held, the release of prisoners should be agreed to only if, in addition to securing the soldier's release, other gains should be secured, such as a commitment to stop the Qassams (21 percent thought that the release of the soldier in return for prisoners would be sufficient, and 23 percent believed that even if there was no possibility of a military rescue, no negotiations should be conducted with the kidnappers). Results further showed that 61 percent of Jews (56 percent of the total sample) believed that in exchange for the soldier, Israel should agree to release only a small number of prisoners, even if this condition prevented the deal from happening; by contrast, 29 percent believed that Israel should be willing to release a large number of prisoners in return for the soldier. On whether only prisoners who had not been directly involved in terrorist attacks, that is, with no "blood on their hands," should be allowed to be released, 80 percent of the Jewish public (77 percent of the sample) agreed (were "certain" or "thought"); 62 percent (65 percent of the sample) believed (were "certain" or "thought") that only women, minors, elderly people, the sick, or prisoners who were already close to their release date should be released.

27. Weisglass and Sharon speech at IDC Herzliya.

28. Kuperwasser speech at IDC Herzliya.

29. Aharon Ze'evi-Farkash and Dov Tamari, *How Will We Know? Intelligence, Operations and State Politics* [in Hebrew] (Tel Aviv: Yediot Aharonot, 2011), 21–81.

30. Farkash and Tamari, *How Will We Know?*, 82–83.

31. Farkash and Tamari, *How Will We Know?*, 21–81.

32. The reason for this lack of success was self-inhibitions and international restrictions under the international humanitarian law principle of proportionality, which limits the state's ability to conduct extensive air campaigns against hybrid terrorist organization facilities that are embedded in territories that are saturated with civilian population.

33. Rapaport, *Fire on Our Forces*, 184.

34. "The Second Lebanon War: A Timeline," Israel Defense Forces, July 7, 2016, https:// www.idf.il/en/minisites/hezbollah/the-second-lebanon-war-a-timeline/.

35. Isaac Ben-Israel, *The First Israel-Hezbollah Missile War* [in Hebrew] (Tel Aviv: Program for Security Studies, College of Policy and Government, Tel Aviv University, May 2007), 8, 53.

36. Ben-Israel, *The First Israel-Hezbollah Missile War*, 26.

37. Ben-Israel, *The First Israel-Hezbollah Missile War*, 27.

38. Aluf Ben, Amos Harel, and Yoav Shatran, "The IDF Will Fly in Lebanese Sky Until the Kidnapped Are Released" [in Hebrew], *Haaretz*, updated August 31, 2011, http://www.haaretz.co.il/misc/1.1141451.

39. "Hamas Strengthening and Force Buildup."

40. "Hamas Strengthening and Force Buildup."

41. "The Palestinian Islamic Jihad and Fatah Elements in the Gaza Strip Dispatched a Terrorist Who Carried Out a Suicide Bombing Attack in Eilat" [in Hebrew], Meir Amit Intelligence and Terrorism Information Centre, February 1, 2007, http://www.terrorism-info.org.il/he/article/18656.

42. Amit Cohen, "The Factions Agreed: Deals With Israel Will Be Respected" [in Hebrew], *Ma'ariv*, February 8, 2007, http://www.nrg.co.il/online/1/ART1/541/588.html.

43. Amit Cohen, "Report: the IDF Kidnapped a Senior Hamas Operative from the Heart of Rafah" [in Hebrew], *Ma'ariv*, September 8, 2007, http://www.nrg.co.il/online/1/ART1/633/818.html.

44. Uri Yablonka, "Israel: the Gaza Strip Is a Hostile Entity" [in Hebrew], *Ma'ariv*, September 19, 2007, http://www.nrg.co.il/online/1/ART1/637/779.html.

45. George Bush, "Joint Understanding" (speech, Annapolis Conference, Annapolis, MD, November 27–28, 2007), http://www.knesset.gov.il/process/docs/annapolis_conference.htm.

46. Ali Waked and Hanan Greenberg, "Activity in Gaza: 35 Palestinians Killed, 5 Soldiers Injured" [in Hebrew], Ynet, March 1, 2008, http://www.ynet.co.il/articles/0,7340,L-3513127,00.html.

47. Ali Waked, "Hamas in Cairo: Ready for a Six-Month Truce" [in Hebrew], Ynet, updated April 25, 2008, http://www.ynet.co.il/articles/0,7340,L-3535667,00.html.

48. Ben Caspit, *Evasive: Ehud Barak, the Real Story* (Or Yehuda, Israel: Kinneret Zmora Bitan, 2013), 58–60.

49. Ori Yablonka, "The Cabinet: Giving Calm a Chance But Are Ready for an Operation" [in Hebrew], *Ma'ariv*, November 6, 2008, http://www.nrg.co.il/online/1/ART1/745/272.html.

50. "Hamas Strengthening and Force Buildup."

51. "Intensive Rocket Fire Attacks Against Western Negev Population Centers and the Ashqelon Region After Hamas Announces the End of the Lull Arrangement," Meir Amit Intelligence and Terrorism Information Centre, December 22, 2008, http://www.terrorism-info.org.il/en/18365/.

52. Yanir Yagna, "Shin Bet: 565 Rockets, 200 Mortar Shells Fired at Israel Since Start of Gaza Op," *Haaretz*, January 13, 2009, https://www.haaretz.com/news/shin-bet-565-rockets-200-mortar-shells-fired-at-israel-since-start-of-gaza-op-1.268043.

53. "Operation Cast Lead", Ynet, accessed January 1, 2020, http://www.ynet.co.il/yaan/0,7340,L-1722969-PreYaan,00.html.

54. Caspit, *Evasive*, 32, 34.

55. Caspit, *Evasive*, 47–48.

56. Caspit, *Evasive*, 41, 46.

57. Caspit, *Evasive*, 53–54.
58. Shmulik Hadad, "Galant After the Targeted Killing: We Placed Immense Pressure on Hamas" [in Hebrew], Ynet, January 15, 2009, http://www.ynet.co.il/articles/0 ,7340,L-3657051,00.html.
59. "UN Secretary General: The Sites are Heartbreaking," *Mako*, January 20, 2009, http://www.mako.co.il/news-military/israel/Article-06956d46544fe11004.htm.
60. Asa Kasher, "Operation Cast Lead and the Right War Doctrine" [in Hebrew], *Tchelet* 35 (2009–2009), http://tchelet.org.il/article.php?id=437&page=1
61. Ori Blau and Yotam Feldman, "Operation Cast Lead: This Is How the Military Justice Allowed the IDF to Win" [in Hebrew], *Haaretz*, January 23, 2009, http://www .haaretz.co.il/1.1528798
62. Richard Goldstone, "Reconsidering the Goldstone Report on Israel and War Crimes," *Washington Post*, April 1, 2011, https://www.washingtonpost.com/opinions /reconsidering-the-goldstone-report-on-israel-and-war-crimes/2011/04/01/AFg111JC _story.html.
63. "Terrorism Against Israel from the Gaza Strip Since Operation Cast Lead: Statistics, Characteristics and Trends" [in Hebrew], Meir Amit Centre for Terrorism Information and Intelligence, March 1, 2011, http://www.terrorism-info.org.il/data/pdf /PDF_10_338_1.pdf.
64. Hanan Greenberg, "IDF: Hamas Didn't Perpetrate the Attack—But Is Responsible" [in Hebrew], Ynet, January 27, 2009, http://www.ynet.co.il/articles/0,7340,L-3662796,00 .html.
65. Barak Ravid, "Head of Shabak, Yuval Diskin: Despite Egyptian Efforts, the Smuggling Continues" [in Hebrew], *Haaretz*, September 02, 2009, http://www.haaretz.co .il/news/politics/1.1252987.
66. Amos Harel, Barak Ravid, and Yossi Melman, "Air Force Planes Attacked Dozens of Trucks in Sudan Transporting Weaponry from Iran to the Gaza Strip" [in Hebrew], *Haaretz*, March 26, 2009, http://www.haaretz.co.il/news/politics/1.1252581.
67. Maya Bengal, "The Prime Minister Hinted About Sudan: Active in Farther Places" [in Hebrew], *Ma'ariv*, March 26, 2009, http://www.nrg.co.il/online/1/ART1/871/840. html?hp=1&loc=107&tmp=4011.
68. Interview with Ehud Olmert, February 5, 2014.
69. Bengal, "The Prime Minister Hinted about Sudan."

11. CHANGES IN THE GREATER MIDDLE EAST: THE NETANYAHU ADMINISTRATION (2009-18)

1. "Netanyahu's Speech at Bar Ilan University—Full Version," *Haaretz*, June 15, 2009, http://www.haaretz.co.il/news/politics/1.1266091.
2. "Netanyahu's Speech at Bar Ilan University."
3. "Netanyahu's Speech at Bar Ilan University."
4. "Terrorism Against Israel from the Gaza Strip Since Operation Cast Lead: Statistics, Characteristics and Trends" [in Hebrew], Meir Amit Centre for Terrorism Information and Intelligence, March 1, 2011, http://www.terrorism-info.org.il/data/pdf /PDF_10_338_1.pdf.

5. Tamar Pileggi, "Palestinians Freed in Shalit Deal Killed 6 Israelis Since 2014," *Times of Israel*, July 20, 2015, https://www.timesofisrael.com/palestinians-freed-in-shalit-deal -killed-6-israelis-since-2014/.

6. "Gilad Shalit Exchange for Palestinians Prisoners—As It Happened," *Guardian*, June 25, 2006, https://www.theguardian.com/world/blog/2011/oct/18/gilad-shalit-release -palestinians-live.

7. Ben Caspit, *Evasive: Ehud Barak, the Real Story* (Or Yehuda, Israel: Kinneret Zmora Bitan, 2013), 449.

8. Tuli Shragai and Yishai Avior, "The Price of Prisoner Exchanges" [in Hebrew], *Walla*, May 27, 2008, http://news.walla.co.il/item/1288328.

9. "Report: Israeli Airman Ron Arad Was Tortured to Death in 1988," *Times of Israel*, February 20, 2016, https://www.timesofisrael.com/report-israeli-airman-ron-arad-was -tortured-to-death-in-1988/.

10. Benjamin Netanyahu, *Terrorism: How the West Can Win* (New York: Avon, 1986), 233.

11. Benjamin Netanyahu, *Fighting Terrorism: How Democracies Defeat Domestic and International Terrorists* (New York: Farrar, Straus & Giroux, 1997), 144.

12. Netanyahu, *How the West Can Win*, 233.

13. Netanyahu, *Fighting Terrorism*, 233.

14. Nir Hasson, "Bomb Explodes in Central Jerusalem; 1 Dead, at Least 30 Hurt," *Haaretz*, March 23, 2011, https://www.haaretz.com/israel-news/bomb-explodes-in-central-jerusalem -1-dead-at-least-30-hurt-1.351377.

15. "Palestinian Terrorist Attempts Attack on Tel Aviv Nightclub,", *The Israel Project*, August 29, 2011.

16. Karl Vick and Aaron J. Klein, "Attack in the Israeli Desert. It Wasn't Supposed to End This Way," *Time*, August 18, 2011, http://content.time.com/time/world/article /0,8599,2089467,00.html.

17. Yoav Zitun, "IDF: Killed Terror Chief Planned Mega-Attack," *Ynet News*, September 3, 2012, https://www.ynetnews.com/articles/0,7340,L-4200671,00.html.

18. "Timeline: Israel Launches Operation Pillar of Defense Amid Gaza Escalation," *Haaretz*, November 20, 2012, https://www.haaretz.com/israel-news/timeline-israel -launches-operation-pillar-of-defense-amid-gaza-escalation.premium-1.479284.

19. Nitzan Erlich, "Watch: Netanyahu in a Message to Hamas: 'We Will Continue to Protect Our Citizens' " [in Hebrew], *Kikar Shabbat*, November 14, 2012.

20. Lilach Shoval and Daniel Sirioti, "The Targeted Killing of Ahmad Jabari" [in Hebrew], *Israel Hayom*, November 15, 2011, 21. "Operation Pillar of Defense (2012)," Israeli Defense Forces, November 2012, https://www.idf.il/en/minisites/wars-and-operations /operation-pillar-of-defense/.

22. "Operation Pillar of Defense."

23. "Operation Pillar of Defense."

24. "Findings from Analysis of Terrorists Killed During Operation Pillar of Defense and Investigation of Relations Between Them and Noncombatants Killed Unintentionally" [in Hebrew], Meir Amit Centre for Information and Intelligence, December 16, 2012, http://www.terrorism-info.org.il/he/article/20444.

25. Gabe Fisher, "21 Wounded in Terror Attack on Tel Aviv Bus," *Times of Israel*, November 21, 2012, https://www.timesofisrael.com/chaos-in-tel-aviv-as-bus-explodes/.

26. Attila Somfalvi and Elior Levi, "Israel Initiated Relief; Hamas: We Will Smuggle More Weapons" [in Hebrew], Ynet, November 24, 2011, http://www.ynet.co.il/articles/0,7340,L-4311038,00.html.

27. "General Assembly Votes Overwhelmingly to Accord Palestinian 'Non-Member Observer State' Status in United Nations," United Nations, November 29, 2012, https://www.un.org/press/en/2012/ga11317.doc.htm.

28. Annyssa Bellal, "Armed Conflict Between Israel and Palestine in 2014," in *The War Report: Armed Conflict in 2014* (Oxford: Oxford University Press, 2015), 41.

29. "Rocket Threat on Israel from the Gaza Strip" [in Hebrew], Meir Amit Centre for Information and Intelligence, July 8, 2014, http://www.terrorism-info.org.il/he/article/20666.

30. "Evacuation of Hamas Command from Syria: Update and Initial Analysis of Significance" [in Hebrew], Meir Amit Centre for Information and Intelligence, December 11, 2011, http://www.terrorism-info.org.il/he/article/17811.

31. David D. Kirkpatrick, "Islamists Win 70 Percent of Seats in Egyptian Parliament," *New York Times*, January 21, 2011, www.nytimes.com/2012/01/22/world/middleeast/muslim-brotherhood-wins-47-of-egypt-assembly-seats.html.

32. Isabel Kershner and Michael R. Gordon, "Israeli Airstrike in Syria Targets Arms Convoy, U.S. Says," *New York Times*, January 30, 2013, http://www.nytimes.com/2013/01/31/world/middleeast/syria-says-it-was-hit-by-strikes-from-israeli-planes.html.

33. Benjamin Netanyahu, "United Nations General Assembly Address" (speech, United Nations General Assembly, October 1, 2013), https://mfa.gov.il/MFA/PressRoom/2013/Pages/PM-Netanyahu-addresses-UN-General-Assembly-1-Oct-2013.aspx.

34. Zvi Zinger, "The Names of 26 Palestinian Prisoners to Be Released in First Round Have Been Decided" [in Hebrew], *Megafon*, August 12, 2013, http://megafon-news.co.il/asys/archives/170324.

35. Netanyahu, "United Nations General Assembly Address," October 1, 2013.

36. Benjamin Netanyahu and John Kerry, "Statements by PM Netanyahu and US Secretary of State John Kerry After Their Meeting in Jerusalem" (speech, Jerusalem, December 5, 2013), https://www.netanyahu.org.il/en/news/751-statements-by-pm-netanyahu-and-us-secretary-of-state-john-kerry-after-their-meeting-in-jerusalem.

37. Netanyahu and Kerry, "Statements by PM Netanyahu and US Secretary of State John Kerry."

38. Benjamin Netanyahu, "Speech at Likud Conference" (speech, Likud Conference, December 18, 2013).

39. Benjamin Netanyahu, "Benjamin Netanyahu's Speech at a Weekly Knesset Meeting, 4.5.14," Benjamin Netanyahu official website, May 4, 2013,

40. Ben-Dror Yemini and Asaf Gabor, "Abu Mazen Surprises: 'We Do Not Support Boycotting Israel" [in Hebrew], *Maariv*, December 19, 2013, http://www.nrg.co.il/online/1/ART2/532/565.html.

41. Nimrod Bosso, "Ministry of Housing and Administration Granted Permits for Building of 2,100 Houses Past the Green Line" [in Hebrew], *The Marker*, November 3, 2013, http://www.themarker.com/realestate/1.2155999.

42. Benjamin Netanyahu, "Prime Minister's Speech at Start of Weekly Government Meeting" (speech, Jerusalem, Israel, April 6, 2014).

43. Jackie Hori and Barak Ravid, "Fatah and Hamas Signed Reconciliation Agreement: 'End of Palestinian Split' " [in Hebrew], *Haaretz*, April 23, 2014, http://www.haaretz.co.il/news/politics/1.2303136.

44. Benjamin Netanyahu, "Speech at Prime Minister's House" [in Hebrew], Benjamin Netanyahu official website, August 28, 2014, http://www.netanyahu.org.il/-רבד ראש-הממשלה-בפתח-ישיבת-הממשלה-14-3-19וחדשות/879-.

45. Amir Bochbot, "Cleared for Publication: The Navy Captured a Ship Possessing Rockets from Iran to Gaza" [in Hebrew], *Walla*, March 5, 2014, http://news.walla.co.il/item/2726459.

46. "News on Terrorism and the Israeli-Palestinian Conflict (March 12–18 2014)" [in Hebrew], Amit Meir Centre for Information and Intelligence, March 18, 2014, http://www.terrorism-info.org.il/he/article/20632.

47. Lazar Berman, "Israeli Forces Catch Man Wearing Explosive Belt," *Times of Israel*, May 30, 2014, https://www.timesofisrael.com/israeli-forces-catch-man-wearing-explosive-belt/.

48. "Prime Minister Netanyahu: In the Next Government I lead, I Plan to Enact a Law to Change the System of Government" [in Hebrew], Benjamin Netanyahu official website, January 6, 2015, http://www.netanyahu.org.il/22--הממשלה-ישיבת-בפתח חדשות/917-דברי-ראש-הממשלה-14-.

49. Benjamin Netanyahu, "Speech at Rally in Support of French Immigrants to Israel" [in Hebrew], Benjamin Netanyahu official website.

50. Benjamin Netanyahu, "Speech at Likud Supporters Conference in Ashkelon" [in Hebrew], Benjamin Netanyahu official website, February 19, 2015, http://www.netanyahu.org.il/14γ6γ29-הממשלה-ישיבת-בפתח-הממשלה-ראש-דברי-921/חדשות.

51. Jackie Khouri, "Palestinians: Mohammed Abu Khdeir Was Burned Alive" [in Hebrew], *Haaretz*, July 5, 2014, http://www.haaretz.co.il/news/politics/1.2367495.

52. Eli Senyor Ilana Curiel, and Yotam Zitun, "Rocket Fire to the Centre During Netanyahu Speech: 'I Looked to the Sky, Shrapnel Fell in the Garden' " [in Hebrew], Ynet, modified July 11, 2014, http://www.ynet.co.il/articles/0,7340,L-4541823,00.html.

53. Avital Lahav, "Flug Will Recommend to Lapid: There Is No Choice But to Raise Taxes" [in Hebrew], Ynet, August 28, 2014, http://www.ynet.co.il/articles/0,7340,L-4563831,00.html.

54. Tal Inbar, "Operation Protective Edge in Numbers," Israel Defense, August 27, 2014, http://www.israeldefense.co.il/en/content/operation-protective-edge-numbers.

55. "Summarizing 50 Days of Fighting in Numbers" [in Hebrew], *Mako*, updated August 26, 2014, http://www.mako.co.il/news-military/security/Article-83af72ede931841004.htm.

56. Benjamin Netanyahu, "Prime Minister's Speech at the State Rally at Ammunition Hill, to Mark 48 Years of Unification of Jerusalem" [in Hebrew], Benjamin Netanyahu official website, http://www.netanyahu.org.

57. Netanyahu, "Prime Minister's Speech at the State Rally."

58. Eli Ashkenazi, "ISIS Palestine: 7 Guilty of Planning to Operate Branch in Israel" [in Hebrew], *Walla*, January 18, 2015, http://news.walla.co.il/item/2820786.

59. Ron Kampeas, "Family of Avera Mengistu Wants US Help to Get Him Back from Gaza," *Times of Israel*, November 21, 2017, https://www.timesofisrael.com/family-of-avera-mengistu-wants-us-help-to-get-him-back/.

60. Yaser Okvi, "Abu Mazen: We Won't Allow Israelis to Sully Al-Aqsa with Their Feet" [in Hebrew], *Ma'ariv*, September 16, 2015, http://www.maariv.co.il/news/politics /Article-498155.
61. ICT, "Study: Terrorists Post Info on Social Media Before Attacking," December 6, 2018, https://www.gov.il/en/departments/news/study_on_lone_wolf_terror_phenomena _120618.
62. "Intermediate Check Results of Profiles of Perpetrators of Terror Attacks in Judea and Samaria in the Current Terror Wave" [in Hebrew], Meir Amit Centre for Information and Intelligence, November 25, 2015, http://www.terrorism-info.org.il/he /article/20917.
63. Boaz Ganor, "Artificial or Human: A New Era of Counterterrorism Intelligence?," *Studies in Conflict & Terrorism* (February 27, 2019), DOI: 10.1080/1057610X.2019.1568815.
64. Ganor, "Artificial or Human."

12. ISRAEL'S COUNTERTERRORISM POLICY FROM THE PERSPECTIVE OF ISRAELI DECISION MAKERS

1. Daniel Byman, *A High Price: The Triumphs and Failures of Israeli Counterterrorism* (Oxford: Oxford University Press, 2011),381.
2. Interview with Rehavam Ze'evi, November 14, 1999. All interviews noted here were conducted by the author.
3. Ze'evi, interview.
4. Interview with Shlomo Gazit, November 7, 1999.
5. Interview with Yitzhak Shamir, November 1996.
6. Interview with Ariel Sharon, September 13, 2000.
7. Interview with Shimon Peres, February 11, 2000.
8. Peres, interview.
9. Interview with Amnon Lipkin-Shahak, December 12, 1999.
10. Interview with Yaakov Perry, December 4, 1998.
11. Interview with Carmi Gillon, November 24, 1999.
12. Interview with Meir Dagan, December 4, 1998.
13. Interview with Rafi Eitan, October 31, 1999.
14. Interview with Avi Dichter, March 3, 2014.
15. Interview with Shabtai Shavit, November 22, 1999.
16. Interview with Gabi Ashkenazi, February 24, 2014.
17. Ashkenazi, interview.
18. Ashkenazi, interview.
19. Interview with Shaul Mofaz, February 17, 2014.
20. Mofaz, interview.
21. Interview with Benjamin Netanyahu, 1999.
22. Dichter, 2014.
23. Gazit, 1999.
24. Shavit, 1999.
25. Perry, 1998.
26. Netanyahu, 1999.

27. Abu Jihad was commander of Fatah's armed wing, the "Western Sector," and former deputy to Arafat. He was assassinated in Tunis in 1988.
28. Peres, 2000.
29. Interview with Ehud Olmert, February 5, 2014.
30. Interview with Nitzan Nuriel, February 2, 2014.
31. Nuriel, interview, 2014.
32. Gillon, 1999.
33. Dichter, 2014.
34. Dagan, 1998.
35. Lipkin-Shahak, 1999.
36. Salah Shehade was one of the leaders of Hamas's military wing who was killed in Gaza in 2002.
37. Ashkenazi, 2014.
38. Mofaz, 2014.
39. Mofaz, 2014.
40. Mofaz, 2014.
41. Public Committee Against Torture in Israel v. Government of Israel (HCJ 769/02).
42. Dagan, 1998.
43. Dagan, 1998.
44. Yahya Ayyash, the "Engineer," was at the top of Israel's most-wanted list at the time. He was responsible for carrying out suicide bombings in Israel and was assassinated by Israel via a booby-trapped cell phone. His killing was followed by four revenge attacks by Hamas operatives.
45. Peres, 2000.
46. Dichter, 2014.
47. Netanyahu, 1999.
48. Lipkin-Shahak, 1999.
49. Gillon, 1999.
50. Pressler, 1999.
51. Shavit, 1999.
52. Arens, 1996.
53. Mofaz, 2014.
54. Dagan, 1998.
55. Dagan, 1998.
56. Netanyahu, 1999.
57. Gazit, 1999.
58. Mofaz, 2014.
59. Lipkin-Shahak, 1999.
60. The interview with Shimon Peres took place prior to Israel's withdrawal from Lebanon.
61. Peres, 2000.
62. Tamir, 1999.
63. Ahituv, 1999.
64. Amit, 1999.
65. Perry, 1998.
66. Nuriel, 2014.
67. Nuriel, 2014.

68. Dichter, 2014.
69. Tamir, 1999.
70. Amit, 1999.
71. Perry, 1998.
72. Olmert, 2014.
73. Ashkenazi, 2014.
74. Lipkin-Shahak, 1999.
75. Shavit, 1999.
76. Sharon, 2000.
77. Arens, 1996.
78. Peres, 2000.
79. Shavit, 1999.
80. Gillon, 1999.
81. Perry, 1998.
82. Ahituv, 1999.
83. Ahituv, 1999
84. Ahituv, 1999.
85. Netanyahu, 1999.
86. Dagan, 1998.
87. Shamir, 1996.
88. Dichter, 2014.
89. Dichter, 2014.
90. Gillon, 1999.
91. Lipkin-Shahak, 1999.
92. Shavit, 1999.
93. Sharon, 2000.
94. Olmert, 2014.
95. Netanyahu, 1999.
96. Peres, 2000.
97. Shavit, 1999.

SELECTED BIBLIOGRAPHY

Alon, Mati. *The Return to Zion*. Bloomington, IN: Trafford, 1995.

Alon, Yigal. *Kelim Shluvim*. [In Hebrew.] Tel Aviv: Kibbutz Meuhad, 1980.

Avneri, Aryeh. *Pshitut Hatigmul*, pts. 1 and 2. [In Hebrew.] Tel Aviv: Sifriyat Madim, 1954.

Azoulay-Katz, Orli. *Haish Shenitzeach et Azmo* [The man who defeated himself]. Tel Aviv: Yediot Aharonot, 1999.

Barak, Aharon. *Judicial Discretion*. New Haven, CT: Yale University Press, 1989.

Bar-On, Mordechai. *The Gates of Gaza: Israel's Defense and Foreign Policy 1955–1957*. [In Hebrew.] Tel Aviv: Am Oved, 1992.

Barzilai, Gad. *Democracy in Wartime*. [In Hebrew.] Bnei Brak, Israel: Kibbutz Poalim, 1992.

Beilin, Yossi. *To Touch Peace*. [In Hebrew.] Rishon L'Zion, Israel: Yediot Aharonot, 1997.

Ben-Gurion, David. *The Sinai Campaign*. [In Hebrew.] Tel Aviv: Am Oved, 1959.

Ben-Israel, Isaac. *The First Israel-Hezbollah Missile War*. [In Hebrew.] Tel Aviv: Program for Security Studies, College of Policy and Government, Tel Aviv University, May 2007.

Ben-Rafael, Eliezer. *Israel-Palestine: A Guerrilla Conflict in International Politics*. Westport, CT: Greenwood, 1987.

Bergman, Ronen. *Authority Given*. [In Hebrew.] Tel-Aviv: Yediot Aharonot, 2002.

——. *Rise and Kill First*. New York: Random House, 2018.

Byman, Daniel. *A High Price: The Triumphs and Failures of Israeli Counterterrorism*. Oxford: Oxford University Press, 2011.

Caspit, Ben. *Evasive: Ehud Barak, the Real Story*. [In Hebrew.] Or Yehuda, Israel: Kinneret Zmora Bitan, 2013.

Caspit, Ben, and Ilan Kfir. *Ehud Barak*. [In Hebrew.] Bnei Brak, Israel: Galei Alpha Communications, 1999.

Drucker, Raviv, and Ofer Shelah. *Boomerang: The Failure of Leadership in the Second Intifada*. [In Hebrew.] Jerusalem: Keter, 2005.

Eitan, Rafael. *The Story of a Soldier*. [In Hebrew.] Tel Aviv: Sifriyat Maariv, 1985.

Eldar, Mike. *Shayetet 13: The Story of the Naval Commando*. [In Hebrew.] Tel Aviv: Sifriyat Maariv, 1993.

Friedman, Thomas. *From Beirut to Jerusalem*. New York: Farrar, Straus & Giroux, 1989.

Ganor, Boaz. "Artificial or Human—A New Era in Counter-Terrorism Intelligence" *Studies in Conflict & Terrorism* (February 27, 2019), https://www.tandfonline.com/doi/abs/10.1080/1057610X.2019.1568815.

——. *The Counter-Terrorism Puzzle: A Guide for Decision-Makers*. New Brunswick, NJ: Transaction, 2005.

——. "Israeli Counterterrorism in the Shadow of Oslo." *Policy View*, no. 17 (December 10, 1995).

Gazit, Shlomo. *Trapped Fools: Thirty Years of Israeli Policy in the Territories*. London: Frank Cass, 2003.

Gillon, Carmi. *Shabak Bein Hakraim*. [In Hebrew.] Tel Aviv: Yediot Aharonot, 2000.

Harel, Amos, and Avi Issacharoff. *The Seventh War*. [In Hebrew.] Tel Aviv: Yediot Aharonot, 2004.

Harkabi, Yehoshafat. *Fatah in the Arab Strategy*. [In Hebrew.] Tel Aviv: Maarachot, 1969.

Hart, Alan. *Arafat: The Definitive Biography Written in Co-Operation with Yasser Arafat*. London: Sidgwick & Jackson, 1994.

Hass, Amira. *Drinking the Sea at Gaza*. [In Hebrew.] Tel Aviv: Kibbutz Meuhad, 1996.

Havakook, Yaakov, and Shakib Saleh. *Islamic Terrorism: Profile of the Hamas Movement*. Jerusalem: Israeli Defense Ministry, 1999.

Inbari, Pinhas. *Broken Swords*. [In Hebrew.] Tel Aviv: Ministry of Defense Publishing, 1994.

——. *A Triangle Over Jordan*. [In Hebrew.] Tel Aviv: Sifriyat Maariv, 1984.

Israeli, Raphael. *PLO in Lebanon, Selected Documents*. London: Weidenfeld & Nicolson, 1983.

Kurz, Anat. *Islamic Terrorism and Israel: Hezbollah, Palestinian Islamic Jihad and Hamas*. [In Hebrew.] Tel Aviv: Papyrus, Tel Aviv University, 1993.

Lustick, Ian. "Terrorism in the Arab-Israeli Conflict: Targets and Audiences." In *Terrorism in Context*, ed. Martha Crenshaw. University Park: Pennsylvania State University Press, 1995.

Maimon, David. *The Terror That Was Defeated: The Suppression of Terror in the Gaza Strip, 1971–1972*. [In Hebrew.] Bnei Brak, Israel: Steimatzky, 1993.

Merari, Ariel, and Shlomi Elad. *Hostile Terror Activities Abroad: Palestinian Terrorism Outside of Israel, 1968–1986*. [In Hebrew.] Bnei Brak, Israel: Hakibutz Hameuchad, 1986.

Mishal, Shaul, and Reuven Aharoni. *Stones Aren't Everything: The Intifada and the Leaflet Weapon*. [In Hebrew.] Tel Aviv: Hakibbutz Hameuchad, 1989.

Morris, Benny. *Israel's Border Wars, 1949–1956*. [In Hebrew.] Tel Aviv: Am Oved/Sifriyat Ofakim, 1996.

Naor, Arye. *Begin in Power: A Personal Testimony*. [In Hebrew.] Tel Aviv: Yediot Aharonot, 1993.

Naveh, Danny. *Government Secrets*. [In Hebrew.] Tel Aviv: Yediot Aharonot, 1999.

Netanyahu, Benjamin. *Fighting Terrorism: How Democracies Defeat Domestic and International Terrorists*. New York: Farrar, Straus & Giroux, 1997.

——. *Terrorism: How the West Can Win*. New York: Avon, 1986.

Pedhauzer, Ami. *The Israeli Secret Services and the Struggle Against Terrorism*. New York: Columbia University Press, 2009.

Perry, Yaakov. *Haba Lehargekha*. [In Hebrew.] Tel Aviv: Keshet, 1999.

Qurie, Ahmed. *Peace Negotiations in Palestine: From the Second Intifada to the Roadmap*. London: I. B. Tauris, 2015.

Rabin, Yitzhak. "Political Illusions and Their Price." In *The Lebanon War*. [In Hebrew.] Tel Aviv: Hakibbutz Hameuchad, Kav Adom, 1983.

——. *Service Book*. [In Hebrew.] Tel Aviv: Sifriyat Ma'ariv, 1979.

Rapaport, Amir. *Fire on Our Forces*. [In Hebrew.] Tel Aviv: Ma'ariv, 2007.

Rubin, Barry. *Conflict and Insurgency in the Contemporary Middle East*. New York: Routledge, 2010.

Rubin, Barry, and Judith Colp Rubin. *Chronologies of Modern Terrorism*. New York: Routledge, 2008.

Samia, Yom-Tov. *Leadership in Moments of Truth*. [In Hebrew.] Tel Aviv: Conţenţo de Semriķ, 2014.

Sasser, Michael. *Conversations with Rehavam Gandhi Ze'evi*. [In Hebrew.] Jerusalem: Yediot Aharonot, 1992.

Savir, Uri. *The Process: Behind the Scenes of a Historic Decision*. [In Hebrew.] Tel Aviv: Yediot Aharonot, 1998.

Sayigh, Yezid. *Armed Struggle and the Search for State*. Oxford: Clarendon, 1997.

Schueftan, Dan. "The PLO and the Lebanon War: An Interim Assessment." In *The Lebanon War*. [In Hebrew.] Tel Aviv: Hakibbutz Hameuchad, Kav Adom, 1983.

Shabi, Aviva, and Roni Shaked. *Hamas: From Belief in Allah to the Road to Terrorism*. [In Hebrew.] Jerusalem: Keter, 1994.

Shalev, Aryeh. *The Intifada: The Reasons, the Characteristics and the Implications*. [In Hebrew.] Tel Aviv: Papyrus, 1990.

Shalom, Zaki. *David Ben-Gurion, the State of Israel and the Arab World 1949–1956*. [In Hebrew.] Sde Boker, Israel: Ben-Gurion Heritage Institute, 1995.

Shay, Shaul. *The Shahids: Islam and Suicide Attacks*. Piscataway, NJ: Transaction, 2004.

Shiff, Ze'ev, and Ehud Ya'ari. *Intifada*. [In Hebrew.] Jerusalem: Schocken, 1990.

Sprinzak, Ehud. *Between Extra-Parliamentary Protest and Terror: Political Violence in Israel*. Jerusalem: Jerusalem Institute for Israel Studies, 1995.

——. *Israeli Society and the Challenge of Islamic Terrorism*. [In Hebrew.] Tel Aviv: Israeli Intelligence Heritage and Commemoration, 1997.

Straschnov, Amnon. *Justice Under Fire*. [In Hebrew.] Tel Aviv: Yediot Aharonot, 1994.

Susser, Asher. *The PLO After the Lebanon War*. [In Hebrew.] Tel Aviv: Hakibutz Hameuchad, 1985.

Tal, Israel. *National Security: The Few vs. the Many*. [In Hebrew.] Tel Aviv: Dvir, 1996.

Ze'evi-Farkash, Aharon, and Dov Tamari. *How Will We Know? Intelligence, Operations and State Politics*. [In Hebrew.] Tel Aviv: Yediot Aharonot, 2011.

INDEX

Page numbers in *italics* indicate figures or tables.

booby traps: by Israel, 29, 55, 152, 254, 382n44; by terrorists, 52, 216, 250, 252
boomerang effect: Ayyash killing and, 16, 151–53, 311–12, 382n44; Gillon on, 312–13; Musawi killing and, 311, 313–14; as psychological warfare, 311–12; as revenge, 105, 149–53, 284, 311–15, 339
border police. See *Mishmar Hagvul*
Bringing Home the Goods Operation, 237–38
British, 1–2
B'Tselem. *See* Israeli Information Center for Human Rights in the Occupied Territories
Bush, George H. W., 120
Bush, George W., 238; on disengagement, 234–35; Middle East Roadmap of, 219–21, 231–33, 236, 248–49; on Sharon, 212, 230, 258–59

Café Apropo, Tel Aviv, 174–75, 178
Camp David summit, 196–98, 201–2, 206–7, 228
Canada, 185
carrot and stick policy, 45, 58, 149, 191
Castel Brigade, 80
Cast Lead Operation, 251–56, 258–60, 270
casualties, 3, 7, 80, 153–54, 200, 225–26, 369n9
ceasefires, 81; Hamas and, 249, 283–84; number of, 284; UN resolutions on, 29, 246–47, 252–53
Central Intelligence Agency (CIA, U.S.), 176–78, 210
Ciechanover Committee, 184–85
"cities of refuge," 129, 138–39
Civil Administration, 75
civil defense groups, 69
Civil Guard, 69–70, 340–41
civilian targets, 32
Clinton, Bill (U.S. president), 176, 178, 186, 188, 196, 200–202, 228
closures, 44, 114–17, 154–57, 163
Coastal Road Massacre, 77
collaboration accusations: with Israel, 99, 102–4, 130, 143, 195, 252, 363n68; on terrorism, 32, 42, 57, 102, 104, 166, 339

collective punishments, 114–17
communications intelligence (COMINT), 288, 338
Confrontation of the Fedayeen, 3
counterterrorism, 6, 224; Arafat responsibility influencing, 208; on capabilities vs. motivation, 333–34; CIA on, 176–78, 210; court system on, 100, 109, 325, 329, 341; Dagan on, 190; democratic considerations vs., 292, 294, 334; domestic cooperation on, 338–39; domestic pressure vs., 292–93, 294; effectiveness vs. legitimacy in, 336; in Gaza Strip, 248; goals of, 297–304, 329–32, 335; intelligence and, 21, 153, 338; international cooperation in, 3, 21–22, 32, 37–40, 56–59, 72, 81, 339; Israelis helping, 69–70, 340–41; land mines and, 29, 47, 69, 254; liberal-democratic values and, 21–22, 334; B. Netanyahu on, 168–69, 285–86; Olmert on, 330; Peres on achievements and, 331; policy and, 3–4, 14–17, 39–40, *337*; Rabin activities on, 17; on rationale, 315–19, 333, 338; Sharon and, 228–29, 330; targeted killings and, 204–5, 339–40; on terror motives, 341–42; trade-offs of, 296, *296*; transitions in, 293, *294–95*; worldview on policies and, 17, 331, 335. *See also* High Court of Justice (Israel)
Counterterrorism Dilemmas Conceptual Model, 351n42; on activities and governments, 25; on Barak, E., 228–30, *229*; on Begin, 86–88, *87*; on Ben-Gurion, 37–40, *39*; domestic factors on, 23–24, *24*; on Eshkol and Meir, *58*, 58–60; international factors in, 22–24, *24*; on liberal-democratic values, 22–24, *24*; on Netanyahu, B., 193–94, *194*, 289–91, *290*; on Olmert, 257–60, *259*; on Peres, 86–88, *87*, 161–64, *163*; on Rabin, 72–73, *73*, 161–64, *163*; restraint dilemma axis of, 23–24, *24*; on Shamir, 86–88, *87*, 117–19, *119*; on Sharett, 37–40, *39*; on Sharon, 228–30, *229*, 257–60, *259*

COLUMBIA STUDIES IN TERRORISM AND IRREGULAR WARFARE

Bruce Hoffman, Series Editor

This series seeks to fill a conspicuous gap in the burgeoning literature on terrorism, guerrilla warfare, and insurgency. The series adheres to the highest standards of scholarship and discourse and publishes books that elucidate the strategy, operations, means, motivations, and effects posed by terrorist, guerrilla, and insurgent organizations and movements. It thereby provides a solid and increasingly expanding foundation of knowledge on these subjects for students, established scholars, and informed reading audiences alike.

Ami Pedahzur, *The Israeli Secret Services and the Struggle Against Terrorism*

Ami Pedahzur and Arie Perliger, *Jewish Terrorism in Israel*

Lorenzo Vidino, *The New Muslim Brotherhood in the West*

Erica Chenoweth and Maria J. Stephan, *Why Civil Resistance Works: The Strategic Logic of Nonviolent Conflict*

William C. Banks, editor, *New Battlefields/Old Laws: Critical Debates on Asymmetric Warfare*

Blake W. Mobley, *Terrorism and Counterintelligence: How Terrorist Groups Elude Detection*

Jennifer Morrison Taw, *Mission Revolution: The U.S. Military and Stability Operations*

Guido W. Steinberg, *German Jihad: On the Internationalization of Islamist Terrorism*

Michael W. S. Ryan, *Decoding Al-Qaeda's Strategy: The Deep Battle Against America*

David H. Ucko and Robert Egnell, *Counterinsurgency in Crisis: Britain and the Challenges of Modern Warfare*

Bruce Hoffman and Fernando Reinares, editors, *The Evolution of the Global Terrorist Threat: From 9/11 to Osama bin Laden's Death*

Boaz Ganor, *Global Alert: The Rationality of Modern Islamist Terrorism and the Challenge to the Liberal Democratic World*

M. L. R. Smith and David Martin Jones, *The Political Impossibility of Modern Counterinsurgency: Strategic Problems, Puzzles, and Paradoxes*

Elizabeth Grimm Arsenault, *How the Gloves Came Off: Lawyers, Policy Makers, and Norms in the Debate on Torture*

Assaf Moghadam, *Nexus of Global Jihad: Understanding Cooperation Among Terrorist Actors*

Bruce Hoffman, *Inside Terrorism*, 3rd edition

Stephen Tankel, *With Us and Against Us: How America's Partners Help and Hinder the War on Terror*

Wendy Pearlman and Boaz Atzili, *Triadic Coercion: Israel's Targeting of States That Host Nonstate Actors*

Bryan C. Price, *Targeting Top Terrorists: Understanding Leadership Removal in Counterterrorism Strategy*

Mariya Y. Omelicheva and Lawrence P. Markowitz, *Webs of Corruption: Trafficking and Terrorism in Central Asia*

Aaron Y. Zelin, *Your Sons Are at Your Service: Tunisia's Missionaries of Jihad*

Lorenzo Vidino, *The Closed Circle: Joining and Leaving the Muslim Brotherhood in the West*

Arie Perliger, *American Zealots: Inside Right-Wing Domestic Terrorism*

Joseph M. Brown, *Force of Words: The Logic of Terrorist Threats*

GPSR Authorized Representative: Easy Access System Europe, Mustamäe tee
50, 10621 Tallinn, Estonia, gpsr.requests@easproject.com